DARA Z. STROLOVITCH

# Affirmative Advocacy

RACE, CLASS, AND
GENDER IN INTEREST
GROUP POLITICS

*The University of Chicago Press*
Chicago and London

DARA Z. STROLOVITCH is assistant pro-
fessor of political science at the University of
Minnesota. Her 2002 dissertation, upon which
this book is based, in 2003 received the Best
Dissertation Award from the Race, Ethnicity,
and Politics Section of the American Political
Science Association, as well as the Gabriel G.
Rudney Memorial Award for Outstanding Dis-
sertation in Nonprofit and Voluntary Action
Research from the Association for Research on
Nonprofit Organizations and Voluntary Action.

The University of Chicago Press, Chicago 60637
The University of Chicago Press, Ltd., London
© 2007 by The University of Chicago
All rights reserved. Published 2007
Printed in the United States of America

16  15  14  13  12  11  10  09  08  07      1  2  3  4  5

ISBN-13: 978-0-226-77740-5 (cloth)
ISBN-13: 978-0-226-77741-2 (paper)
ISBN-10: 0-226-77740-5 (cloth)
ISBN-10: 0-226-77741-3 (paper)

Library of Congress Cataloging-in-Publication
Data

Strolovitch, Dara Z.
    Affirmative advocacy : race, class, and gender
in interest group politics / Dara Z. Strolovitch.
        p.  cm.
    Originally presented as the author's thesis
(doctoral)—Yale University, 2002.
    Includes bibliographical references and index.
    ISBN-13: 978-0-226-77740-5 (cloth : alk. paper)
    ISBN-10: 0-226-77740-5 (cloth : alk. paper)
    ISBN-13: 978-0-226-77741-2 (pbk. : alk. paper)
    ISBN-10: 0-226-77741-3 (pbk. : alk. paper)
    1. Pressure groups—United States.
2. Minorities—United States—Political activity.
I. Title.
    JK1118.S78 2007
    322.40973—dc22
                                    2006037083

To my grandparents, Harry and Esther, *aleihem hashalom.*

# Contents

# Illustrations

## TABLES

# Abbreviations and Acronyms

## ORGANIZATION NAMES

The organizations that participated in the survey and interviews were promised anonymity. The organizations listed here are referenced by name in the text based on incidents and quotations that have been published previously or are in the public domain.

| | |
|---|---|
| AARP | American Association of Retired People |
| ACLU | American Civil Liberties Union |
| AFL-CIO | American Federation of Labor–Congress of Industrial Organizations |
| APRI | A. Philip Randolph Institute |
| BPN/USA | Business and Professional Women/USA |
| BSCP | Brotherhood of Sleeping Car Porters |
| CLASP | Center for Law and Social Policy |
| DAN | Direct Action Network |
| GLAAD | Gay and Lesbian Alliance Against Defamation |
| LCCR | Leadership Conference on Civil Rights |
| NAACP | National Association for the Advancement of Colored People |

| | |
|---|---|
| NAACP LDF | National Association for the Advancement of Colored People Legal Defense Fund |
| NAPALC | National Asian Pacific American Law Center |
| NCLR | National Council of La Raza |
| NCWO | National Council of Women's Organizations |
| NGLTF | National Gay and Lesbian Task Force |
| NJCRAC | National Jewish Community Relations Advisory Council |
| NOW | National Organization for Women |
| NOW LDEF | National Organization for Women Legal Defense and Education Fund |
| NWPC | National Women's Political Caucus |
| NWSA | National Women's Studies Association |
| WILPF | Women's International League for Peace and Freedom |
| ZPBS | Zeta Phi Beta Sorority |

## LEGISLATION, GOVERNMENT ENTITIES, AND OTHER ACRONYMS

| | |
|---|---|
| DOMA | Defense of Marriage Act |
| EEOC | Equal Employment Opportunity Commission |
| ENDA | Employment Non-Discrimination Act |
| FCC | Federal Communications Commission |
| FMLA | Family and Medical Leave Act |
| HIV/AIDS | Human Immunodeficiency Virus/Acquired Immunodeficiency Syndrome |
| HUD | Housing and Urban Development |
| LGBT | Lesbian, Gay, Bisexual, Transgender |
| NAFTA | North American Free Trade Agreement |
| NEPDG | National Energy Policy Development Group |
| OSHA | Occupational Safety and Health Administration |
| PAC | Political Action Committee |
| PRWORA | Personal Responsibility and Work Opportunity Reconciliation Act |
| SNESJO | Survey of National Economic and Social Justice Organizations |
| TANF | Temporary Assistance to Needy Families |

# Cases

# Acknowledgments

I have incurred many debts in writing this book, and it is impossible to convey in words the depth of my gratitude to all those who have provided help, advice, and encouragement over the years. My most profound thanks go to the officers and professional staff at each of the 286 advocacy organizations who generously gave of their time to respond to my survey, and the forty officers who so graciously met with me for face-to-face interviews. Without the benefit of their time and their insights—and without their tireless work in pursuit of social, political, and economic justice—this project simply would not have been possible.

This book began as my dissertation, and it owes a tremendous debt to the extraordinary guidance, support, and inspiration I received from my graduate advisers and other faculty members at Yale. Rogers Smith gave me invaluable encouragement and support throughout the dissertation and book-writing processes. He has been remarkably available, patient, and helpful, reading draft after draft and taking the time to help me figure out what it was that I really wanted to write about. His kindness and generosity are unparalleled, and his unfailing faith in his students and in the value of our ideas has given many of us the confidence to find our voices and follow our passions in our research. I also am deeply grateful to Cathy Cohen, whose own work and example inspired much of this project and who helped me navigate and negotiate the intricacies of doing engaged research. Her commitment, with Rogers Smith, to the Center for the Study of Race, Inequality, and Politics at Yale provided the physical and intellectual space in which graduate students could pursue our interests in an engaged, supportive, and constructively critical community of scholars. Donald Green deserves very special thanks for his help at many stages of this research, and for being exceptionally accessible and available. He helped me work through a range of conceptual and methodological issues and also generously provided crucial resources without which I never could have completed the survey. Debra Minkoff also provided inspiration and guidance for the project. David Mayhew, Marty Gilens, Eric Patashnik, and Greg Huber gave me valuable feedback and advice at early stages of the research. Several faculty members at other institutions also read and commented on my survey in its early phases, and they have continued since then to provide invaluable comments, advice, and encouragement. Jeffrey Berry bears special mention in this regard, as do Burdett Loomis and Jane Junn. Kay Lehman Schlozman and Ken Kollman not only provided me with valuable feedback on the survey but also generously shared their own data with me.

My graduate school colleagues have provided boundless support, critique, inspiration, and, above all, much cherished friendship. They have served as readers, critics, mock-survey respondents, and make-believe audiences, and their commitments to their own academic and political work are truly motivating. I feel incredibly lucky to have such wonderful collaborators in endeavors intellectual, political, and personal. Janelle Wong has provided advice and support at every juncture, and I was particularly grateful for her wise counsel as I conducted the interviews for this project. In addition to helping in innumerable ways with the survey and interviews and reading many drafts of every chapter, Dorian Warren helped me wrestle with the conceptual framework for the project. I am eternally grateful to Naomi Murakawa, who has read every chapter several times and the entire manuscript in full more than once (and then once more), each time offering fresh insights and imparting gravitas that helped me refine my arguments and focus on what was truly at stake in them. Other graduate school colleagues to whom I am immensely thankful for reasons both scholarly and not-so-scholarly include Rebecca Bohrman, Elizabeth Cohen, Hawley Fogg-Davis, Paul Frymer, Helena Hansen, Perlita Muiruri, Mark Overmeyer-Velazquez, Jessica Pisano, Steve Pitti, Amy Rasmussen, Alicia Schmidt-Camacho, Sarah Song, and Meredith Weiss. I owe very special thanks to Terri Bimes, Lori Brooks, Lisa Garcia-Bedolla, Tamara Jones, Rogan Kersh, Andy Rich, and Eric Schickler, each of whom offered warmth, wisdom, and generosity when I first arrived in New Haven. I am particularly indebted to Rebecca Bohrman, Naomi Murakawa, Amy Rasmussen, and Dorian Warren, who, through their unremunerated envelope stuffing, helped me field my survey on a shoestring budget.

Many people have helped shape this project through their thoughtful comments, conversations, critiques, and suggestions about various portions of the manuscript. I am very grateful to Maryann Barakso, Liz Beaumont, Jeffrey Berry, Sarah Binder, Teri Caraway, Dario Castiglione, Dennis Chong, Cathy Cohen, Joshua Cohen, Lisa Disch, Suzanne Dovi, Jamie Druckman, Paul Frymer, Don Green, Zoltan Hajnal, Michael Heaney, Rodney Hero, Lisa Hilbink, Camille Holmes, Valerie Hunt, Larry Jacobs, Tim Johnson, Alethia Jones, Jane Junn, Sally Kenney, John Kingdon, Ken Kollman, Regina Kunzel, Burdett Loomis, Jane Mansbridge, David Meyer, Naomi Murakawa, Kevin Murphy, Taylar Neuvelle, August Nimtz, Catherine Paden, Kathryn Pearson, Dianne Pinderhughes, Adolph Reed, Andrew Rehfeld, Betsy Reid, Reuel Rogers, David Samuels, Kira Sanbonmatsu, Lynn Sanders, Kay Lehman Schlozman, Phil Shively, Kathryn Sikkink, Rogers Smith, Jessica Trounstine, Dorian Warren, Mark Warren, Kent Weaver, Laurel Weldon, Janelle Wong, and Iris Young. Sally Kenney read and commented on numerous chapters, some more than once, offering honest, insightful, and practical comments and advice. Lisa Disch read several chapters, providing fresh observations and unique insights about ways to frame and integrate the empirical and normative arguments. Scott Abernathy, Jamie Druckman, Chris Federico, Marty Gilens, Don Green, Samantha Luks, Joanne Miller, and David Silver also provided invaluable advice and assistance with various aspects of the data analyses. The students in my graduate seminars on Interest Groups and Social Movements, especially those who took the class in the fall of 2005, supplied useful comments and unique perspectives. Hilen Meirovich, Angie Bos, Adriano Udani, Sheryl Lightfoot, and Serena Laws provided very able research assistance at various stages, and Patricia Rosas helped a great deal with copyediting. Regina Bonnaci at Zogby International administered the telephone survey of organizations. Ella Futrell and Sally Tremaine, both at Yale, and Judy Leskela Iverson, at the University of Minnesota, patiently helped with the administration of my grants. Pam Lamonaca and Barbara Dozier at the Institute for Social and Policy Studies at Yale and Cheryl Rackner Olson,

Judith Mitchell, Jen Salvati, Angelina Fugelso, Alexis Cuttance, Karen Kinoshita, Susannah Smith, and Angie Hoffman-Walter at the University of Minnesota provided much-needed technical support.

I was extremely fortunate to spend a year as a research fellow at the Brookings Institution while I conducted much of the research for this book. Brookings senior fellows E. J. Dionne and Kent Weaver merit special thanks for their very helpful interest in my work. They, along with Ming Hsu, also helped immensely by connecting me to several interview respondents. Thomas Mann and Paul Light provided invaluable encouragement and resources, as did Sarah Binder, who, with Rachel Caulfield, Grace Cho, and Dennis Ventry, also provided helpful feedback on early versions of several chapters. Sherra Merchant gets very special thanks for helping me with the transcriptions of the interviews.

I also was lucky to spend a year as a visiting faculty fellow at Georgetown's Center for Democracy and the Third Sector (now the Center for Democracy and Civil Society), where Steve Heydemann, Virginia Hodgkinson, and Marc Morjé Howard were tremendously welcoming and provided me with generous support, space, and resources. While I was a fellow there, Dario Castiglione and Mark Warren organized a wonderful workshop on representation at which I received helpful feedback from each of them, as well as from Joshua Cohen, Suzanne Dovi, Jane Mansbridge, Andrew Rehfeld, Laurel Weldon, and Iris Young. I submitted the next-to-final version of this manuscript only a few weeks after Iris Young's untimely passing. As will be clear to anyone who reads even the first chapter, this book was inspired a great deal by her work, which I first encountered as an undergraduate in a feminist theory course, and which has continued to motivate many of my questions about politics and political science ever since.

My colleagues in the Political Science Department at the University of Minnesota provided a congenial and stimulating environment in which to complete this manuscript. John Freeman and John Sullivan furnished crucial resources and release time, while Mary Dietz, Bud Duvall, Jim Farr, Colin Kahl, Dan Kelliher, Wendy Rahn, Martin Sampson, and Phil Shively provided advice and encouragement at crucial junctures. I also have been fortunate to take part in the University of Minnesota's vibrant interdisciplinary community. I was particularly lucky to be a resident fellow at the University of Minnesota's Institute for Advanced Study, where Dean Steven Rosenstone and Director Ann Waltner have created a wonderful environment for interdisciplinary research and scholarly exchange. I also have benefited a great deal from my affiliations with the Center for

Advanced Feminist Studies, the American Studies Department, the Gender, Women, and Sexuality Studies Department, and the Center for Women and Public Policy at the Humphrey Institute. I am especially grateful to Ron Aminzade, David Chang, Susan Craddock, Tracey Deutsch, Karen Ho, Sally Kenney, Keith Mayes, Hiromi Mizuno, Jennifer Pierce, and Rachel Schurman for their collegiality, intellectual engagement, and advice. Kevin Murphy deserves special mention for his support and feedback on a wide range of topics, as do Bob Burns and Rod Ferguson, who often saw to it that I remembered to eat dinner.

This book was made possible in no small part by the generous grant and fellowship support that I received from the following sources: the Social Sciences and Humanities Research Council of Canada; the Nonprofit Sector Research Fund at the Aspen Institute; the Center for the Study of Race, Inequality, and Politics at Yale; the Institute for Social and Policy Studies at Yale; the Enders Fund at Yale; the Irving Louis Horowitz Foundation; the Brookings Institution; the Center for Democracy and the Third Sector at Georgetown University (now the Center for Democracy and Civil Society); and the University of Minnesota.

I thank Kay Lehman Schlozman and Traci Burch for allowing me to quote from their unpublished paper. I also thank the *Journal of Politics*, the Southern Political Science Association, Blackwell Publishing, and CQ Press for permission to make use of portions of the following materials, which have appeared elsewhere in other forms:

> "A More Level Playing Field or a New Mobilization of Bias? Interest Groups and Advocacy for the Disadvantaged." In *Interest Group Politics*, 7th ed., edited by Allan Cigler and Burdett Loomis. Washington, D.C.: CQ Press, 2007.
>
> "Do Interest Groups Represent the Disadvantaged? Advocacy at the Intersections of Race, Class, and Gender." *Journal of Politics* 68, no. 4 (2006): 893–908.

At the University of Chicago Press, John Tryneski and Rodney Powell provided a great deal of encouragement and support for this project. I am grateful to Lori Meek Schuldt for help with copyediting and to the anonymous reviewers for their engaged reading, for their enthusiasm for the project, and for their enormously valuable comments, critiques, and suggestions.

My parents, Sheva and Ernie, have helped in many ways on this long journey. In addition to being a wonderful brother, Devon Strolovitch is a great linguist, a fabulous citation checker, and a truly inspired radio producer.

Regina Kunzel has touched my life in so many remarkable ways, and both it and this book are much richer for knowing her. I have benefited immeasurably from her tremendously generous and loving support, wisdom, humor, patience, and copyediting. She also introduced me to Jack and Lucas, who helped as well (when they were not conspiring to spill water on my laptop).

If, in spite of all the aforementioned generosity and assistance, any errors have found their way into the pages of this book, they are the sole responsibility of the author.

# ONE

# Introduction

In June 2002, William "Hootie" Johnson, chair of the Augusta National Golf Club in Augusta, Georgia, received an unexpected letter from Martha Burk, then chair of the National Council of Women's Organizations (NCWO). The NCWO is the largest coalition of women's groups in the United States, with two hundred member organizations encompassing more than six million members. Established in 1983 in response to the failure to ratify the Equal Rights Amendment to the Constitution of the United States, the organization has been at the forefront of many battles over women's rights since its founding. Writing on behalf of this large and influential organization, Burk urged Johnson to open his men-only golf club to women. Augusta soon would be hosting the Masters Golf Tournament, an occasion that Burk hoped would prompt Johnson to adopt a more inclusive policy. Many of the sponsors of the event, she suggested, including Coca-Cola, IBM, Citigroup, and General Motors, certainly would not appreciate the publicity that would result were she to call attention to Augusta's current discriminatory practices.

For his part, Johnson did not appreciate being told what to do, much less Burk's thinly veiled threat of a possible NCWO-sponsored boycott of the tournament's sponsors. Rather than trying to avoid the threatened publicity by quietly and privately negotiating with Burk, Johnson lashed back publicly and in no uncertain terms, stating that the club would not admit women "at the point of a bayonet" (Lewis 2003; McGrath 2002). Within days, the news media were abuzz with coverage of the showdown. As the tournament drew closer, reporters invoked the parallels between sex-based and race-based exclusions and asked golfer Tiger Woods what he thought of Burk's demands. Although Woods stated publicly that he thought Augusta should admit women, he made it clear that he would not boycott the tournament, saying, "Is it unfair? Yes. Do I want to see a female member? Yes." But, he pointed out, private clubs have the right to set their own membership policies. Noting that Augusta had admitted its first African American member only twelve years prior, Burk called upon Woods to take a firmer stance and to boycott the event in solidarity with women (Ferguson 2002).[1]

Public reaction to the face-off was decidedly mixed. Burk was called everything from an antifamily, man-hating lesbian to a feminist hero (Lewis 2003; M. Nelson 2003), and Johnson, too, was both praised and pilloried. And while many commentators echoed Woods's feeling that as a private organization, Augusta was within its rights to determine its membership, others were shocked to learn that such wholesale and egregious exclusions were still being practiced and, it seemed, were perfectly legal in the twenty-first century.

The showdown between Johnson and Burk is a revealing parable about the persistent inequalities in the contemporary United States. Among the last bastions of white, male, Protestant privilege, as well as sites of networking, deal making, and power brokering, golf courses are highly symbolic and highly evocative realms of exclusion. Moreover, by invoking the defense of Augusta's status as a "private" organization, Johnson and his defenders conjured the specter of historic deployments of the rights of private organizations in southern states. Claims to such rights were used to protect the Ku Klux Klan and the racially exclusionary "white primaries" used by the allegedly "private" Democratic Party as a key method to disenfranchise black voters in many states (including Georgia, home to the Augusta golf course, where white primaries persisted until 1946, when they were declared unconstitutional by the United States Supreme Court in *King v. Chapman*). More recently, southern public schools had cast themselves as private organizations in order to resist the racial integration mandated by the 1954 Supreme Court decision in *Brown v. Board of Education of Topeka*, thereby preserving their right to exclude black students.

At the same time as they confront strongholds of discrimination and exclusion such as golf courses, these kinds of actions on the part of advocacy groups such as the NCWO raise questions about the roles of these organizations as representatives of marginalized groups in U.S. politics. Taking on institutions such as Augusta is part of a long and important history in which advocacy groups have targeted high-profile institutions in order to make symbolic points about discrimination and to set precedents that undermine the legal bases of more far-reaching forms of exclusion and discrimination. However, by devoting extensive and high-profile attention to fighting for a benefit that would be enjoyed by the very limited population of women who would be able to join an exclusive, private, and very expensive golf club such as Augusta, the NCWO through its actions also raised important questions about the priorities and practices of contemporary social and economic justice advocacy groups.

This book explores the conflicts and contradictions in the practices of advocacy organizations as they fight for social and economic justice in the new millennium, when waning legal exclusions coincide with heightened social, political, and economic inequalities within the populations they represent. In an era of subsiding de jure discrimination but vast de facto inequality, how do advocacy organizations decide which battles to prioritize? Faced with limited resources but encompassing large and internally complex constituencies, how do organizations working for women, racial minorities, and low-income people decide which groups and subgroups warrant the most attention? This book answers these questions by systematically examining the issues and strategies of advocacy organizations that speak for marginalized populations in American politics. Taking seriously the injunction of political, social, and legal theorists that we think of the ensemble of systems of oppression together as a totality, I bring together normative political theory and empirical social science research methods to examine representation in American interest group and social movement politics.

Writers since Alexis de Tocqueville have recognized that American civic organizations are a key component of a healthy democratic society and citizenry (Tocqueville [1835] 1965). Tocqueville and his intellectual descendants argue that civil-society organizations, including everything from unions to bowling leagues, promote democratic values such as freedom of speech and association, social capital, civic participation, leadership skills, trust in government, and cross-class alliances (see, for example, Dionne 1998; Putnam 2001; Rocco 2000; Skocpol 2003; Verba, Schlozman, and Brady 1995; Mark E. Warren 2001; Mark R. Warren 2001).

One form of civic organization—national-level advocacy or social movement organizations—has historically been a crucial conduit for the articulation and representation of disadvantaged interests in U.S. politics, particularly for groups that are ill served by the two major political parties (Frymer 1999). Advocacy organizations have presented historically marginalized groups with an alternative mode of representation within an electoral system that provides insufficient means for transmitting the preferences and interests of those citizens. For many years, these organizations often were the sole political voice afforded groups such as southern blacks and women of all races, who were denied formal voting rights until well into the twentieth century. Long before women won the right to vote in 1920, for example, organizations such as the National American Woman Suffrage Association (formed in 1890) and the National Woman's Party (formed in 1913) mobilized women and lobbied legislators on their behalf, providing some insider access for the mass movements with which they were associated. Similarly, the National Association for the Advancement of Colored People (NAACP, formed in 1909) provided political and legal representation for African Americans in the South who, after a brief period of voting following Reconstruction and the passage of the Fifteenth Amendment in 1870, were largely disenfranchised and denied formal representation until the passage and enforcement of the Voting Rights Act of 1965.

While advocacy organizations often were the only voice for these groups, they were nonetheless comparatively weak, greatly outnumbered and outresourced by business, financial, and professional interest groups.[2] The 1960s and 1970s, however, witnessed an explosion in the number of movements and organizations speaking on behalf of disadvantaged populations (Berry 1977). Mass mobilization and increased representation led to greater opportunity and mobility for many women, members of racial minority groups, and low-income people. Organizations advocating on their behalf pursued lawsuits, regulations, and legislation aimed at ending de jure racial and sex-based discrimination and increasing resources and opportunities for those groups, and many of their efforts bore fruit.

In 1963, for example, the Equal Pay Act prohibited sex-based wage discrimination. The following year saw the passage of the 1964 Civil Rights Act, which barred discrimination in public accommodations, in government, and in employment, and established the Equal Employment Opportunity Commission (EEOC) to investigate complaints of discrimination and impose penalties on offenders. That same year, the United States Congress passed the Economic Opportunity Act, the centerpiece of President Lyndon

Johnson's War on Poverty, creating programs to attack poverty and unemployment through, for example, job training, education, legal services, and community health centers. In 1965, the Voting Rights Act prohibited racial discrimination in voting, amendments to the Immigration and Nationality Act liberalized national-origins quotas in immigration, and the Social Security Act established Medicare and Medicaid, providing health care for elderly and low-income people. That was also the year that President Johnson signed Executive Order 11246, calling on federal government contractors to "take affirmative action" against discrimination based on "race, creed, color, or national origin." Two years later, in 1967, this order was extended by Executive Order 11375 to include sex-based discrimination. Title IX of the Education Amendments of 1972 banned sex discrimination in schools. In 1973, the Supreme Court struck down the restrictive abortion laws that were on the books in most states at that time and upheld a 1968 EEOC ruling prohibiting sex-segregated "help wanted" ads in newspapers. Also in 1973, Congress passed the Equal Credit Opportunity Act, prohibiting discrimination on the basis of sex, race, marital status, religion, national origin, age, or receipt of public assistance in consumer credit practices.

With these developments came increased resources, newly fortified rights, more political power, and greater levels of mobilization than ever before for groups such as women, racial minorities, and low-income people. As a consequence, they became what Anne Larason Schneider and Helen Ingram call "emergent contenders" in American politics. Emergent contenders are groups that have gained some political, economic, and social power but have not yet completely shaken their powerlessness, stigmatized identities, or political and social marginalization (Schneider and Ingram 1997). Decades after advocacy groups helped government officials lay the legal and legislative groundwork that made possible these changes, however, important questions remain about how well these organizations represent their constituents. How much power and access do the organizations in the community of social and economic justice interest organizations have relative to that of organizations representing more-advantaged constituencies (Gray and Lowery 1996; Schlozman 1984; Schlozman and Burch forthcoming)? How far-reaching is the impact of the policy issues that these organizations pursue? How effectively do advocacy organizations empower those members of marginalized groups who will be in the best position to uplift less-powerful members of their communities (Dao 2005; DuBois 1903)? How much access do these organizations have to elected officials, and how successfully do they pursue their policy goals? Are formal organizations and insider tactics the "enemies of protest" (Clemens 2005) that lead to oligarchy, conservatism, moderated demands, and demobilization (Cigler 1986; Costain 1981; McCarthy and Zald 1973; Michels 1911; Piven and Cloward 1977; Polletta 2002; Staggenborg 1988)? How well do such organizations serve to build social capital, boost civic participation, or bring people together across class lines (Berry 1999; Putnam 2001; Skocpol 2003)? Each of these questions focuses on a critical aspect of how successfully organizations represent their constituents.

This book contributes to our understanding of these broad questions about representation by tackling concerns that have been up to now unaddressed in the literature. It prioritizes questions about the degree to which movements and organizations claiming to speak for marginalized groups attend to the particular challenges associated with advocating on behalf of disadvantaged subgroups of their own marginalized constituencies. That question, introduced by recent political, social, and legal theory, is reflected in popular and widely circulating questions about advocacy organizations. Is it true, as many allege, that civil rights organizations focus on "middle-class" issues? Is feminism a movement of and for affluent white women? Do economic justice organizations marginalize low-income people of color?

## OVERVIEW OF ARGUMENT AND MAJOR FINDINGS

Legal scholar and critical race theorist Kimberlé Crenshaw has termed the multiply disadvantaged subgroups of marginalized groups such as women, racial minorities, and low-income people "intersectionally marginalized" (Crenshaw 1989), an insight that has prompted considerable interest and attention on the part of political and social theorists (see, for example, Moraga and Anzaldua 1981; Baca Zinn and Dill 1996; Combahee River Collective [1977] 1981; Hancock 2004, 2007; Hull, Scott, and Smith 1982; Lugones 1992, 1994; Mohanty 1988; Spelman 1988; M. Williams 1998; Young 1997, 2000). Recognizing that important inequalities persist *among* racial, gender, and economic groups, intersectional approaches highlight inequalities *within* marginalized groups. For example, the low-income women who are unlikely to manage to afford the membership fees at the Augusta National Golf Club constitute an *intersectionally disadvantaged subgroup* of women, as they face marginalization both economically and based on gender.

Despite widespread interest in the concept of intersectionality, it has proven difficult to assess empirically. To do so, I examine three key questions fundamental to evaluating the representation of marginalized groups in the United States: First, how active are advocacy organizations when it comes to policy issues that affect intersectionally marginalized subgroups of their constituencies? Second, when they are involved with such issues, in what ways are they active—in particular, at which political institutions do they target their advocacy, and what kind of coalitions do they form? Third, how do organizations define their mandates as representatives, and what are some of the steps that can be taken by organizations to strengthen representation for intersectionally marginalized groups?

To answer these questions, I collected new quantitative and qualitative data using a survey of 286 organizations as well as in-depth face-to-face interviews with officers and professional staff at 40 organizations. To collect the survey data, I designed the first quantitative study that focuses on the organizations that together make up the social and economic justice interest community, the 2000 Survey of National Economic and Social Justice Organizations (hereafter referred to as the SNESJO). Coupled with the information that I collected through the in-person interviews and analyzed in light of insights based in theories of intersectionality as well as theories of representation, these data allow for the first large-scale and in-depth examination of the extent to which these advocacy organizations represent disadvantaged subgroups of their constituents.

The data paint a complicated and nuanced portrait of social and economic justice advocacy organizations and the challenges that they face as they work to represent marginalized groups in the contemporary United States. First, the evidence reveals that it does not suffice to distinguish only between advantaged and disadvantaged groups. To understand the priorities and activities of advocacy organizations, we must distinguish among *four* types of issues affecting four differently situated constituencies: *universal issues*, which, at least in theory, affect the population as a whole, regardless of race, gender, sexual orientation, disability, class, or any other identity; *majority issues*, which affect an organization's members or constituents relatively equally; *disadvantaged-subgroup issues*, which affect an organization's constituents who are disadvantaged economically, socially, or politically compared to the broader constituency; and *advantaged-subgroup issues*, which also affect a subgroup of an organization's constituents but one that is relatively advantaged compared to the broader constituency.

Distinguishing among these four policy types reveals that advocacy organizations are much more active on policy issues affecting a majority of their constituents than they are on issues that affect subgroups within their constituencies. This finding might seem to suggest that these organizations conform to a traditional conception of majoritarian representation that is based on the idea that attention should be devoted to constituents in proportion to their numbers. Such an interpretation is challenged, however, by the more startling finding that shows that organizations apply a double standard when it comes to the levels of energy that they devote to issues affecting differently situated subgroups of their constituencies. Issues affecting advantaged subgroups are given disproportionately high levels of attention, whereas issues affecting disadvantaged subgroups are given disproportionately low levels. In fact, once we account for other effects, issues affecting advantaged subgroups receive more attention than majority issues. Moreover, although organizations are extremely active when it comes to issues affecting advantaged subgroups regardless of the breadth of impact of the issue, the level of activity on issues affecting disadvantaged subgroups depends on the proportion of constituents that is affected by these issues.

So, for example, the survey data show that women's organizations are only slightly more active on violence against women—a majority issue—than they are on affirmative action in higher education—an issue affecting a subgroup of relatively advantaged women. Organizations are much *less* active, however, when it comes to welfare reform, an issue affecting a subconstituency of *intersectionally disadvantaged* women. Instead of working on issues affecting disadvantaged subgroups directly, officers at these organizations assume that representation for these subgroups will happen as a by-product of their efforts on other issues and that the benefits of other efforts will "trickle down" to disadvantaged constituents.

At the same time, I find that organizations that speak on behalf of marginalized groups do not lack interest in advocating on behalf of disadvantaged subgroups within their constituencies. To the contrary, concerns about representing disadvantaged subgroups weigh heavily on the minds of organization officers, and the majority of them are genuinely committed to the goal of advocacy for their multiply disadvantaged constituents. Indeed, most of the officers I interviewed view representation as far more than a process of interest aggregation or a duty to represent the majority will.[3] Rather, they conceive of representation as a form of advocacy, and they express principled commitments to using their roles as representatives as a means to achieve social justice (Fenno 1978; Urbinati 2000). As a consequence, most of these officers feel a responsibility to advocate for and to "do right" by disadvantaged subgroups of their constituencies. However, while many demonstrate a commitment to incorporate such advocacy into their roles as representatives, fewer operate this way in practice. Instead, attention to the concerns of intersectionally disadvantaged constituents is superseded by the fact that most organizations do not regard the intersectionally-constituted inequalities and issues that affect these constituents as central to their agendas. Consequently, officers at these organizations marginalize and downplay the impact of such issues, framing them as narrow and particularistic in their effect, while constructing policy images of issues affecting advantaged subgroups as common interests that have a broad impact (Baumgartner and Jones 1993, 26).

Because of these framings and constructions, organizations are far more willing to expend resources and political capital on behalf of advantaged subgroups than they are on behalf of disadvantaged ones. As a result, organizations are active not only at different *levels* when it comes to issues affecting intersectionally disadvantaged subgroups of their constituencies, they are also active in different *ways* when it comes to these issues. The differences between the tactics used for each subgroup exacerbate the lower levels of activity on behalf of intersectionally disadvantaged subgroups. In contrast to the popularly held stereotype that depicts profligate litigation by progressive organizations, I find that these organizations are actually quite hesitant to target the judiciary. However, while overall levels of court use by advocacy organizations are quite low, these organizations are substantially more likely to use the politically and financially expensive courts on behalf of advantaged subgroups of their constituencies than they are on behalf of disadvantaged subgroups. Finally, coalitions are ideally suited to pursuing issues affecting intersectionally disadvantaged groups and issues that cut across the constituencies of a range of organizations, and organizations do indeed pursue much of their work on issues affecting disadvantaged subgroups through coalitions with other groups. However, while organizations often work in alliances with other groups on disadvantaged-subgroup issues, they devote lower levels of energy to their coalitional efforts on these issues than they devote to coalitions dedicated to working on issues affecting advantaged subgroups.

Thus, although they constitute a critical source of representation for their intersectionally marginalized constituents, advocacy organizations are considerably *less* active, and active in *substantially different ways*, when it comes to issues affecting disadvantaged subgroups than they are when it comes to issues affecting more advantaged subgroups.

## AFFIRMATIVE ADVOCACY

Although the trends that I uncover are widespread, they are not ubiquitous, nor are they intentional. Indeed, the story of interest groups as representatives of intersectionally marginalized groups is more one of possibility than it is one of failure, and some organizations do speak extensively and effectively on behalf of intersectionally disadvantaged subgroups of their constituencies. Evidence from the survey and interviews demonstrates that what separates these organizations from those that fail to provide extensive representation for intersectionally disadvantaged groups is their commitment to a set of practices and principles that together constitute a framework of representational redistribution that I call *affirmative advocacy*.

Like affirmative action in education or employment, which is intended to redistribute resources and level the playing field for disadvantaged individuals in these arenas, the principle of affirmative advocacy recognizes that equitable representation for disadvantaged groups requires proactive efforts to overcome the entrenched but often subtle biases that persist against marginalized groups in American politics. This recognition compels those organizations that appreciate it to redistribute resources and attention to issues affecting intersectionally disadvantaged subgroups in order to level the playing field among groups. Among the practices they adopt to accomplish this redistribution are creating decision rules that elevate issues affecting disadvantaged minorities on organizational agendas; using internal processes and practices to improve the status of intersectionally disadvantaged groups within the organization; forging stronger ties to state and local advocacy groups; promoting "descriptive representation" by making sure that staff and boards include members of intersectionally marginalized subgroups of their constituencies; resisting the silencing effects of public and constituent opinion that are biased against disadvantaged subgroups; and cultivating among advantaged subgroups of their constituencies the understanding that their interests are inextricably linked to the well-being of intersectionally disadvantaged constituents. Through procedures and mores such as these, organizations engage in a form of redistributive representation that blurs the boundaries between advocacy and representation and that is itself a prefigurative form of social justice (Urbinati 2000, 2002). In these ways, organizations advance an innovative conception of representation that has great potential to equalize both representation and policy outcomes by offsetting the power of relatively advantaged subgroups.

I derive the substance and component measures encompassed within the affirmative advocacy framework inductively from empirical evidence about the practices of organizations found in the survey and interview data. Many of the principles and commitments that are embodied by the practices of affirmative advocacy, however, reflect ideas in political, social, and legal theories about interests, identities, representation, and redistribution. The framework draws on and brings into conversation a broad range of scholarship in these areas, including the contention of political theorist Iris Young (1992; 2000) that oppressed groups should receive extra representation, and legal scholar Lani Guinier's notion of "taking turns," which counters the dominance of purely majoritarian systems of voting and democratic governance. The framework also has a rough analogue in the "difference principle" articulated by political philosopher John Rawls in his classic book, *A Theory of Justice* (Rawls 1971). Rawls offered this principle to rebut utilitarian ideas that hold that distributive schemes should bring "the greatest good for the greatest number." Among Rawls's central arguments is that rather than following the majoritarian logic of utilitarianism, institutions should instead be designed to benefit the least well-off members of society and that inequalities are justifiable only to the extent that they meet this criterion.[4]

My examination of organizations that represent marginalized groups suggests that analogous principles animate the *representational* schemes of the organizations that most vigorously advocate for intersectionally disadvantaged subgroups. These organizations prioritize advocacy and representation that benefit their least well-off constituents, redistributing representational resources and energy to issues that affect intersectionally disadvantaged subgroups of their constituencies. As affirmative advocates, organizations harness a version of what Michael Dawson (1994) calls "linked fate" in order to better represent disadvantaged subgroups. That is, they engage in a form of what Nancy Schwartz (1988) labels "constitutive representation," cultivating among advantaged subgroups of their constituencies the understanding that their interests are bound up with the well-being of intersectionally disadvantaged constituents, nurturing a sense of what I call *intersectionally linked fate.*[5]

In their attempts to simultaneously work within but also transform the opportunity structure offered by interest group politics, organizations that engage in affirmative advocacy resist the incentives to remain unidimensional in their advocacy and to replicate the cleavages within marginal groups that exist in the larger society (C. Cohen 1999). As such, these organizations provide alternatives to the utilitarian, majoritarian, rationalist, and adversarial assumptions that dominate discussions about representation and interest group politics (Mansbridge 1983). Examining these organizations therefore presents us with an alternative conception of representation, one that compels us to take account of the centrality of advocacy, redistribution, and social justice as some of its key components (Urbinati 2000; 2002).[6]

## PLAN OF THE BOOK

*Affirmative Advocacy* examines both the challenges and the opportunities that the relatively young constellation of organizations representing marginalized groups presents for the political representation of *all* members within these groups, emphasizing key questions about the ways in which the relative size, resources, and status of a constituency influence the level of advocacy that an organization devotes to that group. In addition to contributing to such an understanding of the extent to which disadvantaged groups have a voice in national politics, the data that I have collected provide the first detailed portrait and overview of organizations that represent marginalized groups in national politics, presenting new information about their policy agendas, tactics, and organizational features.

The study analyzes provocative, but to date untested, theoretical claims about intersectionality and brings these analyses to bear on questions about civil society and representation. In so doing, it is in dialogue with a large body of empirical and theoretical work about representation that has taught us a great deal about the extent of constituent-representative accountability and congruence (either dyadic or collective; see, for example, Achen 1978; Ansolabehere, Snyder, and Stewart 2001; D. Arnold 1993; Bartels 1991; Druckman and Jacobs 2006; Erikson, Wright, and McIver 1993; Ferejohn 1986; Fiorina 1981; Jackson and King 1989; W. Miller and Stokes 1963; Jacobs and Shapiro 2000; Page and Shapiro 1992; Stimson, MacKuen, and Erikson 1995); the possibilities for deliberation associated with different representational arrangements (see, for example, Fishkin 1991; Gutman and Thompson 1996; Habermas 1987; Schwartz 1988; Urbinati 2000); the representational styles of elected officials (see, for example, Burke [1774] 1889; Fenno 1978; Mansbridge 2003; Pitkin 1967); the relationship between economic advantage and policy responsiveness (see, for example, Bartels 2005; Gilens 2005; Jacobs and Page 2005); and the circumstances under which elected officials who are people of color or women behave differently or have greater or lesser power and influence than their white and male counterparts (see, for example, Canon 1999; Carroll 1991, 2002; Diamond 1977; Fenno 2003; Fraga et al. 2005; Gay 2001, 2002; Gilliam 1996; Hawkesworth 2003; Kathlene 1994; Kenney 1996; Lublin 1997; Prestage 1977; Reingold 1992; Sierra and Sosa-Riddell 1994; Smooth 2001; Swain 1993; Thomas 1994; Walsh 2002; Whitby 1997).

While my study draws on the insights of these important bodies of work, it also reorients traditional questions about political representation by moving away from the typical focus on elected officials, concentrating instead on organizations that represent marginalized groups in national politics. The book also tries to refocus our expectations about what constitutes "good" representation by engaging Melissa Williams' (1998) evocative conception of representatives as *mediators*. Williams argues that representation is most centrally a form of mediation in which representatives intercede on behalf of their constituents' interests in the state's policies and actions. I argue that among the main responsibilities of organizations representing marginalized groups in their roles as mediators is to serve as *affirmative advocates* on behalf of their intersectionally disadvantaged constituents.

To assess how effectively organizations fulfill this mediator role, the study explores the advocacy activities of organizations across the three branches of the federal government, exploring the opportunities for mediation and representation that each branch offers. By considering these activities together with analyses of coalitions as well as with assessments of the levels and meanings of representation afforded disadvantaged subgroups, I evaluate the representation that is produced by all of these factors as a greater whole than the sum of its constituent parts. After assessing the state of representation for marginalized groups, I draw on the empirical analyses and evidence to recommend measures that can be taken by advocacy organizations to expand their capacities for advocacy on behalf of their full constituencies. Unifying these recommendations is the principle of *affirmative advocacy*, a framework that encourages organizations to proactively address the challenges associated with achieving equitable representation for intersectionally disadvantaged groups.

In the chapters that follow, I use the data collected through the SNESJO and the interviews to examine how well organizations represent their constituents. Chapter 2 discusses the role of advocacy organizations as representatives for marginalized groups and elaborates the theoretical framework for the book. It explains the policy typology and study design, and it explores some of the limitations of the data and analytic framework. Chapter 3 introduces the reader to the contemporary universe of organizations representing women, racial minorities, and low-income people in national politics. It compares the information about them from my study with data from previous surveys and with publicly available information, using this as the basis for a discussion of their roles in representing marginalized groups. Chapter 4 shows that organizations are much more active on majority issues and on issues affecting advantaged subgroups than they are on policy issues that affect disadvantaged subgroups of their constituents. Chapter 5 examines the use of the courts by advocacy organizations and assesses whether the political institutions that are targeted by these organizations vary by issue type. It then evaluates the consequences of this variation for the resulting quality of representation afforded to intersectionally disadvantaged groups as well as for concerns about the use of the courts to bring about social change. Chapter 6 explores coalitions among organizations, asking whether such alliances are an alternative vehicle for activity on issues affecting disadvantaged subgroups. Chapter 7 concludes the book with a discussion of the "best practices" associated with high levels of activity on behalf disadvantaged subgroups and uses these practices to make the case for the principle of affirmative advocacy.

TWO

# Closer to a Pluralist Heaven?

Nothing less than the meaning of political representation for marginalized groups is at stake in the questions about the priorities and activities of advocacy organizations that motivate this book. In raising these questions, this book draws on and contributes to more than a half century of scholarly debates about the role of political organizations as representatives within national politics. Some of the most fundamental disagreements about the role of these organizations have revolved around questions about whether these "pressure groups" alleviate or exacerbate inequalities in other political realms.

Many of the scholars of American politics who first considered these questions departed from Madisonian hand-wringing about the "violence of faction," and were instead quite sanguine about the role of pressure groups in American politics. Proponents of a "pluralist" view of American politics in the 1950s and 1960s, such as David Truman (1951) and Robert Dahl (1967) saw power as broadly diffused and were optimistic that interest groups and advocacy organizations would form to represent groups when their interests were at stake (see also Bentley 1908; Herring 1929; Latham 1952). Viewing "pressure groups ... to be the essence of politics" (J. Wilson [1974] 1995, 3), they were confident that these organizations would be sufficiently powerful to protect and advance the interests of the groups that they represented so that no single interest would win or lose all of the time.

In spite of this optimism, marginalized groups had few formal political organizations representing their interests in national politics before the 1960s. Although, as I suggested in chapter 1, groups such as women, racial minorities, and low-income people relied heavily on advocacy organizations, the actions and influence of organizations such as business associations that spoke for more powerful and antiegalitarian interests put marginalized groups at a severe disadvantage relative to other interests (Baumgartner and Jones 1993; Minkoff 1995). E. E. Schattschneider ([1960] 1975) argued, for example, that interest groups exacerbated rather than eased inequalities in political access.[1] Through the process that Schattschneider termed the "mobilization of bias," the concerns of weak groups were "organized out" of politics by elites who manipulated the agenda toward their own interests. As a consequence, he asserted, the interests of weak groups were not merely opposed but were actually excluded from the political agenda. "The flaw in the pluralist heaven," he wrote, "is that the heavenly chorus sings with a strong upper-class accent." He estimated that approximately 90 percent of the population could not access what he called "the pressure system," the informal but extensive system of organizations mobilized to influence national politics (Schattschneider [1960] 1975, 35; see also Michels 1911; Mills 1956; Lindblom 1963; Lowi 1969).

## INTEREST GROUPS AND REPRESENTATION
## FOR MARGINALIZED POPULATIONS

True as it was when he wrote it, Schattschneider's well-known rejoinder to the optimism of pluralists such as Truman and Dahl was soon challenged by the social movements of the 1950s, 1960s, and 1970s. These movements mobilized historically marginalized and excluded groups—in particular, women, racial minorities, and low-income people—and led, in turn, to an explosion in the number of formal organizations representing these populations in national politics (Berry 1977; Costain 1992; Geron, De La Cruz, and Singh 2001; Hero 1992; Imig 1996; Josephy, Nagel, and Johnson 1999; Marquez and Jennings 2000; McAdam 1982; Minkoff 1995; Morris 1984; Pinderhughes 1995; Piven and Cloward 1977; Schlozman 1984; Robert Smith 1996; Torres and Katsiaficas 1999; C. Wong 2006). For example, the period between 1960 and 1999 saw the formation of 56 percent of currently existing civil rights and racial minority organizations, 79 percent of currently existing economic justice organizations, and 65 percent of extant women's organizations.[2] At the beginning of the twenty-first century, there were more than seven hundred organizations representing women, racial minorities, and low-income people in national politics (Strolovitch 2006). These include more than forty African American organizations, more than thirty Asian Pacific American organizations, and well over one hundred women's organizations. Organizations such as these continue to make up only a small portion of the broader interest group universe that counts more than seventeen thousand national organizations and that encompasses organizations representing much wealthier and more powerful interests such as business, professional, financial, ideologically conservative, and foreign policy organizations (Baumgartner and Leech 1998; Gray and Lowery 1996; Heaney 2004; Schlozman and Burch forthcoming; Tichenor and Harris 2005). Nonetheless, organizations such as the National Association for the Advancement of Colored People (NAACP), the National Organization for Women (NOW), the Center for Law and Social Policy (CLASP), the National Council of La Raza (NCLR), and the National Asian Pacific American Law Center (NAPALC) have become a significant and visible presence in Washington politics. Organizations such as these provide an institutionalized voice to and compensatory representation for the concerns of formerly excluded groups that still have insufficient formal representation in national politics (Boles 1991).

Because of their mandate to give voice to the voiceless, the explosion in the ranks of these organizations brought with it the promise of a new era in which the interest group system would ensure—as the pluralists claimed—that everyone, even those underserved by electoral politics, would be represented (Baumgartner and Jones 1993). The extent to which this promise has been fulfilled, however, has been the source of much debate. In addition to persistent concerns about the biases and inequalities in the broader pressure group system (Danielian and Page 1994; Schlozman 1984; Schlozman and Burch forthcoming), the growth in the number of organizations representing marginalized groups has brought with it new concerns about the biases *within* organizations claiming to speak on behalf of marginalized populations. There is broad (though by no means unanimous) agreement that the increase in the number of organizations speaking for marginalized groups has helped these populations in significant ways. However, a great deal of work suggests that in spite of their potential, these organizations replicate the elite bias that was lamented by Schattschneider (Berry 1999; Cohen 1999; Kurtz 2002). While Schattschneider was concerned primarily with biases toward wealthy and powerful interests within the broader pressure group system, new misgivings have surfaced about biases within the organizations that claim to remedy the inequities resulting from such biases. These reservations take six main forms and encompass concerns about the implications of organizations that emphasize social issues over economic ones or conversely emphasize economic issues over social ones; worries about the conservatizing impact of organizational formalization on protest-oriented social movements; concerns about the implications of socioeconomic biases in political participation for the ability of organizations to speak for broad populations; suspicions about the repercussions of strategic considerations; and arguments about the effects of intersectional marginalization for representation on behalf of disadvantaged groups.[3]

## ECONOMIC ISSUES VERSUS SOCIAL ISSUES

The first cluster of misgivings revolves around critiques of a middle-class bias in the agendas of organizations representing formerly excluded groups. In *The New Liberalism*, for example, Jeffrey Berry (1999) argues that liberal advocacy groups have abandoned the pursuit of economic justice and are instead dominated by activity on "post-materialist" issues (Inglehart 1977; also known as quality of life, social, or *identitarian* issues) such as the environment, which, he argues, are of interest mainly to middle-class people. In her recent book, *Diminished Democracy*, Theda Skocpol (2003) expresses a related concern about the decline in nationally federated cross-class membership organizations. She argues that the staff-led identity-based organizations that have mushroomed since the 1960s have abandoned low-income and working-class people as well as their policy concerns.[4] These worries also are voiced by political theorists such as Nancy Fraser, who views movements for more equitable redistribution as having been displaced and disarmed by a "politics of recognition" that is overly concerned with identity-based struggles (Fraser 1997).

## SOCIAL ISSUES VERSUS ECONOMIC ISSUES

A second set of concerns is essentially the mirror image of this first cluster, and it alleges that organizations concerned with class and economic issues marginalize issues of race, gender, and sexuality such as affirmative action, abortion, and lesbian, gay, bisexual, and transgender rights (LGBT) (Duberman 2002). These two lines of criticism reverberate through contemporary partisan politics, with some analysts claiming that the Democratic Party fails to appeal to its natural base of low-income voters because it neglects class issues and focuses instead on issues of identity, catering to constituencies such as racial minorities and pro-choice feminists (Gitlin 1995; Frank 2004; Wallis 2005). Others counter that the Democrats are too willing to sacrifice these latter constituencies in pursuit of swing voters who support Democratic economic positions but who have conservative views when it comes to policy issues such as abortion, affirmative action, and LGBT rights (Frymer 1999).

## THE IRON LAW OF OLIGARCHY

A third constellation of reservations about the extent to which advocacy organizations represent disadvantaged subgroups overlaps with these first two and stems from what some scholars claim are the conservatizing effects of formal, professionalized, and institutionalized organizations on the participatory, democratic, and radical social movements out of which they grow (Gamson and Schmeidler 1984; Michels 1911; Piven and Cloward 1977; Staggenborg 1988; Valocchi 1990, 1993). These concerns echo those of the early twentieth-century sociologist Robert Michels (1911). Michels argues that as the skilled leaders needed by organizations (or parties, in his study) stay in office for longer periods of time and become increasingly professionalized, the organizations that they lead become increasingly centralized and bureaucratized.[5] In the process, the interests of leaders begin to diverge from those of their members, and they become more concerned with their own positions and organizational maintenance than with the political goals of the organization. In a similar vein, Frances Fox Piven and Richard Cloward (1977) argue that permanent and professionalized organizations inhibit protest, mass defiance, militancy, and radical dissent, all of which, they argue, are responsible for the gains made by movements. These organizations instead abandon oppositional politics, embrace moderate goals, and use institutionalized tactics.[6] According to both Michels and Piven and Cloward, then, the clear consequence of the proliferation of advocacy organizations is decreased movement efficacy and an abandonment of issues affecting disadvantaged groups.

## SOCIOECONOMIC BIASES IN POLITICAL PARTICIPATION

Levels of advocacy on behalf of disadvantaged subgroups are also likely to be low because of the socioeconomic biases associated with political and organizational activity in the United States. Sidney Verba, Kay Lehman Scholzman, and Henry Brady, for example, find much lower levels of organizational membership among women, African Americans, Latinos, and people with lower levels of income and education (Verba, Schlozman, and Brady 1995). Consequently, the median member of most advocacy groups is likely to be white, male, affluent and well educated, and organization leaders are likely to try to appeal to the interests and preferences of such a member. Many of these socioeconomic and demographic biases—particularly biases toward the highly educated and affluent—are even more pronounced when it comes to the members of staffs and boards who make the decisions for their organizations about policy advocacy (Abzug and Galaskiewicz 2001; DiMaggio and Anheier 1990; O'Regan and Oster 2005; Pease 2003; Rutledge 1994; J. Wilson [1974] 1995). Because governance structures and decision-making processes often mean that organizations reflect the attributes of their staffs and members (Berry 1977), even well-intentioned organization leaders might not hear from members of disadvantaged subgroups within their constituencies, further depressing the chances that these organizations will address issues that concern them (Barakso 2004; Mansbridge 1983; Michels 1911).

### STRATEGIC CONCERNS

Although not primarily concerned with representation for disadvantaged subgroups, evidence from other areas of scholarship about interest groups and social movements suggests a set of strategic reasons to be concerned that organizations will not be active when it comes to issues affecting disadvantaged subgroups. Many of these reasons are related to the aforementioned socioeconomic biases in political participation, and they also derive from insights from two main sources: Anthony Downs's book *An Economic Theory of Democracy* (1957) and James Q. Wilson's equally influential work *Political Organizations* ([1974] 1995).

*Median Members* | In his classic book, Anthony Downs argues that political parties and candidates choose policy positions that appeal to the "median voter" in order to maximize the number of voters casting ballots for them (see also Black 1948). From a Downsian perspective, interest groups similarly want to maximize member support and therefore try to appeal to their "median member." As a consequence, interest groups are likely to ignore targeted issues affecting numerically small subgroups—whether weak or strong—in favor of issues that have a wide impact and that affect their median member. Similarly, in order to avoid alienating allies, contributors, members, and potential members, organizations avoid issues that are unpopular or controversial among their members or the public, as are many of the issues affecting disadvantaged groups (Kollman 1998; Rothenberg 1992; M. Smith 2000; Schlozman and Tierney 1986).

*Organizational Maintenance* | James Q. Wilson suggests another set of strategic considerations that are likely to depress advocacy on behalf of disadvantaged subgroups. Echoing Michels, he argues that the decisions of organization leaders are structured in large part by concerns about organizational maintenance and survival—considerations about, for example, the need to secure contributions, hold on to members, and maintain legitimacy. Wilson contends further that these concerns make organization leaders risk-averse and compel them to cater to those who can contribute time and money (J. Wilson [1974] 1995; see also Barakso 2004; Gibson and Bingham 1985; McCarthy and Zald 1973; Moe 1981; Salisbury 1969; Staggenborg 1988; Walker 1983, 1991). As Verba, Schlozman, and Brady (1995) show, potential contributors and volunteers are likely to come from relatively advantaged social and economic strata and are consequently less likely to be sympathetic to the demands and needs of disadvantaged subgroups.

*Political Opportunities and Reputational Concerns* | The need to respond to threats and to exploit political opportunities and policy windows in order to advance their policy goals might serve to further dampen organizations' attention to disadvantaged-subgroup issues (Austen-Smith and Wright 1994, 1996; Baumgartner and Leech 1998; Goldstone and Tilly 2001; Jenkins and Perrow 1977; Kingdon 1995; Kollman 1998; McAdam 1982; Meyer 1990, 1993; Meyer and Staggenborg 1996; Smith 2000; Tarrow 1996; Van Dyke and Soule 2002; Van Dyke 2003).[7] In addition to these reasonable desires for policy successes, there are reputational advantages associated with policy wins (Chong 1991; Kingdon 1995; McAdam 1982; C. Tilly 1978). As a result of such considerations, organizations are likely to prefer high-profile, politically salient, and winnable issues over more low-profile issues or issues that might not result in victories (Costain 1992; Freeman 1975; Kingdon

1995; McAdam 1982; Tarrow 1996). Policies affecting disadvantaged subgroups are often politically salient or high on the policy agenda, but when they are, they are almost by definition political "losers" (if they were not, these subgroups would no longer be quite so disadvantaged), so pursuing the interests of such subgroups on these issues is rarely a surefire route to policy success.

*Niches* | In line with these strategic rationales, the niche theories of William Browne (1990) and Virginia Gray and David Lowery (1996) suggest another set of reasons that organizations will not be very active on behalf of disadvantaged subgroups of their constituencies. These scholars argue that to maintain a competitive advantage and a well-established identity among patrons, members, and government officials, interest groups focus on narrow policy "niches," preferring a monopoly over a few issues to wide involvement within their policy domains (Baumgartner and Jones 1993; Browne 1990; Heinz et al. 1993; for a contrary view, see Heaney 2004). Organizations therefore favor issues that are similar to those that they have previously addressed and that are recognizable as "their" issues by members and policy makers, avoiding issues that transgress the boundaries around traditional and identifiable policy issues (Barakso 2004; Baumgartner and Jones 1993; Kingdon 1995; J. Wilson [1974] 1995).

*Capture* | Finally, taken as a whole, the strategic arguments described in this section suggest that attention to issues affecting disadvantaged subgroups is rendered unlikely because there is little competition for the support and membership of the members of these subgroups. They are thus "captured" by those organizations that are willing to claim them in any way, depriving weak subgroups of the "exit option" that stronger members can use to exact attention by threatening to withdraw their support (Frymer 1999; Hirschman 1970).

## INTERSECTIONAL MARGINALIZATION

A final approach to understanding how well organizations represent their disadvantaged constituents is informed by the recognition of what scholars have termed *intersectionality* (which I began to describe in chapter 1). Theories of intersectionality were developed initially by feminists of color who were frustrated with a feminist movement that privileged and essentialized the experiences and positions of white women, representing these experiences as those of "all women," and also with a civil rights movement that similarly privileged and essentialized the experiences and positions of black men (Collins 1990; Davis 1981; hooks 1981). More generally, intersectional theories reject the notion that one particular form of domination or social relation—be it race, class, patriarchy, or heteronomativity—is the primary source of oppression (Kurtz 2002, 38). While not denying the importance of "group identities" based on categories such as race, gender, class, or sexuality, proponents of intersectional frameworks insist that "what makes a group is less some set of attributes its members share than the [class, gender, race, nationality, religion, etc.] relations in which they stand to others" (Young 2000, 90).[8] As a consequence, while they recognize that important inequalities persist *between* marginalized and dominant racial, gender, or economic groups, intersectional approaches highlight the ways in which social and political forces manipulate the overlapping and intersecting inequalities *within* marginal groups. They also emphasize the consequent unevenness in the effects of the political, economic, and social gains made by marginalized groups since, and as a result of, the social movements and policy gains of the 1960s and 1970s highlighted earlier in this chapter and in chapter 1 (McCall 2005). Examples of intersectionally marginalized groups include African American gay men, who face discrimination based on both race and sexuality, and low-income women, who are disadvantaged both economically as well as based on gender.[9]

From an intersectional perspective, the quandaries within the community of organizations representing marginalized groups cannot be understood as a zero-sum trade-off between economic issues on the one hand, and social issues on the other (what some scholars have characterized as an "either/or" approach that regards economic and social injustices as mutually exclusive), nor should they be construed as the inevitable outcome of rational or strategic choices. It is not simply that socially liberal organizations neglect economically disadvantaged people or that economically oriented organizations marginalize issues of race, gender, and sexuality. Instead, adherents of an intersectional approach contend, the problem is that all of these organizations are traditionally organized around single axes of discrimination and are sectoral in their analyses of social problems. As a result, these organizations fail to recognize that subgroups of their constituents are caught at the crossroads of multiple forms of disadvantage. Consequently, organizations erase and fail to address issues that affect subgroups of their constituencies whose marginalized positions are constituted by the *intersections* of different forms of disadvantage (Crenshaw 1989; C. Cohen 1999; Kurtz 2002).

## UNDERSTANDING INTERSECTIONALITY

Groups can be marginalized or lack power along any of a variety of axes within what Patricia Hill Collins has called the "matrix of domination" (Collins 1990): they might lack financial resources; they might now be or have been in the past the objects of de jure or de facto discrimination; they might lack electoral power and therefore have no or few elected representatives; or they might lack "cultural capital" because they are socially stigmatized by the broader society or the dominant culture (M. Williams 1998, 15), because their moral standing is questionable, or because they do not conform to "middle-class or dominant constructions of moral, normative, patriarchal citizenship" (C. Cohen 1999, 13–14). They also may be few in number (i.e., a minority), though—as illustrated by the examples of billionaires, who are a minority of all Americans, and by women, who constitute a majority of the population—minority status on its own is not necessary or sufficient to qualify a group as marginalized. In addition, membership in marginalized groups helps structure patterns of social and political inequality, and membership in these groups is not usually experienced as voluntary or mutable (M. Williams 1998, 15).

Theories and lived experiences of intersectionality tell us that these many forms of oppression and disadvantage are not static or able to be ranked, and they do not operate along single axes in simple or additive ways. Instead of functioning as separate, fixed, and parallel tracks, these systems are at once dynamic and structural, and they create cumulative inequalities that define, shape, and reinforce one another in ways that constitute the relative positions and opportunities of differently situated members of marginalized groups (C. Cohen 1999, 51; Crenshaw 2000, 8; Parenti 1978, 76). The term *intersectionality* itself derives from a "traffic" metaphor employed by Crenshaw to illustrate the functioning and impact of multiple forms of marginalization. Race, gender, and other forms of discrimination, she explains, are "roads" that structure the social, economic, and political terrain. These roads, though often framed as distinct and mutually exclusive, in reality overlap and intersect, creating "complex intersections" at which two or three or four "disempowering dynamics" meet.

Those situated at the juncture of multiple "roads" of oppression and disadvantage (such as those based on race, gender, and economic status) are subject to injuries by "the heavy flow of traffic" traveling simultaneously from many directions and along multiple roads (Crenshaw 2000, 9). The effects of the injuries resulting from these manifold forms of discrimination are compounded, exponential, and unique products that are different from and far greater than the sum of their parts, creating unique dimensions of disempowerment and differently situated subgroups (Crenshaw 1989, 57). Because they are mutually constituted, specific forms of disadvantage cannot be understood or addressed in isolation. Since all forms of subordination are interconnected, understanding each one requires doing what legal scholar Mari Matsuda describes as "asking the other questions." For example, when we see something that "looks racist," she says, we should also ask, "Where is the patriarchy in this?" When something looks sexist, we need also to look for the heterosexism in it. If something is homophobic, we must also understand the class interests embedded in it (Matsuda 1991, 1189).

Rather than asking these "other questions," existing legal and political paradigms more often elide such connections and intersectionally constituted forms of discrimination. Because the consequences of intersectional discrimination affect marginal members of already marginal groups, they tend to be obscured, analyses of their effects are consequently few, and policy solutions to them remain undeveloped. As Ange-Marie Hancock explains, focusing on single causes leads to attempts to "treat multiple diagnosis problems with a single magic policy prescription," thereby creating a permanent set of marginal groups who remain unaided by the proposed solutions (Hancock 2007, 70). Trying to understand and address the effects of gender, for example, without taking race and class into account obscures many issues that are unique to or that disproportionately affect disadvantaged subsets of women. Gender discrimination in the labor force, for instance, intersects with other forms of subordination such as those based on race, sexuality, or class and cannot be effectively understood or addressed without addressing all of these dimensions.

Consider the concentration of low-income women of color in low-wage and unsafe jobs in the United States. If we treat this concentration purely as a function of gender discrimination, we ignore its racial, ethnic, and class determinants. Conversely, if we treat the concentration as a function solely of racial discrimination, without acknowledging its disparate impact on men and women, we obscure the gendered nature of racial discrimination and class structures. Either possibility leads to a piecemeal and therefore incomplete understanding of, and incomplete solutions to, the many vulnerabilities that conspire together to *create* and *reinforce* one another through these labor force inequities that concentrate *some* women, but not *all* women, in jobs such as these. Neglecting the multiple dimensions of this concentration also obscures the ways in which "intersecting forms of domination produce locations of both oppression and opportunity" for differently situated subgroups such that more privileged women and people of color might in fact benefit from or contribute to such inequalities (Baca Zinn and Dill 1996).

While marginalization occurs along multiple intersecting and overlapping axes such as gender *and* race *and* poverty, the *political response* to oppression and disadvantage in the United States, with few exceptions, has been to organize interest groups and to pursue public policies that are dedicated to addressing *single* axes of oppression—gender *or* race *or* poverty. There are certainly a number of national organizations, such as the National Black Women's Health Imperative, that have explicit missions to represent the interests of intersectionally marginalized groups (in this case, black women). However, the vast majority of interest groups are organized along a single axis or cleavage, such as race, gender, union membership, poverty status, or sexuality. Of the more than seven hundred organizations listed in a wide range of print and online directories and categorized as organizations representing marginalized groups at the national level in 2000, I found fewer than twenty that were organized explicitly around more than one axis of marginalization.[10] Organizations representing one main axis of identity or one form of inequality or marginalization, such as NOW, the NAACP, and others, are clearly the norm at the national level.[11]

An intersectional understanding exposes the fact that the interests associated with these identities and inequalities are not givens in nature but are instead constructions that result from social and political processes and experiences (Appiah and Gutman 1996; Baker 1998; Boswell 1997; Fausto-Sterling 1993; Jacobson 1998; J. Katz 1995; Kimmel 1995; Lorber 1995; Omi and Winant 1994). From this perspective, the single-axis interest groups that so dominate advocacy politics do not represent unitary constituencies with clearly defined and bounded interests. Instead, the broad constituencies spoken for by these organizations are coalitions of intersecting and overlapping groups that are organized around one particular axis that is *constructed* or *framed* as what they have in common. As Iris Young explains, however, attempts to define a common group identity tend "to normalize the experience and perspective of some of the group members" while "marginalizing or silencing that of others" (Young 2000, 89). Consequently, organizing around one axis usually means that these allegedly "common interests" (or what Cathy Cohen calls "consensus issues") are actually those that affect or are "rooted in the experiences of" the more privileged members of a group, and the policy issues addressed by these organizations are likely to be those that affect these more privileged members as well (Cohen 1999, 23).[12] The claims and needs of intersectionally disadvantaged groups, on the other hand, are constructed and framed as being *outside* the purview of these single-axis organizations, and they therefore fall through the cracks between the axes of most existing advocacy organizations.

To illustrate this dynamic, consider once again the example of the concentration of low-income women of color in low-wage jobs. Although this issue has a disproportionate effect on women, it is less likely to be seen as a gendered problem or to be addressed as such by women's organizations because it does not reflect the experiences of women from dominant racial, ethnic, and class groups in the United States. Because of its disproportionate effect on women, however, an intersectional approach also leads us to expect that this issue is less likely to be addressed by organizations that represent racial minorities or low-income people. Moreover, were any of these single-axis organizations to address this issue, they would be likely to focus on it as a one-dimensional problem of *either* race or gender or class. A single-axis approach consequently fails to appreciate and address the intersectional causes and effects of this concentration on the intersectionally marginalized women who bear the brunt of its impact. Replicated over numerous issues and organizations, this dynamic yields a paucity of attention to the issues that affect intersectionally marginalized groups (and a great deal of attention to issues that affect advantaged subgroups) by the interest groups that claim to speak for them. As a consequence, the benefits of the policy gains made possible by the advocacy activities of these organizations are distributed unevenly among members of these groups, a situation that Cathy Cohen (1999) has labeled "advanced marginalization." As a consequence, members of constituencies who are privileged "but for" one axis of disadvantage reap the greatest benefits of efforts of advocacy groups, which thereby amplify the inequalities *within* the populations they represent, leading to heightened stratification. While some members of marginalized groups will be better off, others will be worse off, both

vis-à-vis dominant society and relative to other members of the marginalized group (C. Cohen 1999).

## POLICY TYPOLOGY

Each of the six approaches that I have outlined above bodes ill for intersectionally marginalized groups, and together they provide many reasons to suspect that the single-axis interest groups that predominate at
the national level are ill equipped to represent intersectionally marginalized subgroups of their constituents. Much of the scholarship supporting
these suspicions, however, is either theoretical (Crenshaw 1989; Williams
1998; Young 1997, 2000; see also Carter, Sellers, and Squires 2002; Hancock 2007), based on ungeneralizable case studies (Cohen 1999; Kurtz 2002;
Weaver 2000; L. Williams 1998), or focused on organizations other than
ones speaking on behalf of women, racial minorities, and low-income people. For example, Jeffrey Berry (1999) examines the policy activities of public interest groups but focuses largely on environmental organizations,
paying minimal attention to organizations representing groups such as
women, racial and ethnic minorities, and low-income people. In addition,
his study focuses on the congressional testimony of these organizations,
and so while invaluable, it does not give us a full picture of the agendas and
advocacy tactics of organizations representing the disadvantaged. Theda
Skocpol's important book, *Diminished Democracy* (2003) focuses its analyses on all organizations of one particular organizational structure—large,
federated, national membership organizations. As a consequence of these
research designs, extant evidence cannot refute the claims made by many
advocacy organizations that they actually *do* represent their disadvantaged
constituents, nor can it adjudicate between contending explanations about
why they do not.

Moreover, while helpful for understanding how organizations represent
disadvantaged subgroups, extant intersectional frameworks are limited,
relying as they do on dichotomous distinctions that differentiate only
between, on the one hand, *single-axis issues* (or, in Cathy Cohen's terminology, "consensus issues") that affect the whole group and, on the other
hand, *intersectional issues* (or, in Cohen's terminology, "cross-cutting issues") that affect disadvantaged members (C. Cohen 1999).[13] Dichotomous
frameworks such as these conflate two separate categories, failing to distinguish the interests of the majority from the interests of advantaged
subgroups. As a consequence, these two-part frameworks do not examine

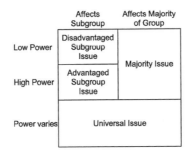

**Fig. 2.1.** Policy typology.

whether there are differences in the levels of advocacy devoted to policy issues affecting a majority of members compared to those affecting advantaged subpopulations within marginalized groups, nor do they interrogate the specific effects associated with axes of privilege.

Insights from strategic frameworks that emphasize organizational maintenance and the need to appeal to the median member suggest additional dimensions that help extend these dichotomous frameworks. From such a Downsian approach, representation corresponds to majority rule, and it is therefore the breadth of an issue's impact that determines how active an organization will be. From this perspective, as the number of members that are affected by an issue decreases, so will the level of attention that an organization devotes to the issue.[14] While a useful supplement to intersectional understandings, such a strategic approach is insufficiently attentive to the issues of power and marginalization emphasized by intersectional paradigms. Strategic paradigms therefore conflate small advantaged subgroups with small disadvantaged subgroups, suggesting low levels of activity on behalf of both.

The elisions of both intersectional and Downsian paradigms can be addressed, and the strengths of each approach harnessed, by expanding the key aspects of both frameworks to produce the four-part public policy issue typology that I introduced in chapter 1 (see fig. 2.1). The four categories in this typology are (1) *universal issues*, which at least in theory, affect the population as a whole, regardless of race, gender, sexual orientation, disability, class, or any other identity; (2) *majority issues*, which affect an organization's members or constituents relatively equally; (3) *disadvantaged-subgroup issues*, which affect a subgroup of an organization's constituents who are disadvantaged economically, socially, or politically compared to the broader constituency; and (4) *advantaged-subgroup issues*, which also affect a subgroup of an organization's constituents but one that is relatively strong or advantaged compared to the broader constituency.

For example, universal issues include policy issues such as health care reform or Social Security. Though not everyone is affected in exactly the same way by either of these issues, issues such as these, as their name implies, are relatively "equal opportunity" in their potential impact, both among members of constituencies of the organizations in this study and outside of these constituencies. Majority issues, in contrast, have particular effects on the constituents of the organization in question. However, among these constituents, a majority issue is also an equal opportunity issue, equally likely to affect any member of an advocacy organization's constituency even if it does not affect a numerical majority. An example of such an issue is violence against women in the case of women's organizations. This issue is of potential concern to all women, all of whom have relatively equal potential to be victims, even if not every woman herself is or will be a victim in her lifetime.[15]

While both universal and majority issues are, in different ways, equal opportunity issues, neither disadvantaged-subgroup nor advantaged-subgroup issues can be characterized in this way. Instead, when it comes to these issues, different subgroups of an organization's constituency arc *unequally* likely to benefit from or to be harmed by such issues. In the case of disadvantaged-subgroup issues, they are more likely to benefit or harm a subgroup of an organization's constituents that is disadvantaged relative to other constituents. For example, welfare reform is a disadvantaged-subgroup issue in the case of women's organizations. That is, many of the causes of poverty are related to gender-based oppression and discrimination, and the majority of people directly affected by this policy are women (and their children), but the majority of women are not affected by it, nor are all women equally likely to be affected by it. Instead, welfare reform has a disproportionately high chance of affecting specific subgroups of women—in particular low-income women and women of color, that is, intersectionally disadvantaged subgroups of all women.

In contrast to disadvantaged-subgroup issues, advantaged-subgroup issues, while also unequal in their potential impact, are more likely to benefit or harm a subgroup of an organization's constituents that is advantaged relative to other constituents. So, while issues falling into this category affect a subgroup of the broader group or involve multiple axes of identity, many of those axes may be associated with advantage or privilege (e.g., middle-class, male, white, heterosexual) rather than with disadvantage or marginalization. In addition, although they affect a subgroup of an organization's constituency, issues falling into the advantaged-subgroup category are more likely than disadvantaged-subgroup issues to be constructed or framed as majority issues.[16] An example of an advantaged-subgroup issue is affirmative action in higher education as an issue for women's organizations. While this policy issue is gendered and intended to benefit women, not all women are equally likely to benefit from affirmative action policies in higher education. Instead, the benefits of such programs are more likely to go to middle-class and affluent women, who are far more likely than low-income women to attend college, graduate school, and professional school.

In labeling these issues advantaged-subgroup issues, I mean in no way to suggest that the constituents affected by these issues are advantaged relative to the general population. It is important to keep in mind that for the most part, all of the organizations being considered here represent groups that are marginalized or disadvantaged in some way relative to the population as a whole. The disadvantages faced by members of advantaged subgroups, however, are not necessarily compounded by other axes of marginalization.

In addition, classifying issues and groups in a typology assumes to some degree that the categories within this typology are socially and politically meaningful and that they help us understand oppression as a "systematic, structured institutional process" (Young 1997, 17). Nonetheless, because the concepts of interest to social scientists are rarely based on categories that inhere in nature, any classification scheme or typology is constructed and therefore subjective to some degree. We have come to accept, for example, the contingency, malleability, and constructedness of concepts such as race and gender that we previously assumed were clear and easily measurable (Baker 1998; Boswell 1997; Fausto-Sterling 1993; Jacobson 1998; Kimmel 1994; Lorber 1995; Omi and Winant 1994). Debates about the ever-changing racial and ethnic categories of the United States Census of Population are but one example of this phenomenon (K. Williams 2006).

The concepts of interest in this study are no less malleable, contingent, or debatable, and, as a result, both the categories in the aforementioned policy typology and the issues assigned to each category (as will be discussed shortly) are unavoidably plastic. There are many other policy categorization schemes through which we might analyze organizations' choices about issue advocacy, such as whether the issues addressed are economic or social, regulatory, distributive, or redistributive (Peterson 1981), or whether they have to with domestic policy or foreign policy. That each of these alternatives would tell us something important about interest groups, representation, and public policy need not undermine the value of the story that I tell using the typology that I put forward here.

Even if we accept the classification scheme that I have proposed, the fact that I limit the intersections that I examine to two axes (for example, the intersection of race and gender, or the intersection of class and sexuality) in spite of the myriad possible points of intersection raises questions about whether I am focusing on certain manifestations of intersectional disadvantage at the expense of others. Does this classification scheme leave out, for example, important questions about representing women who are low-income and also have a disability, or low-income gays and lesbians of color? As Ange-Marie Hancock notes, "all categories can be fractured into ever-exponentially increasing sub-categories once intersectionality is addressed empirically" (Hancock 2007, 66). Consequently, some reductiveness is necessary to keep the empirical analysis manageable, and I can realistically test only a limited number of intersections.

## STUDYING REPRESENTATION

Although theories of intersectionality have elicited extensive interest in the social sciences and humanities, there have been fewer large-scale and systematic efforts to assess these theories empirically (for some exceptions, however, see Fraga et al. 2005; Hawkesworth 2003; and Smooth 2001). As Hancock points out, most quantitative analyses that have taken an intersectional approach have done so using surveys and other instruments that were intended for other purposes and therefore were not designed to capture the overlapping and intersecting categories suggested by intersectional frameworks (Hancock 2007, 66–67; see also McCall 2005).

In order to operationalize the concepts associated with intersectionality (as well as with the other approaches outlined earlier), the central issues of the book are addressed using original data and a multiple-methods approach. First, to examine systematically how well organizations represent disadvantaged subgroups of their constituencies, I collected new data using a telephone survey of national advocacy organizations representing women, racial minorities, and low-income people in national politics.[17] Because I targeted the full population of the relevant organizations in this universe and asked questions about a range of public policy issues, the survey

has yielded data that allow for the first systematic and generalizable analysis of the relationship among constituency, issue type, and advocacy in
organizations working for underrepresented groups. To supplement the
quantitative data, I conducted in-depth semistructured, anonymous, face-
to-face interviews with officials at forty organizations between March 22
and August 3, 2001. I briefly describe both the survey and the face-to-face
interviews here. For more extensive information about both the interviews
and the survey design, execution, and question wordings, please see appendices A, B, and C.

## THE 2000 SURVEY OF NATIONAL ECONOMIC AND
## SOCIAL JUSTICE ORGANIZATIONS

I collected the survey data using the 2000 Survey of National Economic
and Social Justice Organizations (SNESJO). I designed the survey instrument, and the telephone interviews were conducted in 2000 by Zogby
International. Survey interviews were completed with officers of 286 organizations out of a universe of 714 organizations (for a 40 percent response
rate).[18] Table 2.1 shows the distribution of the organization types in both
the universe of social and economic justice organizations and the resulting
sample of organizations that participated in the survey and interviews (see
table 2.1). I chose to include in the survey both organizations with individual members (what are often referred to as *citizen groups* and which I will
call *membership organizations*) and organizations that do not have a mass
base (what Robert Salisbury [1984] calls "institutions" and which I refer to
as *nonmember organizations*).[19]

I compiled a database of organizations using information from published directories of organizations, media sources, and movement publications. These sources also were used to collect preliminary data about the
groups in order to test for nonresponse and other types of bias in the resulting data. The questions in the SNESJO focused on organizations' activities
on public policy issues of the 1990s that have had significant implications
for rights and resources for marginalized groups such as women, racial
minorities, immigrants, LGBT people, and low-income people. To contextualize these activities and facilitate comparisons with existing work, the
SNESJO replicates key questions from earlier surveys (Berry 1977; Heinz
et al. 1993; Knoke and Adams 1984; Kollman 1998; Laumann and Knoke
1987; Schlozman and Tierney 1986; Walker 1991), including questions about

TABLE 2.1  Distribution of national advocacy organizations (nationally and in samples), by organization type

| ORGANIZATION TYPE | ORGANIZATIONS IN THE UNITED STATES | | SAMPLE | | FACE-TO-FACE INTERVIEWS | |
|---|---|---|---|---|---|---|
| | # | % | # | % | # | % |
| Asian Pacific American | 32 | 4.5 | 13 | 4.5 | 3 | 7.5 |
| Black/African American | 40 | 5.5 | 20 | 7 | 4 | 10 |
| Latino/Hispanic | 43 | 6.3 | 16 | 5.6 | 2 | 5 |
| Native American/American Indian | 35 | 5.3 | 13 | 4.5 | 1 | 2.5 |
| Civil rights—Other[a] | 70 | 10.1 | 33 | 11.5 | 5 | 12.5 |
| Immigrants' Rights | 8 | 1.1 | 6 | 2.1 | 1 | 2.5 |
| Labor[b] | 175 | 24.6 | 42 | 14.7 | 4 | 10 |
| Economic justice[c] | 153 | 21 | 66 | 23.1 | 8 | 20 |
| Public interest[d] | 21 | 3 | 11 | 3.9 | 4 | 10 |
| Women's rights/feminist[e] | 137 | 18.6 | 66 | 23.1 | 8 | 20 |
| Total | 714 | 100 | 286 | 100 | 40 | 100 |

Sources: The database of organizations was compiled by author based on information in the following print and online directories: the Electra Pages (electrapages.com); the Encyclopedia of Associations (Gale Research 2000);the Leadership Conference on Civil Rights (lccr.org); the National Directory of Asian Pacific American Organizations (Organization of Chinese Americans 1999); the National Directory of Hispanic Organizations (Congressional Hispanic Caucus, Inc. 1999); Public Interest Profiles (Foundation for Public Affairs 1999); Washington Information Directory (CQ Press 1998); Washington Representatives (Columbia Books 1999); and Who's Who in Washington Nonprofit Groups (Congressional Quarterly 1995); the Women of Color Organizations and Projects National Directory (Women of Color Resource Center 1998).
[a] Includes broadly based civil rights and civil liberties organizations; lesbian, gay, bisexual, and transgender (LGBT) rights organizations; criminal justice organizations; Arab/Muslim organizations; antiracist organizations; some religious minority groups; and multi-culturalism organizations.
[b] Includes unions.
[c] Includes antipoverty, welfare rights, anti-homeless, and anti-hunger organizations.
[d] Includes consumer, environmental, and "good government" organizations that advocate in the areas of racial, gender, or economic justice.
[e] Includes women of color, reproductive rights, and women's health organizations.

internal factors such as organizations' resources, activities, and ideology, as well as measures of external factors such as the effects of shifts in partisan control of political institutions.

The SNESJO addressed only domestic policy issues, and, in order to assess the type of representation provided by organizations, issues were further limited to ones that can be pursued at the national level and through all three branches of the federal government (the legislative, executive, and judicial branches). Using a two-step method, I also stipulated that the policy issues must have been on the national political agenda during the period covered by the study (i.e., issues had to involve pending court cases being heard by the Supreme Court, pending legislation being debated in Congress, or pending policy being set in an executive branch department or agency). To select appropriate questions, I compiled a list of issues from *Congressional Quarterly* for 1990, 1993, 1996, and 1999 and another from the "Supreme Court Roundup" (a regular feature in the *New York Times*) for 1990–2000. After selecting all issues that were potentially relevant to the groups in the survey, I then searched the 1990–2000 volumes of the *Congressional Record* and of the *Federal Register* to confirm that the issues were on the agendas in the legislative and executive branches as well, noting how many times each issue had been mentioned in each of these sources. I repeated this reverse search for the "Supreme Court Roundup." Although appearing in any one of these sources would constitute sufficient evidence that issues were on the political radar screen and thus could reasonably be expected to be on the agenda of advocacy groups, all twenty-two issues that I selected were found in at least two of the sources, and twenty of the twenty-two issues were found in all three sources. While there are certainly biases inherent in basing the selection of policies on these sources, this method avoids issues for which a lack of activity could be explained simply as a function of issues not being "on the agenda." In order to determine which issues should be addressed to each type of organization, I constructed a grid in which I arrayed each organization type along one axis and each issue type along the other axis. After listing all of the various subgroups of a constituency that could be affected by each policy issue, I then selected four policy issues for each organization type, the first three of which included one majority issue, one advantaged-subgroup issue, and one disadvantaged-subgroup issue (see table 2.2). The same universal issue— Social Security—was used as the fourth issue for all groups, thus also serving as a control issue.

So, for example, respondents from Asian Pacific American organizations were asked about hate crime as a majority issue, as all Asian Pacific Americans are, theoretically, equally likely to be victims of hate crime. Respondents from these organizations were asked about affirmative action in government contracting as an advantaged-subgroup issue, as this issue affects primarily Asian Pacific American business owners, a relatively privileged subgroup of all Asian Pacific Americans. Finally, they were asked about violence against women as a disadvantaged-subgroup issue, as it intersects gender and race and affects Asian Pacific American women, an intersectionally disadvantaged subgroup of Asian Pacific Americans.[20]

TABLE 2.2 Specific policy issues used in SNESJO questions, by organization type and issue category

| ORGANIZATION TYPE | MAJORITY ISSUE | ADVANTAGED SUBGROUP ISSUE | DISADVANTAGED SUBGROUP ISSUE | UNIVERSAL ISSUE |
|---|---|---|---|---|
| Asian Pacific American | Hate crime | Affirmative action in government contracting | Violence against women | Social security |
| Black/African American | Racial profiling | Affirmative action in higher education | Welfare | Social security |
| Latino/Hispanic | Census undercount | Affirmative action in higher education | Welfare | Social security |
| Native American/American Indian | Tribal sovereignty | Affirmative action in higher education | Violence against women | Social security |
| Civil rights—Other[a] | Hate crime | Affirmative action in higher education | Discrimination against LGBT people | Social security |
| Immigrants' Rights | Green-card backlog | Availability of H1B visas | Denial of benefits to immigrants | Social security |
| Labor[b] | Minimum wage | White-collar unionization | Job discrimination against women and minorities | Social security |
| Economic justice[c] | Welfare | Minimum wage | Public funding for abortion | Social security |
| Public interest[d] | Campaign finance reform | Internet privacy | Environmental racism | Social security |
| Reproductive rights/women's health | Late-term abortion | Abortion coverage by insurance/HMOs | Public funding for abortion | Social security |
| Women's rights/feminist[e] | Violence against women | Affirmative action in higher education | Welfare | Social security |

*Sources:* Issues were selected by the author based on information from *Congressional Quarterly* (1990, 1993, 1996, and 1999); the *New York Times* "Supreme Court Roundup" (1990–2000); the *Congressional Record* (1990–2000); and the *Federal Register* (1990–2000).

[a] Includes broadly based civil rights and civil liberties organizations; lesbian, gay, bisexual, and transgender (LGBT) rights organizations; criminal justice organizations; Arab/Muslim organizations; antiracist organizations; some religious minority groups; and multiculturalism organizations.

[b] Includes unions.

[c] Includes antipoverty, welfare rights, anti-homeless, and anti-hunger organizations.

[d] Includes consumer, environmental, and "good government" organizations that advocate in the areas of racial, gender, or economic justice.

[e] Includes women of color organizations.

*Operationalizing Intersectionality* | Operationalizing concepts such as intersectionality, power, and marginalization, no matter how contingently we conceptualize them, is challenging. Doing so in a study such as this one is further complicated by the fact that I am applying conventional social science methods to operationalize concepts that call into question the very kinds of categorization schemes and positivist claims dictated by social science (Hancock 2007, 66–67). There are consequently inherent tensions between my reliance on categories such as race, gender, and class for the data collection and empirical analyses, on the one hand, and the fact that the normative and theoretical frameworks underlying the study call into question the boundedness of the categories on which I rely, on the other. While I acknowledge these tensions and the questions that they might raise about how the analyses and results might differ had I drawn different boundaries, the exigencies of social science require that categories and boundaries be delineated for analytic purposes. This is a first but nonetheless critical step that represents a significant advance in a quantitative analysis of this sort.

*No Slippery Slope* | Moreover, deconstructivist approaches, of which intersectionality is a subset, do not uniformly suggest that we jettison categories as analytic tools. Rather, such approaches most often challenge *static* or *naturalized* understandings of categories such as gender, race, and sexuality. While intersectionality emphasizes the diversity within, the overlap between, and the contingency and constructedness of these categories, it does not question whether such categories are socially and politically meaningful. Indeed, rather than arguing that we should abandon these classifications as analytic categories, advocates of an intersectional approach want us to recognize the *salience* of social and demographic categories in order to more thoroughly appreciate their political implications (Dietz 2003; Hancock 2007, 66–67; McCall 2005).

## FACE-TO-FACE INTERVIEWS

The statistical analyses of quantitative data allow for broad, systematic, individual-level analyses of public policy advocacy and political representation in the United States across a diverse range of organizations and policy issues. While the survey data allow me to isolate the particular effects of a variable on an organization's activities, I gathered more detailed information about issues that had been covered by survey questions, including questions about constituencies, coalition work, representation, and choices of policy issues and advocacy tactics, by supplementing the SNESJO data with information from in-person, open-ended interviews (see table 2.1). The information obtained during these interviews provides more in-depth, qualitative information about advocacy organizations and their policy activities and goals. As a consequence, the less-structured, more open-ended responses in the face-to-face interviews offer a window into the nuances of how, why, and in what context organization officers make the decisions that they do about how to allocate organizational energy and resources. (Please see appendices A and C for additional information about the face-to-face interview methodology).

## SOME NOTES ON PUBLIC INTERESTS, SPECIAL INTERESTS, AND THE COMMON GOOD

Before proceeding with the rest of the book, in which I present the results of the analyses and discuss their substantive implications, a few issues related to the classification of the individual policy issues within the four categories warrant further discussion, as do some of the assumptions that underlie these classifications and what they suggest about the "interests" at stake in each one. For example, Social Security commonly is depicted as a textbook case of a universal issue and is a policy that is regularly portrayed as being "in the public interest." However, as I discussed earlier, differently situated individuals are affected differently by Social Security, and its actual universality is subject to many questions and debates about the inclusivity of its effects, such as whether its benefits go disproportionately to middle-class recipients.

That the effects of universal issues can vary based on the social, political, or economic location of the beneficiaries also draws our attention to the common but nonetheless complicated distinction that often is drawn between "public" (or "common") interests, on the one hand, and "special" interests, on the other hand.[21] While the interests involved in issues such as Social Security and clean air are commonly portrayed as being *broadly* shared and for the "common good," many of the policies that are the focus of the organizations in this study (such as affirmative action, reproductive rights, and public assistance to the poor) more often are portrayed as *narrowly* defined and therefore as being "special" interests that are *in conflict with* the broad public interest (Pitkin 1967, 191). As Iris Young and others have argued, however, movements and organizations that aim to combat social, political, and economic inequalities contend that appeals to a unitary or common good "often bias the interpretation of the common good in ways that favor dominant social groups" while perpetuating the marginal status of nondominant groups by positioning them "as deviant Other" and constructing their claims as "special interests" (Young 2000, 81). I will demonstrate in ensuing discussions that such distinctions between "broad" and "narrow" interests are also at work in these ways within organizations that represent marginalized groups, reproducing similar biases that favor advantaged subgroups of these constituencies.[22]

## INTERSECTIONALITY AND GROUP INTERESTS

Along with addressing the contingencies associated with public interests, the practice of assigning "group interests" also calls for some clarification. In particular, it is important to unpack the assertion implicit in these designations that the issues in the policy typology affect or are in the interests of the constituencies of the organizations to which they have been assigned. As the earlier discussion of intersectional marginalization suggested, there are many complications associated with assessing the impact of policy issues and determining what is in the "interests" of the members of broad and internally diverse groups that are defined by social or demographic characteristics such as race, class, or gender. How can we know for certain, for example, that (as the selection of hate crime as the majority issues for Asian Pacific American organizations asserts) all Asian Pacific Americans are relatively equally likely to be victimized by hate crime and that it is therefore in their interest for organizations that speak for them to be active on this issue?

Similarly, as Anne Phillips notes, we might accept as relatively straightforward "the notion that women have at least some interests distinct from and even in conflict with men's" (Phillips 1998, 234). However, women comprise a large and diverse group, and they have many differing opinions about the issues that affect them (Sears and Huddy 1990). Kristin Luker and Jane Mansbridge have documented, for example, that different subsets of women take diametrically opposed views of their interests when it comes to the issues of abortion and the Equal Rights Amendment (Luker 1984; Mansbridge 1986; see also Sapiro 1981). While "pro-choice" women regard reproductive rights as an essential component of women's equality, "pro-life" women believe just as strongly that abortion harms women's social status. Many members of marginalized groups reject a number of the policy goals pursued in their names by organizations that claim to represent their interests, and others deny altogether that their demographic characteristics affect their political identities, attitudes, or life chances (Young 2000). Implicit in the designation of an issue such as violence against women as a majority issue for the women's organizations in this study, however, is the assertion that all members of the large and diverse category "women" have an interest in measures designed to curtail gender-based violence. While it may indeed be relatively safe to assume that "all women" have a "group interest" in being protected from violence, an intersectional approach also alerts us to the fact that many of the legal interventions that are commonly used to protect women from violence might not meet the interests of all women. Scholars such as Angela Davis (2000) and Kimberlé Crenshaw (1994) have pointed out, for example, that low-income women and women of color might be reluctant to rely for protection from abusive partners on the police or other law-enforcement officers, at whose hands they might equally fear violence. They also may hesitate to call the police to intervene lest doing so perpetuate stereotypical notions of men of color as perpetrators of violence. Immigrant women might be reluctant to leave abusive spouses out of fear of being deported (Crenshaw 1994).[23]

Along similar lines, designating affirmative action in higher education as an advantaged-subgroup issue for women's organizations implicitly asserts that privileged women *all* share a broadly defined interest in this issue. However, not all privileged women are in a position to benefit from affirmative action; many are well beyond their college and graduate school days and are therefore unlikely to take advantage of such programs. Moreover, while women generally and white women in particular have benefited a great deal from affirmative action in higher education and might well share a broad concern about maintaining women's access to college and universities, many women in fact oppose such programs, either on principle or because they believe that they are harmed rather than helped by them. Plaintiffs in many of the most high-profile lawsuits against affirmative action in colleges and professional schools, for example, have been white women who have claimed to have been harmed by affirmative action programs geared toward admitting members of racial minority groups.[24]

## OBJECTIVE AND SUBJECTIVE INTERESTS

Even if we could identify a comprehensive and definitive set of objectively plausible "women's interests" (or "African American interests," or "low-income people's interests"), it is often the case that such interests do not coincide with the expressed preferences, or *subjective* interests, that people claim for themselves (Mansbridge 1983; Pitkin 1967, 161; Schlozman and Tierney 1986). For example, scholars from W. E. B. DuBois (1935) to David Roediger (1991) have argued that it would have been in the interests of nineteenth-century white workers to ally with black workers to demand higher wages from their employers. However, the "preferences" of white workers for racial segregation and white supremacy and their perception that their own social status was augmented by the continued elevation of whites over blacks more often prevented them from pursuing the cross-racial economic alliances and higher wages that were arguably in their objective interests.

However important it is to acknowledge that there are often differences between the things people want and the things that an outsider might believe they *ought to* want, it is also important to note that scholars such as Ian Shapiro argue persuasively that there are nonetheless identifiable sets of basic interests such as security, nutrition, health, and education that groups require. Along similar lines, Rogers Smith asserts that "people do have basic, recognizable types of substantive interests," which, he argues, include "material well-being, some forms of political protection and political power, and senses of ethically constitutive identity" (Rogers Smith 2004, 309). As Shapiro acknowledges, any account that specifies what these basic interests are will be controversial because these interests are always at least partly "socially constructed" and "may vary with time and circumstance" (Shapiro 1999, 85). Such concessions need not undermine the quest to fulfill these interests, he contends.

Indeed, scholars continue to debate whether it is possible to speak about individuals' or groups' objective interests at all. Some scholars, most notably rational choice theorists, argue that it is impossible to define objective interests because we cannot attribute interests to individuals in the absence of prior knowledge about their identities, beliefs, preferences, and intentions. Instead, they contend, we should focus on expressed preferences (Calhoun 2002; Reeve 2003; Scott and Marshall 2005). Others, however, assert that we cannot equate expressed preferences with real interests because people may be misled, misinformed, or simply irrational about their wants and needs. Proponents of this view argue that we should instead think about interests as what Jane Mansbridge calls "enlightened preferences"—the policy choices that people *would* make were they liberated and fully informed (Mansbridge 1983). Although, as Phillips cautions, such approaches

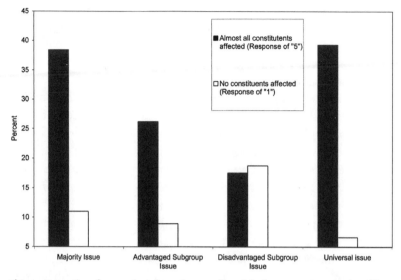

**Fig. 2.2.** Perception of proportion of constituents affected, by issue type. Organization officers were asked, "On a scale of 1 to 5, where 1 is 'none' and 5 is 'almost all,' what proportion of your members/constituents would you say is directly affected by the following issues?" Data in the black columns reflect the percentage of respondents giving the answer "5." Data in the white columns reflect the percentage of respondents giving the answer "1" (data from SNESJO).

edge "uncomfortably close to notions of 'false consciousness'" (Phillips 1998, 234) and might therefore rightly be critiqued as vanguardist and patronizing, normative theorists nonetheless tend to concur that we ought not rely on expressed preferences as the sole indicators of an individual's or group's interests.

Although it is not possible for me to establish definitively that some issues are squarely in the "interests" of a particular social group or of the constituents of a particular organization, nor is there a definitive way to verify whether my policy issue classification scheme is perfect, the data from the SNESJO can shed some light on these questions. Examining responses to the survey question asking respondents what proportion of their constituents is affected by each issue type provides some evidence that the issues that I have chosen have been classified correctly and that the categories of the typology do capture the variation in the ways these issues impact the organizations' constituents (see fig. 2.2).

We would expect, for example, that both majority and universal issues will affect large portions of constituents, and indeed, the largest proportion of respondents (close to 40 percent) said that the majority and universal issues affect "almost all" of their constituents. Advantaged-subgroup and disadvantaged-subgroup issues should affect fewer constituents; indeed, only 26.2 percent of respondents said that "almost all" of their constituents are affected by the advantaged-subgroup issue, and only 17.5 percent gave this response about the disadvantaged-subgroup issue. Although an inexact measure of their actual impact, their responses to this question lend credence to the categorization of the policy issues and suggest that the associated measures are capturing politically meaningful concepts, constructed and noisy as they are.[25]

## CONCLUSION

The foregoing discussion has not resolved the long-standing dilemmas associated with relying on demographic categories or imputing interests to the broad and diverse groups contained within them for analytic purposes, nor has it settled the notoriously difficult quandaries related to imputing these interests in cases in which we have incomplete knowledge about or there is a contradiction between objective and subjective interests. These questions, which long have been the subjects of political and scholarly discussion, will continue to concern me in subsequent chapters, and I will heed the warnings raised by these and other debates, attending to them as appropriate.

Nonetheless, it is not my objective here, nor in the rest of this book, to settle these long-standing questions. Consequently, like most social scientists and political analysts, I will continue to rely on contingent and constructed categories such as race, class, gender, and sexuality and to impute political interests to those who fall into them. I will also, however, point out cases in which these categories obscure more than they illuminate, and I will draw attention to the social and political constructedness of these interests and identities (Schlozman and Tierney 1986). Indeed, by foregrounding the many different social, economic, and political locations occupied by the members of ascriptive groups such as women, racial minorities, and low-income people, and by highlighting the constructedness, contingency, and plasticity of these categories, the policy typology and, more broadly, the intersectional framework within which it is based implicitly resist essentialist notions that hold that the individuals falling into these categories share inevitable and naturally occurring common identities and interests. Acknowledging the constructedness of these interests also foregrounds the ways in which forces such as ideologies, political leaders, affiliations, identities, and positions within power relations shape individuals' and groups' perceptions of their interests, their political goals, and their conceptions about the proper means to achieve these goals (Bachrach and Baratz 1962; Connolly 1972; Dahl 1967; Disch 2006; Gaventa 1982; Hayward 2000; Lukács [1923] 1971; Lukes 1974; Manin 1997; Schattschneider [1960] 1975; Schlozman and Tierney 1986; Shapiro 1999; Rogers Smith 2004; Young 2000).

I will address these and other important dimensions of the ways in which advocacy organizations construct, articulate, and aggregate interests and identities. It is important to bear in mind, however, that the objects of this study—advocacy organizations that represent marginalized groups—act on that assumption that, for all of their internal diversity and variation, members of these groups do share interests in particular policy issues and in overcoming their marginalization and that they are connected by what Michael Dawson has described as "linked fate" (Dawson 1994; M. Williams 1998). As such, these organizations operate based on the belief that members of marginalized populations are, at a minimum, better off individually and collectively when they mobilize as groups and attempt to achieve a voice in politics and public policy than they would be in the absence of such efforts (see Mansbridge 1983, 26). Indeed, as important as it is to heed the cautions associated with notions of group interests and group representation, members of marginalized groups continue to rely on both of these concepts because, as Iris Young reminds us, "in the context of practical affairs," such measures are often the best way to "gain a voice for many wrongly excluded issues, analyses, and positions" (Young 2000, 122–23).

This project shares these normative assumptions about representation and the interests of marginalized populations at the same time as it interrogates many of the ways in which these interests are defined and deployed. As such, rather than engaging in a wholesale questioning of whether members of marginalized share any interests that can be represented within political institutions and policy-making processes, the arguments and analyses in this book question which of the *range* of possible interests and identities the organizations that claim to speak for these groups decide to emphasize and to deploy. Rather than dispensing altogether with categorizations and classifications, I assess the implications of the schemes that *are* employed for the representation of intersectionally disadvantaged members of marginalized groups.

To these ends, chapter 3 addresses the roles of group identification and perceptions of linked fate in muddying the distinctions between objective and subjective interests among members of marginalized populations. The analyses in this and successive chapters also will detail the ways in which organizations representing these populations define and deploy the "groupness" on which they rely to make their political claims. Subsequent discussions also will demonstrate the ways in which the "common interests" of marginalized groups are thus designated because they have been *constructed* as such, pointing to the roles played by advocacy organizations themselves, as well as the roles of other policy makers and policy elites, in these processes of interest formation and construction (Schlozman and Tierney 1986, 20).

I turn now to the first part of this enterprise, presenting data from the survey and interviews to explore the contemporary universe of national social and economic justice organizations. Combining this information with a normative discussion about group representation, I discuss the role of advocacy organizations as representatives of marginalized groups in American politics.

# THREE

# Intersectionality and Representation

*Intersectionality* is a relatively new term within political theory and social science research, but concerns about multiply disadvantaged subgroups are long-standing.[1] Throughout the nineteenth and twentieth centuries and extending into the twenty-first, American political movements and organizations that claimed to speak on behalf of marginalized groups have faced allegations that they ignored the needs, interests, and identities of constituents who face more than one type of discrimination or disadvantage, a legacy that sociologist Sharon Kurtz has characterized as a "repeated, painful failure of social movements to come to terms with multiple, simultaneous domination" (Kurtz 2002, 29). For example, Sojourner Truth's 1851 address to the Women's Convention in Akron, Ohio, famous for her repeated refrain, "Ain't I a woman?" pointed out the fact that voting rights for African American women were excluded from the agenda of the women's suffrage movement, sacrificed to the fear of alienating conservatives and southern whites (men and women) who opposed voting rights for blacks (Davis 1981; Giddings 1984; Truth [1851] 1976). Until very recently, many labor unions actively supported anti-immigration policies based on a narrowly protectionist strategy. In the 1960s, New Left groups, such as Students for a Democratic Society, relegated female participants to traditionally female roles within their organizations, such as typing notes and serving coffee. Second-wave feminist organizations of the 1960s and 1970s asked lesbians to keep quiet lest they validate a hostile public's stereotype that all feminists were lesbians. Accompanying each of these allegations and exclusions have also been demands from members of intersectionally disadvantaged subgroups for recognition of the overlapping and intersecting nature of discrimination based on race, gender, sexuality, and class. For example, speaking at the semicentennial of the National American Woman Suffrage Association in 1898, Mary Church Terrell spoke to the multiple exclusions faced by black women and told the audience that she rejoiced "not only in the prospective enfranchisement of my sex but in the emancipation of my race" as well (Terrell [1898] 2003).

Organizations and movements of the nineteenth and first half of the twentieth century could respond to such demands for recognition by claiming that, as organizations speaking on behalf of weak, minority, and marginalized groups, they were constrained by the need to first gain a place at the political table. That claim is less persuasive in the face of the achievements of organizations representing women, racial minorities, and low-income people during the latter half of the twentieth century that I discussed in chapter 2. With the lifting of many of the legal barriers to their political, economic, and social participation, and more elected officials and organizations representing their interests than ever before, groups such as low-income people; women; lesbian, gay, bisexual, and transgender (LGBT) people; African Americans; and Latinos are now what Anne Larason Schneider and Helen Ingram call "emergent contenders" in U.S. politics and policy making. While each of these groups has suffered a historically compromised position in the American polity, the organizations that currently speak for these populations bear a striking resemblance to more traditionally powerful lobby groups. Indeed, based only on a list of addresses, it is impossible to distinguish antipoverty organizations from business lobbies, civil rights organizations from professional organizations, or feminist groups from Christian conservative organizations. A majority (61.4 percent) of the organizations in this study are located in the greater District of Columbia area (Washington, D.C.; Maryland; and Virginia), and many are on or near "Gucci Gulch," the K Street corridor that is home to some of the most powerful lobbying firms and interest groups in the country. Organizations such as the National Organization for Women (NOW), the National Association for the Advancement of Colored People (NAACP), and the American Federation of Labor–Congress of Industrial Organizations (AFL-CIO) once may have been considered radical by mainstream political actors. Their geographic proximity to these lobbyists signifies the extent to which many of them have become political "insiders" that lobby members of Congress and command the attention of cabinet members and committee chairs.

While they might look similar on the surface, organizations advocating on behalf of marginalized groups differ from other interest groups in fundamental ways. The most important distinction is that the organizations under consideration here derive their legitimacy from their claims to represent weak and marginalized groups rather than by channeling or augmenting the power and influence of already powerful groups. In so doing, they advance a new conceptualization of representation. In this chapter, I describe some of the salient features that characterize the contemporary universe of organizations advocating for women, racial minorities, and low-income people, emphasizing their self-perceptions as compensatory representatives for underrepresented groups as well as the responsibilities that this role entails. Combining a normative discussion about representation with empirical evidence about the goals and activities of interest groups, I delineate expectations about representation for intersectionally disadvantaged groups by the advocacy organizations that claim to speak for them.

Foremost among these expectations, I argue, is that these organizations will use the access, influence, and political capital that they derive from the claim to represent marginalized groups to represent and act as mediators on behalf of intersectionally disadvantaged subgroups of the populations for whom they claim to speak. In other words, one way we might evaluate the work of advocacy organizations is by assessing the extent to which they use their status and influence for the benefit of the least well-off among their constituents. The data show that organization officers believe in and take seriously this expectation, even if they do not always meet it when it comes to mediating on behalf of intersectionally disadvantaged groups.

## THE COMMUNITY OF ORGANIZATIONS REPRESENTING MARGINALIZED GROUPS

In spite of their origins in outsider movements, many of the organizations that advocate for marginalized groups have come to look a lot like political insiders. Nonetheless, a comparison with data from previous studies of interest groups shows that the organizations in this study remain outmoneyed by organizations representing other, more traditional interests. In addition, they have fewer resources and fewer organizational and

TABLE 3.1    Political and financial characteristics of organizations in SNESJO

| CHARACTERISTIC | MINIMUM | MAXIMUM | MEAN | SE MEAN | KOLLMAN (1998) (MEAN VALUES) |
|---|---|---|---|---|---|
| Importance of influencing national public policy[a] (1–5 scale) | | | 4.43 | 0.05 | |
| Conservative-Liberal[b] (1–10 scale) | | | 6.89 | 0.13 | |
| Budget | $0 | $10,000,000 | $555,406 | 100,022 | $4,029,289 |
| Budget used for advocacy (%) | 0 | 100 | 29.4 | 1.92 | |
| Number of members | 11 | 1,000,000 | 69,631 | 6341 | 141,637 |
| Number of paid staff | 0 | 500 | 39.4 | 4.90 | 110 |
| N=286 | | | | | |

*Sources:* SNESJO; Ken Kollman (1998) *Outside Lobbying: Public Opinion and Interest Group Strategies.* Princeton: Princeton University Press.

[a] Organization officers were asked, "On a scale of 1 to 5, if 1 is 'not important' and 5 is 'very important,' how important is influencing national public policy as a part of your organization's mandate and activities?"

[b] Organization officers were asked, "On a scale of 1 to 10, where 1 is very conservative and 10 is very liberal, how would you describe your organization?"

TABLE 3.2    Select characteristics of organizations in SNESJO

| SELECTED CHARACTERISTICS | % WITH CHARACTERISTIC IN SNESJO | SCHLOZMAN AND TIERNEY (%) (1986) | KOLLMAN (%) (1998) |
|---|---|---|---|
| Located in Washington, DC area | 61.4 | | |
| Hold tax-exempt status | 89.0 | | |
| Employ legal staff | 31.8 | 75.0 | |
| Registered to Lobby congress | 34.1 | | |
| Employ lobbyists | 25.0 | | |
| Have one or more PACs | 19.0 | 54.0 | 64.0 |
| N=286 | | | |

*Sources:* SNESJO; Kay Schlozman and John Tierney (1986) *Organized Interests and American Democracy.* New York: Harper & Row; Ken Kollman (1998) *Outside Lobbying: Public Opinion and Interest Group Strategies.* Princeton: Princeton University Press.

political tools than do other interests such as corporate, business, and professional organizations (see tables 3.1 and 3.2). Fewer than one-third (31.8 percent) of the organizations surveyed in the SNESJO employ a legal staff, compared with three-quarters of the organizations in Kay Lehman

Schlozman and John Tierney's 1986 study of interest groups.[2] Only one-quarter of the organizations in the SNESJO employ lobbyists (although 34.1 percent are *registered* to lobby members of Congress), and only one-fifth have political action committees (PACs). Schlozman and Tierney, in contrast, found that 54 percent of the organizations in their 1986 study had PACs, and Kollman in his 1998 research noted that 64 percent of organizations had affiliated PACs.

In addition to these continuing disparities, the growth in the number of social and economic justice organizations has been outpaced by the growth in the number of business and professional organizations—the same organizations that dominated the interest group universe in the years before the mass mobilizations of the 1960s and 1970s and the increase in the number of organizations representing marginalized groups (Baumgartner and Leech 1998; Berry 1989; Schlozman 1984; Schlozman and Burch forthcoming; Schlozman and Tierney 1986; Walker 1991).

Although they have fewer resources, organizations representing women, racial minorities, and low-income people are very politically engaged, devoting, on average, just under one-third of their budgets to advocacy activities. In addition, influencing national policy is extremely important to these organizations, and they tend to be quite liberal, scoring an average of just under 7 on the survey's ten-point scale of ideology (where 1 is "very conservative" and 10 is "very liberal").[3]

In addition to these differences in resources and characteristics, the organizations in this study also exhibit a different understanding of their political roles than do other types of interest groups. Specifically, organizations representing marginalized groups claim a distinctive mandate when it comes to advocating for their constituents in politics and policy making. Like their corporate and professional analogues, organizations that speak on behalf of marginalized groups exist to advocate for their members and constituents in national politics and policy making. However, unlike these other groups, they do so in a political universe in which the constituents for whom they speak, while formally enfranchised, continue to be marginalized and underrepresented within political institutions. In spite of the fact that there are more women and racial minorities in elected offices today than there have been at any point in American history, members of these and other marginalized groups continue to make up only a small percentage of elected and appointed officials (see fig. 3.1). For example, while women constitute approximately 51 percent of the American population, in 2006 they held only 15 percent of the 435 seats in the United

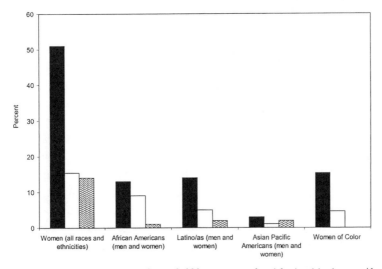

**Fig. 3.1.** Percentage of congressional seats held by women and racial minorities in 2006 (data from www.cawp.rutgers.edu/Facts/Officeholders/elective.pdf; www.ethnicmajority.com).

States House of Representatives and only 14 percent of the 100 seats in the U.S. Senate. Only eight states had women governors in that year, and only 22.5 percent of seats in state legislatures were held by women.[4] Similarly, even though the 1982 reauthorization of the Voting Rights Act contained "results-oriented" amendments that have led to the creation of majority-minority districts (intended to increase the number of members of minority groups holding elected office), members of racial minority groups also continue to be underrepresented in Congress. While African Americans made up approximately 13 percent of the U.S. population in 2006 they held only 9 percent of House seats and a mere 1 percent of Senate seats. Latinos comprised about 14 percent of the overall population but occupied only 5 percent of House seats and 2 percent of Senate seats. Women of color, who made up about 15 percent of the population, held just slightly over 4 percent of House seats and no Senate seats. Numbers are similarly low for Asian Pacific Americans, Native Americans, low-income people, and LGBT people.

The repercussions resulting from the dearth of elected representatives for marginalized groups are compounded by other limits to equitable representation and full democracy in the American electoral system. Geographically based congressional districts, for example, make difficult the election of representatives of groups whose members do not live in res-identially distinct areas (Canon 1999; J. Cohen and Rogers 1992; Guinier 1994; Rehfeld 2005; Mark E. Warren 2001, 2004). Women, for instance, share many interests (qualified as these interests are by the considerations about the difficulties of ascribing interests to groups such as these that I discussed in chapter 2) but rarely are concentrated geographically in particular congressional districts (though women often do comprise over half the voters in a district).[5] In addition, the winner-take-all elections that are used to elect members of the U.S. Congress are biased against electoral successes for candidates from minority parties, which often represent the interests of racial and ethnic minorities in proportional representation systems such as those found in many European countries (Guinier 1994; Young 1992). As a consequence, in spite of record numbers of women and minorities in Congress and other elected offices, it remains difficult for these representatives to have a major impact on formulating or passing legislation that would benefit these groups (Guinier 1994; Swain 1993; Swers 2002). The two-party dominance of national politics that is encouraged and reinforced by the American electoral system leads to the "capture" of disadvantaged groups by whichever of the two parties is even slightly more hospitable to them, minimizing their influence within party politics as well (Frymer 1999; Sanbonmatsu 2002; Swers 2002; Thomas 1994).

Moreover, as the theories of intersectionality that I described in chapter 2 help us understand, salient groupings that help define political interests and preferences—such as those based on race, ethnicity, class, citizenship, and gender—are not static, mutually exclusive categories. Instead, these groups are defined by contingent, dynamic, and intersecting interests. Because individuals belong to many intersecting and overlapping groups, an individual's "interests" typically exist along more than one dimension. For example, a predominantly Latino electoral district might elect a Latino member of Congress, but that does not guarantee that this representative will attend to the specific concerns of Latinas, low-income Latinos, or gay and lesbian Latinos (Fraga et al. 2005). Geographically based elections are thus ill equipped to transmit the multifaceted interests and preferences of groups whose identities and interests are intersectionally constituted.

Advocacy organizations help fill in some of these gaps in electorally based representation by transcending geographic boundaries and providing compensatory and surrogate representation for groups of people with shared interests but inadequate formal territorially based political representation (Jenkins 1987; Kersh 2001; Rehfeld 2006; Mark E. Warren 2004). As Scott Ainsworth writes, while elected representatives have a geographic basis for representation, interest groups "focus on functional divisions" that are often spread across the entire country (2002, 69). So, for example, an

African American member of Congress from New York represents African Americans in his or her district. Although he or she might try to act as a surrogate or a "virtual" representative for African Americans nationwide, his or her primary responsibility is to the members in his or her district (Burke [1792] 1889; Fenno 2003; Gay 2002; Mansbridge 2003; Pitkin 1967). African American interest groups, on the other hand, represent African Americans from states and districts all over the country (Ainsworth 2002).

Consequently, as voluntary organizations that seek to influence legislatures, courts, government agencies, and public opinion, national advocacy organizations speaking for underrepresented groups attempt to persuade geographically based members of Congress to take action on issues that might not otherwise be included on the political agenda by mobilizing voters. To do so, they use a wide range of tactics such as directly lobbying legislators, engaging in letter-writing campaigns, testifying at committee hearings, and providing policy makers with information and research. In addition to influencing legislators, advocacy organizations attempt to influence the executive branch by lobbying presidents and their advisers regarding pending legislation or by providing agencies with comments and testimony about proposed regulations. When efforts to influence the legislative and executive branches fail, advocacy organizations also use the courts, filing amicus curiae briefs or bringing test cases and class action suits to represent their constituents. Although their power to set the agenda, frame policy debates, and shepherd policy changes is, of course, limited by a range of important factors that I will address at length in chapters 4 and 5, advocacy organizations help compensate for inadequate levels of formal political representation for marginalized groups in all of the aforementioned ways.

## MEMBERS AND CONSTITUENTS

The organizations in this study use the foregoing tactics to provide advocacy and representation for members of marginalized groups. However, as I explained in chapter 2, this book examines both membership and nonmembership organizations. Consequently, evaluating the roles of these organizations as representatives requires taking into account some of the differences between the organizations that fall into each of these two categories. Although the organizations in each classification share many qualities and have many similar purposes, there are some differences between them that bear mention (see table 3.3). For example, the membership organizations (also called *citizen groups*) in this study are, on average, more

TABLE 3.3 Comparison of selected characteristics of membership and non-membership organizations

| CHARACTERISTIC | MEMBERSHIP ORGANIZATIONS (N=178) | | NON-MEMBERSHIP ORGANIZATIONS (N=108) | |
|---|---|---|---|---|
| | % | MEAN | % | MEAN |
| Importance of influencing national public policy[a] | | 4.51 | | 4.3 |
| Conservative-Liberal[b] | | 6.9 | | 6.8 |
| Located in Washington, DC area | 57.8 | | 67.7 | |
| Organizations with tax-exempt status | 86.9 | | 94.9 | |
| Organizations employing legal staff | 32.6 | | 30.3 | |
| Organizations registered to lobby Congress | 38.1 | | 26.9 | |
| Organizations employing lobbyists | 30.3 | | 15.3 | |
| Organizations with one or more PACs | 24.2 | | 7.1 | |
| Budget | | $692,984 | | $363,222 |
| Budget used for advocacy (%) | | 29.6 | | 28 |
| Number of paid staff | | 39.5 | | 31.5 |

Source: SNESJO.

[a]Organization officers were asked, "On a scale of 1 to 5, if 1 is 'not important' and 5 is 'very important,' how important is influencing national public policy as a part of your organization's mandate and activities?"

[b]Organization officers were asked, "On a scale of 1 to 10, where 1 is 'very conservative' and 10 is 'very liberal,' how would you describe your organization?"

likely to employ lobbyists and to have political action committees than are nonmembership organizations (referred to by Robert Salisbury as "institutions" and encompassing the organizations composed of other organizations as members that that he calls "associations"). Membership organizations are also wealthier than nonmembership organizations and have larger staffs. Nonmembership organizations, on the other hand, are more likely than membership organizations to be located in Washington, D.C.

One particular set of differences between membership and nonmembership organizations has important implications as we consider the role of advocacy organizations as representatives of marginalized groups. Most significantly, while membership organizations have, by definition, a constituency that comprises identifiable, dues-paying members to whom the organizations are ostensibly accountable, the same is not true of nonmembership organizations. For example, the NAACP currently claims 400,000 individual members; its sibling organization, the NAACP Legal Defense Fund (NAACP LDF), has no individual members (although like many nonmembership organizations, it does have individual donors).

Consequently, membership organizations arguably have a far more clearly delineated constituency than nonmembership organizations do. While true in theory, the NAACP example demonstrates that in practice this contrast between the constituencies of membership and nonmembership organizations is, to some degree, a distinction without a difference, at least in this regard. In spite of their differing organizational forms, the missions of most of the organizations in this study, membership and nonmembership alike, transcend the boundaries of dues-paying members or donor lists. For example, the mission statement of the NAACP states that it exists "to ensure the political, educational, social and economic equality of rights of all persons and to eliminate racial hatred and racial discrimination." The analogous statement by the NAACP LDF says that at its founding, its "primary purpose was to provide legal assistance to poor African Americans," but that "its work over the years has brought greater justice to all Americans." Both organizations make broad claims about representing broad groups that are not limited to members or donors. Unlike business and professional organizations, it is rarely the case that organizations such as these have narrow missions that are geared exclusively toward securing benefits for their members. Instead, the organizations discussed here are by and large the kinds of interest groups that Jeffrey Berry labels "public interest groups," organizations that make claims to speak for broad social and economic groups and that lobby for benefits that do not "selectively and materially benefit the membership and activists of the organization" (Berry 1977, 7).[6] Labor unions, which bargain for material benefits that often extend exclusively to their members, typically are not classified as public interest groups. However, by setting industry standards, the increased wages and benefits attained by unions for their members also help (and are intended to help) nonunion workers (Gerber 1999; Mishel and Walters 2003). Moreover, outside of their roles in collective bargaining for wages and benefits, unions closely resemble Berry's public interest groups in their political activities and policy goals. In this capacity, unions are connected to, and indeed have often been in the forefront of, broad movements for economic and social justice (Novkov 2001; Warren 2005).

Indeed, as I will demonstrate in this chapter, the organizations considered in this study share a commitment to working for policies that benefit whole classes of people or broad social groups or for policies that address ideological concerns such as the environment or peace. This does not mean that the membership organizations among them do not pay particular attention to the specific interests and preferences of their dues-paying members, nor does it mean that the nonmembership organizations among them do not attend to the desires of their benefactors. In fact, as I will show in many of the analyses that follow, organizations do just these things under many circumstances. However, it is nonetheless the case that all of the organizations under consideration here can be described as having constituencies that go beyond these formal members or donors. As such, while I will distinguish between member and nonmember organizations as necessary in the analyses and discussions that follow, I also will consider them together as a group when appropriate.

While their common traits of having broad constituencies and representing the interests of broad social and economic groups allow us to treat these organizations similarly, these same qualities complicate matters somewhat as well. The farther we move away from bounded populations, such as residents of congressional districts or dues-paying members of member-based organizations, the more tenuous are our evaluations of whether representation is taking place. So, while the organizations in this study may claim to represent broad social and economic groupings and populations such as "women," "racial minorities," "workers," or "environmentalists," there is really no way to verify whether they actually do represent these populations. Do the members of these broad groups identify with these organizations? Do they even know of their existence? Would they identify their own interests as being the same ones as those being pursued by these organizations?

These are all important and provocative questions about the relationships between advocacy organizations and the populations that they claim to represent. For the purposes of the arguments and analyses in this book, however, it is less important whether those being spoken for identify with the organizations that claim to speak for them than it is that these organizations claim to speak for them in the first place. As I began to discuss in chapter 2, what I am assessing is how well the organizations that claim to represent these groups fulfill the missions that they claim for themselves and with which the polity entrusts them. As such, I am to some degree drawing direct connections between membership in marginalized groups, on the one hand, and membership in interest groups, on the other, two categories that political theorist Melissa Williams (1998) argues are distinct. Williams categorizes membership in interest groups as voluntary, shifting, and a matter of degree and describes membership in marginalized groups as "involuntary, immutable, and dichotomous" (M. Williams 1998, 116). While not all members of a marginalized group will be formal *members* of the interest groups that claim to speak for this group (in fact, very small proportions of potential members ever join these organizations), in my definition, they are all *constituents* of these organizations, and we therefore can evaluate the claims and actions of these organizations in this light.[7]

With these considerations in mind, in describing and analyzing these organizations and the populations they claim to represent, I differentiate among three categories. When referring to the formal dues-paying or otherwise formally determined members of organizations, I use the terms *members of organizations* or *organization members*. I refer to the members of the broad social and economic groups that are represented by these organizations as *members of* groups or populations, such as low-income people or women. To describe the broad constituencies to which both membership and nonmembership organizations lay claim, I use the term *constituents*.

## REPRESENTATION AND RESPONSIBILITY: NORMATIVE BENCHMARKS

Although advocacy organizations do much to fill in the gaps in electoral politics, many of the same features that make these organizations effective representatives for marginalized groups also make it difficult to hold these organizations responsible as representatives. For example, for all of their inadequacies, elected representatives are formally accountable to their constituents through elections. Advocacy organizations vary widely in how accountable they are to their constituencies, however; most are not subject to the formal and legally binding accountability that derives from elections that confer policy-making powers. Organizations must, of course, answer to their boards of directors. Some organizations, labor unions in particular, have legally binding elections through which they select their officers. However, neither of these mechanisms provides accountability that is equivalent to that which is enforced by the imperfect but nonetheless constitutionally mandated and protected elections faced by members of Congress. Lacking the mechanism of elections that gives voters the power, limited as it is, to "throw the bums out," it is difficult for constituents to impose any obligations and responsibilities on the advocacy organizations that claim to speak for them.

In membership organizations, members can, in theory, vote "with their feet" and simply leave organizations with which they are dissatisfied, seeking or forming ones that better serve their interests (Ainsworth 2002, 69). However, as I discussed in chapter 2, intersectionally disadvantaged subgroups are, to borrow Paul Frymer's term, "captured" by the organizations that claim to represent them and therefore lack this meaningful exit option. In addition, elected officials are distinct from others who claim to represent constituents in that they are legally bound to work for every constituent in their district, regardless of whether these constituents voted for them or identify with their political party.[8] Interest groups, by comparison, are under no legal obligation to represent or respond to people who are not members of or donors to their organization (Ainsworth 2002). Difficulties such as these make it important to delineate expectations about the ways in which we want advocacy organizations to represent their constituents, particularly in light of the faith vested in them by members of marginalized groups and considering the claims made by these organizations to speak for these groups.

While it is true that most interest groups are not legally bound to act on behalf of nonmembers, organizations representing marginalized groups typically claim to speak for the entire population in whose name they make claims. They also claim that these groups share common interests that they, as representatives, are able to identify and represent. Organizations such as the NAACP, for example, claim very explicitly to speak for "all African Americans," while the AFL-CIO states that it works for "working people in the global economy."[9] Not only do these organizations make claims to speak for these broad constituencies, but most claim further that they are advocates for the weak and marginalized and that they are motivated by a desire to advance social justice and equality (Berry 1977). Indeed, their political legitimacy and power derive from these claims.

In light of such claims by advocacy organizations and given the legitimacy and power that these claims beget (Kersh 2001), what might we expect of organizations that claim to represent marginalized groups? The following sections delineate two central sets of expectations of advocacy organizations to their constituents: (1) the expectation that they will nurture feelings of intersectionally linked fate among constituents and (2) the expectation that they will engage in processes of representation as mediation.

## LINKED FATE AND COLLECTIVE IDENTITY

Organizations representing marginalized groups trade in the claim that the populations for which they speak are bound, to greater or lesser degrees, by what political scientist Michael Dawson (1994) calls "linked fate." Dawson developed this concept to explain the distinctly high levels of cohesiveness

in the political attitudes and behavior of African Americans—cohesiveness
that persists in spite of increasing social, economic, and political disparities that have resulted in what might be characterized as divergent "objective" interests among members of African American communities. He
argues more generally that when members of a marginalized group have
a shared history of exploitation, discrimination, and political disenfran-
chisement, they come to perceive "that their own self-interests are linked
to the interests" of the groups to which they belong (Dawson 1994, 77). As a
consequence, they use their perceptions of the interests of these groups "as
a proxy for their own interests," even in cases when these group interests
would not be thought of as being in their objective interests (Dawson 1994,
61). Social movement theorists ascribe a similar role to the emotions associated with collective identities, which they argue are both necessary for
and created by mobilization (Melucci 1989). Collective identities generate
solidaristic feelings and perceptions of shared grievances and status, thus
leading movement participants to "adopt as their own the good of others in
their group" (Mansbridge 1983, 27). [10] Thinking about their own well-being
in this way can lead in turn to favoring policies that are perceived to promote the welfare of the group even when these policies provide individuals
"with no personal benefits and may involve them in considerable cost"
(Mansbridge 1983, 27). In these ways, both linked fate and collective identities suggest alternatives to purely rational or individual calculi and lenses
through which members of marginalized groups evaluate policy options,
formulate preferences, and identify interests (Gould 2004; Jenkins 1999;
Kurtz 2002; Mansbridge 1986; Polletta and Jasper 2001; Taylor and Whittier
1999).[11]

Collective identities and linked fate cohere around shared histories,
status, grievances, and interests (B. Anderson 1991). However, the precise
content of these grievances is not self-generating. Rather, it is usually determined by political actors—including advocacy organizations—who help
construct it by framing issues, claims, and interests in particular ways.[12]
These frames—what Erving Goffman calls "schemata of interpretation"—
are deployed for a range of purposes: to attract members and donors, inspire
and mobilize constituents, attract media and policy-maker attention, and
influence policy debates (Goffman 1974; Goodwin and Jasper 2003, 52; Snow
and Benford 1988, 1992; Tarrow 1992, 2005).[13]

By drawing boundaries around issues, frames highlight some elements
of a policy issue while they downplay others. For example, in 1995, in the
wake of the vote on California's anti–affirmative action Proposition 209,

Jesse Jackson (president of what was then called the National Rainbow Coalition and is now called the Rainbow/PUSH coalition) and Patricia Ireland (then president of NOW) tried to recast the terms of public debate about affirmative action in order to increase support for it. To do so, they emphasized the benefits of affirmative action to women while they downplayed its benefits to members of racial minority groups (Skrentny 1996, 229; Strolovitch 1998).

As this example suggests, among the ways in which organizations use frames is to try to influence what scholars including Deborah Stone, Frank Baumgartner, and Bryan Jones call the "policy image" of the issues they pursue, reframing them for the public in ways that are favorable to their constituents or that increase the chances that they will attain their desired policy outcome (Baumgartner and Jones 1993; D. Stone 1989). In similar fashion, advocacy organizations also use frames to try to influence the ways in which their constituents think about issues and more broadly to signal to them which issues are relevant to their interests. However, as Margaret Levi and Gillian Murphy point out, "the way an issue is framed inherently includes and excludes some interests" (Levi and Murphy 2006, 656). As such, the ways in which organization leaders decide which issues are in the interests of their constituents includes the interests of some subgroups while defining the interests of other subgroups as being outside their mandate.

Together, the concepts of linked fate, collective identities, and framing are helpful in understanding the ways in which advocacy organizations determine the issues they will address. There are, however, some important differences between these processes as they manifest at the organizational level and the ways in which these same processes help determine individual attitudes. Individual members of marginalized groups may use a linked-fate heuristic in their political considerations to greater or lesser degrees. As I began to explain in chapter 2, however, advocacy organizations that represent these groups rely on the logic of linked fate both as a filtering mechanism, through which they determine the scope and content of their policy agendas and the interests of the populations they represent, and as the basis on which they are able to claim that they articulate these interests (Banaszak 1996; Barakso 2004; Clemens 1997; McFarland 1976).[14]

As should be clear by now, however, assumptions that the fate of all members of a community are linked often work to conceal inequalities within these communities in some of the same ways that appeals to the public interest (that I discussed in chapter 2) tend to be framed so that they favor the interests of dominant social groups while they perpetuate the marginality of subordinate groups. Because of crosscutting differences within populations, Cathy Cohen explains, not all members of marginalized communities are considered "equally essential to the survival of the community" or "equally representative proxies of individual interests" (C. Cohen 1999, xi). Instead, these common fates and interests more often are defined as those of advantaged members. As such, the majority and advantaged-subgroup issues associated with these interests are the ones that are framed as being worthy of the community's political support, and these issues are the ones most likely to be pursued by the interest groups that speak for these communities.

Underlying this process is an implicit appeal by organizations to their intersectionally disadvantaged constituents that these constituents should understand their interests as being bound up with those of advantaged members of their communities. Disadvantaged members are further expected to identify with the successes of these advantaged members, whose achievements are understood in some way to trickle down to them—a version of what Maureen Scully and Douglas Creed (2005) have called "imaginative empathy." As a consequence, it is also assumed that members of these disadvantaged subgroups will support efforts to secure policies that promise to benefit their advantaged cousins, even if members of these subgroups are unlikely to benefit from these efforts themselves.

While advocacy organizations expect their intersectionally disadvantaged constituents to demonstrate collective consciousness and group solidarity by identifying "up" the hierarchy, the analogous forms of "groupness" and solidarity are not demanded of advantaged members. For example, women's organizations regularly frame access to birth control and abortion as being issues that are of concern to all women, and they frame their advocacy on such issues as consequently benefiting all women as well. Lesbians, however, are far less likely than heterosexual women to require birth control or abortion-related services.[15] It is nonetheless assumed by feminist organizations that lesbians will see their fates as being tightly linked to those of heterosexual women, that they will understand the centrality of these issues to a feminist agenda, that they will support feminist organizations in their efforts to preserve abortion rights, and that they will embrace victories in this policy area as their own victories as well.

The analogous dynamic is rarely assumed when it comes to issues that affect lesbians. With a few important exceptions (such as NOW, whose

Web site prominently features its work to legalize same-sex marriage), feminist organizations rarely assume that heterosexual women see their fortunes as being linked to the fortunes that befall lesbians. Even when they are active on such issues, they do not universalize issues such as same-sex marriage or protection against workplace discrimination based on sexual orientation. They rarely take it for granted that the heterosexual women in their constituency will consider such issues as being central to a feminist agenda, and they do not expect that these women will throw themselves wholeheartedly into efforts to mobilize support for them. Neither do the leaders of these organizations assume that their heterosexual constituents will revel in the successes and mourn the losses around policy issues that affect lesbians. They might even worry that they would lose support and members were they to voice such expectations; because of capture, however, they are unlikely to have such concerns vis-à-vis the possibility of lesbian defectors who are asked to mobilize around issues such as abortion.[16]

My point here is not that lesbians should refrain from supporting and from taking an active role in defending reproductive rights but rather to point out that most deployments of linked fate are essentially unidirectional and pointed "up" rather than "down" the hierarchy. Part of the potential of advocacy organizations, then, is to frame issues in a way that nurtures a sense of intersectionally linked fate among their differently situated constituents as well as among the organizations in their interest communities. That is, advocacy organizations are well positioned to expand the ways in which they frame issues and deploy their demands for solidarity and framings of collective identity so that they benefit the least well-off by including identification not only *up* the hierarchy but *down* and *across* hierarchies as well (Rawls 1971; see also Bell 1990; Chesler 1996; Rothenberg and Scully 2002; Thompson 2001).

## REPRESENTATION AS MEDIATION

Political theorist Melissa Williams's work on the obligations of elected legislative representatives to their constituents is suggestive in this regard. Representation, she argues, is in its essence a form of mediation between constituents' concerns and interests, on the one hand, and the state's policies and actions, on the other hand. How this mediation takes place depends on the representative's sense of his or her obligation to his or her constituents. What, Williams asks, are the responsibilities of a representative to those he or she claims to represent and "speak for" (M. Williams 1998)?

In this section of the chapter, I outline a response to this question about representation and advocacy, using evidence from the survey and interviews about the goals and activities of interest groups as the basis for my answer. Based on this evidence about these practices, I delineate expectations about interest group representation for intersectionally disadvantaged groups, implicit in which is an innovative conceptualization by advocacy organizations of representation as a form of social justice. A key component of this formulation is the notion that effective and equitable representation by advocacy organizations requires that they act as mediators on behalf of their constituents in four key ways: (1) between marginalized groups and the state; (2) between marginalized groups and members of the general public; (3) among the differently situated subgroups that compose their own internally diverse constituencies; and (4) between their own constituents and organizations representing other marginalized groups. By mediating in these ways, officers at advocacy organizations can use their organizations to reverse the more typical dynamic in which disadvantaged constituents are asked to identify with the interests and well-being of advantaged ones. Instead, advocacy groups can frame issues and constituencies in ways that help constituents understand the intersecting connections between forms of disadvantage in order to nurture a sense of *intersectionally linked fate* in which advantaged subgroups identify the interests and well-being of disadvantaged subgroups with their own.

In her discussion of political theorist Hannah Pitkin's landmark work on representation (Pitkin 1967), Iris Young (2000) argues that legitimate representation "consists in exercising independent judgment but in the knowledge and anticipation of what constituents want." The constituents of organizations representing marginalized groups profess to want social and economic justice of some sort. Moreover, as I have argued previously, the moral force of advocacy organizations' claims to give voice to marginalized groups is based on the assumption that they will work to achieve this social justice by compensating for the minimal formal representation afforded these groups in electoral politics and institutions. Based on this claim, advocates for marginalized groups are charged with *mediating* between their constituents and the government by giving voice to the concerns of these constituents, whose perspectives have been historically excluded from policy debates, when their interests are at stake in the policy process.

Melissa Williams argues that a central goal of incorporating the interests of marginalized groups into public policy deliberations in these ways is to foster inclusive debates that might persuade others, particularly members of privileged social groups, to look beyond their immediate self-interest (see also Mansbridge 1983). In particular, she hopes that incorporating marginalized groups more centrally into policy deliberation will lead members of privileged groups to supplement their self-interested impulses with a recognition of the interests that they share with members of marginalized groups. Foremost among these shared interests, she argues, is "a shared interest in justice" (M. Williams 1998, 144; see also Urbinati 2000).

Williams emphasizes the ways in which elected representatives can facilitate this recognition within legislatures and among members of the general public. Advocacy organizations can and do mediate in these ways as well, acting as emissaries on behalf of their underrepresented and marginalized constituencies within government and the broader polity. These organizations are even *more* strongly positioned than elected representatives to give voice to intersectionally marginalized groups *within* their own constituencies as well as within the larger interest communities of which they are a part. As such, we might expect advocacy organizations to mediate among the many members of what an intersectional approach helps us recognize are internally diverse constituencies in order to help them achieve the goal of social justice. In particular, we might expect organizations to mediate between weaker and stronger subgroups of their constituencies, making a case for the needs and interests of weaker subgroups in the same way that they do for their marginalized constituency vis-à-vis the dominant general public. Finally, in addition to mediating among the subgroups *within* the marginalized populations that they represent, organizations might also use their positions within their interest communities to mediate *among* the organizations representing other marginalized groups as well.

By mediating in these ways, advocacy organizations can frame issues and mandates so that they encourage constituents to draw connections between issues and groups that these constituents might not make on their own. In so doing, organizations can use their political access and influence to benefit the least well-off among their constituencies. To do so, they can nurture collective identities and forms of solidarity that encourage privileged members to substitute an understanding of their interests that encompasses the well-being of disadvantaged subgroups.

## SPEAKING FOR OTHERS

Because the organizations in this study advocate for members of groups who are politically, economically, or socially marginalized, considerations of their responsibilities to their constituents must confront an issue that complicates their roles as representatives. In many cases, the mere fact that the representative has access to policy makers removes him or her to some extent from the forms of marginalization to which he or she is claiming to give voice (Tom 1995; Mark E. Warren 2001, 2004). Linda Martìn Alcoff (1991) summarizes this dilemma, asking, "Is it ever valid to speak for others who are unlike us or who are less privileged than us?" This question has engendered a great deal of debate, particularly within historically marginalized communities (Guidry and Sawyer 2003). For example, the partic-ipation of many whites in the civil rights movement of the 1950s and 1960s was viewed by many African Americans as perpetuating the paternalistic notion of noblesse oblige, the idea that privilege brings with it a duty to help the less fortunate. The move from the civil rights activism of the 1960s to the embrace of the idea of black power was, at least in part, an insistence by many African Americans that they advocate on their own behalf and minimize the role of white activists within the movement. Similarly, some contemporary organizations have as their ultimate goal the hope that their constituents will eventually garner the strength and resources necessary to represent themselves. The executive director of an economic justice group told me, for example, that his organization's goal is to work "with people living in poverty so they themselves have a voice, so that they can represent themselves rather than [having the] people speaking for them [do it]."[17]

Recognizing the problems and challenges inherent in the claim to speak for those who are less advantaged ought not to lead to abandoning what Al-coff characterizes as "a political responsibility to speak out against oppres-sion." Rather, keeping in mind the caution not to do so paternalistically, "the very fact of" privilege brings with it the responsibility to advocate for disadvantaged groups (Alcoff 1991, 99). In the case of the organizations in this study, part of that privilege derives directly from the legitimacy that organization officers are accorded based on their claims to speak for marginalized groups. As such, although it is important for officers in these organizations to recognize the limitations of their abilities to truly speak *for* the members of disadvantaged subgroups of their constituencies, it is equally important that they acknowledge that there is a need for them to advocate *on behalf of* these subgroups because they are uniquely positioned to do so. "In some cases," Alcoff reminds us, "certain political effects can be gained in no other way" (Alcoff 1991, 107; see also Urbinati 2000, 2002).

Conventional approaches to representation and interest groups lead many observers to ask why we should expect these organizations to act altruistically rather than strategically. Why should organizations aspire to speak for marginal subgroups of their constituents rather than for the majority or for those who, through their abilities to contribute time and money, command the most attention? Indeed, organizations cannot represent every member at all times, nor can they focus exclusively on disadvantaged subgroups to the exclusion of majorities. However, by announcing broad policy agendas and a determination to speak for all members of a given constituency, advocacy organizations claim implicitly to speak for less-privileged members of these groups (Spalter-Roth and Schreiber 1995). As such, characterizing representation for disadvantaged subgroups as an act of altruism underscores one of the main points about intersectionality. The notion that it is altruistic to work on behalf of disadvantaged subgroups of a constituency rests on the assumption that these members are *not a part of* the group and that it is an act of selfless charity rather than one of responsibility and common interests to advocate for them. Unless organizations qualify their claims and say, for example, "we speak for white, heterosexual, middle class women," their claims to represent broadly based groups such as women, African Americans, and low-income people *include* claims and assumptions that they will advocate on behalf of disadvantaged subgroups of these populations.

## CONSTITUENCIES AND ISSUE AGENDAS

While we might feel compelled to absolve organizations of expectations that they will represent intersectionally disadvantaged subgroups if they were to make no claims to speak for broadly defined constituencies, few organizations construe their constituencies as being so narrowly circumscribed. Instead, evidence from the survey and interviews demonstrates that officers at most organizations feel a responsibility to speak on behalf of many subgroups within their constituencies. Indeed, an examination of officers' ideas about the constituencies for whom they speak and the policy areas in which they are interested reveals that these organizations conceive of representation in a manner that embraces social justice as a central goal and that recognizes the ways in which traditional forms of electoral representation underserve the populations for whom they speak. Advocacy on behalf of these underserved populations, therefore, is a central and necessary component of this alternative conception of representation.

To assess their own ideas about the scope and content of their representational obligations, survey respondents were asked a series of questions about the extent to which their organizations represent the interests of a range of population groups (see fig. 3.2). All respondents were asked about the same groups, which by design included some populations that are "core constituencies" for each organization (for example, women in the case of women's organizations, low-income people in the case of economic justice organizations), as well as groups of people who are almost certainly contained within each organization's constituency but whose identities, from a single-axis perspective, are not likely to be seen as central to the mission of the organization (for example, African Americans in the case of women's organizations, or women in the case of economic justice organizations).

Respondents' answers to these questions demonstrate that most organizations approach their roles as representatives very broadly. Most of the organizations in the study try to address the concerns of many groups—on average, eight of the ten groups about which they were asked in the survey. Just under half—43 percent—claim to address the public policy concerns of all ten groups. Further evidence that these organizations feel a responsibility to represent people beyond their members and constituents is evident in responses to a question that asked survey respondents about whether their organizations generally focus on policy issues that affect their constituents directly or whether they generally focus on issues that affect people beyond their constituencies. Two-thirds of respondents surveyed claim that they are eager to advocate for public policies that benefit people beyond their constituencies.[18]

In similar fashion, in face-to-face interviews, interviewees confirmed their organizations' commitments to expansive constituencies that transcend members and donors. A public policy specialist at a labor organization, for example, made it clear that representing the actual members of his organization was only the tip of the iceberg in terms of the impact he hoped his work would have. His organization's immediate constituency, he explained, "is the national unions that are affiliates." However, he went on, "our interests are the advancement of working people. Not only our members, but generally." He continued, "There's no group in American society that wouldn't be of concern to us, with the possible exception of those who are so rich, they don't need to work. They don't need our help."[19] The president of a large industrial labor union echoed these claims. Asked whether his organization works on behalf of the workers in his unions or on behalf of working people more generally, he said, "There's [no difference] between the two. Our members are the workers in general . . . what we do and how we do it to advance the interests of our members, we hope has a spin off for the rest of society and that we raise the floor for everyone. That makes it easier for us to begin our continuing efforts of bargaining and organizing."[20]

Almost all respondents framed their constituencies and missions in similarly broad ways, claiming that while their organizations might focus on a particular group, their goals for influencing public policy extend far beyond that particular population. For example, asked on whose behalf her group is active, the field organizer at a feminist organization said, "Well, *women* [is] the obvious answer, but that's not necessarily the only answer. Basically those who are being discriminated against based on systems of oppression, including people of color, people of various sexual orientations, SES statuses[socioeconomic statuses], marital statuses, you name it— we work to end discrimination on any basis."[21] Most poignantly, the executive director of an African American organization explained,

> Our direct constituency is probably the dues-paying members of the [organization], but I will also tell you that we don't have the luxury of thinking that we only can serve those issues because all members are impacted by these problems. . . . [So] we also work for the citizens of the communities in which we work. Because if there's racism within the institution . . . when it comes to people of color, then those same disparities are manifested in the way the dominant group works in the community also. . . . All of these are our constituents because the issues that we work on ultimately impact on all of them indirectly or directly.[22]

This theme was repeated by the executive director of a civil rights organization that focuses on criminal justice issues. Asked on whose behalf the group is active, he replied, "Narrowly we're working for defendants and offenders and their lawyers." However, he continued, "[we also] like to think of [the constituency] as pretty large. . . . Ultimately, I argue that our constituency is the general public," although, he added, smiling, "some of it wouldn't agree with us." As the organization that, he claimed, "identified the impact of race or the relationship between race and punishment in the American criminal justice system," another important constituency for this group is "African Americans and other minorities that are over-represented in the criminal justice system." But he also argued that part of the constituency is composed of people who are not affected directly by the criminal justice system—sympathetic individuals with ideological commitments who are, as he put it, "concerned about the amount of punishment there is and the number of people in prison." That, he said, is "another broader constituency. . . . People we know support us financially, who've never been in prison or jail."[23]

## POLICY MANDATES

In addition to claiming broad *constituencies*, organizations representing marginalized groups also embrace broad *policy mandates* as a part of their roles as representatives of these constituencies. In contrast to the policy specialization and preference for narrow policy niches that increasingly characterize business and professional organizations (and that I will discuss at greater length in chapter 4), issue pluralism is the norm for organizations representing women, racial minorities, and low-income people (Browne 1990; Gray and Lowery 1996). To assess the scope of their perceived policy mandates, survey respondents were asked a series of questions about their organizations' interest in nine broad policy areas (see fig. 3.3). As with the questions about the populations that they represent, all respondents were asked about the same general issue areas, which deliberately included some issues that are clearly central to their missions (for example, women's issues in the case of women's organizations and antipoverty policy in the case of economic justice organizations) as well as issues that almost certainly affect members of their constituencies but which are less likely to be seen as central to their missions (for example, immigration policy in the case of women's organizations and women's equality in the case of economic justice organizations). Respondents' answers to these questions demonstrate that most organizations construe their policy mandates very broadly. Organizations are at least minimally interested in an average of 6.8 out of the eight general public policy areas asked about in the survey, and they are, on average, "very interested" in three.

Many officers I spoke with during face-to-face interviews emphasized the broad policy agendas of their organizations. For example, the chair of the board of an Asian Pacific American professional organization depicted

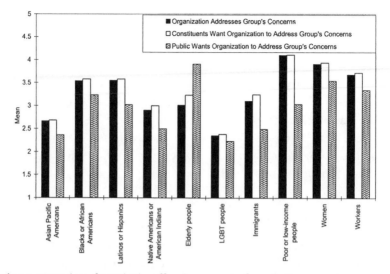

**Fig. 3.2.** Comparison of organization officers' assessments of organization responsiveness, constituent responsiveness, and public responsiveness to constituencies. Data in the first column reflect the mean responses of organization officers to the question, "Please tell me, on a scale of 1 to 5, with 1 being 'not at all' and 5 being 'a great deal,' to what degree does your organization address the policy concerns of each of the following groups?" Data in the second column reflect the mean responses of organization officers to the question, "Please tell me, on a scale of 1 to 5, with 1 being 'not at all' and 5 being 'a great deal,' to what degree would you say that your members [or the] people your organization serves want your organization to address the policy concerns of each of the following groups?" Data in the third column reflect the mean responses of organization officers to the question, "Now, on a scale of 1 to 5, with 1 being 'not at all' and 5 being 'a great deal,' to what degree would you say that the general public thinks that the policy concerns of these same groups deserve to be addressed?" (data from SNESJO).

his organization as being interested in *all* issues of racial and ethnic discrimination, not just those that affect Asian Pacific Americans. "Many of the issues that Asian [Pacific] Americans have are very similar to the issues that African Americans or Hispanic Americans have," he argued. "Hispanic Americans, certainly with respect to language rights and with respect to immigration issues, and African Americans in terms of profiling, stereotyping types of issues."[24]

Similarly, the executive director of an African American organization explained that he considers how active his organization will be on potential issues in the context of his group's main policy area, which is "criminal justice issues' impact on people of color." Consequently, issues such as "the death penalty . . . incarceration . . . police brutality, racial profiling, discrimination in the workplace" all fall "very neatly within the context of how they impact on communities of color within the criminal justice context." However, he continued, issues such as these are embedded within a "broader context" that includes other issues such as "childcare for children or housing for people or adequate compensation for work." Therefore, he said, "we need to also speak to [those issues] because they impact on our lives and our lives' quality."[25] As a policy analyst at a large labor organization put it, "We have positions on an extremely broad range of issues" because so many issues have implications for his group's constituents. Consequently, he continued, "there aren't many that we don't" have a position on.[26]

Position taking on an issue is clearly not coterminous with devoting high levels of energy and resources to advocacy on that issue. Indeed, as David Mayhew (1974) explains, position taking may in fact be used for the purposes of making low-cost or symbolic gestures on an issue with little intention of real engagement. However, organizational position taking on an issue indicates that an organization sees a connection between that issue and its general policy mandate. Consequently, if an organization is not active on an issue on which it has taken a position, it is reasonable to ask why not and to investigate whether this is more often the case when it comes to some types of issues than it is when it comes to others. It is important not to allow rationalist assumptions about the ways in which we *expect* these organizations to behave to prevent us from recognizing some of the unique ways in which they actually *do* behave as they negotiate the opportunities and constraints of the political environment in their efforts to pursue justice for marginalized groups.

## MEDIATING

The advocacy organizations in this study, then, generally take very broad views of their missions and constituencies. Evidence from the survey data and face-to-face interviews also demonstrates that organization officers recognize and embrace their roles as mediators in a variety of different and important ways. This recognition can be seen in the responses to another series of survey questions in the SNESJO that asked respondents whether they represent various population groups. The answers to these questions show that organization leaders believe that their organizations exist at least in part to compensate for the general public's biases against marginalized and stigmatized groups. Specifically, respondents were asked about the extent to which the general public thinks the concerns of a range of populations

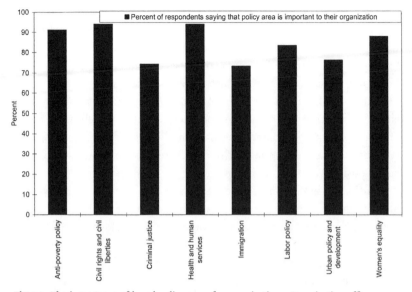

**Fig. 3.3.** The importance of broad policy areas for organizations. Organization officers were asked, "On a scale of 1 to 5, where 1 is 'not important' and 5 is 'the most important,' how important is each of the following issues to the activities and political concerns of your organization?" Data reflect the percentage of respondents giving answers from 2 through 5 (data from SNESJO).

ought to be addressed in public policy debates. Responses to these questions differ markedly from responses to questions asking respondents about the groups that their organizations actually do represent (see fig. 3.2). For example, when asked to rank the groups their constituents *want* them to represent, surveyed leaders listed low-income people in first place. When asked to do the same for groups their organizations *actually* represent, they also ranked low-income people first. However, when asked to rank the groups whose interests the *general public* wants to see represented, they listed elderly people first and low-income people fifth.[27] This disparity between their actions and their sense of the preferences of the general public reveal a self-perceived mediator role that takes seriously the responsibility to advocate on behalf of groups that the public would just as soon ignore.

Although respondents quite clearly embrace this particular public aspect of their mediator role, there is less evidence that the organizations considered here embrace a commitment to mediating among the subgroups *within* their constituencies. Survey respondents also were asked about the extent to which their constituents think the concerns of the same populations ought to be addressed. Unlike their responses about the public's feeling about these groups, responses to the questions about their constituents' views are nearly identical to their responses to the questions about the groups that their organizations represent (see fig. 3.3). As such, these data suggest that officers and professional staff at these organizations see themselves as being charged with giving voice to, rather than transforming, the views and preferences of their constituents.

While the survey data do not show a widespread commitment to mediating on behalf of groups within their constituencies, some interviewees told a somewhat different story. The statements of these interviewees suggest that at least some officers make efforts to educate their constituents and communities about issues and try to nurture a sense of intersectionally linked fate among them, rather than simply acting as delegates charged with representing their constituents' stated preferences. For example, the chair of the board of an African American organization told me that, in his opinion, "Black people are very conservative on abortion, the death penalty, on gay rights." Thus, he said, part of his job is to push his members to think about these issues in different ways, and to "pull it apart [for them] and say well 'why do you like [the death penalty]?' [Eventually] they'll say, 'I don't.'"[28] Along similar lines, the executive director of a women's labor organization explained that she certainly takes her members' stated preferences into account in deciding which issues the group will address. However, she said, the organization often supports "things that not all of our members probably agree with, but we feel are in keeping with a progressive organization that has the goals that we have."[29]

This mediator role comes through particularly clearly in the following statements by the president of a labor organization, who described the challenges he faced in the early 1990s as he worked to persuade a majority of his members to ratify the union's official opposition to the North American Free Trade Agreement (NAFTA). Free trade, he explained, threatens the jobs of the union's members who work in manufacturing industries. However, his union also represents workers in the air transport industry, and these members thought that NAFTA actually would create jobs in their sector of the economy. "Well, those workers," he said, "think that maybe this [free] trade idea isn't such a bad deal." "We have to educate them," he explained, to understand that "while it may be a good deal for you, it's a bad deal for these members over here."[30] In the end, the members from the air transport industry saw the issue within a broader context and came to identify their own interests with those of their fellow workers who were likely to be disadvantaged by the economic changes brought on by free trade. The union was able to take an official position against the trade agreement with a wide margin of support from its members (although of course NAFTA ultimately became law).

The intention here is not to argue that advocacy groups should take it upon themselves to "convert" their members' views on particular policy issues nor to argue that every organization should or can represent every subgroup or work on every issue. Rather, the point is that advocacy groups are uniquely positioned to mediate among members of what an intersectional approach helps us recognize are internally diverse constituencies composed of differently situated subgroups. As such, organizations can mediate between weaker and stronger subgroups, making a case for the needs and interests of weaker subgroups in the same way that they are charged with doing for their marginalized constituencies vis-à-vis the dominant general public (Urbinati 2000, 2002). Although it is not the norm, by being nonrepresentative, these organizations can and, as the foregoing examples suggest, often do foster feelings of intersectionally linked fate among the many subgroups of their constituencies. In so doing, they advance a form of representation as advocacy that redistributes resources and energy in ways that benefit their least well-off constituents.

## CONCLUSION

Although similar on the surface, organizations representing marginalized groups are different than—and play a different role than—other types of interest groups. They claim to represent the voiceless, and their statements make it clear that these claims reflect genuine commitments and desires to do so. So, in addition to normative desires that organizations might use their access, legitimacy, and political capital to represent all members of the populations on whose behalf they claim to advocate, the data show empirically that most organizations sincerely want to do so. Most organizations lay claim to broad-based constituencies that include all members of the groups for whom they advocate, and they hope that their efforts will have a broad policy impact. Moreover, officers at these organizations understand and accept their roles as mediators between their constituencies and other constituencies within their interest community, as well as between their constituencies and the broader polity. Though not as widespread, there is additional evidence that some of these organizations act as mediators and that they try to foster intersectionally linked fate among the many groups that together comprise their constituencies.

Taken together, this evidence provides an empirical basis for expectations that organizations will represent intersectionally disadvantaged subgroups of their constituencies. Moreover, the evidence shows that in their attempts to fulfill these expectations, advocacy organizations advance a conceptualization of representation that embodies the pursuit of social justice as a central goal. In the name of social justice, these organizations call upon themselves to be *nonrepresentative* by violating norms of proportionality and pure preference-transmittal. Instead, organizations aspire to advocate in a compensatory way for intersectionally disadvantaged subgroups of their constituencies. In these ways, organizations advance a distinctive concept of redistributive representation in which legitimacy is derived not merely from the proportion of their constituency that supports their actions (which is often the yardstick used to assess the representativeness of elected officials) but also from the extent to which their actions advance the goal of justice for marginalized groups (Urbinati 2000, 2002).

Given these goals, concerns about how well these organizations represent intersectionally disadvantaged members become even more germane. How can we reconcile these claims with the claims of so much theory and so many case studies that organizations representing marginalized groups ignore intersectionally disadvantaged constituents?

A cynical (or, some might contend, a realistic) interpretation of this discrepancy is that officers and staff at advocacy organizations—even organizations that are committed to equality and social justice—are rational political actors who, like elected officials, are simply trying to maintain their organizations, maximize their credibility, and appeal to as broad a base as they can. In addition, as appellants to these same elected officials, it is incumbent upon them to lay claim to being the voice of as many potential donors and voters as possible. Voters and donors are, after all, their currency when it comes to trying to influence elected officials. This interpretation is not without validity, but it captures only a very small piece of a much more complicated story about the disjuncture between the well-intentioned claims made by the officers depicted in this chapter and the elitist organizations that are the object of so much derision. It is to this story that I turn in the next chapter.

# FOUR

# Trickle-Down Representation?

We met for lunch at a popular Dupont Circle restaurant, on one of those humid summer days that reminds you that Washington, D.C., was built on a wetland. My lunch companion, the chair of the board of a civil rights organization, had just returned from his organization's annual convention. As we ate, he reflected upon some of the decisions made at the convention about this organization's public policy agenda. Among them had been a decision to move away from social service programs—such as SAT prep, credit counseling, and teen pregnancy prevention—which had come to dominate much of the group's efforts, and to focus instead on policy advocacy, or what he called "justice programs" that focus on public policy advocacy. "If you can change justice," he said, "you won't need as much service." How, I asked, does his organization decide which justice-related issues to pursue and which of the many subgroups of its constituency it will represent? He replied,

> I'm very sensitive to the charge—which I used to make, but which I really think is unfounded—that we represent middle-class blacks exclusively. I reject the argument that the civil rights gains of the '60s benefited only middle-class Americans. I know that's not true.... We think that what we do benefits all African Americans up and down the income stream.

Probably not as much for people at the very, very bottom. We do fight racial discrimination, at least, for people in the working [world].... And to some extent, people not in the working world are beneficiaries of what we do, because we lobby for increased government payments in the whole social-welfare apparatus.... So, even people down at the very bottom are beneficiaries of what we do.[1]

Although his answer did not speak directly to the question that I had posed, it does address the questions that motivated the research for this book: Who do organizations such as his represent, and how well? Moreover, his answer indicates that this question was on his mind and suggests that he knows that others wonder about this issue as well. His response attests to the centrality of this question for political actors and for the public—it is not just political scientists and democratic theorists who wonder about the biases in the "pluralist heaven."

Over the course of our lunch, we discussed the specific procedures his organization uses to define its policy agenda. I asked him about his organization's level of involvement in influencing policy related to the issue of racial profiling. He said that this was a priority for his group and explained, "Sometime over the last three or more years, this issue became a real concern for us." I then asked him about his organization's efforts to influence public policy on affirmative action in higher education. He listed several major efforts that his group had taken to try to preserve or enhance current policy in the face of legislative and judicial attempts to roll it back. His organization had filed amicus curiae briefs in relevant court cases, it had made efforts to defeat ballot initiatives in California and Washington State, and it had lobbied against proposed federal legislation as well as against state legislation in Florida. "It's a major, major issue," he said.[2]

Referring to his statement about lobbying for increases in social spending, I asked whether his group had been involved in the debates and events leading up to the 1996 Personal Responsibility and Work Opportunity Reconciliation Act (PRWORA), commonly known as the Welfare Reform Act. "Yes," he said, "we opposed the Clinton plans." He paused for a moment, and then continued, "Probably not as vigorously as we should have ... [and] we didn't pay as much attention to the aftereffects as we should have done." Had there been any discussion at the recent convention about action the organization might take to remedy its low level of involvement with this issue, I asked? Perhaps they were gearing up to work on influencing the 2001 reauthorization of the law? "I don't think so," he said, "it's not a top issue." Why not? I inquired. "A combination of things. . . . We're doing so much else. This is something else shouting for our attention. Even though it's important, it's [gesturing away from himself with his hand] over there. We can't take it on or the details are complicated, and we're not quite sure. . . . So, it's not a matter of indifference as it is busyness and other things on our plate and no room for this important issue."[3]

My exchange with the civil rights leader helps make sense of the competing claims about the extent to which organizations represent and mediate on behalf of intersectionally disadvantaged constituents. In the case of this particular civil rights organization, the logic underlying the different levels of energy it devotes to each issue captures three key characteristics of how organizations advocating for the underrepresented make decisions about the representation of their disadvantaged constituents.

First, it is clear that these organizations do not lack interest in advocating on behalf of disadvantaged subgroups within their constituencies. To the contrary, my lunch companion and his organization have good intentions and *want* to do right by people he characterized as being "at the very bottom." Moreover, concerns about representing disadvantaged subgroups are on the minds of organization officers. His response about representing low-income blacks spoke to the salience of the concern, felt by the leadership of many organizations, that disadvantaged constituents are not being represented adequately. However, this concern is superseded by a second notable characteristic: This organization does not view issues affecting disadvantaged constituents as central to its agenda. As the chair of the board put it, these concerns are seen, quite literally, as being "over there"—as peripheral rather than central to these organizations' key concerns. Adding categories "complicates" issues—it is easier to stick with single categories of analysis. As a consequence, the organization's leadership downplays the impact of disadvantaged-subgroup issues, which serves to marginalize them even further.

Third, instead of working on disadvantaged-subgroup issues directly, officers at these organizations assume either that *other* organizations will work on them or that representation for disadvantaged subgroups will occur as a by-product of their efforts on other issues and that the benefits of their other efforts will "trickle down" to intersectionally disadvantaged constituents. As a consequence, when organizations *do* work on issues affecting intersectionally disadvantaged groups, this work tends to be more symbolic and less vigorous than it is when it comes to other issues. In the case of this particular civil rights organization, officers want and intend for it to speak for more than just middle-class African Americans. Nonetheless, the organization expends considerably more effort to protect affirmative action in college admissions than it does to protect public assistance to the poor. Although it is concerned about welfare and antipoverty policy and while it recognizes that these issues are important to a disproportionate number of African Americans, it simply does not give priority to those matters on its public policy agenda. Instead, the officers at this organization assume that their work on affirmative action, an issue that benefits mainly a relatively advantaged subgroup of African Americans, will benefit their entire constituency. They fail to apply the same logic to an antipoverty policy, such as welfare reform, that also benefits a subgroup of African Americans but in this case a disadvantaged one. When it comes to welfare reform, they engage in symbolic activities such as taking a position on it, but they do not devote substantial time or resources to these efforts (Mayhew 1974).

These three dynamics manifest across the community of organizations advocating for marginalized groups. Data from the Survey of National Economic and Social Justice Organizations (SNESJO) make it possible to analyze the level of advocacy on issues affecting disadvantaged subgroups represented by these organizations. When combined with information from the face-to-face interviews with organization officers, it is apparent that while advocacy groups provide some representation for their disadvantaged constituents, they are *substantially less active* when it comes to issues affecting disadvantaged subgroups than they are when it comes to issues affecting advantaged subgroups. In spite of sincere desires to represent disadvantaged constituents, they do not view the issues that affect these constituents as central to their agendas and view extra axes of disadvantage as complicating. As a consequence, officers at these organizations marginalize and downplay the impact of such issues, framing them as being outside their niches and as narrow and particularistic in their effect, while framing issues affecting advantaged groups as if they affect a majority of their constituents and have a broad and generalized impact.

Although this process depresses activity on issues affecting intersectionally disadvantaged subgroups, it is not entirely decisive. Other factors and practices lead many organizations to advocate extensively on behalf of intersectionally disadvantaged subgroups of their constituencies. As I began to demonstrate in chapter 3, the leaders of most organizations are genuinely committed to representing the voiceless and to mediating on their behalf in the policy process. The analyses in this chapter show that, under some circumstances, these commitments lead organization officers to re-sist political forces that conspire against representation for disadvantaged subgroups. As such, their dedication offsets a significant portion of the mo-bilization of bias against these constituents in politics and public opinion.

## RETHINKING THE MOBILIZATION OF BIAS: INTEREST GROUPS AND THE DISADVANTAGED

As my exchange with the chair of the board of the civil rights group makes clear, concerns about the elitism—or the perceived elitism—of organiza-tions such as the one he heads are not merely academic. Although such explicit acknowledgment of these concerns is rare, such apprehensions un-derlie many discussions about interest groups among the staff members of these organizations as well as among members of the general public. The "explosion" in the number of feminist, civil rights, and economic justice organizations has brought with it unprecedented levels of representation for women, racial minorities, and low-income people. For several decades, organizations such as the National Association for the Advancement of Col-ored People (NAACP) and the National Organization for Women (NOW) and their associated legal defense funds have played a central role in legal and legislative efforts to end de jure racial and sex-based discrimination and to increase resources and opportunities for the underrepresented. However, as I discussed at greater length in chapter 2, the increase in the number of these organizations has been accompanied by criticism and concern about the biases and inequalities within organizations claiming to speak on behalf of marginalized populations.

Taken together, the theoretical work on intersectionality, broad studies of organizations, sociological literature about social movements, and case studies of policy issues and single organizations that I discussed at length in chapter 2 suggest many reasons to anticipate low levels of activity on issues affecting intersectionally disadvantaged subgroups, and they also imply several possible explanations for these low levels. However, no quantitative study has yet examined advocacy on behalf of marginalized groups in an explicitly comparative and intersectional framework, across groups and issues. It is consequently difficult to gauge the nature of the disparities and the severity of the problem, and it is more difficult still to adjudicate between the competing explanations of these low levels that are posited by the various approaches.

The lack of systematic evidence also makes it impossible to refute defini-tively the claims made by many organizations that they *do* try to represent disadvantaged members of their constituencies—claims that constitute a robust response to the argument that we simply should not expect interest groups to advocate on behalf of intersectionally marginalized constituents. As demonstrated by the data presented in chapter 3, officers at most or-ganizations embrace broad policy mandates and claim to represent and to be mediators for many subgroups within their constituencies. Key to the mission statements of many organizations, for example, is a claim to rep-resent all members of the social or economic group on whose behalf they speak. The NAACP, for instance, claims, "For 90 years, the NAACP . . . has served as *the* voice for African Americans" (emphasis added).[4] Implicit in this statement is the claim that this organization is the voice for all African Americans—male and female, gay and straight, rich and poor—and that it will attend to issues affecting all of these subgroups. Some organiza-tions claim explicitly to work on intersectional issues. For example, Kerry Lobel, former executive director of the National Gay and Lesbian Task Force (NGLTF), stated that her organization tries "to represent people who are disadvantaged in a number of ways because they don't always have a voice in politics" (Bull 1998). Similarly, NOW states that it is "dedicated to making legal, political, social and economic change in our society in order to achieve our goal, which is to eliminate sexism and end *all oppression*" (emphasis added). To achieve this extremely broad goal, it does not restrict itself to pursuing goals only on what are traditionally considered "women's issues." Instead, the organization has five official priorities: "the passing of an equal rights amendment to the U.S. Constitution, opposing racism, advocating for abortion and reproductive rights, supporting lesbian and gay rights and ending violence against women."[5]

Of course, the contradictions between such assertions by organizations, on the one hand, and the theoretical claims of political scientists, on the other hand, do not in themselves provide a theoretical basis for em-pirical expectations. A conventional and eminently reasonable interpreta-tion of the assertions made by advocacy organizations might be that they are strategic utterances by savvy political actors who, like elected officials, want to maximize their credibility and appeal by advertising to a broad base. However, the incongruities between the two characterizations cast doubt on the assumption that organizations simply will not be active when it comes to issues affecting intersectionally disadvantaged subgroups, and they also underscore why it is important to assess whether they are.

In addition, while we certainly should not take the statements of political organizations and their leaders at face value and risk overlooking strategic reasons that might lead them to profess a desire to represent particular subgroups or an interest in a specific policy issue, neither should we ignore or dismiss these claims. As I have explained previously, it is important that rationalist expectations not obscure the actual actions of organizations that do advocate on behalf of disadvantaged subgroups of their constituencies.

Moreover, it is not only statements by organization officers that challenge the assumption that interest groups will not represent intersectionally disadvantaged constituencies. Some scholars suggest that important incentives *encourage* organizations that advocate for underrepresented populations to address disadvantaged-subgroup issues. Representing disadvantaged constituents increases an organization's legitimacy because it buttresses claims to speak for the whole group for which it advocates (C. Cohen 1999; Kurtz 2002; Willis 1998). Reaching out to disadvantaged constituents and serving as mediators on their behalf also can increase the size of an organization's membership, help it build coalitions, and ultimately help it survive (J. Wilson [1974] 1995). There is even some empirical evidence that various advocacy groups do in fact dedicate themselves to representing disadvantaged subgroups of their constituencies. For example, Michael Katz argues that feminist organizations, accused of being a movement of and for affluent women, "turned to poverty" in the 1970s as a way to incorporate working-class women and women of color (1989, 71). Similarly, Donna Cooper Hamilton and Charles V. Hamilton (1992) find that African American civil rights groups have always been dedicated to representing their poor constituents and that they are devoted to economic justice as well as to racial justice, evidenced by their activities on both civil rights and antipoverty policies as far back as the New Deal (see also Baumgartner and Leech 1998; Imig 1996; McCann 1986).

Katz's and Hamilton and Hamilton's findings do not demonstrate that these organizations have been active on behalf of *all* intersectionally marginalized subgroups, nor does this evidence provide any indication that they will continue to do so. Nonetheless, their studies do provide important empirical reasons to believe that some organizations might be active on issues affecting some intersectionally marginalized subgroups.

As such, their findings provide evidence that it is anything but a foregone conclusion that interest groups will ignore disadvantaged constituents.

## ANALYSIS

The four-part policy typology that highlights the power, size, and status of the constituency affected by a public policy issue (introduced in chapters 1 and 2) helps adjudicate between the various possibilities suggested by extant research about the levels of advocacy that organizations devote to issues affecting intersectionally disadvantaged groups. To that end, I use the survey data to test the hypothesis that the level of activity that organizations devote to an issue depends more on the relative *advantage* of the subgroup affected by the issue than it does on the relative *size* of the affected group. If true, we should find that organizations are less active when it comes to issues affecting intersectionally disadvantaged subgroups than they are when it comes to majority and advantaged-subgroup issues. If, however, it is the size of the affected subgroup that is most important, levels of activity should rise and fall based on the proportion of constituents affected, resulting in high levels of activity on majority and universal issues and in relatively equal levels of advocacy for advantaged and disadvantaged subgroup issues.

In order to compare their levels of activity on public policy issues, each survey respondent was asked how active, on a scale of 1 to 5, their organization had been on each of four designated policy issues. Recall from chapter 2 that I selected each issue to represent one of the four categories within the issue typology: majority, advantaged-subgroup, disadvantaged-subgroup, and universal. For example, for Asian Pacific American organizations, hate crimes were categorized as a majority issue because, theoretically, all Asian Pacific Americans are relatively equally likely to be victims of a hate crime. Affirmative action in government contracting was categorized as an advantaged-subgroup issue for this group, as it affects primarily Asian Pacific American business owners, a relatively privileged subgroup of all Asian Pacific Americans. Violence against women was selected as a disadvantaged-subgroup issue, as it affects Asian Pacific American women, a subgroup that is intersectionally disadvantaged by race and gender. While the majority, advantaged-subgroup, and disadvantaged-subgroup issues vary by organization type, the same universal issue—Social Security—was used for all groups.

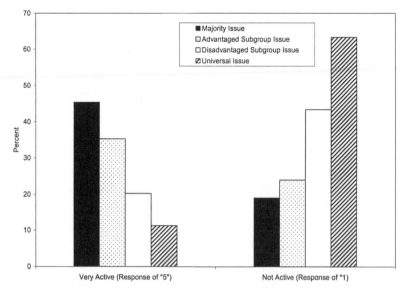

**Fig. 4.1.** Percentage of organizations that are "very active" or "not active," by issue type. Organization officers were asked, "Please tell me, on a scale of 1 to 5, where 1 is 'not active' and 5 is 'very active,' how active has your organization been on each of the following policy issues in the past ten years?" The four columns on the left reflect the percentage of respondents giving the answer "5." The four columns on the right reflect the percentage of respondents giving the answer "1" (data from SNESJO).

Examining the mean levels of activity by issue type, as well the proportion of organizations that are "very active" and "not active" on each one, provides some preliminary information about the extent of advocacy when it comes to issues that affect intersectionally disadvantaged subgroups (See figs. 4.1 and 4.2). Measured in terms of both the percentage and the mean, organizations are most active on the majority issue (81 percent of organizations are active) and next most active on the advantaged-subgroup issue (76 percent are active), followed by the disadvantaged-subgroup issue (57 percent are active). The universal issue comes in last (37 percent are active).[6]

Although the figures show quite clearly that activity levels vary by issue type and that organizations are not very active on disadvantaged-subgroup issues, percentages and means alone do not allow us to test directly the various explanations about why this is the case. A multivariate analysis, however, can isolate the effects of issue type on an organization's level of advocacy on each type of issue by controlling for other variables that might influence their policy activities, such as organizational characteristics and resources. To conduct such an analysis, the dependent variable measuring

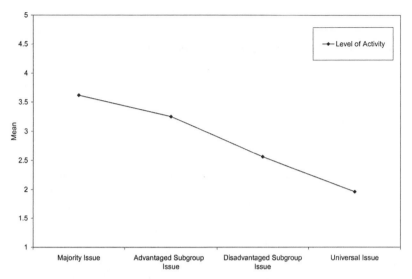

**Fig. 4.2.** Mean levels of organization activity, by issue type. Data reflect the mean response to the question, "Please tell me, on a scale of 1 to 5, where 1 is 'not active' and 5 is 'very active,' how active has your organization been on each of the following policy issues in the past ten years?" (data from SNESJO).

levels of activity on each of the four policy issues (minus each organization's average level of activity on the other three issues) is regressed on a range of independent and control variables that operationalize several internal organizational and external political explanations for variations in organizations' level of policy activity.[7]

In order to first examine directly at the macro level whether levels of policy activity do indeed vary by policy type in the ways that intersectional theories suggest that they will, I created four dummy variables to capture each type of policy issue (labeled *Universal issue, Majority issue, Advantaged-subgroup issue,* and *Disadvantaged-subgroup issue*), designating universal issues as the excluded category.[8] To test Downsian claims that groups try to focus on issues that will have the broadest impact on their constituents, I include a measure of the proportion of constituents that are affected by each issue (*Constituents affected*). One implication of theories of intersectionality is that activity on an issue will vary based on both the power of the subgroup affected by it and the proportion of constituents affected by it. To account for this possibility, I created dummy variables for the interaction between *Constituents affected* and each policy type (*Constituents affected X Majority, Constituents affected X Advantaged-subgroup, Constituents affected X Disadvantaged-subgroup*).[9]

Of course, organizational maintenance-related concerns about resources, funding, legitimacy, and public attitudes, among other factors, also likely affect activity on a policy issue. Fears of losing members or contributors might make organization leaders reticent about taking action on issues if large portions of their constituents disagree with their groups' positions on the issues or if organization officers do not believe that their constituents are concerned about the issues (Kingdon 1995; Kollman 1998; Rothenberg 1992; J. Wilson [1974] 1995). To test for such organizational maintenance effects, I included variables that measure the proportion of constituents that agree with an organization's position on each issue (*Constituents agree*) and that are concerned about each issue (*Constituents concerned*).

Advocacy organizations do not make decisions in a vacuum, and their activity levels might also be affected by political opportunities and threats such as how much attention an issue is receiving in Congress, from the administration, in the courts, or among their political allies more generally (Jenkins and Perrow 1977; Kingdon 1995; McAdam 1982; M. Smith 2000). Reputational concerns stemming from the desire to be associated with policy successes might lead organizations to be particularly attentive to political threats and opportunities on potentially "winnable" issues (Chong 1991; M. Smith 2000; J. Wilson [1974] 1995). To ensure that inactivity is not merely a function of a lack of political threats or opportunities, the survey design includes only issues on the political agenda (see appendix B). In addition, to control for the effect of the *variation* in the salience of issues on the political agenda on levels of attention from advocacy organizations, I also have included a measure (*Agenda salience*) of the number of entries for the issue (in hundreds) in *Congressional Quarterly*, the "Supreme Court Roundup" feature of the *New York Times*, and the *Federal Register* during the period covered by the study.[10]

Other factors in the external political and social environment that are related to political opportunities and constraints are also likely to affect activity on policy issues. Perceived levels of the public's support for, or opposition to, an organization's stand on an issue might also affect its activity levels, as might the level of controversy surrounding an issue (Bauer, Pool, and Dexter 1963; Kollman 1998; M. Smith 2000; J. Wilson [1974] 1995). Thus, based on estimates by the surveyed leaders, the model also includes a variable that measures how controversial an issue is in the public's eyes (*Controversial*) and what proportion of the public agrees with the organization's position on the issue (*Public agrees*).[11]

The niche theories advanced by Virginia Gray and David Lowery (1996) and by William Browne (1990, 1998) suggest that organizations choose to work on particular policies based on the opportunities available to them in relation to the issue coverage of other organizations. I included two measures to examine whether the desire to develop and maintain niches influences organizations' decisions about policy advocacy. The first is a count of the total number of organizations in the advocacy sector of which the group is a part (*Primary niche*). The second variable is a count of the number of organizations in the advocacy sector that intersects with that of the organization in question regarding the disadvantaged-subgroup issue about which they were asked (*Secondary niche*). So, in the case of women's organizations, the first variable is the total number of women's organizations, while the second is the number of economic justice organizations, which is the organization type that they are likely to consider in thinking about a welfare "niche."

The analysis also includes several controls for organizational features and capacities such as size and resources. Because organizations with more resources might have the capacity for activity on more issues than would groups with fewer resources, I included controls for organizational capacity, operationalized using two measures: the percentage of an organization's budget that is devoted to advocacy and the number of paid staff.[12] Finally, organizations with individual members are likely to respond differently to constituents and to the public than are those organizations that do not have individual members. To capture these differences, I ran separate models for member (Model 1) and nonmember (Model 2) organizations and controlled for the number of members (in thousands) in the case of member organizations.[13]

The regression models are presented in table 4.1. Overall, the results bolster and help explain the findings suggested by the means and percentages, revealing that organizations are active at low levels on issues affecting disadvantaged subgroups of their constituencies.[14] The low levels of attention to these issues cannot be accounted for by the fact that they affect or are of interest to a subgroup of constituents. Instead, an intersectional approach helps a great deal in explaining variations in levels of advocacy across policy issues, showing that it is crucial to take into account the combined effects of the size, advantage, and status of the constituents affected by these issues to understand why issues affecting disadvantaged subgroups are given short shrift. While many other factors in the model—such as

**TABLE 4.1** Predicting levels of activity on policy issues

| | VARIABLE MEAN (STD. DEV.) | MODEL 1: MEMBERSHIP ORGANIZATIONS | | MODEL 2: NON-MEMBERSHIP ORGANIZATIONS | | | | MODEL 3: ECONOMIC AND SOCIAL ISSUES | |
| | | | | INTERACTIVE | | NON-INTERACTIVE | | | |
| | | ORDERED LOGIT COEFFICIENT | RSE | ORDERED LOGIT COEFFICIENT | RSE | ORDERED LOGIT COEFFICIENT | RSE | ORDERED LOGIT COEFFICIENT | RSE |
|---|---|---|---|---|---|---|---|---|---|
| *Intersectionality Variables* | | | | | | | | | |
| Majority issue | 0.250 (0.433) | −0.217 | 0.712 | 1.458 | 1.425 | 2.978*** | 0.530 | −0.220 | 0.743 |
| Advantaged-subgroup issue | 0.250 (0.433) | 1.329* | 0.712 | 1.719** | 1.413 | 1.902*** | 0.418 | 1.594* | 0.730 |
| Disadvantaged-subgroup issue | 0.250 (0.433) | −0.999 | 0.673 | 0.0289 | 1.690 | 1.135** | 0.434 | −1.089 | 0.699 |
| Constituents affected X majority | 0.865 (1.678) | 0.607*** | 0.198 | 0.392 | 0.330 | | | 0.570** | 0.204 |
| Constituents affected X advantaged-subgroup | 0.838 (1.617) | 0.220 | 0.201 | 0.035 | 0.328 | | | 0.159 | 0.202 |
| Constituents affected X disadvantaged-subgroup | 0.685 (1.397) | 0.571** | 0.196 | 0.297 | 0.408 | | | 0.559** | 0.201 |
| *Strategic Variables* | | | | | | | | | |
| Constituents affected | 3.420 (1.366) | −0.321** | 0.145 | −.0245 | 0.310 | 0.156 | 0.128 | −0.320* | 0.149 |
| Constituents concerned | 3.898 (1.192) | 0.403*** | 0.087 | 0.472*** | 0.143 | 0.461*** | 0.143 | 0.396*** | 0.092 |
| Constituents agree | 4.107 (1.115) | 0.178* | 0.099 | −0.093 | 0.143 | −0.066 | 0.140 | 0.145 | 0.099 |
| Public agrees | 3.101 (1.005) | 0.003 | 0.091 | 0.073 | 0.196 | 0.071 | 0.191 | 0.036 | 0.095 |
| Controversial | 3.590 (1.221) | −0.001 | 0.071 | 0.359** | 0.120 | 0.358** | 0.116 | −0.007 | 0.072 |
| *Political Opportunity Variables* | | | | | | | | | |
| Primary Niche[a] | 110.823 (54.279) | 0.001 | 0.001 | 0.005* | 0.002 | 0.004** | 0.002 | 0.002 | 0.001 |
| Secondary Niche[b] | 126.657 (47.039) | −0.003* | 0.002 | 0.001 | 0.002 | −0.001 | 0.002 | −0.000 | 0.002 |
| Agenda salience[b] | 572.137 (534.468) | 0.023* | 0.002 | 0.005 | 0.027 | 0.006 | 0.025 | 0.025* | 0.002 |
| *Control Variables* | | | | | | | | | |
| Number of members | 67.708 (166.282) | −0.001 | 0.000 | | | 0.001 | | −0.000 | 0.000 |
| Percent of budget to advocacy | 29.373 (29.493) | −0.000 | 0.003 | 0.002 | 0.003 | 0.001 | 0.003 | 0.000 | 0.003 |

|  | Model 1 | Model 2 | Model 3 | Model 4 | Model 5 |
|---|---|---|---|---|---|
| Number of paid staff | 39.358 (81.829) | | | | |
|  | 0.000 | 0.001 | 0.001 | 0.001 | 0.000 |
| Economic v. Social[c] | | | | | −0.0174 |
|  | | | | | 0.259 |
| Initial log likelihood | −710.203 | −353.090 | −353.090 | −353.090 | −682.757 |
| Log likelihood at convergence | −625.566 | −299.403 | −300.875 | | −599.611 |
| Chi-square (degrees of freedom) | 132.21*** (17) | 111.43*** (16) | 99.15*** (13) | | 135.21*** (18) |
| Cut point 1 | −1.146 | 1.033 | 1.756 | | −1.182 |
|  | 0.675 | 1.37 | 0.991 | | 0.670 |
| Cut point 2 | 1.018 | 3.470 | 4.215 | | 1.000 |
|  | 0.698 | 1.400 | 0.946 | | 0.696 |
| Cut point 3 | 3.149 | 5.747 | 6.482 | | 3.192 |
|  | 0.684 | 1.458 | 0.989 | | 0.681 |
| Cut point 4 | 5.371 | 8.022 | 8.714 | | 5.415 |
|  | 0.724 | 1.505 | 1.009 | | 0.722 |
| Pseudo R² | 0.12 | 0.15 | 0.15 | | 0.12 |
| N | 507 | 255 | 255 | 255 | 490 |

*Sources:* SNESJO; Congressional Quarterly; the *New York Times* "Supreme Court Roundup"; the *Congressional Record*; and the *Federal Register*.

*Note:* Coefficients are Ordered Logit coefficients. Each case represents the level of one organization's activity on one of the four issues about which they were asked in the SNESJO. Robust standard errors (RSE) are therefore used to correct for clustering of the standard errors as there are four observations for each organization. The dependent variable uses responses to the survey question: "Please tell me, on a scale of 1 to 5, where 1 is not active, and 5 is very active, how active has your organization been on each of the following policy issues in the past ten years?" Respondents were asked about four policy issues that correspond to the four possibly issue types in the policy typology. The effects of each type is shown through the dummy variables "Majority issue," "Advantaged-subgroup issue," and "Disadvantaged-subgroup issue." Universal issues are the excluded categories. The dependent variable is coded 1–5, so a positive sign on a coefficient indicates an increase in activity, while a negative sign indicates a descrease. To take account of the general "activeness" of each organization, the mean level of activity on the three issues not being predicted was subtracted from each activity level (the resulting values were then re-aggregated into five categories). Differencing out each organization's average level of activity in this way minimizes the bias that would be introduced by including a measure of activeness as an independent variable as well as minimizing the "noise" that would result from failing to take account of overall activeness. VIFs and tolerance levels show no signs of multicolliearity.

[a] *Primary Niche* is a count of the total number of organizations in the advocacy sector of which the group is a part; *Secondary niche* counts of the number of organizations in the advocacy sector that intersects with that of the organization in question regarding the disadvantaged-subgroup issue about which they were asked.

[b] *Agenda salience* is calculated based on information from *Congressional Quarterly* (1990, 1993, 1996, and 1999); the *New York Times* "Supreme Court Roundup" (1990–2000); the *Congressional Record* (1990–2000); and the *Federal Register* (1990–2000).

[c] The variable measuring economic and social issues is coded: Social = 0, Economic = 1.

* Relationship is significant at p < .10; ** Relationship is significant at p < .05; *** Relationship is significant at p < .01.

concerns for organizational maintenance, the need to respond to political opportunities and threats, and the desire to carve out niches—also affect levels of advocacy, in most cases they exacerbate the biases against issues affecting intersectionally disadvantaged subgroups. These results apply to both membership and nonmembership organizations, although slightly different factors are at play for each case.[15]

## SMALL BANG, BIG BUCKS: ISSUE TYPE, LEVEL OF IMPACT, AND THE DYNAMICS OF REPRESENTATION

The most striking finding in this analysis is that organizations do not allocate their advocacy activity in ways that benefit the greatest numbers of constituents. In fact, under some circumstances, quite the opposite is true. When we examine the variables that test the relationships that are at the heart of this book—how the size, status, and power of the constituency affected by an issue influences the level of advocacy devoted to that issue— we find that activity does *not* necessarily increase as the proportion of constituents affected by an issue increases. In fact, in some cases the broader the potential impact, the *less* attention an issue receives.

*Membership Organizations* | The implications of the regression results for membership organization are more clearly illustrated if we convert the coefficient estimates into probabilities (see fig. 4.3).[16] Transforming the estimates in this way allows us to predict the chances of activity and inactivity as these vary by issue type. Figure 4.3 shows that, holding all other variables in the model at their means, there is a 2 percent chance that an organization will be active at the highest level (a response of "5" on the 1-to-5 scale of activity) in the case of universal issues and that these chances increase slightly, to 3 percent, in the case of disadvantaged-subgroup issues. The probability that an organization will devote such a high level of activity to an issue rises to 6 percent if the issue in question is a majority issue and increases again to 12 percent for advantaged-subgroup issues. Indeed, organizations are twice as likely to devote their greatest efforts to advantaged-subgroup issues when compared with majority issues. Comparing the probabilities for advantaged- and disadvantaged-subgroup issues shows that, at average levels of impact, organizations are three times more likely to devote their highest levels of advocacy to issues affecting advantaged subgroups of their constituency than they are to issues affecting disadvantaged ones.

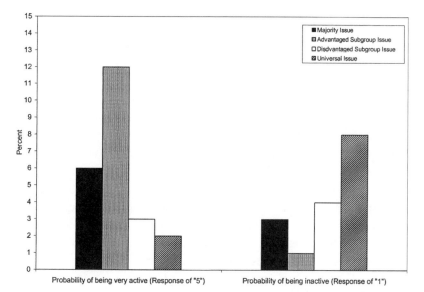

**Fig. 4.3.** Predicted probability of activity and inactivity, by issue type. Organization officers (of membership organizations only) were asked, "Please tell me, on a scale of 1 to 5, where 1 is 'not active' and 5 is 'very active,' how active has your organization been on each of the following policy issues in the past ten years?" The four columns on the left reflect the probability of giving the answer "5" (holding the other variables in the model constant). The four columns on the right reflect the probability of giving the answer "1" (holding the other variables in the model constant) (data from SNESJO).

The implications of this disparity, and the value of combining strategic and intersectional approaches, are illustrated further by calculating probabilities that show the contingent effects of *Constituents affected* as they vary by policy type. Consider a majority issue with a low level of impact on an organization's constituents ("1" on the 1–5 scale of impact). Under these circumstances (and holding all other variables at their means), there is a 23.3 percent chance that an organization will be very active on this issue (4 or 5 on the 1–5 scale of activity). This probability increases to 78.8 percent in the case of a majority issue with a *high* level of impact ("5" on the 1–5 scale of impact). In the case of disadvantaged-subgroup issues, the chances of activity at these levels increase from 14.6 percent to 45.6 percent as we move from low to high levels of impact. In the case of advantaged-subgroup issues, however, levels of activity are likely to be very high (62.8 percent chance of a high level of activity), even when impact is at its lowest level. Moreover, the probability of a high level of activity on an issue that affects an advantaged subgroup increases much less starkly (to 78 percent) as we move from low to high levels of impact. In fact, the probability that an organization will be active at a high level is greater in the case of an advantaged-subgroup issue with almost no impact on its constituents than it is for a disadvantaged-subgroup issue that affects "almost all" of its constituents.

Together, these results reveal a double standard applied by membership organizations in determining the level of advocacy that they devote to policy issues—a double standard that benefits privileged subgroups at the expense of other members. Specifically, the interaction effects demonstrate that breadth of impact is crucial for increasing levels of advocacy when it comes to majority and disadvantaged-subgroup issues but has far less of an effect in the case of issues affecting advantaged subgroups. When it comes to issues that affect advantaged subpopulations, advocacy is high even at very low levels of impact. However, when it comes to the other two issue types—majority issues and disadvantaged-subgroup issues—organizations are active at high levels only when they perceive that more constituents are affected.

These findings suggest that a Downsian approach is a necessary but insufficient component of an explanation for levels of policy advocacy. On its own, such an approach obscures the interactive effects of breadth of impact and subgroup power and status. That is, if the driving motivation were simply a strategic concern to have "broad" impact, we should see low levels of activity on issues affecting both disadvantaged and advantaged subgroups. Instead, regardless of their breadth of impact, advantaged-subgroup issues receive much more attention than disadvantaged-subgroup issues. As such, an intersectional explanation is crucial to fully understanding variations in levels of policy advocacy: organizations do not increase their efforts simply in response to an increase in the proportion of constituents affected. Instead, this maxim holds only for majority issues and issues affecting disadvantaged subgroups; issues affecting privileged subgroups receive high levels of attention regardless of whether the proportion of an organization's constituents that is affected is low or high. Indeed, under many conditions, issues affecting advantaged subgroups receive more attention than majority issues as well.

*Nonmembership Organizations* | The situation is somewhat different when we examine the results for nonmembership organizations. In this case, none of the interaction effects is significant. A noninteractive model, then, seems more appropriate for nonmembership organizations. Nonetheless, the underlying message of the pattern for membership organizations remains: organizations apply a double standard that benefits privileged subgroups at the expense of disadvantaged ones.

## POLICY IMAGES AND FRAMING

The face-to-face interviews provide even more support for combining intersectional and strategic understandings of policy advocacy and for the hypothesis that the level of activity an organization devotes to subgroup issues is due more to the power of the subgroup affected than to the proportion of constituents that it affects. In addition, juxtaposing the survey data with information from the interviews allows us to see the dynamics that produce the uneven levels of activity. Taken together, these two types of data suggest further that a substantial portion of the variation in the distribution of activity across issues and constituencies is due to the ways in which advocacy groups frame issues (Collier and Brady 2004). Whereas survey respondents generally recognized that majority issues affect more constituents than do advantaged-subgroup issues, in face-to-face interviews, respondents framed advantaged-subgroup issues *as if* they were majority issues that affect many more constituents than they actually do. In contrast, the respondents framed issues affecting disadvantaged subgroups as having an impact on an extremely narrow portion of the constituency.

For example, among the women's organizations in the SNESJO, 38 percent of the interviewed leaders said that the majority issue, violence against women, affects "almost all" of their constituents. Far fewer, 13.6 percent, said that the disadvantaged-subgroup issue, welfare reform, affects almost all constituents, and only 9.8 percent said that the advantaged-subgroup issue, affirmative action in higher education, affects almost all constituents. Levels of activity, however, do not reflect these assessments. Advantaged subgroups benefit disproportionately while disadvantaged subgroups are disproportionately neglected. Whereas 86 percent of women's organizations are active on violence against women, the majority issue, almost as many—79.5 percent—are active on affirmative action in higher education, even though respondents recognize that this issue affects fewer constituents. A far smaller proportion of women's organizations—only 60.5 percent (strikingly, still a majority)—are active on welfare reform, although they recognize that this issue has almost the same impact on their constituencies as affirmative action in higher education. However, as I will show in the following section, respondents in the interviews framed both violence against women and affirmative action in higher education as affecting *all* women and therefore as being in women's "common interest." In contrast, they framed welfare reform as a "special interest" that has a very *narrow* impact even though, like affirmative action in higher education, it affects a subgroup of all women. Notably, welfare reform affects a stigmatized and marginalized subgroup of women defined by a second axis of disadvantage. Affirmative action in higher education, on the other hand, affects a relatively advantaged subgroup defined by a second axis of relative privilege. In reality, the proportion of women affected by each of these issues is relatively similar. For example, according to the 2002 Current Population Survey, approximately 17.5 percent of women over the age of twenty-five have college degrees, while approximately 12.6 percent of all women live below the poverty line, as do 26.5 percent of female-headed households and 22.9 percent of women living alone.[17]

Consider this typical judgment by the field organizer at a women's organization. Asked why her organization is so active on the majority issue of violence against women, she framed the issue as one that affects most women: "It's so prevalent, and it's so dire, it affects so many women," she said, "It really prevents so many women's freedom and success and equality."[18] When asked about the advantaged-subgroup issue of affirmative action in higher education, however, the vice president of another women's group also framed the issue as a common interest that affects *all* women, not just the relatively advantaged subset of women who attend college, graduate school, or professional school. She said, "I think it's a priority because . . . affirmative action is one of the reasons that women and minorities have made so much progress. . . . It has a huge impact and . . . [it affects] *all* women who are in the workforce or go to college or start their own business and are competing for government contracts—that's a lot of women." She went on to say that women on public assistance "don't go to college, but that's a smaller and smaller set of people."[19] Her statement downplays the number of women who are too disadvantaged to take advantage of affirmative action, and it maintains the framing of the issue as one of concern to "all women."

Finally, when asked about her organization's activity on welfare reform, a disadvantaged-subgroup issue, this field organizer's comments captured the tenor of many comments and was particularly revealing. "[We are] not as active [on that as we are on] some of the other projects," she said. "We work in coalition with organizations that do work on welfare reform, but it's really just not our cup of tea. . . . We definitely see welfare reform as [a] gendered issue. It's definitely something that we're concerned with and have been involved in but just not on the same level."[20] This evocative statement about welfare not being her organization's "cup of tea" is probably unintentionally honest, conjuring as it does images of respectable womanhood that marginalize intersectionally disadvantaged women.[21]

These statements about welfare reform, affirmative action, and violence against women are characteristic of general trends in the connections drawn by respondents between the impact of various policy issues on their levels of advocacy on those issues. As such, these statements help explain the patterns of involvement in policy issues reflected in the data from the SNESJO. The qualitative and quantitative data taken together illuminate how the respondents frame and justify their reasons for being involved in some issues and not others. Specifically, they play *up* the impact of majority and advantaged-subgroup issues and play *down* the impact or relevance of disadvantaged-subgroup issues. Essentially, there is little return for increases in the impact of advantaged-subgroup issues because organization leaders strategically conflate power and impact. In effect, organization leaders substitute the higher status of advantaged groups for the relatively narrow impact of the issues that affect them. As such, the leadership can justify giving priority to both majority and advantaged-subgroup issues by framing them both as interests common to all women that have a broad impact. Issues affecting disadvantaged-subgroups, on the other hand, are framed as special interests that are both narrow and particularistic, justifying their low levels of activity. Because, as I showed earlier, the survey data reveal that advocacy on a disadvantaged-subgroup issue depends in part on the proportion of constituents affected by it, framing these issues narrowly exacerbates the biases against activity on them. Such framings mirror the juxtapositioning of special interests against those of the common good that, as I discussed in chapter 2, often are used by the larger polity to justify a lack of attention to issues affecting marginalized groups.

Though important, advocacy organizations play only a limited role in the overall political system and therefore have limited power to set the agenda or to initiate or frame debates on their own (Bauer, Pool, and Dexter 1963; Heclo 1978; Kingdon 1995; M. Smith 2000; Snow and Benford 1992; Tarrow 1992, 1994; J. Wilson [1974] 1995). It is therefore not surprising that the women's organizations cited earlier frame welfare, affirmative action, and violence against women in ways that echo politically dominant constructions of these issues (Kingdon 1995; Tarrow 1994). Certainly the practice of adopting moderate frames that echo those of dominant social and political tropes can be rhetorically powerful, and such framings have, not surprisingly, been an important part of the strategies and successes of many social movements (Frymer, Strolovitch, and Warren 2006). Such frames can be particularly important during inhospitable political periods. Roberta Spalter-Roth and Ronnee Schreiber found, for example, that during the 1980s, women's organizations felt that they had to adapt to the antifeminist backlash of the era by avoiding "radical" language. Instead, they presented their goals in moderate, universalistic, and even "pro-family" terms. In spite of their commitments to understanding gender inequality as a structural rather than an individual problem, they presented their concerns in what Spalter-Roth and Schreiber characterize as "the dominant language of liberal individualism" (1995, 115–16).

Echoing the frames and constructions that circulate more broadly in national debates is a strategic move that can help organizations fend off threats or take advantage of political opportunities, attaching their favored policy alternatives to agenda items "that others may have made prominent" (Kingdon 1995, 50). As I discussed in chapter 3, however, scholars such as Deborah Stone, Sidney Tarrow, and Frank Baumgartner and Bryan Jones remind us that this is not the only way in which organizations engage in framing. Another common strategy used by advocacy organizations to advance their goals is to endeavor to *reframe* debates and to reconstruct "policy images" in ways that refute or disarm the dominant discourses that marginalize their constituents (Baumgartner and Jones 1993; D. Stone 1989; Tarrow 2005). The director of legal and public policy at a women's organization said, for example, "If we don't" frame issues, "then other people will frame them for us." Anticipating that possibility, her organization tries very hard to preemptively frame issues, and to do so "in a way that doesn't reinforce old stereotypes."[22] Women's organizations have worked hard to frame abortion as an issue of agency and "choice," for example, to combat the framing of abortion as an act of immoral selfishness and irresponsibility (Luker 1984). The field organizer quoted earlier who portrayed violence against women as a concern that has a broad impact engaged in a similar attempt to destigmatize this issue. In light of the efforts that organizations often devote to reframing issues for the benefit of their constituents and policy agendas, the narrow framing of welfare is conspicuous for its congruence with politically dominant framings.

## EXACERBATING THE BIAS?

It is clear that low levels of advocacy on disadvantaged-subgroup issues are strongly related to the power of those affected and to the tendency on the part of organizations to downplay the effects that these issues have on their constituent groups. Nevertheless, other factors also exacerbate the biases against disadvantaged subpopulations. Some of these factors manifest differently in membership organizations than they do in non-membership groups, but the net result is the same: disproportionately low levels of advocacy on behalf of intersectionally disadvantaged groups and disproportionately high levels of attention to the issues affecting their advantaged counterparts.

### CONSTITUENT CONCERN

First, in membership and nonmembership organizations alike, constituent concern about an issue leads to increased advocacy on that issue. The interviews support this finding and confirm that organizations conform to traditional notions of representation in this way. That is, they are more active on issues that they perceive as being important to their constituents, something that they gauge either by means of constituent surveys or by evaluating the number of constituents who call or write with opinions on a given issue. The executive director of an African American organization, for example, told me that his group took a proactive approach to trying to determine its constituents' attitudes and policy priorities, conducting regular polls to identify issues that are important to them. Several other respondents said, however, that they make the decision to mobilize around an issue when they begin "getting lots of phone calls" about it. The executive director of an Asian Pacific American organization explained that her group became involved in advocacy to change the regulations governing H-1B work visas (for skilled workers) because "our community wanted us to lead on [it] . . . that's kind of what sparked our interest to . . . get involved."[23] In contrast, the executive director of an economic justice organization told me that his organization has never done anything regarding public funding for abortion or reproductive health more generally because it is not an issue that they "particularly get a lot of pressure from our constituencies to work on and it's not high on our list."[24]

Pegging levels of activity to constituent concerns is understandable and congruent with traditional notions of representation and concerns about organizational maintenance. However, this practice has problematic implications for advocacy on disadvantaged-subgroup issues because concern about these issues is, on average, lower than it is for majority and advantaged-subgroup issues. For example, while 58 percent of respondents reported that "almost all" of their members are concerned about the majority issues about which they were asked, and 45 percent gave this answer regarding the advantaged-subgroup issues, only 30 percent believed that almost all of their members are concerned about their designated disadvantaged-subgroup issues. The effect of these uneven levels is further compounded by the fact that interest groups, like members of Congress, are more likely to address issues that are important to those "passionate minorities" of their constituencies who have the motivation and the resources to make themselves heard (Kollman 1998). Because advantaged subgroups are likely to have the resources necessary to make organizations aware of their concerns, organizations perceive more constituent interest in issues that are of concern to those subgroups (Verba, Schlozman, and Brady 1995). This perception, in turn, contributes to the disproportionately high levels of attention devoted to advantaged-subgroup issues.

## CONSTITUENT AGREEMENT

Both membership and nonmembership organizations respond to constituent concerns about policy issues, but the former also pay particular attention to whether their constituents *support* the organization's positions on these issues. The higher the proportion of constituents in agreement with a membership organization's position on an issue, the more active the organization is likely to be on that issue. Constituent agreement does not, however, have a significant effect on the activity levels of nonmembership organizations. This discrepancy between membership and nonmembership organizations makes sense: organizations that depend on member support fear alienating their constituents, a concern that does not have the same urgency for nonmembership organizations.

In the interviews, many respondents from membership-based organizations affirmed this relationship and explained that they are unlikely to take action on an issue unless their constituents agree with the organization's position on it. For example, a policy analyst at a labor organization told me, "Anything that is going to be internally divisive for us tends to be something that we're less likely to take a strong position on." For this organization, the aversion to divisive issues manifests itself as a focus on "issues affecting working people and their families" and an avoidance of what the respondent called "social and civil rights issues."[25] Likewise, the executive director of an Asian Pacific American organization commented, "We have to be very careful. We don't want to turn off or upset our community.... What's the point of having an advocacy organization if you're turning them off?" In particular, she said, violence against women is an issue "that we steer away from" because, in her opinion, it is "not a topic that is openly discussed ... in our community."[26]

It is part of an organization's mandate to reflect and respond to its constituents' attitudes and policy preferences, and, once again, such responsiveness is in keeping with traditional notions of representation and the exigencies of organizational maintenance. However, the foregoing examples suggest that constituents' dissent is more likely to prevent advocacy when it comes to issues affecting disadvantaged-subgroups—in the cases just mentioned, Asian Pacific American women within Asian Pacific American organizations and low-income women and people of color within labor organizations. Consequently, organizations' patterns of response and nonresponse to constituent preferences suggest that they pass up important opportunities to supplement their responsiveness with more active mediation on behalf of disadvantaged subgroups of their constituencies. Rather than nurturing the understanding among more-advantaged constituents that their fortunes and interests are linked to less-advantaged members of their communities, they reinforce the marginalization of intersectionally disadvantaged groups by validating the idea that these issues, and the people they affect, are not worthy of the organization's attention.

Although the foregoing statements reflect and reinforce the statistical finding that activity rises and falls with constituent support, these trends are by no means ubiquitous. Instead, the comments of several other officers remind us of the important findings that I discussed in chapter 3, regarding organization leaders' beliefs that their organizations should compensate for biases against marginalized groups by acting as mediators on their behalf. Many officers, for example, expressed a commitment to taking the lead on issues rather than following the leads of their constituents. For example, the executive director of an African American organization commented that in his view, leadership entails a responsibility "to promote [an] issue regardless of whether it's popular or not."[27] In a more specific example, the president of a large union explained that his organization decided to address affirmative action and gender discrimination in hiring, salaries, promotion, and job classification even though, at the time, "that

wasn't always a popular issue with some of the male members" who dominated the union's membership. "Ultimately," he continued, these resistant
members "came to understand that it was the right thing to do" because
his organization "told the truth" about the issue. Now, he said, "we get
participation and great acceptance from our members" about gender issues in the workplace. In his view, this kind of constituent education is an
important part of his role. "You can't run from issues," he said. "A good
union will never run from the issues."[28]

While the responses of many organizations to constituent opinion exacerbate biases against intersectionally disadvantaged subgroups, this example demonstrates that there are also important instances of leaders who
work instead to resist and even reverse these attitudes by framing issues and
educating advantaged constituents about the ways in which their interests
are tied to those of disadvantaged subgroups. In the case of the aforementioned union leader, for example, he refused to defer to the unsympathetic
attitudes of male members who were unreceptive to addressing gender-
related workplace issues. By insisting that the union work on these issues
and by educating his members about the issues in the process, this officer
demarginalized women and the workplace issues that affect them. Framing these issues as central to the concerns of the organization as he did, he
signaled to members that women are worthy of the organization's energy.

## THE POLITICAL ENVIRONMENT

Although constituents' opinions on an issue affect membership organizations' levels of policy advocacy, *public* opinion does not have a significant
effect on either membership or nonmembership organizations (though
the slope is positive in both cases). This finding suggests that low levels of
activity on disadvantaged-subgroup issues are not a function of the fact
that public support is, on average, lower when it comes to such issues than
it is for majority and advantaged-subgroup issues. By refusing to curtail
their activities in response to unsupportive public attitudes, organizations mediate on behalf of intersectionally disadvantaged groups within
the broader polity.

In line with not bending to public opinion, another result of this analysis
shows that heightened levels of controversy significantly augment levels
of activity, at least in the case of nonmembership organizations (the effect
is positive but insignificant for membership organizations). This unantic-
ipated effect is likely the result of the double-edged nature of controversy,

which can help create political opportunities that are simultaneously risky and potentially productive. On the one hand, advocacy on a controversial issue can risk arousing the public's ire about an issue to which it might otherwise pay little attention. On the other hand, the work of Mark Smith (2000) suggests that controversy can help increase the salience of an issue, opening up opportunities to address it by stimulating attention and debate.

The interviews echo these contrasting possibilities—disagreement and controversy seem to drive organizations to avoid some issues, while stimulating action on others. For example, asked whether concerns about controversy affect their organizations' involvement in public policy issues, many respondents made statements such as, "I would say that this is not an organization that shies away from controversy."[29] The executive director of an economic justice organization told me that his organization in fact is "looking for controversy, usually" so that the organization can arouse and harness public interest in an issue and "lead a debate on it."[30] While many respondents claimed that controversy was inevitable and often a boon, others expressed quite the opposite sentiment. "I doubt we'd ever take on something that controversial," the executive director of another economic justice organization confided.[31]

In general, however, the officers with whom I spoke seemed far less hesitant to take on controversial issues when such issues are understood to relate directly to their organizations' raisons d'être. For example, the chair of the board at an Asian Pacific American organization said that in a controversial case such as that of Wen Ho Lee (the Taiwanese-American Los Alamos physicist who was accused of espionage), it was "very controversial, [but] we felt like we had to be out in front [on it] . . . because . . . it's affecting an Asian American, has a disparate impact on Asian American scientists, and so it would be odd, almost, if we didn't have [a] voice in it." However, he said, other issues are "so controversial that we don't [even] take a position." "For example," he said, "we would never take a position on abortion. Two reasons—one is [that] it's politically very, very sensitive. Two, and more importantly, it doesn't have a special impact on the APA [Asian Pacific American] community."[32]

Although in general, respondents were not reluctant to take on controversial issues, as is the case with concerns about constituent agreement, the foregoing example demonstrates that controversy is more likely to depress activity on issues that affect an intersectionally disadvantaged subgroup— in this case, Asian Pacific American women. Moreover, as the foregoing statement from the chair of the board suggests, in order to justify a lack of involvement leaders often frame controversial issues affecting intersectionally disadvantaged subgroups as either having a very narrow impact or lacking a specific impact on the organization's primary constituency.

This particular case, however, underscores how subjective and malleable such criteria can be. The Wen Ho Lee racial-profiling case has a disparate impact on the Asian Pacific American population and is highly symbolic given the history of the ways in which allegations of disloyalty have been deployed to discriminate against Asian Pacific Americans. However, this particular form of racial profiling is primarily likely to affect relatively advantaged members of that community—defense industry employees, academics, and research scientists. In addition, this chair of the board's assertions notwithstanding, many Asian Pacific American feminists and women's health activists claim that the abortion issue *does* have a particular impact on women in the Asian Pacific American community because they face considerable constraints, structured by limited access and community norms against abortion (Nowrojee and Silliman 1997). Moreover, in spite of being framed as a special interest that affects fewer Asian Pacific Americans than the Wen Ho Lee case, reproductive rights arguably affect a *larger* portion of the community, as there are far more Asian Pacific American women than there are Asian Pacific American scientists and defense industry workers. Although the broader issue underlying the firing and investigation of Wen Ho Lee is racial discrimination in the workplace, the impact of this issue is universalized, while the impact of abortion is downplayed and particularized.

Once again, because the level of advocacy depends so heavily on the proportion of constituents perceived to be affected by a disadvantaged-subgroup issue, downplaying the effects of such issues further depresses levels of activity on such issues by exacerbating the biases against the affected subgroup that are already present in the broader political environment. Moreover, rather than taking the occasion to insist upon conveying an understanding that links the fate of Asian Pacific Americans women to the more general fate of the Asian American community, this officer passed up an opportunity to mediate on behalf of this intersectionally disadvantaged subgroup of his constituency.

In general, then, advocacy on behalf of disadvantaged subgroups is low, and strategic considerations such as attentiveness to constituent attitudes suppress it further. However, because membership and nonmembership organizations each respond to slightly different pressures, these biases offset each other and reduce, at least to some degree, the mobilization of bias among elites, among the mass public, and within the advocacy universe. Membership organizations are much more responsive to the attitudes of their constituents than are nonmembership organizations, while nonmembership organizations seem almost to thrive on controversy in ways that membership organizations do not. In addition, because levels of activity are not based on public agreement with their position on an issue, advocacy organizations mitigate the negative effects of public opinion on politically unpopular groups and issues. Together, these results illustrate some of the ways in which the practices of advocacy organizations defy majoritarian and rationalist incentives, providing a window into innovative conceptions of representation on behalf of marginalized groups.

## POLITICAL THREATS, POLITICAL OPPORTUNITIES, AND THE IMPORTANCE OF TAKING A STAND

The foregoing findings suggest that levels of activity are not a function of officers' perceptions that issues are popular among members of the mass public. In the case of membership organizations, however, the salience of an issue on the political agenda has a slightly but significantly positive effect, suggesting that the popularity of an issue among policy makers can be an important determinant of activity (the effect is positive but not significant for nonmembership organizations). This result indicates that membership organizations respond strategically to political threats and try to exploit political opportunities that open "policy windows" for their goals (Kingdon 1995; McAdam 1982; Meyer 1990, 1993; Tarrow 1996; C. Tilly 1978).

In fact, many interview respondents told me that they were more likely to pursue issues that were politically salient, particularly if their involvement in these issues was likely to have an impact and lead to success. Answering questions about why they addressed particular policy issues, respondents repeatedly made statements such as, "We don't generally take on things that we think there's no hope of accomplishing anything on;" "You always have to think about whether you'll be successful . . . Can we win this one? . . . Is it worth it?" and "Where we think we can make a real difference . . . there is a greater likelihood that we'll get in there and that we'll devote more resources to it."

While most respondents said that they responded to threats and opportunities in the hope of achieving successes, many also made it clear that short-term success was not their only goal. The field organizer at a women's organization, for example, laughed as she said, "We really don't have a good track record for picking things based on" whether they will be "easily attained."[33] In fact, many respondents made comments suggesting that they were very likely to "lead with [the] heart more than with [the] head," taking action on issues that one respondent characterized as "nonstarters" out of a desire to take a stand or with an eye toward pushing for changes over the longer term. The executive director of a Latino organization said, for example, that his organization often gets involved in issues "just for symbolic purposes, because . . . it's important to lay a marker and say this is where we stand even though we may lose."[34] An economist in the public policy department at an economic justice group told me that in his experience, organizations very often take action on issues "for long-term and educational purposes" even in cases in which "the immediate likelihood of prevailing isn't great."[35] The legislative director of a reproductive rights organization explained that her organization will sometimes go as far as to file a motion on an issue "knowing full well we might not win" but on which the organization feels strongly that it has "to make the political point, that this is something that's unconstitutional or illegal."[36]

Issues affecting intersectionally disadvantaged groups are often ones that might be labeled, in the terminology of one of the respondents quoted previously, "nonstarters." Failing to devote attention to these hard issues, however, relegates them to this status ad infinitum. As such, the commitments to pursuing difficult issues that are articulated by the aforementioned organization officers are evidence of their dedication to working for and representing disadvantaged subgroups of their constituents over the long term and demonstrate their dedication to these subgroups in hard times. In this light, these efforts are qualitatively different from the symbolic and low-level efforts that organizations often devote to disadvantaged-subgroup issues. Rather than engaging in symbolic gestures such as position taking or petition signing in lieu of real commitment, the engagement described here prioritizes advocacy for the least well-off. While this advocacy might yield few policy victories in the short term, it serves to redistribute representational resources to the most difficult issues and least advantaged constituents, which is necessary for progress on these issues in the longer term. Organizations must respond to their political environments, and therefore they focus a great deal of energy on pursuing winnable issues and fending off impending threats. Nonetheless, many organizations supplement these strategic aims with the goal of using representation as a means to social justice, thereby increasing the attention they devote to disadvantaged-subgroup issues.

It is important to note as well that organizations do not always react to political opportunities or threats to existing programs when their constituents are affected. Moreover, the chances that organizations will react vigorously to threats and opportunities are often lower when it comes to issues affecting intersectionally disadvantaged subgroups. In the case of the 1996 welfare reform legislation discussed earlier, for example, many women's and civil rights organizations claimed to have been caught off guard by President Clinton's efforts to dismantle this entitlement, and they did not jump into the fray until after the law had passed and the program had devolved to the states. Some analysts claim that feminist organizations soft-pedaled their opposition to the PRWORA out of gratitude to President Clinton for having signed the Family and Medical Leave Act (FMLA) of 1993, which provides employees with twelve weeks of unpaid leave following a birth or adoption or to care for a spouse, child, or parent who is ill. The implications of their silence on welfare reform are compounded by the fact that while the FMLA is a crucial piece of feminist legislation, it provides only for unpaid leave. Consequently, it is unlikely that the low-income women most likely to be affected by welfare reform would be in a position to take advantage of the benefits provided by the FMLA.

## POLICY NICHES

Threats and opportunities within political institutions can increase the attention paid by organizations to particular policy issues. In addition to these conditions in the macro-level political environment, conditions *within* advocacy communities are related to levels of advocacy as well. Niche theories suggest that organizations might abstain from high levels of activity on an issue if they believe that many others within their interest community are attending to it. Such an aversion to replicating the efforts of other groups might lead organizations to choose to allocate their advocacy activities and resources in ways that do not replicate the issue coverage of other organizations.

Niche-related decision making could have particularly important implications when it comes to issues affecting intersectionally disadvantaged subgroups of an organization's constituency because the "ownership" of such issues is often ambiguous (C. Cohen 1999). Consequently, officers often believe that that these issues fall within the jurisdiction and niches of organizations other than their own. For example, the officers at the women's organizations who were questioned about their advocacy regarding welfare reform policy seemed to think that this issue "belongs" to economic justice organizations, reducing the chances that they will address this issue.

Many of the officers I spoke to were indeed concerned not to squander scarce resources by replicating the work being done by other organizations. The vice president at a women's organization said quite bluntly, "If there is an issue that some other women's group is front and center on and very expert in and has it covered, it doesn't make sense for another women's legal group to do that."[37] Similarly, the field organizer at another women's organization explained that in order for her group to get involved in an issue, "there has to be a demonstrated need. If we know of other organizations that are taking on the issue, we try to do it from a totally different angle."[38] The vice president of a women's legal organization expressed much the same sentiment, explaining, "There are a lot of factors that go into deciding what we focus our resources on at any given moment. But one where we've developed expertise and where outsiders look to us for that expertise is not something that we're usually going to diminish our focus on."[39] Asked whether her organization is involved in efforts to restore public funding for reproductive health services (a disadvantaged-subgroup issue for this organization), the senior program adviser of an economic justice group explained that her organization did nothing on the issue. "It isn't like there aren't a lot of organizations who are very capable of doing this," she noted. "You make your choices. . . . It's not an issue of controversy. It's just [that] it's not clear what the value added would be."[40]

Several respondents explained that this desire to maintain or create a niche often drives decisions about which issues they will avoid or devote little time to. The executive director of a civil rights coalition explained, for example, that on the day that I interviewed him, he had had to decide which of two possible meetings he would attend a few hours earlier. The first, he said, was a meeting with Senate staffers about racial profiling. The other meeting that he was scheduled to attend was at the White House, to talk about the Bush administration's lack of support for American participation in the United Nations Conference against Racism that was to be held in Durban, South Africa, that summer. "I chose to do the latter," he explained, "not because I don't think that profiling is important, but . . . [because] I recognized that racial profiling has many good strong staffers who are working on this." The United Nations conference, however, "had a very limited number of people who were available. So it became important for me to contribute my voice there."[41]

The results of the analysis of the survey data corroborate these interview statements about the importance of policy niches—but with some illuminating wrinkles that vary by issue type and by whether the organizations in question are membership or nonmembership organizations. In the case of membership organizations, the coefficient associated with the primary policy niche (the number of organizations in the advocacy sector with which the group is most centrally associated) is positive but not significant, while the coefficient associated with the secondary policy niche (the number of organizations in the advocacy sector that intersects with that of the organization in question regarding its designated disadvantaged-subgroup issue) is negative and significant. These results suggest that it is sometimes the case that membership organizations refrain from activity on an issue based on the perception that other organizations are likely to take it on, but that this is true mainly in the case of disadvantaged-subgroup issues.

The pattern is somewhat different in the case of *nonmembership* organizations. Among these groups, the effect of the primary niche is positive and significant, suggesting that these organizations might be prone to "bandwagon effects" that lead them to increase their activity on some issues if there are many other potential advocates for it in their primary policy sector. This finding echoes John Kingdon's assertion that political actors look to one another for signs about what is important (Kingdon 1995, 150).[42] Although this effect might augment activity on majority issues, the lack of a significant effect for *Secondary niche* in this analysis suggests that niche considerations do not depress nonmembership organizations' activity on disadvantaged subgroup issues in the way that they do for membership organizations. Among these latter groups, the role of niches provides further evidence of a double standard in the way that some organizations employ otherwise understandable strategies in response to their political environments. It is undoubtedly inefficient for every group in the community of social and economic justice organizations to devote their resources to the same set of policy issues. However, for membership organizations, such concerns about issue coverage by others in a policy sector seem to apply only to issues affecting disadvantaged subgroups. When it comes to taking into account the possibility that other groups will be active on issues in their primary sector, membership organizations seem to abide instead by the adage "the more, the merrier."

The survey measures of policy niches are rather blunt instruments, but evidence of the double standard that they suggest is apparent in the interviews as well. In a particularly illustrative case, the political director of a large membership organization advocating for lesbian, gay, bisexual, and transgender (LGBT) people explained that some issues are so central to the mission and identity of her organization that there is no question about whether they will become involved with them. "No one had to take a vote," she said, "to say we ought to work on employment discrimination issues. Right now, it's perfectly legal in 39 states in this country to fire someone for being gay or lesbian. It's a matter of putting food on your table." Similarly, she continued, no one "took a vote" to decide that her organization "should be a leader on HIV/AIDS issues. It just happened."

Since HIV/AIDS is a central concern for her constituents, I asked her whether her organization had been involved in efforts to make free or low-cost AIDS medications available to low-income people who are HIV-positive (an intersectionally disadvantaged subgroup of this constituency). She replied that her organization is involved in this issue "tangentially" but that it is "certainly not a leader on those issues." "There are other organizations out there who are far . . . better suited to get involved in the patent issue than we are," she explained, "organizations . . . that have a deeper understanding of the federal relationship with pharmaceutical companies and others to help make the case."[43]

It is undoubtedly true that there are other groups that have more expertise when it comes to pharmaceutical issues, but it is equally true that there were other organizations that might have been better suited to take on a medical issue such as HIV/AIDS (although as we now know, few did [C. Cohen 1999; Shilts 1987]). The contrast between this respondent's invocation of niches and techincal expertise as justifications in the case of the disadvantaged-subgroup issue reminds us that there is no objectively determined set of issues that are central to a group's mission or niche. Rather, it is respondents' *perceptions* about and *constructions* of their missions and niches that are key, perceptions and constructions that are influenced a great deal by the same factors that suppress levels of activity on some issues while boosting activity on other issues.

Creating niches and taking on issues that do not replicate the efforts of other organizations in the interest community are reasonable decision rules under some circumstances. The criteria that inform these standards, however, often are based upon subjective assessments that are themselves connected to the same biases that suppress levels of advocacy on issues affecting disadvantaged subgroups. In this case, HIV/AIDS is a central issue for the organization because of its effect on gay men. However, the organization is not active on the issue of low-cost HIV/AIDS drugs—an issue that is most likely to affect low-income HIV-positive people—because it is not similarly framed as being central to its mission. Instead, it is framed as being a techical pharmaceutical issue rather than a social justice issue, and hence outside of the organization's niche, and organization leaders assume that other organizations can and will address this issue. They therefore feel justified in being only tangentially involved in efforts to make HIV and AIDS medications accessible to low-income people, a category that includes many of the gay men who are ostensibly constituents of this organization.

*Niches as Opportunities for Disadvantaged-Subgroup Issues* | Although the survey data suggest that the aggregate effect of niche behavior in the case of membership organizations is to suppress advocacy on disadvantaged-subgroup issues, under some circumstances the desire to find a policy niche can have the opposite effect on policy activity. Because intersectional issues are less likely than other types of issues to be addressed by advocacy groups, they are often "wide open" and available as niches for organizations in search of one (Heaney 2004). This finding presents particularly ripe opportunities for organizations that are dedicated to filling in the gaps in representation for disadvantaged groups.

Examples of such a strategy are evident among several of the organizations whose officers I interviewed. For instance, the director of public policy at a women's organization explained that, in deciding how to focus its efforts, her organization asks, "What are the niches . . . where no one is doing any work and where we may bring something unique?"[44] It was this line of reasoning that led them to focus on addressing the particular effects of violence against women on women with disabilities and on women who are HIV-positive, two intersectionally disadvantaged subgroups of women. Similarly, the chair of the board of a civil rights organization explained that he "jumped" at the opportunity to get involved in efforts to address the implications of privatizing Social Security for African Americans "because that was the first time . . . I'd seen this put in a racial way." Though Social Security is an inherently important issue, he explained that this niche allowed him to throw his and his organization's "weight behind it," and provided him with an opportunity to fill what he saw as an important gap in the discussion about this issue. Had it been framed "entirely race neutral," he made clear, it would have been difficult to justify "a position for or against" privatization.[45]

In a related vein, the executive director of one of the few women's health organizations in the sample that had been very vigorously working to

restore public funding for reproductive rights said that her group prioritizes work on this issue because "when you look within the reproductive
health community . . . that [issue] tends to be lower down on the list of
what people are asking for." Because most "pro-choice advocates tend not
to make funding as high a priority as some other issues," she explained,
this gives her organization "an added reason for us to be advocates" on
this issue.[46] The legislative director at another reproductive rights organization also referenced the importance for her organization of carving
out a specialty in addressing issues of reproductive rights as they affect
low-income women and women of color. This focus, she argued, frames
the issue of abortion differently than it is framed by the other reproductive
rights groups with which her organization sometimes works.

Low-income women and women of color have been active in reproductive rights movements and share many of the same concerns as middle-class
and white women in majority issues such as maintaining access to legal
and late-term abortions. Indeed, in light of data that show that abortion
rates are higher among black women and Latinas, it might even be argued that low-income women and women of color have a *greater* interest
than middle-class and white women in these issues.[47] Having also been
subject to sterilization abuse and other efforts to curtail their reproductive choices, however, low-income women and women of color also face
reproductive-related concerns that have been less fully addressed by the
mainstream reproductive rights movement (Bass 1998; J. Nelson 2003). "In
the mainstream cultural frame," the previously quoted legislative director
explained, abortion is presented as "a white woman's issue" that is prin-
cipally understood as "the right to not have children." This emphasis, she
said, ignores "the minority implications of" reproductive rights, including
issues such as sterilization and, as she put it, "the right *to have* children,"
which has often been denied to low-income women and women of color.

Based on this focus, this organization concentrates its advocacy efforts
on "reproductive equity projects" that address issues such as the disproportionate impact on low-income women and women of color of policies
that block public funding for abortion. They also work with welfare rights
groups on issues such as the family cap provisions that deny or reduce
cash assistance to recipients of public assistance who have additional children while they are receiving benefits. "We're one of the few [reproductive
rights] groups that do look at that," she said.[48] While niches lead some
organizations away from activity on issues affecting intersectionally disadvantaged subgroups of their constituencies, then, some organizations

instead exploit the overall lack of attention to issues affecting these sub-groups, fostering activity in these areas as a way to develop a unique identity and a policy niche.[49]

*Niches and Universal Issues: The Paradox of Social Security* | Although an intersectional approach to understanding power and marginalization is extremely helpful in understanding patterns in levels of advocacy when it comes to majority, advantaged-subgroup and disadvantaged-subgroup issues, levels of activity for the universal issue—Social Security—are some-what paradoxical. As a universal issue that respondents said benefits more of their constituents than any of the others, both Downsian and inter-sectional approaches predict high levels of advocacy and attention to it. However, a smaller proportion of organizations are active and levels of activity are lower on this issue than is the case for any other issue type. While we might explain these low levels of involvement as the result of inattention to economic justice policy on the part of organizations con-cerned with issues such as race and gender, activity on Social Security is relatively low even among organizations for which it has traditionally been a core issue, such as economic justice organizations (just over 30 percent are active; see tables 4.2 and 4.3). Labor organizations are more active on Social Security than any other type of organization (55 percent are active), but they are less active on this issue than on the others about which they were asked. Activity is also low among organizations that regard Social Se-curity as particularly important for their constituents, as is the case with women and racial minorities. Women of all races and men of color rely more heavily on Social Security than white men do, in large part because they are far less likely than white men to have private pension accounts.[50] The executive director of a large Latino organization told me, for example, that "Social Security represents a much larger percentage of retirement income for Hispanics than it does for other groups in the population" but that his organization is nonetheless not active on this policy issue.[51] Re-spondents from many women's and African American organizations made similar comments about the disproportionate reliance on Social Security among their constituents, but few of them address this policy either.

Statements from the face-to-face interviews help illuminate the dy-namics that work to generate such unexpectedly low levels of activity on a universal issue such as this. The interviews suggest that this inattention is the result of a niche-related free rider problem that has particular implica-tions for intersectionally disadvantaged groups. In a typical manifestation of free riding, an actor tries to avail himself or herself of a public good while trying to avoid contributing to the collective action necessary to obtain or maintain that good. In this case, however, officers concerned about organizational maintenance believe that it would be wasteful to expend scarce resources on this issue because they believe that others in their interest community have it "covered." Although these leaders believe that Social Security is an important issue that affects "everyone," they assume (wrongly, it turns out) that they ought not to expend scarce resources on it because "someone else" will work to resolve the issue.

For example, asked why her group was not active on Social Security, the executive director of a women's health organization said, "It's a combination of feeling like it was just a little too far afield from our health agenda and hoping the other groups would be taking care of it."[52] Similarly, the executive director of an economic justice organization said that Social Security was simply not on his radar screen because "it's an issue that I wouldn't have any expertise [about]. There are a lot more powerful players in town than [us] involved with it."[53] The executive director of an economic justice organization acknowledged, "It affects [our constituents]. A lot of them only have Social Security to look forward to." In spite of what he acknowledged was the disproportionate importance of Social Security for his constituents' retirement, his organization is not active on the issue because, as he put it, "there are issues that you've got to let pass you by."[54]

We should not construe the low levels of Social Security–related advocacy on the part of the organizations in this survey as evidence that this issue is not being addressed by other organizations. Indeed, organizations that advocate on behalf of elderly and retired people such as the large, prominent, and powerful American Association for Retired People (AARP) have advocated vociferously and successfully to protect and enhance Social Security (Campbell 2003). However, as some of the interviewed officers explained earlier, issues exist within the broader question of Social Security reform that have particular and disproportionate effects on disadvantaged subgroups of retired people, such as women and racial minorities. Organizations such as AARP, however, have tended not to prioritize advocacy on policies that address the particular ways in which the timing and quality of retirement are structured by issues such as race, gender, and sexuality. Although these organizations have increased their efforts to address such issues, they have tended to focus more on public education and outreach than on lobbying and policy advocacy. And to the extent that such efforts exist, they seem to be fairly recent, evidenced by the chair of the board quoted earlier who suggested that he was excited about becoming involved in a campaign to oppose privatization of Social Security but that this was the first time he had seen efforts to address the racial implications of this issue. Indeed, advocacy on the universal issue of Social Security seems to manifest many of the same biases observed when it comes to the other issue types.

## ECONOMIC VERSUS SOCIAL ISSUES

Differentiating among universal, majority, advantaged-subgroup, and disadvantaged-subgroup issues helps a great deal in understanding the varying levels of attention that advocacy groups devote to certain policy issues. As I suggested in chapter 2, however, other scholars suggest that a somewhat different policy typology explains low levels of advocacy activity on some policy issues. In their view, the ascent of the identity-based and quality-of-life-oriented movements of the 1960s has shifted the focus of progressive organizations away from economic issues (Aronowitz 1992; Berry 1999; Edsall 1991; Fraser 1997; Gitlin 1995; Reed 2000; Skocpol 2003). Instead of focusing on traditional liberal issues such as wages, benefits, pensions, job training, improved working conditions, income maintenance, and basic health coverage, these organizations have, in Jeffrey Berry's words, created a "new liberalism," one that is focused on postmaterialist issues having to do with race, gender, sexuality, and the environment (Berry 1999, 55).

To examine directly whether levels of activity vary depending on whether issues are economic or social in nature, I coded the policy issues in the SNESJO to indicate whether each one is primarily economic or primarily social (*Economic issue* and *Social issue*, with social issues coded "0" and economic issues coded "1").[55] I then reran the ordered logit regression model (for membership organizations only) with this additional measure (see model 3 in table 4.1).

The results of this analysis provide evidence that the variation in levels of activity is indeed a product of intersecting forms of marginalization rather than the consequence of a shift in attention from economic issues to social issues. Adding the new variable has almost no effect on the direction, magnitude, or significance of any of the other measures, including the measures of the categories in my policy typology (the only real difference is a loss of significance for the measure of constituent agreement). The coefficient for the new measure is negative, indicating that economic issues might receive slightly less attention than social issues. However, this coefficient does not reach a conventional level of statistical significance, showing that the variation in organizations' level of policy advocacy cannot be attributed entirely to a surfeit of attention to social issues.

These results are in no way at odds with the argument that identity-based and quality-of-life-oriented organizations pay insufficient attention to issues of economic justice for low-income people. Indeed, the relatively low levels of activity on welfare reform on the part of organizations representing women that I discussed earlier can be seen as an example of that very phenomenon. However, the intersectional framework operationalized by the four-part policy typology suggests that the trends identified by scholars who are concerned about low levels of attention to economic issues are capturing one side of a multifaceted problem that goes beyond a lack of attention to economic issues by organizations that are concerned about race, gender, sexuality, or the environment.

From an intersectional perspective, the lack of attention to economic issues is due to the fact that economic disadvantage is one of many possible manifestations of intersectional marginalization. As Sharon Kurtz writes, "critics who take issue with identity politics would more accurately be described as contesting *single*-identity politics: fragmented politics that don't capture complicated, overlapping, fluid identities" (emphasis in original; Kurtz 2002, xxix). As such, an intersectional approach suggests that we will see the analogous problem among economic justice organizations as well and that these groups will sideline issues that affect subgroups of their economically disadvantaged constituencies who are intersectionally marginalized based on other axes such as race, gender, or sexuality. Moreover, intersectionality also suggests not only that the problems will manifest along economic and social lines but also that economic justice organizations give short shrift to economic issues that affect intersectionally disadvantaged subgroups and that identity-based groups will do the same when it comes to disadvantaged-subgroup issues that are more social in nature.

Each of these hypothetical scenarios is borne out by the data (see tables 4.2 and 4.3). In addition to the low levels of activity on welfare reform on the part of women's and African American organizations discussed previously, we also see low average levels of activity on identity-based issues on the part of economically oriented organizations. Labor organizations, for example, are less active when it comes to job discrimination against

TABLE 4.2 Mean level of activity on each issue type, by type of organization

| | MEAN LEVEL OF ACTIVITY, 1–5 SCALE | | | |
| ORGANIZATION TYPE | MAJORITY ISSUE | ADVANTAGED SUBGROUP ISSUE | DISADVANTAGED SUBGROUP ISSUE | UNIVERSAL ISSUE |
| --- | --- | --- | --- | --- |
| Asian Pacific American | 3.71 | 3.00 | 2.43 | 1.57 |
| Black/African American | 4.13 | 4.53 | 3.71 | 2.07 |
| Latino/Hispanic | 4.58 | 4.25 | 2.92 | 2.08 |
| Native American/American Indian | 4.00 | 3.76 | 2.92 | 1.67 |
| Civil Rights—Other[a] | 3.32 | 2.86 | 2.68 | 1.64 |
| Labor[b] | 3.84 | 4.00 | 3.48 | 2.91 |
| Economic Justice[c] | 3.37 | 3.39 | 1.16 | 1.90 |
| Public Interest[d] | 2.25 | 2.38 | 2.13 | 1.75 |
| Women's Rights/Feminist[e] | 3.61 | 3.39 | 2.88 | 2.09 |

*Source:* SNESJO. Organization officers were asked, "Please tell me, on a scale of 1 to 5, where 1 is not active, and 5 is very active, how active has your organization been on each of the following policy issues in the past ten years?"

*Note:* Data reflect the mean response on the 1–5 scale.

[a] Includes broadly based civil rights and civil liberties organizations; lesbian, gay, bisexual, and transgender (LGBT) rights organizations; criminal justice organizations; Arab/Muslim organizations; antiracist organizations; some religious minority groups; and multiculturalism organizations. Also includes immigrants' rights organizations.

[b] Includes unions.

[c] Includes antipoverty, welfare rights, anti-homeless, and anti-hunger organizations.

[d] Includes consumer, environmental, and "good government" organizations that advocate in the areas of racial, gender, or economic justice.

[e] Includes women of color, reproductive rights, and women's health organizations.

TABLE 4.3  Percentage of organizations active on each issue type, by type of organization

| | PERCENT ACTIVE | | | |
| ORGANIZATION TYPE | MAJORITY ISSUE | ADVANTAGED SUBGROUP ISSUE | DISADVANTAGED SUBGROUP ISSUE | UNIVERSAL ISSUE |
| --- | --- | --- | --- | --- |
| Asian Pacific American | 76.9 | 84.6 | 69.2 | 30.8 |
| Black/African American | 85.0 | 90.0 | 90.0 | 45.0 |
| Latino/Hispanic | 100.0 | 100.0 | 62.5 | 50.0 |
| Native American/American Indian | 100.0 | 69.2 | 69.2 | 15.4 |
| Civil Rights—Other[a] | 74.4 | 64.1 | 64.1 | 23.1 |
| Labor[b] | 78.6 | 78.6 | 71.4 | 54.8 |
| Economic Justice[c] | 69.7 | 71.2 | 12.1 | 30.3 |
| Public Interest[d] | 72.7 | 45.5 | 63.6 | 27.4 |
| Women's Rights/Feminist[e] | 84.8 | 77.3 | 65.2 | 39.4 |

*Source:* SNESJO. Organization officers were asked, "Please tell me, on a scale of 1 to 5, where 1 is not active, and 5 is very active, how active has your organization been on each of the following policy issues in the past ten years?"

*Note:* Data reflect the percentage of respondents giving answers between 2–5.

[a]Includes broadly based civil rights and civil liberties organizations; lesbian, gay, bisexual, and transgender (LGBT) rights organizations; criminal justice organizations; Arab/Muslim organizations; antiracist organizations; some religious minority groups; and multiculturalism organizations. Also includes immigrants' rights organizations.

[b]Includes unions.

[c]Includes antipoverty, welfare rights, anti-homeless, and anti-hunger organizations.

[d]Includes consumer, environmental, and "good government" organizations that advocate in the areas of racial, gender, or economic justice.

[e]Includes women of color, reproductive rights, and women's health organizations.

women and racial minorities, an issue affecting intersectionally disadvantaged workers, and economic justice organizations show extremely low levels of activism when it comes to public funding for abortion—an issue that affects mainly intersectionally disadvantaged low-income women. However, the problem is not merely one of a trade-off between social and economic issues but rather one that concerns intersectional disadvantage more generally. For example, Asian Pacific American and Native American organizations are both much less active when it comes to violence against women, and civil rights organizations are much less active when it comes to discrimination against LGBT people than they are on their designated majority and advantaged minority issues. In each of these cases, both axes of the intersecting inequalities are identity-based, and the result is low levels of policy advocacy on issues affecting intersectionally disadvantaged subgroups of their constituencies.

It is important not to overstate the meaning of these findings, given the bluntness of the measure I use to distinguish between social and economic issues, as well as in light of the differences between this study and related studies by scholars such as Berry and Skocpol. Berry's study, for example, which finds that policy making is increasingly focused on quality-of-life issues such as the environment, approaches this question from the "supply side," focusing on congressional priorities rather than on the agendas of interest groups themselves. In addition, each of our studies examines somewhat different pools of organizations. Most relevant is that the sample of organizations that I examine here includes many groups that are interested in economic policy, such as labor unions, while it excludes many organizations, such as those environmental, animal rights, and consumer groups, that are *not* terribly likely to be interested in economic issues that affect low-income people. The differences between our studies make the implications of our combined results all the more striking, however. That is, while my data show that many groups are active on economic issues, *in spite* of all this activity, Berry finds that congressional policy making is increasingly focused on quality-of-life issues.

Moreover, the point here is not that economic issues affecting low-income people are adequately covered by advocacy groups. Indeed, the results show quite clearly that they are not. However, the evidence presented here suggests rather strongly that the issue is a more general problem having to do with the ways in which power and advantage shape the agendas and activities of advocacy groups. Because low-income people are, by definition, less advantaged than middle-class people (along the specific axis of class), one major manifestation of intersectional disadvantage is a lack of attention to policy issues that affect low-income people in favor of ones that are of interest to middle-class constituents. However, the data also show that this is not the only manifestation of the problem. Instead, it is all issues affecting intersectionally disadvantaged subgroups of all kinds that are given short shrift.

Once again, the interviews help reveal the ways in which intersectional marginalization is manifested in the differences between the issues addressed by organizations that are primarily economically oriented and those addressed by organizations focused on civil rights. In particular, my conversations with organization officers provide evidence that, indeed, the underlying problem does not stem from the mutually exclusive nature of economic and social issues. Instead, the interviews make clear that each of these issue types represents an axis of disadvantage for organizations that focus on either economic or social issues. Officers at these organizations rarely draw connections between the economic and social issues that affect their constituents, and in some cases, they actively *avoid* drawing such connections. As a consequence, they do not appreciate that many of the issues that intersect social and economic policies and disadvantages are ones that affect disadvantaged subgroups of their constituencies. This, in turn, suppresses their organizations' levels of attention to such issues.

An interview that I conducted with the executive director of an economic justice organization was particularly revealing on this point. Asked about his organization's activities addressing the issue of public funding for abortion and other reproductive health services (an issue that intersects social and economic concerns and affects mainly women, an intersectionally disadvantaged subgroup of all low-income people), this respondent answered that there had actually been "none." "Our focus," he explained, "has been on economic questions." Contextualizing this within increasingly common arguments about strategies to build a "Democratic majority" by shifting the focus of the party away from issues such as abortion, affirmative action, and LGBT rights, he explained that "the only way to defend cultural liberalism is with a strong populist economics" that persuades white men to "vote their pocketbook."[56] His response makes clear that because of the gendered connotations of the issue, he does not think of public funding for abortion as an economic issue. The problem is not that this organization fails to address social issues, however, but rather that it fails to recognize the ways in which the issue of reproductive rights *is* in fact an economic issue for the low-income women this group purports to represent. In addition, the organization's broader strategy of staying away from what this respondent characterizes as social issues explicitly rejects the idea that advocacy group officers should cultivate feelings of inter-sectionally linked fate among differently situated constituencies. Rather than approaching an issue such as public funding for abortion in a manner that draws *connections* between what are commonly thought of as separate realms of economic and social policy, the logic embodied in this strategy and in this officer's statements instead buttresses the boundaries *between* issues and groups.

The interviews are also suggestive regarding the potential trade-offs for intersectionally disadvantaged groups when organizations do draw connections between social and economic issues. For example, the executive director of a large civil rights organization told me that while his organization does not "go out of [its] way to hunt down economic justice issues," neither does it actively avoid them. Rather, he explained, the organization's work on such issues is more often "a consequence of the work that we're pursuing in other areas." As an example, he referenced his organization's work on legislation that makes it more difficult to declare personal bankruptcy. He said that while this issue might seem like a purely economic one, his organization considers it a "civil rights issue" as well. The organization approaches it this way because, he explained, many credit card companies "prey on . . . the poorest elements of the communities that we represent . . . poor people, women, people of color." He added, "economic rights issues are coming to the fore . . . as a substitute for some of the race-based activity that continues to be needed but that you have to handle in a different way than we did a few years ago."[57]

In light of political shifts in which efforts to address many issues of race, gender, and sexuality have become increasingly difficult, this "substitu-tion" of class-based issues for racial ones represents an important route—in some cases the *only* route—through which issues affecting disadvantaged subgroups are addressed in national politics. However, it is important to reflect upon what is lost and gained for intersectionally disadvantaged sub-groups when organizations elect to take this course (L. Williams 1998). The findings that I have presented suggest that the risk of this approach is that it might fail to address those elements of economic issues that are related to racial and other forms of inequality and that issues affecting disadvantaged subgroups of the low-income population will be given short shrift. On the other hand, the foregoing examples also demonstrate that organizations that try to address issues that have economic and social implications recognize that in order to represent all of their constituents, they must attend to issues at the intersection of several axes of marginalization—issues affecting disadvantaged subgroups of their broader constituency. Organizations that do not unite issues in this way are far less likely to address issues that affect disadvantaged subgroups of their constituencies because they are less likely to address these intersections.

## BREAKDOWN BY ORGANIZATION TYPES

The multivariate analysis and the information from the interviews provide very strong evidence that issues affecting intersectionally disadvantaged groups receive disproportionately low levels of attention from advocacy organizations when compared with their attention to majority and advantaged-subgroup issues. Nonetheless, there are possible concerns about the selectivity of the policy issues in the survey and about whether the results of this analysis are robust depending on how many items or which combination of them are used or whether they might change if we substituted different policy issues for ones that were selected. Although there is no definitive way to test this possibility without replicating the survey using different policy issues, the comparisons across many different types of organizations and policy issues provide an implicit test of this possibility that is built into the study design.

Tables 4.2 and 4.3 present the levels of activity on each issue type by each type of organization in the study. Table 4.2 shows the mean levels of activity for each issue type, and table 4.3 shows the percentage of organizations that are active on each one. In general, the patterns in levels of activity for the aggregate of organizations hold when we disaggregate the various types of organizations. Across organization types, disadvantaged-subgroup issues receive consistently less attention than majority and advantaged-subgroup issues. The few exceptions to the general trends disappear when we distinguish between the *percentage* of organizations that are active on each issue type (table 4.3) and the *mean levels* of activity by issue type (table 4.2). For example, whereas a greater *proportion* of public interest groups organizations are active on environmental racism (an issue that affects a disadvantaged subgroup of their broader constituency) than they are on Internet privacy (an issue that affects an advantaged subgroup of their constituency), *mean* levels of activity are in line with the findings for the whole sample. That is, the level of advocacy activity on the advantaged-subgroup issue is significantly higher than the level of such activity when it comes to the disadvantaged-subgroup issue.

Similarly, almost as many civil rights organizations are active on affirmative action in higher education (an issue that affects an advantaged subgroup) as are active on workplace discrimination against LGBT people (an issue that affects a disadvantaged subgroup). However, in this case as well, the mean levels of activity are more in keeping with the findings for the whole sample, reinforcing the idea that even when there is broad involvement by many organizations on disadvantaged-subgroup issues, this involvement is relatively superficial compared with activity on majority and advantaged-subgroup issues. Finally, although a slightly greater *proportion* of African American organizations are active on the two types of subgroup issues (affirmative action in higher education and welfare reform) than on the majority issue (racial profiling), the *mean* levels of activity are in line with the findings for the whole sample. By this measure, the disadvantaged-subgroup issue receives slightly less attention than the majority issue and far less attention than the advantaged-subgroup issue.

It is worth noting that the organizations representing women of color in the study also devote their highest levels of attention to advantaged-subgroup issues. With only eight such groups in the sample, it is clearly not possible to generalize from these results. However, this finding does suggest that even organizations that are dedicated to representing intersectionally marginalized groups tend to underrepresent disadvantaged constituents (in this case, low-income women of color).[58]

The fact that the patterns of policy activity are similar across organization types shows that selecting different issues is unlikely to significantly alter the results.[59] However, although each type of organization focuses more attention on majority and advantaged-subgroup issues than on disadvantaged-subgroup issues, it is notable that African American organizations are still an outlier in this regard. Although their mean level of activity on the disadvantaged-subgroup issue (welfare reform) is still quite a bit lower than it is for their activity on the other issue types, African American organizations exhibit the highest mean level of activity on the designated disadvantaged-subgroup issue of all organization types. African American organizations are also the only type of organization for which a greater proportion is active on both the advantaged-subgroup and disadvantaged-subgroup issues than they are when it comes to the majority issue. The large number of African American organizations active on welfare reform underscores the findings of previous research that these organizations traditionally have pursued economic justice issues as a part of their civil rights agenda (Hamilton and Hamilton 1992).

The high levels of engagement of these organizations on a disadvantaged-subgroup issue are a noteworthy departure from more general trends. The disproportionately large percentage of low-income and poor members of African American communities, however, also suggests that this finding about welfare-reform-related activity is not quite as much at odds with the more general results as it might first appear. Recall that the results show that organizations increase their levels of activity on disadvantaged-subgroup issues as the number of constituents affected by these issues increases; with a higher proportion of disadvantaged constituents who are likely to be affected, we would expect higher-than-average levels of attention to this issue. In addition, the *mean* level of African American organizations' activity on welfare reform remains lower than it is for the issues of affirmative action and racial profiling. This discrepancy suggests that much of their activism on welfare reform is more symbolic or superficial than their activism on other types of issues. So, while African American organizations seem more compelled than other organizations to pay at least some attention to welfare reform, they still, in the main, do not make it their priority (L. Williams 1998).

Indeed, as I began to explain earlier, in each case in which a larger-than-expected *proportion* of organizations is active on disadvantaged-subgroup issues, this "lead" vanishes when we examine the mean level of activity on that issue. This consistent disparity between percentages and means indicates that when organizations are active on issues affecting intersectionally disadvantaged subgroups of their constituencies, their levels of engagement are relatively low and their commitments quite shallow. The discrepancy is captured well by the executive director of a broad-based civil rights group who described affirmative action in higher education (an advantaged-subgroup issue) as a "high priority" for his organization.[60] Comparing his organization's activity on this issue to its involvement in the Employment Non-Discrimination Act (ENDA), legislation that would protect LGBT people from job discrimination (a disadvantaged-subgroup issue), he explained that his group had been much less involved with the latter issue. In fact, he told me, his organization had made no independent efforts on this policy issue. He said, "We support ENDA . . . [but] apart from coalitional [efforts], not so much."[61] Although his organization was somewhat involved in the issue, little effort had been devoted to this disadvantaged-subgroup issue, even though antidiscrimination protections are arguably as basic a civil right for LGBT people as affirmative action is for women and racial minorities. Instead, any efforts that this organization had devoted to this issue had been channeled through coalitions with other groups, a topic that will be addressed at greater length in chapter 6.

## CONCLUSION

My conversation with the chair of the board of the civil rights organization, recounted at the beginning of this chapter, captured many of the nuances and ambiguities associated with assessing the efficacy of interest groups as representatives for politically marginalized groups. The evidence suggests that in reality, the situation lies somewhere between the claims of organizations such as his that they speak for all members of their constituencies and the claims of those who argue that national advocacy organizations represent only the interests of their more privileged members. As such, the data illustrate the challenges faced by organizations that are charged with representing marginalized groups in national politics, a responsibility that entails maintaining the resources and insider access that they require to press their claims with policy makers while simultaneously trying to use this access to speak on behalf of "outsider" constituents.

On the one hand, the data reveal that, across organization types, much less advocacy is devoted to issues affecting disadvantaged subgroups than is devoted to either majority or advantaged-subgroup issues. Moreover, controlling for other effects, issues affecting advantaged subgroups frequently receive more attention than majority issues. As an intersectional approach helps us understand, levels of advocacy are closely related to the relative status of the subgroup that is affected. Consequently, the evidence underscores concerns of scholars such as Robert Michels, Theda Skocpol, Frances Piven, and Richard Cloward that formal and professionally run advocacy organizations are imperfect replacements for grassroots movements and mass-membership associations.

The results of the analyses also strongly suggest that the alleged trade-offs between advocacy on social issues and advocacy on economic issues are, in fact, manifestations of the ways in which intersectional marginalization leads organizations of all types to give short shrift to issues affecting disadvantaged subgroups of their constituencies. In the case of organizations that represent constituencies such as women, racial minorities, and LGBT people, intersectional marginalization manifests as a lack of attention to issues affecting low-income people. In the case of economic justice organizations, the problem tends to manifest as a lack of attention to issues of race, gender, and sexuality.

While the pattern of disproportionately low levels of advocacy on behalf of disadvantaged subgroups is clear, however, it does not tell the entire story. Rather, some facets of the survey and interview data reflect an advocacy community that echoes my lunch companion's commitment to using his role as a representative as a means to achieve social justice for his most disadvantaged constituents. Indeed, most of the organization leaders I interviewed see representation as much more than a process of majoritarian interest aggregation. Rather, many claim as part of their organizations' mandates the responsibility to provide compensatory representation for disadvantaged members of their constituencies. Moreover, many of these officers recognize that fulfilling this role demands proactive efforts on their part in order to counter what they understand as biases against these groups in American politics and public policy.

As a result of such efforts and commitments, many of these organizations are less oligarchic than they might appear at first glance. Many organizations are, in fact, quite active on policy issues that affect intersectionally disadvantaged subgroups of their constituencies. In these ways, advocacy organizations continue the work of the mass movements out of which they have grown (movements that also tend to be organized around single-axis issues; Staggenborg 1988). They also go some distance toward offsetting the mobilization of bias in politics and public opinion by trying to take advantage of the opportunities of interest group politics at the same time as they try to transform the opportunity structure associated with them. Some organizations, for example, exploit policy niches in ways that lead to increased attention to disadvantaged-subgroup issues. Others make the most of opportunities for short-term victories but balance this approach with a commitment to fighting longer-term battles for disadvantaged subgroups. Still others mediate on behalf of disadvantaged subgroups by taking up issues even when they are unpopular or controversial among members of the public or, in the case of nonmember organizations, among their own constituents. For these reasons, advocacy organizations are an indispensable form of political representation for women, racial minorities, and low-income people within an electoral system in which they are underrepresented. By emphasizing advocacy, redistributing representational resources, and prioritizing social justice, they also advance an innovative conception of representation that provides an alternative to adversarial, utilitarian, majoritarian, and rationalist approaches to representation and interest group politics.

However, while many organization leaders profess a commitment to representation for intersectionally disadvantaged subgroups, and some even operate this way in practice, levels of advocacy on issues affecting these subgroups are nonetheless disproportionately low. The analyses in this chapter point to several interrelated sources for the discrepancies between the mandates articulated by advocacy officers and the low levels of representation actually afforded disadvantaged subgroups.

First, while the law of oligarchy is not ironclad, the data suggest that the formalization of advocacy organizations does have implications for the representation of intersectionally disadvantaged groups. In particular, the weight placed on constituents' interests in and support for organization positions on policy issues are likely the products of leaders' strategic concerns about resources and organizational maintenance. While understandable, these concerns compel organization leaders to attend to potential contributors and volunteers, who tend to be relatively advantaged. These constituents are unlikely to be concerned about or sympathetic to the demands and needs of disadvantaged subgroups, for whose support there is little competition (Verba, Schlozman, and Brady 1995). The replication of these socioeconomic biases among the members of organization staffs and boards further decreases the chances that organizations will feel pressure to address disadvantaged-subgroup issues (Berry 1977; DiMaggio and Anheier 1990; Michels 1911).

In addition to these internal factors, the evidence also suggests that attention to disadvantaged-subgroup issues is dampened further by external pressures that emanate from the political environment. For example, the need to respond to political threats and the desire to exploit opportunities associated with potential successes often leads organizations away from issues affecting disadvantaged subgroups because such issues are likely to be political "losers." Moreover, much evidence shows that the effects of these internal and external factors are exacerbated by the fact they are applied selectively in ways that reinforce the biases against activity on issues affecting intersectionally disadvantaged groups.

Finally, the sincere commitments of organization leaders to represent intersectionally disadvantaged constituents are superseded by the fact that many organizations do not regard the issues that affect these constituents as central to their agendas. Leaders find that adding categories "complicates" issues when the additional categories are associated with axes of disadvantage but not when the additional axes confer advantages. They also frame concerns in ways that tend to overestimate the breadth of the impact of advantaged-subgroup issues while underestimating the impact of disadvantaged-subgroup issues. This framing allows officers to construct advantaged-subgroup issues as issues in the common interests of their constituents that are broadly related to organizational agendas while constructing disadvantaged-subgroup issues as narrower, complicated, and "special" interests that are, in the words of the civil rights organization officer I quoted at the beginning of this chapter, "over there." Consequently, officers at these organizations marginalize and downplay the impact of such issues while magnifying the impact of issues affecting advantaged subgroups.

It may be strategic for organizations to concentrate their energies on "uncomplicated" issues that they perceive have a broad impact on their constituency. It is certainly critical that organization leaders do what is necessary to maintain their organizations, minimize strain, and maintain their legitimacy with the policy makers they hope to influence. As such, it makes sense that organizations frame issues in ways that resonate with political elites and that they concentrate on issues that are likely to appeal to dues-paying members and contributors who have the most resources, hoping that the effects of such efforts will trickle down to disadvantaged constituents. However, when it comes to issues affecting subgroups of their broader constituencies, organizations employ a double standard. Issues affecting advantaged subgroups are given considerable attention regardless of their breadth of impact, whereas issues affecting disadvantaged subgroups, with some important exceptions, are not. Moreover, these discrepancies persist even once we take into account the relative salience of issues on the agendas of political institutions. Organizations not surprisingly devote a great deal of energy and resources to politically salient issues or to those that they perceive as having the broadest impact, as Downs might predict, but also to those that they *frame* as being broad, regardless of whether they really are. The resulting mobilization of bias *within* the social and economic justice advocacy universe mirrors and reinforces the marginalization of disadvantaged groups within interest group politics, electoral politics, and the broader polity.

These outcomes are not intentional, nor are they inevitable. An alternative that I have begun to sketch out and that I will elaborate in the coming chapters is for organizations to follow the lead of those groups that advocate effectively on behalf of intersectionally disadvantaged constituents and adopt the set of practices that I call *affirmative advocacy*. Together these practices provide a framework within which organizations can balance strategic concerns about organizational maintenance and political opportunities with their mandates to represent and mediate on behalf of disadvantaged subgroups in ways that nurture a sense of intersectionally linked fate among their constituencies. This framework encourages organizations to frame issues affecting disadvantaged subgroups of their constituencies broadly in order to make clear their importance to the constituency as a whole, and it also encourages them to devote *extra* resources and energies to these issues. In order to fulfill their mandate to equalize the representation of *all* women, racial minorities, and low-income people within political institutions and policy making, they can work to reverse the assumption that the benefits of their advocacy on issues affecting advantaged subgroups will trickle down to disadvantaged ones. Instead, they might allocate their resources as if the reverse were true—that time, energy, and money devoted to protecting the rights of, and to expanding resources for, the least well-off will trickle *up* to all sectors of their constituencies.

Although the attention and resources devoted to issues affecting intersectionally disadvantaged groups are important measures of the representation afforded to them by advocacy organizations, these are not the only relevant components of representation. Also important are criteria such as the kinds of activities used and institutions targeted by organizations as they pursue the interests of their constituents. I turn to this component of representation in chapter 5, which evaluates the quality of representation that results from the variation in the political institutions that are targeted by organizations as they pursue their policy goals, focusing in particular on the extent to which and conditions under which advocacy groups turn to the courts in their policy advocacy.

# FIVE

# Tyranny of the Minority?
# Institutional Targets
# and Advocacy Strategies

May 17, 2004, marked the fiftieth anniversary of the United States Supreme Court decision in *Brown v. Board of Education of Topeka*. The ruling in that case declared unconstitutional the doctrine of "separate but equal" that had provided the legal underpinnings for American racial segregation. In his address that day at the grand opening of the Brown v. Board of Education National Historic Site in Topeka, Kansas, President George W. Bush hailed the 1954 decision as one that "changed America for the better, and forever. Fifty years ago today, nine judges announced that they had looked at the Constitution and saw no justification for the segregation and humiliation of an entire race . . . that was a day of justice—and it was a long time coming."[1]

That same date in mid-May 2004 also marked the first day that same-sex couples could be legally married in the state of Massachusetts, following the December 2003 Massachusetts Supreme Court ruling in *Goodridge v. Department of Public Health* that held that it is against the Massachusetts constitution to deny marriage rights to same-sex couples. As a consequence, Massachusetts became the first state in the United States to legalize "gay marriage," and May 17 was the first day that same-sex couples were legally wed in this country. Later that day, President Bush issued a statement that criticized the Massachusetts Supreme Court for its actions on this issue. "The sacred institution of marriage should not be redefined by a few activist judges," he declared. Insisting that "all Americans have a right to be heard in this debate," President Bush repeated his call to the United States Congress to pass "an amendment to our Constitution defining and protecting marriage as a union of a man and a woman as husband and wife."[2]

Juxtaposing President Bush's two statements—the first hailing the court as a crucial vehicle for protecting and advancing minority rights, the second vilifying "judicial activism" for, in his estimation, trampling on the majority's "right to be heard"—highlights a central tension within American politics and constitutional design that has serious implications for the representation of intersectionally disadvantaged groups. In particular, it underscores long-standing questions and lively debates about the proper role of the nonmajoritarian court within American majoritarian democratic politics and policy making, particularly as this role relates to the rights of unpopular and disadvantaged groups in this country.

The judiciary is the branch of the federal government that is most explicitly (though by no means exclusively) charged with protecting rights and with checking the powers and actions of the majoritarian, electorally based legislative and executive branches. As a consequence, the courts often are called upon to protect unpopular minorities from the tyranny of majority rule. Some have argued (most notably Charles Beard) that the minorities the framers likely had in mind were wealthy landowners who, they thought, needed protection from the masses that might wield their populist power against them in the new democracy (Beard 1913; Dahl 1957). However, as the *Brown* and *Goodridge* decisions highlighted here demonstrate, questions about the policy-making activities of the courts, while of broad concern, have particular implications for the protection and representation of disadvantaged groups as well as for the organizations that advocate for and represent them and that are the subject of this book. Proponents of a "legal mobilization" paradigm, such as Michael McCann, argue that legal strategies are crucial for outsider groups because they "help movement activists to win voice, position, and influence" in the policy process and give them a way to "formalize" their roles in policy formulation and implementation processes (McCann 1998, 212). Sally Kenney argues similarly that courts are essential conduits for pursuing women's grievances because the judicial branch plays an important constitutive role in framing issues for policy makers (Kenney 2005). Paul Frymer explains that the courts play an important role when it comes to marginalized groups because Congress often delegates responsibility for their representation and for redressing their grievances to the courts (Frymer 2006). In these and other ways, the courts provide outsider groups with unique opportunities to make claims and to shape the discourses about the policy issues that concern them (Frymer 2006; see also Burstein 1991; Casper 1976; Epp 1998; Handler 1978; O'Connor 1980; O'Connor and Epstein 1983b).

Indeed, although the record of the courts in protecting disadvantaged groups has been inconsistent, advocacy organizations have targeted the judicial branch when other political opportunities have been absent, particularly when they have been unsuccessful in the legislative and executive branches, or in conjunction with these other branches (Barker 1967; Bickel 1986; Cortner 1968; Dworkin 1977, 1986; Handler 1978; Manwaring 1962; McCann 1986, 1998; O'Connor and Epstein 1983b; Sorauf 1976; Vose 1958, 1959;Wasby 1984). *Brown*, for example, was part of an ongoing strategy by the National Association for the Advancement of Colored People Legal Defense Fund (NAACP LDF; under the leadership of Thurgood Marshall) to bring test cases to the Supreme Court that would lead the justices to overturn the 1896 *Plessy v. Ferguson* decision and make real the equal protection guarantees of the Fourteenth Amendment to the Constitution (Tushnet 1987; Wasby 1984). *Goodridge* was part of a similar strategy by the Gay and Lesbian Alliance Against Defamation (GLAAD) to use the (mostly state) courts to establish marriage rights for same-sex couples and to undermine the impact of the Defense of Marriage Act (DOMA) that was passed by Congress and signed into law by President Bill Clinton in 1996.[3] Encouraged by Supreme Court victories during what many regard as the unusually receptive Warren Court era of the 1950s and 1960s, organizations representing marginalized groups made increasing use of judicial strategies to pursue their goals, a practice that has persisted through the eras of the more conservative Burger, Rehnquist, and Roberts Courts (Baum 2001; Casper 1976; Epstein 1993; Kuersten and Jagemann 2000; O'Connor and Epstein 1981–82). As legal scholar Jeffrey Rosen argues, "In the 50 years since *Brown v. Board of Education*, Americans have imagined that the justices could protect vulnerable minorities from the excesses of democratic politics. From affirmative action to school prayer and presidential elections, the court has enthusiastically accepted the invitation to answer the divisive political questions that politicians are unable to resolve" (Rosen 2004, 29).

While advocacy groups might invite the courts to decide such questions, and while the courts might accept the invitation to do so, many critics argue that this virtue of the courts is also its vice. Echoing Alexander Bickel's concern about "counter-majoritarian difficulty" of judicial review (Bickel 1986), they worry that the same insulation from the will of the majority that allows judges to rule on behalf of unpopular minorities also lays the basis for portrayals of their decisions in such cases as undemocratic, anti-majoritarian, and therefore illegitimate (see also Ely 1980, Waldron 2001). Many such critiques of judicial activism—such as the one articulated by George W. Bush at the beginning of this chapter—are lodged by opponents of reproductive rights, LGBT rights, and affirmative action, most of whom would object to these policies from whatever institution they were to emanate (Bork 2003; Scalia 1998). However, ambivalence also emanates from some who support these policies and who sympathize with the goals of the marginalized groups. Many liberal legal scholars have taken issue with what they perceive as an overreliance on court-based strategies by the organizations that represent marginalized groups (D. Bell 1976; Freeman 1978; Scheingold 1974; Tushnet 1991). The ranks of such critics have grown markedly in recent years, at least in part in response to "the conservative entrenchment of federal courts" since the late 1960s (Frymer 2006, 125).

Critical legal scholars such as Scott Cummings, Ingrid Eagly, Richard Abel, and Lucie White argue, for example, that courts inevitably embody and represent the interests of the powerful and that litigation consequently risks co-opting social mobilization and potential community leaders, discouraging client initiatives and leaving "larger social change undone" (Cummings and Eagly 2001; see also Abel 1985; White 1988). Pointing to the high financial costs of lawsuits, these critics argue that when organizations focus their advocacy efforts on the courts, they take resources away from other goals such as mass mobilization. Given the increasing conservatism of the Supreme Court, others simply wonder whether court strategies will lead to favorable rulings on issues that affect marginalized groups (Frymer 2006).

In a vein similar to the more conservative critiques of judicial activism, other progressive skeptics also point to what they perceive as the political costs of court strategies. Some argue that the courts are elitist and overwhelmingly favor dominant groups in society (Hirschl 2004). Others worry that court rulings on behalf of disadvantaged groups that are not in line with public sentiment are elitist and stimulate backlash that ultimately leads to setbacks in the very policy areas they are seeking to advance (Rosenberg 1991).[4] As a consequence, they argue, these victories are Pyrrhic at best, powerful symbolically but not in practice. For example, in a January 2005 op-ed piece in the *New York Times*, sociologist and former senior adviser to Bill Clinton Paul Starr wrote, "The great thing about legal victories like *Roe v. Wade* is that you don't have to compromise with your opponents, or even win over majority opinion." But that, he continues, "is also the trouble." "An unreconciled losing side and unconvinced public," he argues, create the conditions that mobilize opponents to these victories and "may eventually change the judges," thereby undermining these and many other gains (Starr 2005).

In addition to these concerns about the trade-offs involved in using judicial strategies to further the rights of marginalized groups broadly construed, skepticism has also been directed at the particular implications of judicial strategies for intersectionally disadvantaged subgroups of marginalized groups. Critical race legal theorists such as Kimberlé Crenshaw and Elizabeth Iglesias have shown, for example, the limitations of litigation in addressing the intersectionally constituted grievances of women of color in employment discrimination cases (Crenshaw 1989; Iglesias 1996). To prove racial discrimination, Ange-Marie Hancock explains, claimants "cannot argue that a particular policy targets women of color disparately" but must instead demonstrate that it has a "disparate impact on men and women of the racial group." Evidence of gender discrimination similarly entails demonstrating a policy's disparate impact on women *across* racial groups (Hancock 2007, 71). Rather than recognizing the multiple forms of discrimination at play and taking into account their varying effects on differently situated subgroups, courts have more often ruled that if the discrimination in question cannot be ascribed to *either* race *or* to gender, there is no actionable grievance.

## MAJORITARIANISM

As the debates outlined in the previous section suggest, among the many issues at stake in questions about the use of the court on behalf of marginalized groups are concerns and assertions about the relative majoritarianism of each branch of the federal government and about the associated degree of legitimacy of the policies emanating from each one (Bickel 1986). Indeed, one of the distinguishing characteristics of American political institutions is that each branch is marked by its level of majoritarianism relative to the other branches. The judicial, executive, and legislative branches of the federal government therefore can be arrayed on a scale according to their levels of majoritarianism: The legislative branch—with its popularly elected officials serving two-year or six-year terms—is at the high end, and the judicial branch—whose judges hold life-long appointments made by the president—is at the low end. The executive branch falls in the middle of this majoritarianism scale. Although the president is elected by the voters (through their electors), most of the day-to-day activities of executive policy making and implementation are carried out by agencies whose members are appointed by the president rather than being elected by voters. While Senate confirmation hearings for cabinet-level secretaries subject these positions to initial scrutiny by elected officials who are accountable to voters, in general, executive decision makers are not subject to the approval of an electorate.

Thinking about the majoritarianism of the courts as one point on a continuum suggests that questions about judicial tactics might be productively considered within a comparative framework that addresses the *relative* majoritarianism of *each* branch. By making explicit the usually implicit comparisons between the majoritarianism of the courts with that of the legislative and executive branches, we can examine broad concerns about representation and legitimacy in organizational tactics aimed at each of the three branches (Frymer 2006). A comparative framework also makes possible assessments of the opportunities afforded to organizations by each branch and allows us to evaluate the implications of these opportunities for the capacity of organizations to act as mediators and representatives on behalf of their constituents.

In addition to allowing such broad assessments of representation, appraising court use by advocacy organizations by comparing it to their targeting of the legislative and executive branches also provides a valuable lens through which to assess representation for intersectionally disadvantaged subgroups in particular. Critics argue that the nonmajoritarian character of the courts entails political costs that make judicial strategies a poor means of representing marginalized groups. *Because* of these high costs, however, when an organization uses judicial tactics to pursue an issue, it sends strong signals about the issue's importance and about its own willingness to go to bat for the constituents affected by it (Johnson 2003; Kollman 1998; Solberg and Waltenberg 2006). As a consequence, judicial strategies might be thought of as "big guns" that are kept in reserve and brought in when other approaches have failed or are futile.

Considered in this light, judicial strategies provide organizations with opportunities to mediate on behalf of their intersectionally disadvantaged constituents in several significant ways. To the public, such action signals that an organization is in solidarity with an unpopular group. To other members of the constituency, it signals that these issues are central to the concerns of the organization and to its constituency as a whole. To the members of the affected subgroup itself, it signals an organizational commitment of time, resources, and political capital to them and to the issues that affect them (Kollman 1998).

As a consequence, it is important to determine under what circumstances and on whose behalf organizations are willing to incur the costs associated with legal strategies. How willingly do advocacy organizations expend these scarce resources on behalf of intersectionally disadvantaged groups?

In this chapter, I bring these questions about majoritarianism and organizations' targeting of each branch of the federal government to the concerns about political representation and policy advocacy for intersectionally disadvantaged groups that animate this book. To this end, the chapter examines two sets of closely related issues. First, I explore the extent to which and the circumstances under which organizations that speak for marginalized groups target the court relative to their targeting of other political institutions. I then examine whether the political institutions that are targeted by advocacy organizations vary by issue type, and I assess the consequences of this variation as another lens through which to evaluate the political representation afforded intersectionally disadvantaged subgroups. In particular, do organizations' choices about which political branch to target—the legislative, the judicial, or the executive branch—vary based on the power of the affected group, and if they do, do they vary in ways that cannot be explained as matters of jurisdiction, organizational maintenance, or variations in the receptivity or political opportunities associated with each branch? (For further discussion of these questions, see Baumgartner and Jones 1993; Hansford 2004; Kingdon 1995; McAdam 1982; Meyer and Minkoff 2004; Solberg and Waltenberg 2006.) In light of the low *levels* of activity on behalf of intersectionally disadvantaged subgroups depicted in chapter 4, what are the implications of the ways in which organizations distribute their activity among institutions for the kind of representation that these subgroups receive from advocacy organizations?[5]

Given the popular and political attention that court tactics garner, it might seem that organizations that represent marginalized groups rely heavily on litigation and that they use the courts more often than do business and professional organizations. However, based on data from the interviews and the Survey of National Economic and Social Justice Organizations (SNESJO), this appears not to be the case. Instead, Congress is by far the most frequent target of organizations' advocacy activities, while the courts are targeted least often. Popular perceptions and political hand-wringing notwithstanding, organizations representing weak groups do not actually use the courts at distinctively high rates—in fact, as scholars such as Thomas Hansford, Kim Lane Scheppele, Jack Walker, Kay Lehman Schlozman, and John Tierney also have found, these organizations target courts less frequently than do business and professional groups (Hansford 2004; Scheppele and Walker 1991; Schlozman and Tierney 1986).

While organizations representing marginalized groups do not target the judiciary as frequently as they do other branches, they do use court tactics at significantly higher rates when it comes to issues affecting subgroups—both advantaged and disadvantaged—than they do when it comes to majority and universal issues. Most striking is that rates of court use are *highest* when it comes to issues affecting *advantaged* subgroups. Taken together, these findings suggest that popular characterizations of capricious court use by advocacy organizations that wish to steamroll majority preferences in their pursuit of social change are exaggerated and misdirected. Instead, court use by advocacy organizations is markedly infrequent (compared to other tactics), and it is usually reserved for circumstances in which other routes do not work or for occasions when organizations are drawn into lawsuits instigated by opponents of policies that they feel compelled to defend. When there is a chance to pursue their goals legislatively or administratively, advocacy organizations usually choose to follow those routes.

As such, while the use of court tactics by organizations representing marginalized groups has generated reactions ranging from ambivalence to ire (Hilbink 2006), it turns out that it is not the extent of court use by these organizations that is atypical but rather the circumstances under which these organizations target the courts that is distinctive and worthy of scrutiny. This point has been obscured, however, because examinations of these issues rarely differentiate among policy types, thereby concealing the variation in court use and diverting attention from understanding how well organizations represent intersectionally disadvantaged groups. By employing my four-part policy typology and focusing on the representation of intersectionally disadvantaged subgroups, this chapter illuminates the fact that organizations representing these groups do not play fast and loose with court strategies. Nonetheless, while organizations need to use the courts when they cannot succeed via legislative or executive routes, court resources are scarce, and court use often comes with a price. As such, the concentration of judicial and other nonmajoritarian resources on advocacy for advantaged subgroups that I uncover is troubling, exacerbating as it does the inequalities in levels of advocacy that I found, as detailed in chapter 4.

## INTEREST GROUPS AND AMERICAN POLITICAL INSTITUTIONS

American constitutional design—with its checks and balances, separate institutions sharing powers, and guarantees of free assembly—creates multiple points of access and political opportunity for groups and individuals seeking to petition the government to redress their grievances. Interest groups exploit the opportunities afforded by the legislative, judicial, and executive branches, and they participate in the processes of and try to influence the outcomes of each one in myriad ways (Kingdon 1995; Shipan 1997). Interest groups not only try to influence each branch separately but also "initiate action in one arena as a means of stimulating action in another, and when they lose in one institutional arena, they typically pursue their cause in another" (Wright 2003, 49). For example, in the 1940s and 1950s, faced with a hostile Congress, African American civil rights organizations concentrated instead on the federal courts (Frymer 2006; Schlozman and Tierney 1986, 160; Tushnet 1987; Wasby 1984). In the 1960s and 1970s, abortion rights activists pursued a strategy that combined pursuing state-level legislation and referenda with litigation tactics. Such "balancing" is evident when interest groups turn to the courts as a way to overturn unfriendly legislation or regulations or to offset legislative and executive defeats (Cortner 1968). Organizations also target the legislative and executive branches when the *judicial* branch is hostile to their claims. In the 1970s, women's organizations and labor unions turned to Congress and to the Equal Employment Opportunity Commission (EEOC) when the Supreme Court proved unwelcoming to their arguments about the need to protect women against pregnancy discrimination in the workplace in its decisions in cases such as *General Electric Co. v. Gilbert* (1976) and *Nashville Gas Co. v. Nora Satty* (1977). This approach led eventually to the passage by Congress of the Pregnancy Discrimination Act of 1978 (Wright 2003, 55).

Indeed, as I will discuss in the next section, in many cases, no single strategy suffices, and most organizations recognize that they must pursue change through many avenues, exploiting the political opportunities and advantages of each branch or working to change the policy venue in which an issue is addressed (Baumgartner and Jones 1993; Hansford 2004; Kingdon 1995; Meyer and Minkoff 2004).

## THE LEGISLATIVE BRANCH

The legislative branch affords advocacy organizations with many opportunities to represent their constituents, some of which they can initiate themselves while others require invitations from members of Congress. Interest groups try to place policy issues not yet being considered by Congress onto its agenda, and they try to influence legislation at each stage of the legislative process. They lobby members of both the House of Representatives and the Senate and provide information about the policy impact and political consequences of legislation in members' districts (Austen-Smith and Wright 1994, 1996). Advocacy groups try to influence the framing of legislation before bills are introduced, while they are in committee, and when they are being considered by the chamber as a whole. If they are invited, organizations can testify at hearings, and once bills have been passed by both chambers, they can lobby members of conference committees (Esterling 2004; Hojnacki and Kimball 1998, 1999; Schlozman and Tierney 1986).

Many proceedings within the House and Senate can be attended by the public or the media or have easily accessible transcripts. As a consequence, representational activities aimed at Congress are generally quite public and, at least ideally, are subject to more accountability than activities aimed at the other two branches. Legislative tactics often entail relatively large-scale mobilization efforts and present many opportunities for organizations to act as mediators on behalf of their constituents. When organizations lobby Congress, they are, in essence, taking a public stand on behalf of the constituency affected by a policy issue, and they are asking members of Congress to do the same (Kollman 1998).

Because of these attributes, critics who are ambivalent about judicial strategies argue that advocacy groups should focus their activities on the legislative branch because it is the most majoritarian branch, the one most accountable to the public, and its outputs are therefore the most likely to be perceived as legitimate (Rosenberg 1991). In addition, because Congress has the power to implement programs, legislative action is, according to scholars such as Gerald Rosenberg, also more effective. However, while there are certainly some important benefits associated with attempts by advocacy groups to represent their constituents by targeting Congress, legislative tactics are not without their own limitations. Targeting the legislative branch poses particular challenges when it comes to issues affecting intersectionally disadvantaged subgroups because, as I explained at length in chapter 3, legislative districts are rarely drawn to represent intersecting demographics. Members of Congress therefore prefer issues with broad appeal that unify their constituents, not issues that highlight the divisions and differences among them. Consequently, organizations are most likely to target Congress when it comes to issues that affect a majority and least likely when the affected group is small, unpopular, weak, or stigmatized.

In addition, because the majority parties in the House and Senate have the power to set and control the agendas of these two institutions, the most salient limit to targeting Congress has to do with which party is in control of each chamber. Moreover, because of the many steps in the legislative process, Congressional policy making is also often slow, piecemeal, and incremental. Perhaps most centrally, although being subject to the will of the majority can bring increased legitimacy if organizations are successful in their policy goals, the same majoritarianism that creates this legitimacy also can make it difficult for organizations representing unpopular groups to achieve their goals in the first place. Finally, while most concerns about backlash tend to focus on judicial rulings, legislative action is subject to backlash as well—witness the use of the courts by conservatives to undermine legislatively based labor rights since the 1930s (K. Stone 1992; Lovell 2003) and the Violence Against Women Act in the 1990s (*United States v. Morrison* 2000).

## THE EXECUTIVE BRANCH

Like the legislative branch, the executive branch provides many opportunities through which organizations can represent their constituents. While there are limitations to the policy-making capacities of the executive branch, the powers of its many departments, bureaus, agencies, and commissions to execute and enforce legislation have expanded over time as Congress has delegated more and more responsibilities and authority to it. Because Congress so often passes legislation that is vague and short on substantive direction, bureaucratic officials often have de facto policy-making capacities. Congress adds further to these capacities by giving rule-making authority to bureaucratic agencies, whose regulations have the force of law. In addition, the president has important agenda-setting power as well as the power to issue executive orders, to veto legislation, and to issue signing statements that effectively "nullify a wide range of statutory provisions" (Cooper 2005, 516).

As is the case with Congress, some points of executive access can be initiated by organizations themselves, while others can be accessed only by invitation. Organizations can, for example, initiate activities such as lobbying agencies, submitting comments on pending regulations, and even trying to lobby the president and members of the chief executive's cabinet and staff (through, for example, donations to presidential campaigns). In addition, agencies must provide a thirty-day commenting period for all proposed regulations, and organizations can submit comments and attend related rule-making hearings. Agencies often invite organizations with relevant policy expertise to participate in the hearings that they hold about proposed rules, and the agencies also solicit written comments from these organizations (Wright 2003, 52). Officers at organizations also can be invited to serve as members of advisory committees and to take part in procedures for adjudicating agency rules. Most of these activities associated with lobbying the executive branch are not ones that are subjected to high levels of scrutiny. Although many agency proceedings are theoretically open to the public, they get little media attention except in rare cases.

As the main venue for trying to influence implementation, targeting the executive branch has clear benefits. The wide swings in enforcement of Occupational Safety and Health Administration (OSHA) workplace standards and of prosecution of EEOC discrimination cases make clear, for example, that the effects of decisions about enforcement can yield very direct costs or benefits for affected groups (A. Freeman 1998; Melnick 1994). Moreover, scholars such as John Skrentny have shown that executive branch policies and decisions have been crucial in extending rights to marginalized groups such as African Americans, Latinos, women, Asian Pacific Americans, and people with disabilities (Skrentny 2004). Access to the president is particularly useful when the time comes to sign or veto legislation.

However, like representation in the legislative branch, the executive branch has limits as well. Foremost among these limits is that activities that are aimed at the executive branch require a great deal of access and political capital, much of which depends on which party is in power. For most of the organizations in this study, lobbying the executive is a much more viable option when there is a Democrat in the White House (true for eight of the ten years covered by my data). Moreover, even during periods in which Democrats control the executive branch, the processes of formal comment on rules and participation in hearings remain dominated by business and professional organizations. Although the "cozy iron triangles" comprised of alliances among interest groups, congressional committees, and bureaucratic agencies have been mitigated somewhat by sunshine laws and public comment requirements, organizations representing the disadvantaged rarely confront the business and professional organizations that dominate executive lobbying, even in policy areas where regulatory agencies and the bureaucracy in general play a large role (Furlong 1997; Golden 1998; Heclo 1978; Wright 2003). Even when Congress is controlled by a hostile majority party, there are still usually some sympathetic members. This is less true of the executive branch, and as a consequence, lobbying the executive exacerbates many of the problems of legislative politics regarding intersectionally disadvantaged subgroups. Presidents have even more reason than members of Congress to prefer broad issues, issues that are important to their base, or issues that appeal to groups with money or with many likely votes. Consequently, the extent to which executive branch lobbying is amenable to advocacy on behalf of disadvantaged subgroups varies, often based on the party in control of this branch.

## THE JUDICIAL BRANCH

Opportunities to lobby and influence the courts are far fewer and, in various ways, more constrained than they are in the legislative and executive branches, limited mainly to filing suits, providing legal or financial assistance to parties in a case, or filing amicus curiae (friend of the court) briefs. These opportunities are further curtailed because parties to a lawsuit must have an actionable case and standing to sue. The rules governing standing were relaxed in the 1960s and 1970s, providing advocacy groups with more extensive opportunities to bring suits on behalf of plaintiffs and in class actions. However, these rules were tightened up again recently, and it is consequently increasingly difficult for organizations to attain standing to sue. Lawsuits, therefore, are a less viable option today than they have been in the past (Wright 2003, 51). In addition, since 1996, restrictions have increased on the use of legal aid funds for advocacy: no lobbying is allowed (although funds may still be used to "educate" legislators), nor can legal aid funds be used for class action suits (Cummings and Eagly 2001). Organizations without standing can instead file amicus curiae briefs in which they express their views on a lawsuit; however, to do so, they need permission from the parties in the case or from the court itself.[6] In addition to briefs that attempt to influence the decision in a case, organizations also can file briefs encouraging the court to review a case (or not to review it; see Krislov 1963; Caldeira and Wright 1988, 1989, 1990; Songer and Sheehan 1993). However, both litigation and amicus curiae briefs are expensive—one brief alone can cost $50,000 (Caldeira and Wright 1989; Galanter 1974).

What the courts lack in opportunities, however, they make up for in other forms of access and in potential payoff (Schultz 1998; Shipan 1997; Gonen 2003). Organizations that find their access to the executive and legislative branches curtailed when the political party that is most sympathetic to their policy goals is not in control still can turn to the less overtly partisan courts to pursue their goals. Unlike the case with many of the activities in the other two branches, organizations need not have access to officials to try to get an issue on the agenda; if organizations find appropriate plaintiffs, they can file lawsuits on their own.

Opportunities to participate in court also present themselves when challenges are lodged by opponents of policies that advocacy groups wish to defend. This is increasingly true since, as Karen O'Connor and Lee Epstein point out (1983a), conservative advocacy groups have escalated their use of the courts to achieve their own goals in recent decades (see also Baumgartner and Leech 1998, 242–47; Epstein 1985). Moreover, the power of judicial review means not only that the courts can act to protect minority rights but also that they can overturn legislation and regulations that harm disadvantaged groups and can impose higher bars to clear for subsequent legislation and regulation that might impose harms (Cortner 1968; Sorauf 1976; Tushnet 1987; Vose 1958; Wasby 1984). Indeed, in spite of the increasing conservatism of the Supreme Court, the cases decided by the Burger and Rehnquist Courts yielded significant victories for marginalized groups (Baum 2001). Some recent successes have included *Romer v. Evans* (1995), which held that Amendment 2 to the Colorado State Constitution violated the equal protection rights of gay men and lesbians; and *Lawrence and Garner v. Texas* (2003), which overturned the Texas sodomy law that criminalized sexual conduct between members of the same sex.

In addition to providing marginalized groups with access, rights, and protections that have not been attainable through legislation, legal tactics have other benefits as well. Court strategies make use of nonfungible resources such as lawyers, whose pro bono services are chronically in short supply (Cummings and Eagly 2001). Capitalizing on legal expertise was particularly attractive during the uncharacteristically receptive Warren Court era of the 1960s, when foundation money and legal aid funds were plentiful and could not be used for other purposes (Bussiere 1997; M. Davis 1993; Lawrence 1990; Mink 1990). Court tactics also provide rather unique opportunities for tailored arguments on important issues and can be used to make extremely strong and direct statements about fundamental issues and rights (McCann 1994). Because of their political and monetary costs, court tactics also show a real commitment by organizations to issues and the groups they affect (Johnson 2003).

Although the courts can and often do protect minority rights, they are no panacea, and their record in terms of protecting the interests of unpopular groups from the tyranny of the majority has been uneven. For example, the Supreme Court upheld the constitutionality of Jim Crow segregation in its 1896 decision *Plessy v. Ferguson*. Doug McAdam argues that the Court continued to provide "only a weak safeguard against discrimination," deciding cases in ways that limited the civil rights of blacks and gave official sanction to racial discrimination until well into the twentieth century (McAdam 1982, 71). Like members of Congress, justices are products of their time and of their environments, embedded in the same political culture as legislators, and so their decisions often reflect the dominant thinking of the day (Dahl 1957; Johnson 2004). As a consequence, in the *Plessy* decision and many other cases—including *Korematsu v. United States* (1944), which curtailed the citizenship rights of Japanese Americans during the Second World War, and *Bowers v. Hardwick* (1986), which upheld state sodomy laws—the federal courts have reflected, rather than challenged, popular sentiment that was aligned against the rights of unpopular groups (Mishler and Sheehan 1993).

In addition, when the courts *do* flout prevailing public preferences, the sources of their ability to do so—the secrecy of court proceedings, their isolation from public scrutiny, their lack of responsiveness to the pressures of majoritarianism—leave them open to the charges articulated by President Bush regarding the *Goodridge* decision that "activist judges" trample on the public will. As such, they are easily discredited as antidemocratic and as lacking legitimacy (Bickel 1986; Rosenberg 1991). Organizations that pursue their goals through court action are therefore similarly vulnerable to charges that they use the courts as a stealth tactic in order to circumvent democratic channels as they pursue their "special interests." Furthermore, while court *proceedings* can be quite stealthy, judicial rulings themselves are often very high-profile, but without the tempering influence of majoritarian considerations and with little need for public or political dialogue about the issues that are at stake. Critics argue that policy changes achieved through the courts therefore are liable to stimulate a backlash that mobilizes the opposition and actually leads to *more* regressive action and legislation. As Rosen writes, "on the rare occasions that the courts have tried to impose an outcome that is intensely unpopular, it has tended to provoke a strong political response. After the Massachusetts Supreme Court decreed a right to gay marriage . . . , eleven states passed constitutional amendments this past Election Day that ban gay marriage. . . . That is hardly consistent with a vision of judicial heroics" (Rosen 2004, 30). Moreover, many court rulings require enforcement by *elected* officials who *are* subject to the pressures of majoritarianism. As a consequence, many decisions that look good on paper remain unenforced and ineffective. Thus, critics claim that court victories often are empty successes that have more symbolic than practical value (Bartley 1969; Horowitz 1977; Peltason 1971; Rosenberg 1991).

Other sources of ambivalence about court-based advocacy tactics have particular implications for intersectionally disadvantaged subgroups. Critical legal scholars, as I began to explain earlier, argue that legal reform strategies are an *impediment* to social change because the law is, in the words of Cummings and Eagly, "circumscribed within the existing political order" (Cummings and Eagly 2001, 453; see also D. Bell 1976; Freeman 1978; Tushnet 1991). Litigation, they contend, requires "the repackaging of . . . grievances" as rights that can be found in the Constitution (Cummings and Eagly 2001, 456; see also White 1987–88, 1988). Constitutional arguments do not always mesh with the broader political strategies or claims of movements and have proven difficult for many issues. As scholars such as Crenshaw (1989) and Iglesias (1996) have shown, this is especially true of issues and inequalities that intersect categories such as race and gender because courts generally find that discrimination must be attributed to only one of these categories (see also Wing 1997).

## TACTICAL PLURALISM

As a consequence of the many opportunities and hurdles associated with advocacy aimed at each branch, organizations representing weak and politically marginalized groups use a wide range of tactics to advocate on behalf of their constituents, including directly lobbying members of Congress, filing amicus curiae briefs in Supreme Court cases, and submitting comments to agencies. Indeed, most of the gains made by marginalized groups have been brought about through the efforts of organizations that fought for them using a combination of judicial interventions, congressional legislation, and executive action and implementation by a wide range of agencies. Movements and organizations historically have taken advantage of political opportunities and policy windows as they presented themselves, while also working to expand or shift the jurisdiction over issues to new and more sympathetic policy venues (Baumgartner and Jones 1993; Kingdon 1995; Schattschneider [1960] 1975).

This catholic and dynamic approach is certainly true of the organizations in the SNESJO. To assess the range of tactics that they employ, survey respondents were asked to rate on a 1-to-5 scale how often they use each of sixteen tactics. Examining the answers to this series of questions shows that tactical pluralism is the rule for the organizations in this study, which use a very wide range of activities in pursuing their policy goals. On average, these organizations use eleven of the sixteen tactics. Well over half (58 percent) of all organizations make use of at least twelve of these methods (see table 5.1 for list of methods).

Of the tactics aimed directly at a political institution, the most popular activities are almost all ones targeting the legislative branch, while the least popular ones are those targeting the judicial branch. For example, about 75 percent of organizations lobby members of Congress directly, and over 80 percent present testimony at congressional hearings. However, just under 40 percent pursue issues through litigation, and just over half (54 percent) file amicus curiae briefs. Organizations with lawyers on staff more often responded that they "frequently" file both lawsuits and amicus curiae briefs (17.6 percent and 15.6 percent, respectively) than did organizations that do not have a legal staff (1 percent and 2 percent, respectively), but even these rates are fairly low. As such, the organizations in this study report lower rates of litigation than those found in most other studies. For example, 73 percent of the organizations in Kollman's (1998) survey reported filing lawsuits at least occasionally, as did 72 percent of

TABLE 5.1  Organizations' use of tactics

| TACTIC | PERCENTAGE OF ORGANIZATIONS USING TACTIC | PERCENTAGE OF ORGANIZATIONS USING TACTIC "FREQUENTLY" (%) | MEAN |
|---|---|---|---|
| Lobby members of Congress directly | 75.1 | 23.5 | 2.9 |
| Lobby members of executive agencies or the White House directly | 73.0 | 18.6 | 2.9 |
| Lobby by grassroots of members of Congress | 80.4 | 28.8 | 3.17 |
| Work with agencies to draft, enforce and administer regulations, rules or guidelines | 76.1 | 15.8 | 2.84 |
| Work with members of Congress to formulate legislation | 79.7 | 18.9 | 2.96 |
| Litigate in court | 39.8 | 6.3 | 1.82 |
| File amicus curiae briefs in lawsuits brought by others | 54.0 | 6.3 | 2.04 |
| Organize demonstrations, marches, protests, boycotts, strikes, or pickets | 51.6 | 12.3 | 2.19 |
| Participate in public demonstrations, marches, or protests organized by others | 67.8 | 13.6 | 2.5 |
| Issue press releases, talk with the media, or advertise to influence public opinion | 93.3 | 39.3 | 3.82 |
| Enter into coalitions or working with other organizations | 97.9 | 67.1 | 4.4 |
| Testify at congressional hearings | 81.4 | 12.3 | 2.89 |
| Testify at agency hearings | 74.3 | 7.7 | 2.49 |
| Present research results/technical information | 89.8 | 25.3 | 3.4 |
| Work to appoint or elect public officials | 41.3 | 15.4 | 2.1 |
| Serve on governmental advisory commissions/boards | 66.0 | 10.5 | 2.45 |
| Average Number of Tactics Used | | | 11.4 |

*Source:* SNESJO.

Organization officers were asked, "On a scale of 1 to 5, where 1 is never and 5 is frequently, how often does your organization use each of the following influencing methods?"

*Note:* Numbers in the first column reflect the percentage of respondents giving answers of 2–5. Numbers in the second column reflect the percentage of respondents giving an answer of 5. Numbers in the third column reflect the mean response on the 1–5 scale.

the organizations in Schlozman and Tierney's (1986) study, and 56 percent of the organizations surveyed by Walker (1991). Together, these data begin to suggest that concerns about an overreliance on court tactics on the part of organizations representing marginalized groups are overblown.

Comparing data from the SNESJO with information from previous studies demonstrates that the organizations that represent marginalized groups also make much less extensive use of executive tactics than do business and professional lobbies, even in policy areas where regulatory agencies and the bureaucracy in general play a large role (Furlong 1997; Golden 1998; Wright 2003). Low levels of executive targeting are particularly evident when it comes to activities that require an invitation, illustrating the lower levels of access that they have to this branch. For example, in the SNESJO, only three-quarters of organizations (74.3 percent) gave testimony at agency hearings, an activity which was employed by almost all of the organizations in other studies (99 percent of organizations in Schlozman and Tierney's [1986] study, and 88 percent of those surveyed by Berry [1977]).[7] These relatively low levels of tactics targeting the executive branch are all the more striking given that there had been a Democratic administration for nearly eight years at the time that the SNESJO was conducted, which likely increased the extent of executive branch activity on the part of the organizations in the study.[8]

These results concerning specific tactics are echoed in answers to survey questions about institutional targets (see fig. 5.1). Respondents were asked to rate on a 1-to-5 scale how important each branch is as a target of their organization's activity. In this set of responses, the judicial branch is once again the least popular target of advocacy activity, while the legislative branch is again the most popular target (Berry 1977; Scholzman and Tierney 1986; Walker 1991). The legislative branch was ranked "very important" by 48.6 percent of the respondents; the executive branch, by 37.5 percent. However, the federal courts were identified as "very important" by a mere 20 percent of the respondents.[9]

These data paint a picture that departs quite strikingly from the image of profligate litigation by liberal organizations conjured by critics. My interviews with organization officers corroborate and help explain these findings and are in keeping with work by William Haltom and Michael McCann (2004) that shows that concerns about a litigation explosion or crisis are vastly overblown. In a statement that was typical of the sentiments of many officers I interviewed, the executive director of a women's labor organization emphasized the centrality of her organization's work

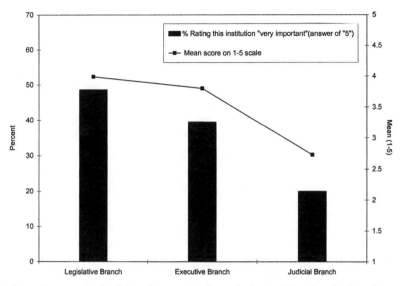

**Fig. 5.1.** Importance of each branch as a target of organizations' activity. Organization officers were asked, "On a scale of 1 to 5, if 1 is 'not important' and 5 is 'very important,' how important is each of the following as a target of your organization's activity?" Data in the columns reflect the percentage of respondents giving the answer "5" (data from SNESJO).

targeting Congress and made clear that her group targets the courts only as a last resort. "On a day-to-day basis," she explained, her organization spends much more time lobbying Congress than it does on any other activity. Explaining that her group does not shy away completely from the courts but rather reserves this option for occasions when it seems most important, she continued, "We do get involved when it looks like it's important to us to get involved in court action too." But the organization does so, she added, "to a lesser extent."[10]

In similar fashion, the executive director of a civil rights organization stated quite bluntly, "We don't litigate." Instead, he said, his organization engages in advocacy "primarily through federal legislation" as well as "administration policies of the executive branch."[11] Most explicitly, the president of a large labor organization explained that his organization prefers "to stay out of court" because the courts "are packed" with members who are unfriendly to labor and are therefore unfair. As a consequence, he explained, his organization pursues "the legislative solution first." Only "if all else fails," he continued, will his organization take what he characterized as its "fight" to court. He went on to explain that he thought that the courts were not the great protectors of minority rights that they are portrayed to be in the public imagination. Instead, he claimed, they are actually a source of injustice. "Labor unions," he argued, "do not receive the same considerations from courts as corporations. It's funny when the courts say that they're the last stand of justice for the people."[12]

These sentiments about the preferences for legislative and, to a lesser degree, executive tactics are emblematic of the ways in which most interviewees characterized their use of the courts. Numerous respondents certainly emphasized that many Supreme Court rulings represent extremely important turning points in establishing rights for their constituencies. However, almost everyone also emphasized that judicial strategies are not a panacea and stressed that the courts can be just as hostile to their arguments and goals as the other branches, depending on the policy at issue and the partisan and ideological composition of the institution in question. In some cases, many of them argued, other branches are actually more amenable than the courts are to their claims.

The comments of the executive director of a civil rights organization are illustrative of this point. "Given the importance of what the courts have meant to the modern civil rights movement," he began, "we have to fight or at least ensure that our views are known and are respected" in the judicial branch. However, he continued, "sometimes legal challenges to existing civil rights legislation require legislative action to rectify them." For example, he explained, "The Supreme Court came down in 1989 with a series of seven decisions that, when taken together, made a huge hole in the fabric of civil rights enforcement. The civil rights community's response was to develop the Civil Rights Act of 1991, ultimately, to reverse those decisions." The bill passed, he said, and it made "a dramatic change in civil rights law" by overriding the detrimental Supreme Court decisions of 1989. "That was a priority," he said, "that was dictated by [the unfriendly actions of] the Supreme Court."[13]

The vice president of a women's organization referenced a similar chain of events. Specifically, she argued that the Supreme Court had issued a series of decisions that betrayed what she characterized as a very "cramped" reading of Title VII, the section of the 1964 Civil Rights Act that prohibits employment discrimination on the basis of race, color, sex, religion, and national origin. To strengthen workplace antidiscrimination protections, organizations lobbied hard to include the provisions in the 1987 Civil Rights Restoration Act and the 1991 Civil Rights Act that "fixed" the results of the Supreme Court's rulings, restoring the protections against employment discrimination that had been decimated by a series of Supreme Court decisions in the 1980s. Most notably, this respondent characterized this set of circumstances as one in which the Court and Congress reversed the roles commonly associated with each one, with Congress playing the role of the institution of last recourse and protector of minority rights in the face of Supreme Court decisions that undermined antidiscrimination laws.[14]

The foregoing statements suggest that ambivalence about court targeting might be time-bound and tied to the political opportunities and ideological makeup of each branch, as well as to the related receptivity of each branch to the claims of the marginalized groups. Indeed, the period covered by this study (1990–2000) was one during which there was a Democratic administration for eight of ten years (1992–2000), as well as a Democratically controlled House of Representatives and Senate for four years (1990–1994). In spite of President Clinton's two appointments, the period of the study also was marked by an increasingly conservative Supreme Court, especially when compared to that of the Warren Court era (1953–69; see Baum 2001; Spriggs and Wahlbeck 1997).[15] This political context might have dampened the propensity of organizations to pursue judicial strategies while boosting their targeting of the administrative and legislative branches.[16]

Political opportunity and ideology are not the only factors affecting organizations' choices of targets, however. In addition to comments related to political opportunities and about feeling unwelcome by the courts or about the limitations of targeting the judiciary, many interviewees claimed that they quite consciously restrained their use of litigation for a range of reasons particular to organizations that have limited resources. For example, the chair of the board of an African American organization explained that while his group used to have seventeen lawyers on staff, at the time of our interview it had only four. As a consequence, the organization has had to roll back its use of litigation as an advocacy strategy—to the detriment, he felt, of the needs of its constituents. The organization, he said, "must get five letters a week from people who want legal help . . . we can't file a lawsuit every time we think a lawsuit needs to be had. Sometimes we can find a firm that will do it pro bono and if we can, we'll do it. If we can't, we just have to go begging or we can't do it."[17]

Many other respondents' statements resonated with the idea that court-related activities are simply too expensive to use capriciously or very often. In an extreme example, the executive director of an economic justice organization said that his group never targets the judiciary because "the cost of getting involved in judicial review is ridiculous. We would have standing on some issues, but we don't have a battery of lawyers to do this stuff."[18] This sentiment was echoed by the field organizer at a women's organization who said that "the thing about litigation is that it costs a lot of money in a way that using other tactics don't, so we're limited in that respect."[19] Her organization has only one lawyer on its staff, and the services of this attorney are reserved primarily for an ongoing litigation project that focuses on keeping women's health clinics open when they are the objects of antiabortion protests and blockades.

Respondents also referenced costs beyond monetary ones that are associated with court strategies (J. Wilson [1974] 1995). In particular, a number of interviewees expressed discomfort with the adversarial character of litigation, emphasizing the consequent political costs of lawsuits. For example, speaking to me in the spring of 2001, in the wake of the 2000 election of George W. Bush, the executive director of an economic justice organization explained that "the first issue is not financial cost." Rather, he said, his main concern is that "lawsuits also entail political cost. . . . Some of those lawsuits might be against the federal government or Secretary Thompson [Tommy Thompson, who was secretary of Health and Human Services during President George W. Bush's first term].[20] He is someone who is going to be a superstar in this administration. . . . I don't want to start a relationship with Thompson on lawsuits."[21]

## TRADE-OFFS AMONG INSTITUTIONS

The survey data and the interview statements make clear that advocacy organizations representing women, racial minorities, and low-income people are anything but dependent on the courts or promiscuous in their targeting of the judicial branch and that their officers do not take litigation lightly. Instead, organizations are ambivalent about targeting the judicial branch and do so at lower rates than they do the legislative and administrative branches—and at lower rates than do other types of organizations (Kollman 1998; Schlozman and Tierney 1986; Walker 1991). In addition, officers at organizations take into account a range of considerations about political opportunities, resources, and political issues and demonstrate that, all else being equal, they have a strong preference for legislative tactics. While they do litigate when Congress and the administration prove hostile to or uninterested in their policy goals, they also recognize the not infrequent hostility of the courts to their concerns as well as the political costs of such nonmajoritarian strategies. Consequently, they also make ample use of legislative and administrative strategies when faced with a hostile or uninterested judiciary, targeting Congress and the executive branch when the judicial branch undermines the rights and resources of their constituents.

Although the findings presented in the preceding sections make clear that each branch of government presents advocacy organizations with many opportunities to represent their constituents as well as an equal number of limitations on their ability to advocate successfully on their behalf, critics have concentrated mainly on pointing out the limitations of judicial strategies, particularly when these strategies are used on behalf of marginalized groups. While all of these criticisms capture important caveats regarding the use of judicial strategies, it is important to contextualize these ambivalences by assessing the shortcomings of court strategies in comparison with the strengths and weaknesses of strategies aimed at other branches.

To that end, it is illuminating to weigh some of the trade-offs associated with strategies aimed at each branch. For example, the corollary to concerns that litigation is expensive is that lobbying Congress and agencies is *inexpensive;* the corollary to concerns about the risks of court decisions that oppose majority opinion is that legislative policy outcomes inevitably *reflect* majority opinion; the corollary to concerns that such decisions stimulate backlash is that legislation and regulation *avoid* backlash; and the corollary to concerns that judicial victories are symbolic ones because they must be enforced by Congress and the administration is the suggestion that policies emanating from these latter two branches are always effectively implemented and enforced. Most centrally, the corollary to arguments that disadvantaged and unpopular groups end up worse off when advocacy organizations use judicial strategies to protect or advance their rights is that they would be *better off* if advocacy organizations refrained from using such tactics on their behalf.

Each of these assertions might be true under some limited circumstances. Some strategies for targeting the legislative branch are indeed relatively inexpensive in comparison to the costs of lawsuits and amicus curiae briefs. Individuals can "lobby" members of Congress, agencies, and even the president, at costs no greater than a phone call or a postage stamp. Organizations can and do mobilize their members and the public to engage in outside lobbying in the form of grassroots letter-writing campaigns, "lobby days," and rallies (Kollman 1998; Wright 2003). However, none of these activities is without its own financial burdens, requiring staff time as well as expenditures for publicity and coordination. Many activities that advocacy groups use to try to influence legislative outcomes, such as campaign contributions to members of Congress, are extremely expensive.

Similarly, while members of Congress are formally accountable to their constituents, we know that there are many ways in which the legislation that they produce often fails to reflect majority opinion (bracketing the difficulty of actually measuring what "majority opinion" is on any given issue). The public does not simply get what it wants from Congress. For example, in spite of the fact that a majority of Americans have for decades favored universal health insurance, legislation that would make this possible has never even approached successful passage in Congress (Jacobs and Shapiro 2000; Skocpol 1997). Even when Congress does produce legislation that coincides with the policy preferences of popular majorities, these laws, like many court rulings, are often more symbolic than substantive (Mayhew 1974). As such, they allow legislators "to make broad appeals to an only half-interested national public while providing loopholes to electorally important interests that pay close attention to legislation and often resist the public policy" (Frymer 2006, 131).

In addition to failing to pass meaningful policies that the public desires, when legislators suspect that their constituents will *object* to legislation that they themselves support, bills often are introduced and passed without much formal consideration or public discussion. In such cases, legislators try to keep pending legislation out of the public eye to the extent possible by, for instance, attaching unpopular initiatives to other legislation. For example, members of Congress routinely attach riders about nongermane policy issues to spending bills. These riders would be likely to fail if they were brought to a vote as stand-alone bills, but they often succeed when they are attached to bills that members are eager to pass or that the president is reluctant to veto (Sinclair 2000). In recent years, such riders have been used to impose new restrictions on abortion and to waive environmental regulations.

Members of Congress also can avoid addressing issues by crafting legislation that is vague and then delegating interpretation and enforcement of this legislation to administrative agencies. Even more relevant to the discussion here, Frymer (2006) argues that rather than passing civil rights legislation directly, Congress often has responded to pressure for such legislation by instead passing laws that explicitly authorize suits by private parties to enforce regulations, that allow greater court oversight of the administrative process, and that provide attorneys' fees and damage awards "for potential plaintiffs." In so doing, members of Congress distance themselves from these policies and essentially delegate "the primary role in [civil rights] enforcement" to less-majoritarian lawyers and courts (Frymer 2006, 135).

Members of Congress also can reduce attention to pending legislation by minimizing the number of hearings related to a bill (M. Smith 2000). The Telecommunications Act of 1996, for example, was the most extensive overhaul of the regulations governing media ownership since 1934. Among the many things it did was to increase the number of television stations that can be owned by one group, loosen restrictions on foreign ownership of radio stations, and eliminate the ownership limits on the number of radio stations (although there are still some limits on the number that can be owned within one market). The act also made it more difficult for citizens' groups to challenge the licenses of radio and television stations, and, by embedding within it the Communications Decency Act of 1996, mandated that the industry "develop a ratings system to identify violent, sexual and indecent or otherwise objectionable programming" (Messere n.d.). The provision of the act that eventually generated the most controversy was what became known as the "digital spectrum giveaway." As its nickname suggests, this provision allowed the Federal Communications Commission (FCC) to allocate extra spectrum for the creation of advanced television free of charge to existing broadcasters. In spite of these major changes, the law was passed by both chambers of Congress and signed into law by President Clinton with almost no media coverage or public hearings (Rich 2005). Executive actions are equally susceptible to accusations of stealthiness, exemplified by President Bill Clinton's Presidential Task Force on Health Care Reform, which many observers argued suffered from a lack of transparency (Skocpol 1997). More recently, the Bush administration's National Energy Policy Development Group (NEPDG, commonly known as the Energy Task Force) was accused of backroom dealing when it refused to reveal the names of the advisers to the group.[22] Evidence of the frequency with which President George W. Bush has used "signing statements" (estimated at more than 750 by the middle of his second term) has drawn new attention to the ways in which such statements can be used by presidents as a line-item veto that quietly but effectively nullifies portions of many laws without having to veto them.[23]

Arguments about the lack of democratic legitimacy of court action are challenged further by data indicating that, generally speaking, the public actually has *less* trust in Congress than it does in the courts. According to the May 23–25, 2005, Gallup Poll for example, 8 percent of respondents said that they had "a great deal of trust and confidence" in the "Legislative branch, consisting of the U.S. Senate and House of Representatives," while twice as many (16 percent) said that they had a great deal of trust and confidence in "the Judicial branch, headed by the U.S. Supreme Court."[24] When considered alongside low rates of voter turnout in congressional elections, it is hard to characterize legislative politics as a model of majoritarian legitimacy.

Assumptions that backlash can be prevented by pursuing policy goals through legislative rather than judicial channels are similarly tenuous. For example, the New Deal legislation that created Aid to Dependent Children and a wide rage of regulations of the financial industry have been the objects of public and legislative opposition almost since their inception. Public ire was similarly piqued in 1989 by congressional legislation that imposed a surtax for Medicare's catastrophic health insurance (Kollman 1998). More recently, in 2005, there was widespread public opposition to legislation aimed at preventing the removal of a gastric feeding tube from Terri Schiavo, a Florida woman who collapsed in her home in 1990. The intervention of Republican members of Congress and Florida Governor Jeb Bush in a dispute among family members over discontinuing life support for Schiavo, diagnosed in 1993 as being in a persistent vegetative state, was widely criticized as the partisan political exploitation of a family tragedy more appropriately resolved in the courts. Backlash against executive regulations and initiatives is similarly common.

As these examples demonstrate, problems of financial costs, nonmajoritarianism, and backlash are not confined to the products of the judicial branch but are instead endemic to the policies and practices of all branches. These problems are particularly evident when the policies in question are intended to benefit or protect disadvantaged and unpopular groups. As such, these concerns should inform our evaluations of *all* advocacy activity on behalf of these groups—not just advocacy through the courts. While we should not dismiss anxieties about costs, legitimacy, democracy, and backlash connected to the nonmajoritarian character of the court, it is equally important not to idealize the representativeness or legitimacy of policies that emanate from the other two branches of the federal government. Castigating court tactics as uniquely costly and antidemocratic presupposes that the processes and outputs of other political institutions are inherently and inevitably inexpensive, representative, democratic, and legitimate. As Frymer reminds us, however, such presuppositions are premised on what he characterizes as a "formalistic" logic of legislative accountability. In this formulation, the fact that "people can vote for legislators" but "cannot vote for federal judges" is taken to mean that "legislators more directly represent the will of the people" (2006, 129). While acknowledging that legislators are not perfect, this logic nonetheless assumes that they are reliably accountable and ignores "the myriad ways in which elected branches are themselves far from representative, both for the well-organized and the disadvantaged." Even when acting "democratically," he argues, "legislators do not 'represent' all sides equally" (Frymer 2005, 4).

This last point about the limits of representative democracy is particularly relevant for disadvantaged groups. Majority rule constitutes one important element of a democratic polity and a legitimate government, but it is not the only element (Frymer 2006). As Lani Guinier reminds us about the limits of majoritarianism, "The majority should enjoy a majority of power, but the minority should also enjoy some power too" (1994, 152). Though far from perfect, the relative isolation of the courts from electoral pressures does allow them to play a distinctive role in protecting and representing unpopular groups in the United States in ways that have allowed populations such as women, racial minorities, religious minorities, and most recently sexual minorities to "enjoy some power" and to more fully participate in and benefit from democratic institutions and outcomes (Frymer 2006; Guinier 1994; Huber and Gordon 2004). As a consequence, for generations, marginalized groups and their advocates in organizations such as the NAACP LDF, the National Organization for Women Legal Defense Fund (NOW LDEF), the American Civil Liberties Union (ACLU), and, in the case described at the outset of this chapter, GLAAD, have turned to the courts for protection when public opinion and elected officials, who are subject to majoritarian preferences, have failed to protect them or act in their interests. Moreover, elected officials *themselves* have relied on the countermajoritarian courts to protect and enhance the rights of marginalized groups when they did not have the ability or the will to do so themselves (Frymer 2006). And indeed, certain legal victories have marked major turning points in the advancement of the rights of underrepresented groups. Those victories have played an extremely important role in the improved social, political, and economic positions of these groups, achieving many advances that would not have been possible through legislative or executive channels. As legal scholar Burt Neuborne argues,

> Over the past fifty years, progressives, in close partnership with the courts, have helped to reinvent this nation, moving from the deeply racist and homophobic 1950s characterized by widespread misogyny, frequent eruptions of police violence, ongoing acts of religious intolerance and recurring spasms of political repression to a contemporary America that, while far from perfect, is at least a place where toleration—racial, political, religious, gender and sexual—has become a mainstream value. (Neuborne 2005, 23)

In this light, judicial activism enhances rather than compromises democracy, and organizations have a responsibility to make their case in court for disadvantaged groups when other channels are unresponsive. Rather than chiding advocacy organizations for undemocratically relying on courts, for squandering their scarce resources, and for stimulating backlash against themselves and their constituents, and rather than asking whether it is right or wrong *in general* to risk backlash or expend resources on court actions, we should consider *the conditions under which* organizations pursue a less-majoritarian route and target the courts, rather than how much they do so. Considered in conjunction with the finding that organizations target the judicial branch at rates far lower than the ones at which they target the legislative and executive branches, the question becomes: Do organizations use the courts in the "right" way—to protect the most vulnerable and unpopular groups when other branches fail to do so, saving the associated resources and political and social capital for the constituencies that need them the most? In other words, what proportion of their court-related resources and energy do organizations devote to addressing issues that affect intersectionally disadvantaged subgroups of their constituencies?

## INSTITUTIONAL TARGETS AND INTERSECTIONAL DISADVANTAGE

To answer this question, I examine the variation in institutional targets of advocacy using a set of questions in the SNESJO that asks respondents to select the federal-level political institution (legislative, executive, or judicial branch) that is the most frequent target of their efforts on each of the

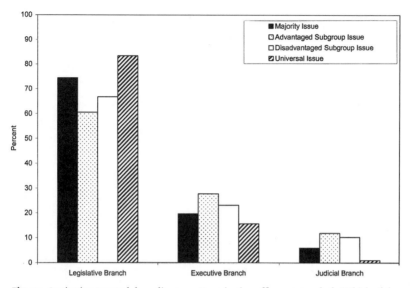

**Fig. 5.2.** Institution targeted, by policy type. Organization officers were asked, "Which of the following political institutions is the most important target of your efforts in trying to influence policy on [the policy issue in question]?" Data in the columns reflect the percentage of respondents selecting that branch for the policy issue in question. The question was posed so that respondents had to select only one of the institutions (data from SNESJO).

four policy issues designated for their organization.[25] As is the case with the general levels of institutional targeting that were presented earlier, the answers to the policy-specific questions reveal that the percentage of organizations targeting the courts is quite low regardless of the issue type in question (see fig. 5.2). However, looking at these results more closely reveals greater complexity. In particular, the data show that rates of court use vary markedly by issue type: while the legislative branch is the most frequent target of activity for all issues, organizations target the courts approximately twice as often when it comes to issues affecting advantaged or disadvantaged subgroups than they do when comes to majority issues. Indeed, there is a clear progression in the extent of this activity that increases steadily as we move from universal issues on the low end to advantaged-subgroup issues on the high end.

Specifically, while only 1 percent of organizations reported that the courts are most important when pursuing the universal issue, 6 percent of organizations claim that the courts are the most important target of their activities when it comes to majority issues, 10 percent target the courts for the disadvantaged-subgroup issue, and almost 12 percent claim that the

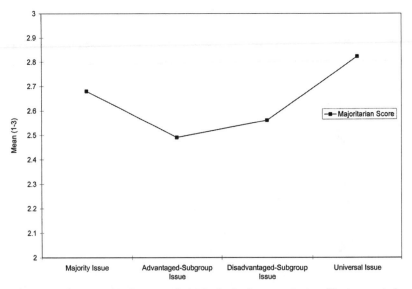

**Fig. 5.3.** Tendency to target the most majoritarian institution. Organization officers were asked, "Which of the following political institutions is the most important target of your efforts in trying to influence policy on [the policy issue in question]?" Answers are coded "1" for the least majoritarian judicial branch, "2" for the executive branch, and "3" for the most majoritarian legislative branch. The majoritarianism scale is calculated based on the average scores for each issue type (data from SNESJO).

courts are the most important target of their activities on the advantaged-subgroup issue. As such, court tactics are most prevalent when it comes to advantaged-subgroup issues. Even though organizations still direct the bulk of their efforts at Congress when it comes to these issues, legislative activity constitutes a far smaller proportion of their activity and judicial activity a far greater proportion of their activity for advantaged-subgroup issues than for any of the other issue types.

Thinking about these results in the context of concerns about the majoritarianism of the channels used to pursue policy goals, a pattern becomes evident: On a scale of 1 to 3, where 1 is the least majoritarian judiciary and 3 is the most majoritarian legislature, the universal issue scores the highest, followed by the majority issue, then by the disadvantaged-subgroup issue, with a slight lead over the advantaged-subgroup issue, which comes in last (see fig. 5.3).[26] Although there are some exceptions, the patterns of targeting and majoritarianism scores generally hold across the various organization types.

The pattern evident in these results is notable because it shows that organizations reserve less-majoritarian tactics for policy issues that affect a subgroup of their constituents, providing further evidence that they do not play fast and loose with such strategies. Instead, officers at organizations reserve such tactics for issues that will be more difficult to pursue were they subjected to majority preferences.

## MULTIVARIATE ANALYSIS

In order to examine whether this same pattern in targeting obtains if we take into account other possible influences on organizations' choices of targets, I used ordered logit regression analysis.[27] The dependent variable in this model (*Target*) is the measure (described previously) of which of the three branches—judicial, executive, or legislative—organizations target in pursuing particular public policy issues.

I regressed this variable on a range of independent variables that tap several concepts that are likely at play in determining which institution advocacy organizations target in their advocacy activities. To examine the relationship between targeting institutions and policy type, I used the dummy variables (described in chapter 2) that measure the type of policy issue under consideration (*Universal issue*, *Majority issue*, *Advantaged-subgroup issue*, and *Disadvantaged-subgroup issue*).[28] Factors other than majoritarianism and policy type are, of course, also likely to influence the choices that organizations make about which institution they will target on a given issue.[29] They include, for example, organizations' general preferences for one institution over another, the level of controversy surrounding an issue, the political party in control of each branch, and whether there are preexisting opportunities to address an issue in a given branch. For example, organizations likely will target more-majoritarian institutions when they perceive public and constituent support, while they will be more likely to target less-majoritarian branches if an issue is unpopular or controversial. To account for this possibility, the model includes measures of the proportion of their constituents that is concerned about the issue (*Constituents concerned*) and the proportion that that agrees with an organization's position on the issue (*Constituents agree*), as well measures of the level of controversy surrounding the issue (*Controversial*) and of the proportion of the public that agrees with the organization's position on the issue (*Public agrees*).

Another likely influence on choices of target is an organization's sensitivity to the political opportunity structure, in particular to the partisan and ideological makeup of each possible target and to its consequent receptivity to the claims of marginalized groups (Hansford 2004; Kingdon 1995; McAdam 1982; Solberg and Waltenberg 2006; Walker 1991). I included two sets of variables to measure these aspects of political opportunity when it comes to activity on a particular issue. First, to examine the effects of sensitivity to partisan shifts within each institution, I included a measure of "partisan sensitivity" based on survey questions that ask respondents whether shifts in party control have altered their targeting of each branch (*Sensitivity to partisan shifts*). By selecting only issues that are already on the political agenda of each institution, the survey design itself controls to some degree for the effects of the political opportunities within each branch. However, to examine whether the variation in the opportunities resulting from the salience of issues on the political agenda of each institution has an effect on organizations' choice of target, I also included measures of the salience of each issue within each branch (*Judicial salience, Legislative salience* and *Executive salience*). As I explained in chapter 4, these measures control for the number of entries for the issue in *Congressional Quarterly*, the "Supreme Court Roundup" feature of the *New York Times*, and the *Federal Register* during the period covered by the study.[30]

The model also includes several controls for organizational features and resources that are likely to affect the choice of target. Jack Walker (1991), for example, found that organizations that rely on a few major patrons are less likely to make use of court tactics than organizations with more varied funding sources, so I also included a scale that tallies organizations' total number of reported sources of financial support (*Number of sources of support*).[31] Walker also found that organizations with large staffs are more likely to use the courts, so I included a measure of how many staff members are employed by the organization. In order to account for the fact that organizational resources help determine the institutions that organizations elect to target, I included controls for whether the organizations have lawyers on staff (which could make them more likely to target the courts; *Legal staff*), and whether they are registered to lobby Congress (which could make them more likely to target this institution; *Registered to lobby*; Solberg and Waltenberg 2006). To take into account the effects of organizations' general institution-targeting proclivities, I included variables based on respondents' answers to questions that asked them to rate, on a 1-to-5 scale, how important each institution is to their organization's overall advocacy activities (*Congress, Administration, Courts*).[32]

Finally, the period of the study coincides with a series of important and high-profile federal cases dealing with affirmative action in higher education, most notably *Hopwood v. Texas*, a case decided in the United States Court of Appeals for the Fifth Circuit in 1996, in which a white female applicant to the University of Texas Law School sued the university, claiming that she was denied admission to the law school because it gave preferential treatment to black and Mexican American applicants in its admissions process.[33] Because affirmative action in higher education is the designated advantaged-subgroup issue for many organizations in the sample, I ran the analysis a second time, excluding cases in which affirmative action was the policy issue in question. The results are presented in the next section, and they remain substantively unchanged (except that the measure of the importance of the courts to organizations' overall advocacy activities does not reach statistical significance in the alternative model).[34]

## FINDINGS

Table 5.2 presents the results of the multivariate analysis. A negative sign on a coefficient indicates a less-majoritarian effect and a greater chance of targeting the courts. A positive sign on a coefficient indicates a more-majoritarian effect and a greater chance of targeting the legislative branch.

These results reinforce the findings indicated by the means and percentages and reveal that even once we take into account other influences, organizations' choices of target do indeed vary by issue type, and they do so in ways that underserve intersectionally disadvantaged subgroups.[35] In addition, the results show that this variation cannot be explained by factors such as political opportunity, partisan sensitivity, or organizational resources. While some of these other factors certainly affect organizations' propensities to target each branch, controlling for all other effects, the measures of issue type are all strongly significant, showing that targeting is strongly influenced by the relationship between the majoritarianism of the institution and the issue type in question.

The negative signs on the coefficients for the three issue types indicate that each one is less likely to be pursued through the legislative branch (and more likely to be pursued judicially) than the universal issue, which is the reference category. The largest of these three coefficients is for the advantaged-subgroup issues, showing that even once we control for other

TABLE 5.2 Predicting targets of activity

| TARGET | VARIABLE MEAN (STD. DEV.) | ALL CASES | | AFFIRMATIVE ACTION EXCLUDED | |
|---|---|---|---|---|---|
| | | ORDERED LOGIT COEFFICIENT | ROBUST STANDARD ERROR | ORDERED LOGIT COEFFICIENT | ROBUST STANDARD ERROR |
| Majority issue | 0.250 (0.433) | −0.778* | 0.464 | −0.732* | 0.474 |
| Advantaged-subgroup issue | 0.250 (0.433) | −1.071*** | 0.383 | −1.134*** | 0.421 |
| Disadvantaged-subgroup issue | 0.250 (0.433) | −0.860* | 0.425 | −0.785* | 0.437 |
| Congress | 3.993 (1.186) | 0.662*** | 0.142 | 0.662*** | 0.150 |
| Administration | 3.790 (1.185) | −0.350** | 0.136 | −0.403** | 0.143 |
| Courts | 2.726 (0.502) | −0.171* | 0.098 | −0.142 | 0.101 |
| Sensitivity to Partisan Shifts | 0.367 (0.482) | −0.092 | 0.239 | −0.287 | 0.269 |
| Public agrees | 3.121 (0.983) | −0.069 | 0.112 | −0.030 | 0.125 |
| Constituents agree | 4.129 (1.108) | 0.008 | 0.118 | 0.024 | 0.136 |
| Controversial | 3.628 (1.214) | −0.099 | 0.106 | −0.076 | 0.115 |
| Number of sources of support | 3.552 (1.713) | 0.148** | 0.075 | 0.111* | 0.082 |
| Number of paid staff | 39.406 (82.638) | −0.002 | 0.001 | −0.001 | 0.002 |
| Legal staff | 0.318 (0.466) | −0.305 | 0.301 | −0.364 | 0.330 |

| | | | | | |
|---|---|---|---|---|---|
| Registered to lobby | 0.341 (0.474) | 0.901* | 0.321 | 0.892** | 0.346 |
| Legislative salience | 459.580 (410.174) | 0.002*** | 0.000 | 0.002*** | 0.000 |
| Executive salience | 125.223 (172.398) | −0.003** | 0.001 | −0.003** | 0.001 |
| Judicial salience[a] | 1.091 (0.968) | 0.027 | 0.168 | −0.002 | 0.172 |
| Initial log likelihood | | −433.31 | | −343.66 | |
| Log likelihood at convergence | | −368.48 | | −295 | |
| Chi-square | | 104.72*** | | 81.16*** | |
| (degrees of freedom) | | (17) | | (17) | |
| Cut point 1 | | −2.343 | | −2.5005 | 1.0972 |
| Cut point 2 | | −0.391 | | −0.4154 | 1.09894 |
| Pseudo $R^2$ | | 0.15 | | 0.14 | |
| N | | 564 | | 482 | |

*Sources:* SNESJO; *Congressional Quarterly*; the *New York Times* "Supreme Court Roundup"; the *Congressional Record*; and the *Federal Register*.

*Note:* Coefficients are Ordered Logit coefficients. Each case represents the target of one organization's activity on one of the four issues about which they were asked. Issues on which organizations were not active are not included, as there would be no possible target of activity in such cases. Robust standard errors (RSE) are used to correct for clustering of the standard errors as there are four observations for each organization. The dependent variable uses responses to the survey question: "Which of the following political institutions is the most important target of your efforts in trying to influence policy on [the issue in question]?" The dependent variable measures which of the three branches—judicial, executive, or legislative—organizations target in pursuing each policy issue. Answers were coded "1" for the courts, the least majoritarian; "2" for the executive branch; and "3" for Congress, the most majoritarian. A negative sign on a coefficient indicates decreasing majoritarianism effect, and a greater chance of targeting the courts. A positive sign indicates a more majoritarian effect, and a greater chance of targeting the legislative branch (targeting the administrative branch falls in between these two). Variable Inflation Factors (VIFs) and tolerance levels show no signs of multicollinearity.

[a] *Legislative salience* is calculated based on information from *Congressional Quarterly* (1990, 1993, 1996, and 1999) and the *Congressional Record* (1990–2000); *Executive salience* is calculated based on information from the *Federal Register* (1990–2000); and *Judicial salience* is calculated based on information from the *New York Times* "Supreme Court Roundup" (1990–2000).

* Relationship is significant at $p < .10$; ** Relationship is significant at $p < .05$; *** Relationship is significant at $p < .01$

effects, organizations are more likely to target the court in the case of such issues than they are for any other issue type. The disadvantaged-subgroup issue is the second most likely issue type to be pursued judicially. The majority issue has the smallest slope effect of the three measures, indicating that it is the most likely to be pursued legislatively (other than the universal issue). These results hold for both membership and nonmembership organizations.

That organizations target the courts more often to pursue their goals on both types of subgroup issues confirms the finding that advocacy groups do indeed put the judiciary to the use for which it was intended, reserving their use of this branch for issues that are less amenable to majoritarian legislative strategies. The most remarkable finding, however, is that even once we account for a range of other influences on organizations' targeting of each branch, they are most likely to use the courts when it comes to advantaged-subgroup issues—even more likely than they are in cases of issues affecting disadvantaged-subgroups.[36]

## PREDICTED PROBABILITIES

The meanings of the regression results come through even more clearly if we convert these coefficient estimates into more decipherable probabilities. This conversion allows us to predict the chances that an organization will target each branch and to examine these chances as they vary by issue type (see fig. 5.4).[37] These predicted probabilities confirm that Congress is, overwhelmingly, the most likely target of advocacy activity for each of the four types of public policy issues. However, when issues affect subgroups, weak or strong, organizations are more likely to use the courts to pursue their goals than they are when issues affect a majority of their constituents. Specifically, there is a 44 percent chance that an organization will target the legislative branch when it is working on a majority issue.[38] This chance decreases to 43 percent if the issue in question affects an intersectionally disadvantaged subgroup of their constituency and decreases even further to 39 percent if the issue in question affects an *advantaged* subgroup of the constituency. Conversely, there is about a 23 percent chance that the judicial branch will be the focus of attention in the case of an issue that affects an advantaged subgroup. The probability of focusing on the courts in cases when an issue affects a *disadvantaged* subgroup is only about 19 percent, which further decreases to 18 percent in the case of a majority issue.

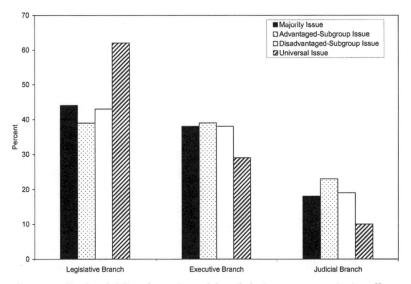

**Fig. 5.4.** Predicted probability of targeting each branch, by issue type. Organization officers were asked, "Which of the following political institutions is the most important target of your efforts in trying to influence policy on [the policy issue in question]?" The columns represent the probability of targeting each branch while holding the other variables in the model constant (data from SNESJO).

Although the differences between these percentages might appear small, they are statistically significant and, more importantly, have substantive implications. Most crucially, the disparities between the probabilities of targeting the courts in the case of advantaged-subgroup issues and disadvantaged-subgroup issues make a bigger difference than we might appreciate at first glance. As I showed in chapter 4, a great deal of attention is devoted to advantaged-subgroup issues, while very little attention is devoted to disadvantaged-subgroup issues, in the first place. As a consequence, the 23 percent chance of court activity in the case of advantaged-subgroup issues is 23 percent of a very high level of activity, while the 19 percent chance of court activity in the case of disadvantaged-subgroup issues is 19 percent of a very *low* level of activity. As such, the substantive implications of these probabilities are quite striking: organizations are more likely to target the courts when issues affect subgroups within their constituencies, but even so, they expend a far greater proportion of their court-oriented resources on behalf of advantaged subgroups of their constituencies. That organizations save their use of court tactics for subgroups is understandable and might be considered congruent with the constitutional role of the courts as protectors of minority rights within a majoritarian democracy. However, it is the fact that organizations are most likely to target both the courts and the executive branch on behalf of advantaged subgroups of their constituencies than they are when it comes to disadvantaged subgroups that is most remarkable. In fact, once we take other factors into account, disadvantaged-subgroup and majority issues are almost equally likely to be pursued through the courts. As such, this finding has important implications for the quality of representation afforded to intersectionally disadvantaged groups.

Specifically, this imbalance in the use of judicial strategies is alarming because it shows that many of the same factors that lead to low levels of advocacy on behalf of intersectionally marginalized subgroups also depress the use of the tactics that are necessary to help these groups overcome majoritarian biases against them. As we saw in chapter 4, officers at advocacy organizations underestimate the impact of issues affecting intersectionally disadvantaged subgroups of their constituencies and overestimate the impact of issues that affect advantaged subgroups. The analysis here suggests that these erroneous estimates increase their willingness to bear the financial costs and political risks of court tactics on behalf of advantaged subgroups because they assume that the potential benefits of these costs will have a broad impact. As such, the concentration of judicial targeting on behalf advantaged subgroups reinforces, rather than alleviates, the low levels of representation for intersectionally disadvantaged groups.

## OTHER FACTORS AT WORK

The regression analysis and predicted probabilities demonstrate clearly that variations in organizations' institutional targeting are strongly related to the relationship between the majoritarianism of each branch and the issue type under consideration. The analysis also shows that other factors help determine the targets of organizations' advocacy activities. I discuss the roles of these other factors in the following section.

### INSTITUTIONAL PROCLIVITIES

First, the three variables rating organizations' general use of each institution show that overall inclinations to target a particular branch also influence the chances that they will target that branch when it comes to a particular policy issue. For example, if organizations tend to focus their advocacy efforts on members of Congress, they also are more likely to target Congress for each individual public policy issue, regardless of whether the issue is a majority issue or an advantaged-subgroup issue. Organizations that tend to focus on either the administration or the courts, on the other hand, are less likely to target their policy advocacy on the four issues in question at Congress.[39] The fact that other variables remain significant even after controlling for these general preferences for targeting each branch shows that although organizations do have preferences when it comes to choosing institutional targets for their advocacy activities on policy issues, this is only one of many influences on their tactical choices for individual policies.

## INTERNAL PRESSURES, EXTERNAL OPPORTUNITIES

The effects of the variables that measure key aspects of the political environment and opportunities reinforce the importance of issue type as a determinant of institutional target. For example, while we might expect that organizations will pursue more controversial issues through the courts rather than subject such issues to more-majoritarian venues, the variable measuring the level of controversy surrounding an issue is not significant (though the slope is negative, as we would expect). In addition, though positive, the measures of both the proportion of an organization's constituents that is concerned about an issue and the proportion that is affected by an issue do not reach conventional levels of statistical significance. The measure of partisan sensitivity is not significant either, although it is negative and therefore in the direction that Walker's findings imply that it should be.[40] The controls for the salience of issues within each institution yield mixed results. The measure of issue salience in the judicial branch has no significant effect, reflecting the fact that an organization can file suits regardless of whether the courts have expressed prior interest in a particular issue. The effect of the measure of salience within the legislative branch is positive and significant, indicating that when an issue is being addressed within the Congress, organizations are indeed more likely to target their advocacy at that more-majoritarian branch. Similarly, the effect of the measure of salience within the administrative branch is slightly but significantly negative, demonstrating an increased likelihood of targeting that *less*-majoritarian branch when opportunities arise there.[41]

Taken together, the results for these variables suggest that factors inside an organization as well as in its external political environment matter a great deal in determining the targets of organizations' advocacy efforts. However, the results also indicate that when all of the issues in question are on the political agenda and being dealt with at relatively similar points in time, the type of policy issue at stake matters a great deal in determining the target for particular policy issues (Hansford 2004).

## INSTITUTIONAL RESOURCES

The variables controlling for institutional resources yield mixed results. First, the number of sources of funding on which an organization relies is positive and significantly related to the majoritarian scale. In other words, the more sources of funding to which an organization has access, the more likely it is to target the legislative branch, suggesting that reliance on one large donor increases the likelihood of court action, as Walker (1991) found. In addition, the number of staff members has a significantly negative relationship with the dependent variable, showing that even at the level of individual public policy issues, having a larger staff increases the use of court strategies. Being registered to lobby Congress is positively and significantly related to the dependent variable, indicating that having the capacity to lobby formally increases the likelihood that organizations will target Congress on a given issue. In a surprising result, however, having lawyers on staff is not significantly related to increased use of court tactics (though the slope is negative and also significantly related at the bivariate level, indicating that there may be some relationship; see Solberg and Waltenberg 2006). This result holds even if primarily legal organizations (for example, legal defense funds for whom litigation is a central activity) are excluded from the analysis.

The interviews suggest that the lack of a significant effect of having lawyers on staff is due to the fact that many organizations employ lawyers to do policy work rather than strictly legal work. That even organizations that employ many lawyers make infrequent use of the courts provides further evidence that these organizations are not excessively litigious. For example, the vice president at a women's organization explained that while most of the staff members at her organization have legal training, "a lot of the work that we do is policy analysis and is relevant to . . . legislation in Congress or in the states. We do a lot of public speaking and public education work . . . on public policy issues which may or may not be from a legal point of view."[42] Similarly, the chair of the board of a racial minority bar association said that in spite of being comprised almost entirely of lawyers, his organization was not well positioned to get involved in lawsuits. "Most often," he explained, "our organization is involved in . . . pre-rulemaking meetings, in the process of formulating bills, regulations, et cetera with executive branch people or congressional people."[43] In spite of being an organization of and for lawyers, this organization still focuses on the legislative and executive branches.

## CONCLUSION

Together with the results of the examination of organizations' general targeting of each branch and the findings in previous work, this analysis demonstrates that compared to their targeting of other branches, advocacy organizations representing marginalized groups do not rely heavily on the courts to advocate for social change or to protect minority rights. It is the circumstances under which organizations target the courts, rather than particularly high levels of judicial targeting, that are remarkable. Organizations are more likely to target the legislative and administrative branches and to invest their court-related energy and resources in issues affecting subgroups of their constituencies, but a disproportionately large share of this activity goes to advantaged rather than disadvantaged subgroups. As such, these findings reveal that the disproportionately high *levels* of activity on behalf of advantaged groups that I found in chapter 4 are matched by a disproportionately heavy use of *nonmajoritarian* activity on their behalf as well. Although the differences are not immense, they are unmistakable, and they show clearly that organizations devote a disproportionately large share of their time, money, energy, and political capital to issues that benefit those constituents who are already the best off. Thus, patterns of institutional targeting often exacerbate rather than alleviate the inequities in representation for intersectionally disadvantaged groups.

## CODA: BEYOND VICTIM BLAMING

In his 2005 *New York Times* op-ed piece cited earlier, Paul Starr (2005) wrote that gay organizations, "dissatisfied with compromise legislation on civil unions and partner benefits . . . thought they could get from judges . . . what the electorate was not yet ready to give." The results of this strategy, he claimed, were "bans on same-sex marriage passing in eleven states and an energized conservative voting base" in the 2004 election. Starr's comments capture the widely held view that targeting courts is a strategically stealthy and antidemocratic tactic that produces backlash against marginalized groups and the politicians who advocate on their behalf. While the findings in this chapter cannot refute this characterization or address directly the question of whether litigation produces more backlash than other advocacy tactics do, the evidence that I have presented complicates the story in some significant ways. By making clear that organization officers are extremely circumspect in their targeting of the courts, the foregoing results suggest that concern about the use of litigation should be directed at the circumstances under which it is used rather than at the fact of its deployment, paying particular attention to the implications of these circumstances for intersectionally marginalized groups.

From this perspective, if there is a reason to be ambivalent about pursuing same-sex marriage rights judicially, it is that in doing so, LGBT advocacy organizations pour high levels of material and political resources into litigating an issue that many observers contend is likely to disproportionately benefit advantaged LGBT people. The harms suffered by same-sex couples by denying them the benefits of marriage are many and important, as are the harms suffered by all LGBT people resulting from the policies that codify such exclusions and from the vitriolic rhetoric that meets efforts to change these laws. However, as scholars such as Cathy Cohen, Lisa Duggen, and Dean Spade have argued, the benefits of marriage would most likely accrue mainly to conventionally coupled, normative gay men and lesbians and to those with financial means (C. Cohen 1997, 2001; Duggan 2005; Spade 2004). Same-sex marriage does less to address the compounded inequalities faced by intersectionally marginalized LGBT people, who are consequently less likely to benefit from associated victories. Moreover, if any backlash is stimulated by efforts to pursue same-sex marriage, intersectionally marginalized LGBT people are likely to bear a disproportionately high share of the negative effects because they are more vulnerable to social, political, and economic forces. Nonetheless, while intersectionally marginalized LGBT people are less likely to benefit from same-sex marriage and are more vulnerable to backlash, they are vulnerable whether this backlash is stimulated by activity targeted at the courts or at Congress.

What is troubling about using the courts to pursue same-sex marriage is not that this issue caused an electoral backlash against the Democrats. Any number of LGBT rights issues pursued through any political venue would have been equally objectionable to a large segment of the American electorate. It is neither fair nor feasible to ask that organizations representing disadvantaged groups abstain from litigation and amicus curiae activity, toiling away to turn the tide of public opinion in their favor so that it becomes possible to achieve their objectives legislatively. To hold advocates for disadvantaged groups responsible for the fact that nonmajoritarian tactics stimulate backlash against their goals is tantamount to blaming the victim. Organizations have a responsibility to represent their constituents vigorously, pursuing all possible avenues on their behalf.

Though imperfect and increasingly tenuous in light of increasing Supreme Court conservatism, legal tactics are nonetheless a key bulwark against majority tyranny. Court strategies provide access for groups whose concerns may be of no interest to, or even offensive to, the broader public, concerns that therefore will be unlikely to receive sympathetic attention from legislators. Legal strategies are therefore one important piece of the tactical arsenal necessary to protect and advance the rights and resources of disadvantaged groups whose needs are not heeded by elected representatives. Court tactics do have costs, but so do tactics associated with targeting the other two branches of the government. When legislative and executive channels do not work, or when adversaries attack important policies through litigation, advocacy groups cannot wave a white flag or wait it out until a legislative approach is feasible. A strategy that aims to change hearts and minds and win the support of a sympathetic majority is important as a long-term goal but not one that should be privileged at the expense of solidarity with and protection of marginalized groups in the present.

It is nonetheless important to reflect on the costs associated with the use of nonmajoritarian tactics, particularly if their use is concentrated on advocacy on behalf of advantaged subgroups. While we should not blame the victim or abandon unpopular groups and issues, neither should we ignore the fact that there are potential pitfalls associated with litigation as a form of advocacy. Relying as they do on less explicitly majoritarian processes than most legislative and executive approaches, judicial strategies can feed the perception that organizations are trying to contravene majority preferences by pursuing public policy changes for some subgroups of their constituencies "below the radar." In fact, in some cases, that is precisely what they are trying to do, and under many circumstances, this strategy is entirely appropriate—indeed, as I have just argued, it might even be mandated. That said, legal resources are scarce, politically costly, and financially expensive. One study estimates, for example, that there are only six thousand full-time legal services staff lawyers in the United States, enough to meet the needs of only 1.3 percent of the four million people who are eligible for free legal services (Cummings and Eagly 2001). The disproportionate use of judicial and other nonmajoritarian tactics for issues affecting *advantaged* subgroups concentrates the use of these scarce resources and the sacrifices of political capital for the benefit of groups that are already the best off.

As such, current practices reinforce the marginalization and inadequate representation of intersectionally disadvantaged subgroups and run counter to the spirit of affirmative advocacy (to be elaborated in chapter 7), which recommends that resources and activities be devoted at disproportionately high rates to the most disadvantaged groups. Applied to questions about institutional targeting, affirmative advocacy entails overallocating court tactics to issues affecting intersectionally disadvantaged subgroups. This does not mean that organizations should eschew court tactics on behalf of advantaged subgroups of their constituencies, that members of these subgroups should themselves abstain from pursuing litigation privately, or that organizations should ignore assaults on important policies such as affirmative action in higher education that provide disproportionate benefits to advantaged subgroups. As the political director of an LGBT organization explained to me, her organization did not make a proactive decision to pursue litigation to allow same-sex marriage. Instead, she said, they had to get involved because "the Republicans in Congress handed us the Defense of Marriage Act [DOMA] and then that spread like wildfire around the country." This action left her organization with what she saw as little choice but to pursue lawsuits that, they hoped, would lead to a ruling that DOMA is unconstitutional (as of this writing, this has yet to occur; see also E. Anderson 2004).[44] A similar predicament has been faced repeatedly by feminist and civil rights organizations when affirmative action programs in colleges and universities have been challenged. Nonetheless, adopting a framework within which "big guns" such as judicial strategies are allocated at higher rates to cases benefiting intersectionally disadvantaged subgroups might enhance organizations' mediation on behalf of these constituents by sending strong signals that they are willing to stand up for and expend their political capital on behalf of these subgroups (Kollman 1998).

The ways in which organizations allocate their use of judicial, legislative, and executive strategies constitute one important measure of the quality of representation that is afforded to intersectionally disadvantaged subgroups. Based on this measure, it seems that the low levels of advocacy on behalf of these subgroups are matched by less-vigorous representation as well. Examining institutional targets is not the only way to assess the vigor of representation, however. One of the many other criteria we might examine is the extent to which organizations devote their coalitional efforts to issues affecting intersectionally disadvantaged subgroups of their constituencies. Because coalitions defy the boundaries around issues and interests that usually define the policy terrain of individual organizations, such alliances offer fitting conditions for organizations to advocate on behalf of intersectionally disadvantaged groups. Chapter 6 addresses this issue, examining coalitions as another lens through which to evaluate the quality of representation afforded intersectionally disadvantaged groups.

# SIX

# Coalition and Collaboration among Advocacy Organizations

The history of the Leadership Conference on Civil Rights (LCCR) is a case study in the promises and challenges of intersectional politics. Founded in 1950, by 2006 the organization was a coalition of 192 member organizations ranging from the A. Philip Randolph Institute (APRI) and the American Association of Retired People (AARP) to the Women's International League for Peace and Freedom (WILPF) and the Zeta Phi Beta Sorority (ZBPS).[1] Established by A. Philip Randolph, founder of the Brotherhood of Sleeping Car Porters (BSCP), Roy Wilkins, who was then executive secretary of the National Association for the Advancement of Colored People (NAACP), and Arnold Aronson, a leader of the National Jewish Community Relations Advisory Council (NJCRAC), the organization has been concerned since its inception with bringing together a wide range of communities to work on an ever wider range of political issues.

In spite of the LCCR's admirable ambitions, its trajectory has not always been smooth, and the unity of the coalition has been threatened at several junctures by internal conflicts. In 1990, for example, the coalition's annual dinner was boycotted and picketed by many of its own member organizations, the result of a dispute over whether to support legislation that would repeal policies imposing sanctions on employers who hire undocumented immigrants. The LCCR had refused to take a position on the issue, but some of its member groups, including the NAACP and the American Federation of Labor–Congress of Industrial Organizations (AFL-CIO), supported employer sanctions (Quiroz-Martínez 2001). Other member organizations, including the American Civil Liberties Union (ACLU) and several Asian Pacific American and Latino organizations, objected to these policies. Boycotting the awards dinner was part of their strategy to pressure the LCCR to formally acknowledge the racially discriminatory effects of employer sanctions, to take a public stand recognizing the rights of immigrant workers as a fundamental issue of civil rights, and to convey these understandings to its constituent organizations.

The strategy was a success. In the years following the boycott, the LCCR coalition adopted a proactively progressive position on immigration and immigrants' rights, and many of its member organizations followed suit. In 2000, the executive council of the AFL-CIO reversed its long-standing position supporting restrictions on immigration and voted to support amnesty for undocumented immigrant workers. In 2006, the LCCR responded vocally to the efforts of President George W. Bush and members of the House of Representatives and the United States Senate to impose new restrictions on undocumented immigrants. The LCCR and its member organizations vigorously and publicly urged members of Congress to jettison proposed legislation such as H.R. 4437, the House bill that would criminalize undocumented immigrants by considering "unlawful presence" a crime and a felony. On March 22, 2006, the National Day of Action on Immigrant Rights, LCCR executive director Wade Henderson spoke at a press conference and encouraged lawmakers to support measures that would facilitate legalizing the status of undocumented immigrants. Verbalizing the grievances that the Asian Pacific American and Latino organizations had lodged sixteen years earlier against the LCCR's own position on this issue, Henderson castigated punitive immigration laws as creating a "two-tier society" and perpetuating "racial and ethnic discrimination."[2]

In spite of—or perhaps more accurately *because* of—conflicts over issues such as immigration, the LCCR has continued to draw together an increasing number of organizations from all corners of the social and economic justice universe. As it has grown, its agenda has expanded to reflect new understandings of the interconnectedness of an impressive array of issues ranging from affirmative action to voting rights for ex-felons, from same-sex marriage rights to Social Security, and from immigration rights to fair housing for low-income people and people of color.

As an organization comprised of other organizations, the LCCR harnesses the energy and resources of all its constituent groups, helping to coordinate their efforts in order to maximize their collective impact and political influence on issues of common concern. Moreover, as the example of its evolving position on immigration policy illustrates, the LCCR's status as a coalition gives it an exceptional capacity to mediate among its member organizations, thereby making these organizations aware of and active on issues of common interest. Under some conditions, the LCCR also is able to stimulate activity on issues that some of these organizations might not ordinarily tackle or to which they might even have been hostile were they operating entirely on their own. In these ways, the LCCR epitomizes not only the promises and possibilities but also the challenges and complications of coalitions as a source of activity and representation for intersectionally disadvantaged groups.

Coalition politics can take many forms, from sharing information to policy networking to creating formal organizational structures that endure over time (Levi and Murphy 2006; Staggenborg 1986). Some coalitions (like the LCCR) are ongoing and enduring formal alliances, while others are transient or ad hoc, focused for a short period on a particular issue or event.[3] Regardless of the specific form that they take, coalitions are "collaborative, means-oriented arrangements that permit distinct organizational entities to pool resources in order to effect change" (Levi and Murphy 2006, 654). Unlike more loosely connected networks of organizations, coalitions typically have "rules for resolving conflict and defining membership" and unite organizations in cooperative advocacy efforts, pooling their resources in solidarity with other movement sectors against common threats or to take advantage of political opportunities (Levi and Murphy 2006, 654; see also Meyer and Corrigall-Brown 2005; Van Dyke 2003). By settling internal conflicts and creating a united front, coalitions allow their member organizations to amplify their voices through cooperative efforts that address shared political interests and policy goals (Berry 1977; Esterling 1999; Evans 1991; Gamson 1975; Hathaway and Meyer 1997; Heaney 2004; Lipsky 1970; Loomis 1986; Salisbury 1983; Salisbury et al. 1987; Spalter-Roth and Schreiber 1995; Staggenborg 1986; Wilson [1974] 1995).[4] In all of these ways, coalitions allow organizations to increase their power, political influence, and, ultimately, their chances of success.

By flouting the usual boundaries around issues and interests and by bringing together organizations and movements with differing priorities, constituencies, and agendas, coalitional politics are, by definition, intersectional politics. As such, they offer a potential laboratory in which to observe the ways in which intersectionally linked fate can be nurtured among the constituents of a wide range of organizations. In their status as what one respondent went so far as to characterize as "a form of interethnic diplomacy," coalitions, by their very nature and purpose, would seem to be perfectly suited to engage in advocacy on behalf of intersectionally disadvantaged groups.[5]

Previous chapters have demonstrated that the levels and type of advocacy activity on the part of organizations representing marginalized groups combine to create a situation in which these organizations significantly underrepresent multiply marginalized subgroups and overrepresent advantaged subgroups. Organizations are far less active when it comes to issues that affect disadvantaged subgroups, and the patterns in their institutional targeting reinforce this neglect by concentrating disproportionately high levels of their expensive and politically costly court activity on overserved, relatively advantaged groups. As illustrated by the case of the LCCR, coalitions in which organizations agree to work together toward a common goal represent a possible remedy to this situation. Because coalitions have the capacity, and indeed the objective, to work on issues that intersect the interests and goals of many organizations and movements, they often alleviate the inequities that favor advantaged subgroups at the expense of disadvantaged ones by giving organizations the opportunity to work on issues and to service constituencies that they might otherwise overlook. Coalitions also provide organizations with the opportunity to serve as mediators among their constituents as well as between their constituents and the constituents of their coalition partners, harnessing these relationships to build trust and solidarity among these overlapping and intersecting constituencies (Levi and Murphy 2006).

As I will show in this chapter, alliances with other organizations represent one of the most promising avenues for meaningful attention to and energetic advocacy on intersectional issues. However, coalitions of organizations are somewhat of a double-edged sword when it comes to advocacy on such issues. On the one hand, coalitions are a key conduit for activity on issues affecting disadvantaged subgroups, creating connections among organizations and the oftentimes narrowly focused single-axis issues on which they concentrate. On the other hand, however, many of the challenges that coalitions typically face—how to balance organizations' individual concerns about organizational maintenance with their contributions to collective efforts; how to address issues such as unequal resources among coalition members, lack of trust among participating organizations, ideological differences among the groups, and disagreements about how to frame policy issues—have particularly knotty ramifications when we examine coalitions as potential sites of advocacy for disadvantaged subgroups (K. Cook, Hardin, and Levi 2005; Levi and Murphy 2006; Rose 2000; Staggenborg 1986). The responses to such challenges often lead to the marginalization of disadvantaged-subgroup issues within coalitions, thereby replicating many of the very dynamics that produce the low levels of activity on these issues within individual organizations that were observed in chapter 4. Coalitions therefore bring into sharper resolution *inter*organizationally the *intra*organizational challenges of intersectionality that that I have discussed in previous chapters. An examination of coalitions, then, offers another vantage point from which to assess the quality of representation afforded intersectionally marginalized constituents as well as a window into how the organizations themselves understand and approach intersectionally disadvantaged issues.

## THE BENEFITS OF COALITIONS FOR ORGANIZATIONS REPRESENTING MARGINALIZED GROUPS

Coalitions offer an array of benefits to organizations that participate in such alliances. Among these advantages, coalitions allow advocacy organizations to combine and compound the strength of their numbers so that their cooperation increases their joint political influence, which is particularly helpful when they are faced with strong, organized opposition (Hathaway and Meyer 1997; McCammon and Campbell 2002; Meyer 1990, 1993, Reagon 1983; Staggenborg 1986; Van Dyke 2003; Van Dyke and Soule 2002). They also allow organizations to share scarce material resources such as funds and staff and to share political resources, such as access to policy makers and membership bases (Browne 1998; Levi and Murphy 2006; Staggenborg 1986). These alliances are also a way to support friends and allies, and they offer organizations a low-cost way to attend to pressure from their memberships for greater involvement on specific issues (Jenkins and Perrow 1977). In addition, coalitions allow organizations to access selective benefits, such as training, technical assistance, and information, that are available only to coalition members (C. Cook 1998, 109; Hula 1995; Levi and Murphy 2006). Groups involved in coalitions can play an important role in the early stages of shaping the agenda and framing the issues around which the coalitions form, and these organizations might also be able to lay claim to some of the spoils resulting from these efforts (Hula 1995; Snow and Benford 1992).

Coalitions offer these benefits to most types of interest groups. Business organizations, conservative organizations, and nonideological organizations all stand to gain when they work together to advance their common interests. While it is true that just about any type of organization can benefit form working in coalition with other groups, historically, coalitions have been especially attractive and beneficial to public interest groups and organizations representing marginalized groups (Browne 1998; Bykerk and Maney 1995; Delgado 1986; Hojnacki 1997, 1998; Sawyers and Meyer 1999; Schlozman 1990; Staggenborg 1986; Tarrow 2005; Van Dyke 2003).[6] For organizations such as these, coalitions hold particularly strong normative, ideological, and strategic benefits. As I will elaborate in this chapter, for organizations that by themselves represent small populations, working within a coalition helps aggregate their collective strength in order to achieve a stronger voice in national politics. In addition, organizations that represent marginalized groups gain increased credibility with policy makers when they ally with other organizations (Woliver 1998). Coalitions similarly can increase the legitimacy of "insider" organizations with a broader array of grassroots constituents. Working in coalitions also advances solidaristic and ideological goals held by many organizations, such as the belief that "no one is free until we all are free."

## STRATEGIC BENEFITS: STRENGTH IN NUMBERS

Coalitions have considerable strategic value for organizations that represent weak, minority, or marginalized groups. By combining their resources and efforts, groups such as women, racial minorities, lesbian, gay, bisexual, and transgender (LGBT) people, and low-income people can work together to promote shared goals or to thwart a common enemy, allowing them to participate in issues that they might not otherwise have the resources to address (Gamson 1961, 1975; Lipsky 1970; C. Tilly 1978; Van Dyke 2003). While coalitions increase the numbers of supporters for all types of organizations, this benefit has particular significance when it comes to marginalized groups for whom the premium on deriving strength from numbers is particularly high. As minority or otherwise weak groups, their constituencies comprise only small portions of the general public, but their numbers increase tremendously when they work with others who have similar interests. For example, in 2004, African Americans, Latinos, Asian Pacific Americans, and Native Americans accounted for approximately 12.8 percent, 14.1 percent, 4.4 percent, and 1.0 percent, respectively, of the total population of the United States. Together, however, these groups comprised approximately a third of the U.S. population (U.S. Census Bureau 2004).

This benefit was cited repeatedly by interviewees as an advantage of working in coalition with other organizations. The political director at a major LGBT organization said, for example, that her organization works in coalition with many civil rights and women's organizations because, as she put it, "we recognized early on that we would be nowhere if we tried to do this alone."[7] In other words, organizations like hers *must* coalesce with like-minded groups if their agendas are to have any hope of success. Similarly, discussing the benefits and drawbacks of coalition work, the chair of the board of an African American civil rights group characterized the best thing about working in coalitions as being "that your forces and your members increase." "Instead of it being just you," he explained, "it's you and somebody else working towards a common goal and new ideas, methods, and strengths."[8]

The comments of the executive director of a large social justice organization underscored the benefits of the large numbers that come from being part of a coalition. He said that no single organization is large enough or strong enough to "achieve an agenda" on its own. However, he continued, his organization is involved in a coalition of thirty-four national environmental groups whose total membership approaches ten million people. Once members of the coalition come to an agreement on an issue, he explained, "we can then talk to Bill Clinton or Bush . . . and we can say, 'We're here for all the environmentalists.' If I just called to say, 'This is [organization name]. Could you talk to me?' they would say, 'I don't think so.'" Politicians are more responsive to coalitions not only because of their numbers but also because of the diversity of constituencies that coalitions signify. Consequently, this respondent continued, when this environmental coalition approaches policy makers, "it's not just elitist environmentalists wanting to go backpacking in fancy national parks. It's people worried about the lungs of asthmatic kids in the black section of Atlanta."[9] This statement suggests that coalitions that gather organizations and movements that do not often ally—such as the "turtles and Teamsters" coalition that brought together environmentalists and labor activists to protest the World Trade Organization Ministerial in Seattle, Washington, in 1999—have great symbolic value that can be particularly effective (Levi and Murphy 2006, 656).

## CREDIBILITY AND LEGITIMACY

This last statement also illuminates another reason why coalitions are popular with advocacy organizations that represent weak groups: coalitions can increase credibility for these organizations, both among politicians and among their own constituents. The policy director of a women's organization alluded to the credibility that can come with a large base of support as a reason that coalitions are so useful. Coalitions "always help," she said, and working with others is really the "only way you get any real change" because "you've got to bring more than just one organizational voice, and you need to bring folks who have grassroots constituency together with folks who are working the state legislatures with the folks who have some academic credentials." "You can't do anything in this town without a coalition," she explained, "I mean, the first question [from policy makers] is, 'Who supports this?'"[10] Such structural features of national politics make coalitions a necessity for all types of interest groups, but they bear particular weight for organizations that have fewer resources and whose constituents are marginalized and often dismissed by political actors.

These statements from organization leaders also highlight two related, though somewhat contradictory, facets of coalitions that make them particularly important to the organizations in this study. To accomplish their policy goals, organizations representing women, racial minorities, and low-income people must negotiate the difficult task of using insider tactics to fight for outsider groups in national politics. To do so, they need the legitimacy that comes from associating with powerful and credentialed individuals and groups. At the same time, these organizations also need to demonstrate that the causes they are pursuing are not narrow and self-interested, and therefore they depend upon the legitimacy of the "grass roots" and the support of their marginalized constituents. Coalitions offer the possibility of both forms of legitimacy—with powerful groups and with more marginalized groups. For relatively mainstream groups, allying with grassroots or "outsider" organizations can increase their credibility among more marginal constituencies who might ordinarily dismiss them as "insiders." For these organizations, joining coalitions that are working on issues that they have not previously thought of as central to their mission also allows them to reach out to new constituencies, thereby broadening their base. Although such outreach is also possible when an organization gets involved in a new public policy issue by itself, allying with other groups can give a newcomer to an issue access to its allies' members while also imparting to the novice organization a level of credibility it would have had a hard time achieving on its own. For example, labor unions seeking to expand their membership base by organizing Mexican and Chinese immigrants have been more successful since joining with Latino and Asian Pacific American organizations in opposing anti-immigrant legislation (D. Warren 2005; J. Wong 2006). Like coalitions among atypical allies, the symbolic value of coalitions between what Margaret Levi and Gillian Murphy characterize as "the great and the small" poses implicit threats to authorities and gives organizations ways to negotiate the often tenuous line between insider and outsider tactics and status (Levi and Murphy 2006, 656).

## ECONOMIES OF SCALE

In addition to expanding their numbers and increasing their credibility, coalitions also allow groups to expand the range of resources available to them, particularly when they are under threat (Meyer 1990, 1993; Staggenborg 1986; Van Dyke 2003; Van Dyke and Soule 2002). Although shared resources and economies of scale are beneficial to all types of organizations, these benefits are particularly important for advocacy organizations representing marginalized groups, which, as I showed in chapter 3, are, on average, more resource-poor than business, corporate, and professional organizations. The executive director of an African American organization commented, for example, "We spend a lot of our time [working in coalitions] because . . . our resources aren't as plentiful as we would like. It really calls for us to work in coalitions and organizations that have similar focus as ours."[11] The executive director of a women's labor group spoke in similar terms about a tax-related coalition that "encompasses women's organizations, civil rights organizations, labor, and environmental groups." "It's a very broad coalition," she observed, "[which] increases its possibility of success . . . just because of the resources that are available."[12] With smaller budgets than business and professional organizations, and with fewer lawyers and lobbyists on their smaller staffs, organizations representing marginalized groups benefit a great deal when they can pool these scarce resources within coalitions.

## IDEOLOGICAL COMMITMENTS AND PREFIGURATIVE POLITICS

Many scholars have found that basic agreement on ideological principles among member organizations is an important condition for coalition work (Gerhards and Rucht 1992; Levi and Murphy 2006; Van Dyke 2003). Ideological commitments that emphasize solidarity and giving voice to the voiceless also encourage coalition work among organizations that prioritize values such as these (G. Arnold 1995; Staggenborg 1986; Van Dyke 2003; see also Mansbridge 1983). Organizations often are compelled by such commitments to transcend their own immediate self-interest in service to broader ideological goals in ways that complement the effects of feelings of linked fate and collective identity that were discussed in chapter 3 (Bawn 1999; Browne 1998; Coles 1996; Van Dyke 2003). For example, the director of civil rights at a labor organization explained that many labor unions have been very active in coalition efforts against vouchers for public schools, even though many of their members would appreciate the vouchers because they "want to put their kids in private school." The labor unions nonetheless participate in the antivoucher coalition, she claimed, because they share an understanding that "public education is a right" that is undermined by vouchers. "So," she explained, "they will go with us on that issue" because their ideological commitment to public education trumps what might seem to be their self-interest in policies allowing vouchers that would help them pay for their own children's private schooling.[13]

In addition to joining coalitions that further specific ideological goals, many of the ideologies embraced by organizations representing marginalized groups emphasize alliances and solidarity as goals *in themselves* (G. Arnold 1995; Bunch 1987; Coles 1996; Flammang 1997; Giddings 1984; Gomes and Williams 1995a; Staggenborg 1986; Van Dyke 2003). As a result, for many progressive groups, allying with other organizations in coalitions provides opportunities to engage in what sociologist Wini Breines (1989) and other have called "prefigurative politics" by embodying in their tactics the changes and ideals that they want to see in the world (see also G. Arnold 1995; Freeman 1972–73).[14] In this way, coalitions are accomplishments in themselves, offering a way to put theory into practice by enacting ideologically salient tropes and frames that emphasize unity, solidarity, and equality—themes such as "sisterhood," "one big union," "no one is free until we all are free," and "the people united" (Taylor 1995). As such, coalitions capture and advance the moral as well as the numerical strengths of social justice work for organizations that advocate on behalf of marginalized populations.

## COALITIONS AND INTERSECTIONALLY DISADVANTAGED SUBGROUPS

For organizations representing marginalized groups, then, coalitions hold particular benefits that make them extremely popular forms of mobilization within this interest community. Given this range of benefits, it not surprising that 98 percent of the organizations in the SNESJO have worked in coalitions at some point, with approximately two-thirds reporting that they have done so "frequently" (see fig. 6.1).[15] Within some categories of organizations, such as Asian Pacific American, African American, and Latino organizations, all organizations reported at least some participation in coalitions. For example, when asked how often her women's organization forms coalitions with other organizations, one field organizer said, "100 percent. . . . All the time. We go out of our way to coalition with other organizations."[16] In fact, almost all the respondents affirmed that coalitions are a key part of their work—even "too much," as one executive director commented wryly, suggesting that perhaps her organization ought to be more selective in its attempts to work with other groups.[17]

In addition to the general attractiveness of coalitions for the organizations in this study, evidence from the survey and interviews suggests that some features of coalitions make them a particularly popular method for addressing intersectional issues. Specifically, although organizations make extensive use of coalitions when it comes to other issue types, coalitions are the most frequently reported activity for issues affecting intersectionally disadvantaged subgroups (see fig. 6.2). Coalitions are therefore the source of a very high percentage of the activity that is devoted to disadvantaged-subgroup issues and are consequently a fertile source of representation for intersectionally disadvantaged subgroups.

The popularity of coalitions as a way to address disadvantaged-subgroup issues is understandable because such partnerships with other organizations offer a low-cost, low-profile way to get involved in an issue. By allying with others, organizations can take part in policy activity on issues about which they would otherwise likely be inactive, and they can do so without expending extensive resources or calling too much attention to their

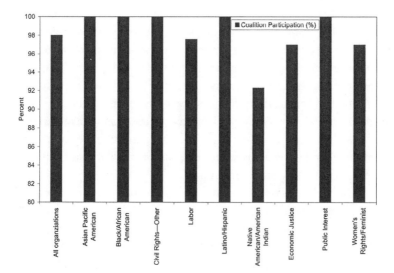

**Fig. 6.1.** Coalition use, by organization type. Organization officers were asked, "On a scale of 1 to 5, where 1 is 'never' and 5 is 'frequently,' how often does your organization use each of the following influencing methods . . . Entering into coalitions or working with other organizations." Data in the columns reflect the percentage of respondents giving answers from "2" through "5" (data from SNESJO).

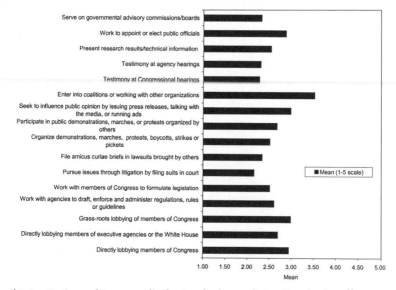

**Fig. 6.2.** Tactics used to pursue disadvantaged-subgroup issues. Organization officers were asked, "On a scale of 1 to 5, where 1 is 'never' and 5 is 'frequently,' how often does your organization engage in the following activities in pursuing its policy goals on the issue of [the policy issue in question]?" Bars represent the mean response for each tactic (data from SNESJO).

efforts (Staggenborg 1986). Alliances can be particularly useful when it comes to disadvantaged-subgroup issues that, as I showed in chapter 4, tend not to be popular among constituents. In fact, many of the officers I interviewed made repeated references to channeling activity on such issues into coalition work. For example, the executive director of an economic justice organization told me that when her members are ambivalent about an issue or when the organization does not want to take the lead on it is "exactly why we enter into coalitions. Our name might be on a sign-on letter, or we might be doing some visits on a particular issue, but . . . we aren't seen as the one out in front on it."[18]

Similarly, the executive director of an Asian Pacific American organization explained that her organization often restricts its work on issues that are controversial among its constituents to coalition efforts. Doing so, she said, is one way to show support for an issue and for the organizations that are working on it, but in a low-profile way. For example, she explained that violence against women (an issue that affects an intersectionally disadvantaged subset of her group's constituency) is a "touchy" subject within the community she represents. As a consequence, she told me, "rather than being out there as an organization" when it comes to addressing this issue, her organization "sign[s] on with some other groups."[19]

## FACILITATING MEDIATION, PROMOTING INTERSECTIONALLY LINKED FATE, AND EXPANDING AGENDAS

In addition to constituting a key source of activity when it comes to issues affecting intersectionally disadvantaged subgroups, coalitions promote trusting relationships among organizations. These relationships in turn can encourage the use of representation as a form of mediation and can nurture a sense of intersectionally linked fate (Gerhards and Rucht 1992; Levi and Murphy 2006; Van Dyke 2003). This sense of connectedness is possible because coalitions foster conditions that highlight connections among issues and constituencies, thereby providing organizations with an opportunity to expand their analysis of the policy issues at hand and to take into account the interests of the overlapping and intersecting constituencies that comprise the coalition (Van Dyke 2003). Coalitions thus can persuade their constituent organizations to take into account issues affecting intersectionally disadvantaged groups that they might not ordinarily consider.

An instance of this process is evident in the case of the LCCR's position on immigration policy described at the beginning of this chapter. Labor groups and African American organizations that are members of this coalition had previously cited fears of worker displacement by immigrants as justification for supporting strategies such as employer sanctions. Immigration rights and civil liberties organizations within the LCCR argued that such measures led to discrimination against workers who "appeared foreign," and a report from the Government Accounting Office found that this was indeed the case (Quiroz-Martínez 2001). The relationships that had been developed among the LCCR's member organizations fostered conditions under which the labor and African American organizations could not avoid confronting the claims and demands of the civil liberties, immigration, Asian Pacific American, and Latino organizations. The claims made by these latter groups addressed, at their core, the importance of recognizing the intersectional disadvantages faced by a subset of workers who are simultaneously marginalized by their status as low-income workers, people of color, and immigrants. Understanding the effects of these intersecting forms of discrimination led to the recognition that employer sanctions relied on racially discriminatory practices that ran counter to the actual objectives of African American organizations. As a consequence, taking into account the claims of Asian Pacific American and Latino organizations broadened understandings of racial discrimination among the other constituent organizations of the LCCR as well as their understandings of what it means to protect workers.

The kind of mediation made possible by coalitions, then, leads to relationships of mutuality and trust that make it more likely that participants will feel responsible, and at times indebted, to other members of the coalition (Levi and Murphy 2006). As a consequence, coalition partners often are able to solicit more involvement from other participating organizations than these groups might choose to contribute to an effort were they working on their own. Although an organization might prefer to participate only nominally in a coalition on a disadvantaged-subgroup issue that falls outside its main areas of interest, its ability to limit its participation under such conditions depends in part upon what the other members of the coalition demand and expect.[20]

For example, when asked if their level of involvement in a coalition varies based on how central to their mission is the issue around which the coalition formed, the executive director of an African American organization answered in the negative, saying, "our coalition partners don't let us [choose our level of participation]. . . . They don't let us take a 'sit-back' position on the issues. They really draw us up front."[21] As an example, he cited his organization's work on welfare reform. At first, he explained, his organization had not even considered getting involved in efforts surrounding the 1996 Personal Responsibility and Work Opportunity Reconciliation Act (PRWORA) that reformed the system of public assistance to low-income people. After being approached by another organization with which his group had worked in coalition on several issues in the past, he agreed to sign his organization onto this group's efforts to influence the pending welfare legislation. Intending mainly to lend his organization's name and passive support to the effort, his organization instead was convinced to take a bigger role in the coalition and ended up, in the words of this respondent, "a part of the main coalition in the whole development process."[22]

## CONNECTING ISSUES

The foregoing example is significant not only because that organization was compelled to participate more fully than it had originally planned but also because its increased involvement helped the group make connections between its core policy interests and other policy issues. In particular, the organization was able to connect issues of criminal justice that form the core of its agenda to broad issues of poverty, unemployment, and income inequality. These new commitments broadened the organization's agenda and, in the words of the executive director, "really opened up our eyes . . . It just really made me see that in the broader context, . . . we are a central part of these issues."[23]

In another example, the executive director of an antipoverty organization told me that when his organization began organizing with antihomelessness advocates, "We went to some of their meetings, we had some of our people who went to testify at their meetings. It was very good" because the members of his organization had the opportunity to meet "other people in similar situations [who were] taking a step to become advocates for their own issues."[24] Most important was that working in coalition with other organizations allowed these members to draw connections between poverty and homelessness and to explore issues at the intersection of these two issues that they had previously thought of as separate.

Similarly, the executive director of a reproductive rights organization explained that her group consciously formed as a coalition of representatives from an array of communities that felt that they had been ill served by reproductive health politics and technologies. In particular, the coalition intended to bring together women's health activists and researchers with low-income women and women of color—groups that often have made it clear that they frequently have felt ignored, abused, and exploited by proponents of birth control and sterilization (J. Nelson 2003). Working in coalition, this executive director argued, the movement is stronger, speaks with a more unified voice, and commands a broad appeal and increased credibility. The broad coalition infuses its work on reproductive rights with considerations about issues of race and class that many argue have tended to have been given short shrift by many pro-choice organizations (J. Nelson 2003; Silliman et al. 2004). In these ways, this coalition has worked to rectify the missteps that have been taken within the reproductive rights community and to build trust among many communities of women, and, crucially, it has tried to ensure that these concerns will continue to be addressed in the future.[25]

## CONNECTING ORGANIZATIONS

As the foregoing examples demonstrate, the cross-fertilization of issues and constituencies born of coalition work stimulates understanding about, and sometimes promotes activity dealing with, issues affecting disadvantaged subgroups that otherwise likely would not be cultivated. In these ways, the relationships nurtured by coalitions can lead to a broader vision, to understandings about how issues are connected, and, ultimately, to more comprehensive solutions to the multifaceted issues that face marginalized groups.

In addition to drawing connections among issues, participants in a coalition often develop connections to one another that in turn foster commitments to the survival and success of the coalition itself (G. Arnold 1995; Levi and Murphy forthcoming). The executive director of a large civil rights organization emphasized to me, for example, "No one wants the death of the coalition on their hands." As a consequence of this concern, he continued, "those who approach this work in good faith really do recognize almost a sacred obligation to be thoughtful about how they pursue their institutional interests so that they don't jeopardize the great value that that coalition brings to many."[26] Allegiances such as these can help foster advocacy and representation for intersectionally disadvantaged subgroups because, as one respondent put it, where there are conflicts, they encourage members of coalitions to "step back from their own peripheral interests and to look more broadly at the interest of the coalition."[27]

Several respondents referenced their commitments to coalitions as having broadening effects on their policy issue participation. The executive director of a women's health organization said, for example, that her organization generally tries "to keep to our niche where it's possible." The group is more flexible, however, when it works in coalitions, particularly if it is clear the coalition will benefit more if the organization reaches outside its niche and does "something beyond what we would have done just based on our own strengths."[28]

When organizations are encouraged to identify with the interests and fates of other groups, they can be encouraged to overcome the narrow framings that, as I have shown in previous chapters, characterize the typical approach to issues affecting disadvantaged subgroups of their constituencies and that suppress activity on these issues.

## FIRST, DO NO HARM

The relationships fostered by coalitions, then, stimulate organizations to broaden their agendas and to join efforts on disadvantaged-subgroup issues that they might otherwise ignore. These relationships also promote connections between organizations that foster loyalty among them, thereby cultivating investments in the success of the coalitions themselves that also can encourage increased attention to issues affecting disadvantaged subgroups. In addition to these proactive effects, the trust and commitments promoted by coalitions also can have a preemptive effect that *prevents* groups from pursuing policy goals that might be *detrimental* to the intersectionally disadvantaged subgroups of their coalition partners (Levi and Murphy 2006). The executive director of a large civil rights coalition explained, "In some instances, you ask forbearance from organizations that would otherwise want to block you from taking positions."[29] Coalitions, he argued, often compel participants to "gauge the issue and its importance to" the overall legislative program of their organizations, reflecting on how important it is that they weigh in on an issue if their position on it does not accord with that of other members of the coalition. This process can allow "the rest of the coalition to move forward" even if some member organizations do not support involvement in a particular issue.[30]

This respondent recounted several policy issues on which opposition from constituent organizations had posed challenges to the coalition.

Because this coalition operates via consensus, such opposition often threatens to stymie advocacy on an issue. In one particularly pertinent case, some of the religious organizations in the coalition opposed its advocacy of federal anti-hate crime legislation and workplace protections for LGBT people. However, after many conversations and meetings, not only did these organizations refrain from vetoing the coalition's advocacy of these protections, they also refrained from doing anything on their own to oppose the legislation. "Sometimes," the executive director of this coalition argued, "the best that you could hope to do is get them [participating organizations] to do no harm."[31] Participating in coalitions improves the odds that groups will abide by this maxim by fostering commitments of trust, solidarity, and linked fate among a wide range of organizations representing many different groups.

## INTERSECTIONALITY AND THE LIMITS OF COALITION POLITICS

Coalitions promote intersectional understandings about issues and constituencies and are a key source of advocacy on issues affecting intersectionally disadvantaged subgroups. However, coalitions present their own challenges to effective advocacy and representation. Much evidence from the SNESJO and the interviews suggests that while they correct many of the inequities in representation for intersectionally disadvantaged subgroups, coalitions also reproduce and bring into sharper resolution many of the same problems associated with advocacy on behalf of these subgroups that have been on display in previous chapters.

Indeed, struggles over intersectionally disadvantaged-subgroup issues are at the heart of the challenges facing coalitions of organizations representing women, racial minorities, and low-income people. Even coalitions that ostensibly are pursuing common goals have to reconcile the interests and objectives of a wide range of organizations that have different constituencies and varying ideologies; use different tactics; have access to varying levels of resources; may not trust one another; and may disagree about everything from issue framing to choice of tactics (K. Cook, Hardin, and Levi 2005; Levi and Murphy 2006; Rose 2000).[32] These and other common hurdles, such as organizations' concerns about their individual organizational maintenance, pose particular challenges when it comes to the efficacy of advocacy for disadvantaged subgroups on the part of coalitions. As a consequence, decisions about how to allocate their scarce time, energy, and resources have implications for precisely the questions that are at issue when it comes to representing intersectionally disadvantaged subgroups within the organizations that comprise the coalition.

In coalitions, these challenges of intersectionality are manifested *inter*organizationally rather than *intra*organizationally. When organizations work together on policy issues, many of the challenges and dynamics within individual organizations that engender low levels of activity on intersectionally disadvantaged issues are replicated within the broader coalition. Consequently, coalitions often are strained by or disband over the same kinds of issues that suppress the activity of individual organizations on issues affecting intersectionally disadvantaged subgroups of their constituencies (G. Arnold 1995; Levi and Murphy 2006; Spalter-Roth and Schreiber 1995).

As outlined in the previous section, the potential benefits of coalition work are numerous and profound; however, where intersectionally disadvantaged interests are concerned, organizations do not always realize the full benefits of coalitions. Overall, organizations' commitment to coalitions addressing disadvantaged-subgroup issues tends to be weaker and more symbolic than it is when it comes to other issue types. In addition, as is the case in individual organizations, the impact of issues affecting intersectionally disadvantaged member groups of coalitions often is particularized and played down, and the concerns of the organizations speaking for these weaker groups frequently are marginalized by advantaged member organizations. So, while coalitions are a key source of activity on such issues, they do not prevent the more general tendency of organizations to give short shrift to the issues that affect their intersectionally disadvantaged constituents. Instead, as I will show subsequently, coalitions perpetuate many of the inequalities in representation at work within individual organizations.

### SYMBOLIC EFFORTS

The organizations that join together in coalitions rarely make equal contributions to the overall effort but rather commit varying levels of energy and resources that depend on organizational maintenance-related criteria such as how much they expect to benefit from a coalition and how central the goals of the coalition are seen as being to their main policy objectives (Levi and Murphy forthcoming). Based on such factors, organizations choose to play either a core or a peripheral role in the alliance's efforts (Hojnacki 1998; Hula 1999; Staggenborg 1986). As a consequence, one defining limitation of coalitions when it comes to advocacy on disadvantaged-subgroup issues is that organizations often devote only symbolic efforts to issues affecting these groups, reserving their "best efforts" in coalition work for the issues that they see as central to their main policy goals. Because, as we saw in chapter 4, disadvantaged-subgroup issues are far less likely than majority or advantaged-subgroup issues to be seen in this way, this tendency has a suppressive effect on levels of effort within coalitions addressing issues affecting intersectionally disadvantaged groups.

These unequal efforts are evident in respondents' answers to survey questions about their participation in coalitions when it comes to particular policy issues. The proportion of organizations engaging in coalition work is relatively equal over each of the four types of public policy issues, ranging from 90 percent in the case of advantaged-subgroup issues to 95 percent in the case of majority issues (see fig. 6.3). However, while the percentage of organizations working in coalitions does not vary much by issue type, the average *level* of participation in coalitions varies a fair bit, and participation levels are lower where disadvantaged-subgroup issues are concerned than they are for either majority or advantaged-subgroup issues. The disparity between the two measures also demonstrates that although organizations are somewhat less likely to join coalitions when it comes to advantaged-subgroup issues than they are for other issues, when they do join coalitions on such issues, they are very active. On the other hand, while a higher proportion of organizations join coalitions as part of their advocacy on disadvantaged-subgroup issues, the resources and energy that they devote to coalition work on such issues is lower than it is when they work in coalition on other issues. As a consequence, their participation in coalitions on disadvantaged-subgroup issues is often relatively shallow and more symbolic than it is substantive.

Interviews support and illuminate this evidence from the survey and illustrate that advocacy organization officers often frame disadvantaged-subgroup issues as narrow, particularistic, and outside their niches. The interviews also are suggestive regarding the ways in which this framing can lead them to devote largely symbolic levels of energy to coalitions around these issues. I asked the executive director of an economic justice organization about his organization's activity on the issue of public funding for reproductive health services. Although these services are particularly

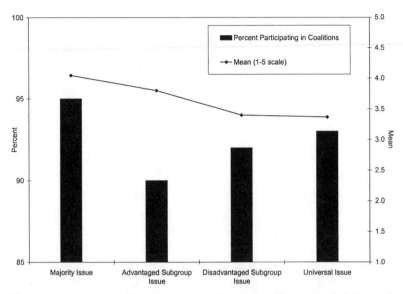

**Fig. 6.3.** Participation in coalitions, by issue type. Organization officers were asked, "On a scale of 1 to 5, where 1 is 'never' and 5 is 'frequently,' how often does your organization engage in the following activities in pursuing its policy goals on the issue of [the policy issue in question]?" Data in the columns reflect the percentage of respondents giving answers from "2" through "5" for each issue type. The trend line shows the mean response for each issue type (data from SNESJO).

important to low-income women, he said that he does not see this issue as being central to his organization's policy concerns. Consequently, when the organization participates in coalitions addressing this issue, it simply signs on to what he characterized as "other people's stuff." As such, he tends not to devote a great deal of time or energy in such cases. Instead, he said, "we're usually pretty clear about areas where we can devote significant amounts of time and where we can't."[33]

CAPTURE

The foregoing respondent's use of the phrase "other people's stuff" is instructive and emblematic, illustrating that organizations often view the coalition work that they devote to disadvantaged-subgroup issues as a form of altruism rather than as part of their mandates as representatives of broad and diverse constituencies. As we saw in chapter 4, when officers at advocacy organizations think about and frame issues as "belonging" to someone else, they rarely take the ownership of them that is necessary to prioritize them. Because framings such as these are much more common in the case of disadvantaged-subgroup issues, officers feel justified in limiting their participation in the coalitions that are formed to address these issues in much the same way they justify low levels of activity on these issues more generally. In addition, organizations with fewer resources within coalitions are often more dependent on, and therefore often more active participants in, these joint efforts than are other organizations. As Susan Staggenborg explains, organizations with fewer resources "may be more likely to put time into a coalition because they can engage in activities in coalition that they cannot do alone" (Staggenborg 1986, 386). These lower-resourced organizations consequently are subject to "capture" by coalitions in much the same way that disadvantaged subgroups are subject to "capture" by organizations (Frymer 1999). As such, weaker organizations have little alternative but to participate in coalitions even if these alliances fail to devote energy and resources to the issues that interest them most.

For example, the executive director of a civil rights organization told me that he often has worked with organizations that are much wealthier and that have much more political access than his own organization. While he and his organization are typically very active members of the coalitions initiated by these other organizations, he said that it is less common for these same organizations to participate at high levels in the coalitional efforts that are initiated by his group unless they happen to involve issues that are central to their agendas. He tolerates the unevenness of their contributions because he appreciates that his organization and the coalition benefit from their association with these more powerful organizations. "It is better to have them in than not," he explained, "even if their involvement is relatively marginal" because "their name enriches the diversity of the group seeking change."[34]

Staggenborg (1986) describes a related instance in her examination of a pro-choice coalition in Chicago. Coalition members were frustrated, she found, by what they perceived as limited contributions to the coalition by the Chicago chapter of the National Organization for Women (NOW). Although Chicago NOW was one of the more highly resourced members of the coalition, it participated primarily by "sending a representative to Alliance meetings." In addition, "while other organizations in the coalition contributed voluntary dues to the Alliance, NOW declined to do so" (Staggenborg 1986, 384–85).

Uneven contributions of time and resources to coalitional efforts are an inevitable element of such alliances. It is understandable that concerns about organizational maintenance and reputation will lead organizations to hesitate about diverting a significant portion of their scarce resources to activities for which they will have to share credit with other groups. Similarly, it is reasonable to expect that these same concerns will lead organizations to devote greater levels of resources and activity to coalitions that address issues that are most central to their agendas (Staggenborg 1986). However logical these decisions are, however, the aforementioned respondent's statements as well as the pro-choice coalition examined by Staggenborg illustrate that such choices often lead to disparities that exacerbate the inequalities between weaker and stronger organizations. When organizations with more resources withhold them from a coalition of which they are a part, they impose unequal burdens on weaker organizations, which are likely to participate more energetically and to devote a greater share of their scarcer resources to the efforts.

## TAKING THE LEAD

How central the goals of a coalition are to the main policy objectives of an organization clearly influences its level of engagement in the alliance. How germane an issue is seen as being to an organization's central concerns is an even more salient criterion when it comes to taking the *lead* in coalitions. Interviewees made repeated references to the fact that their organizations are most likely to head or organize coalitions on the issues that they view as being closest to their core mission. For example, when asked under what circumstances her organization gets involved in coalitions, the executive director of a women's health organization explicitly contrasted two approaches to coalition work. "Sometimes," she said, "it is just, 'all right, we'll lend our name to the coalition.'" In cases when the issue being addressed by the coalition is central to her organization's own agenda, however, "it really is an effort to multiply our strength by working with like-minded allies." In the latter case, coalitions are "a high priority," and her organization gets together "with other groups for whom it is a high-priority area and really put together strategic plans of action."[35] Most significantly, it is in these latter coalitions that this organization's participation is the most likely to endure over the long term. The executive director of a large civil rights organization affirmed the same set of possible approaches to coalition work, summing them up by saying, "Not every organization brings the full weight of their institutional capability to the table on every issue. It varies. What we find is that some organizations take the lead on issues of particular concern for them, and [they] may join in other areas in name only."[36]

The evidence in previous chapters demonstrates that the issues affecting disadvantaged subgroups almost invariably are perceived as less central to organizations' mandates than majority and advantaged-subgroup issues. Because the exigencies of organizational maintenance make organizations much more likely to put forth a great deal of effort in coalitions when they address issues that they consider part of their "core concerns," they are much less likely to take the lead on disadvantaged-subgroup issues because these issues are seen as peripheral to the organization's central policy concerns and goals. In other words, although coalitions provide a low-cost route to addressing issues affecting disadvantaged subgroups of their broader constituencies, organizations often fail to make use of coalitions in ways that attend to such issues in a thorough fashion. Instead, coalitions often reproduce the same biases toward majority and advantaged-subgroup issues that are evident in other types of public policy advocacy.

FRAGILITY

Because organizations are free to modulate their levels of dedication, coalitions have little power to compel organizations to make credible commitments to issues that they do not consider central to their missions or that they regard as "belonging" to someone else (Levi and Murphy 2006). As a consequence, if an issue is not central to the agendas of many organizations, coalitional efforts to pursue it can fall apart very easily (Sawyers and Meyer 1999).

Such fragility is illustrated by the comments of the executive director of a large environmentally oriented social justice organization. I asked this officer about his organization's involvement in policy efforts to address environmental racism (such as the disproportionate locating of environmental hazards in neighborhoods with high concentrations of minority residents). He told me that this issue was peripheral to his organization's main activities but that his group had participated in some environmental justice coalitions. However, he continued, the organization was no longer involved in the issue because the coalitions that addressed it had all fallen apart over time. When I asked him whether his organization usually stops working on an issue if the coalition working on it falls apart, he responded, "No, we keep going no matter what. We work with or without coalitions."[37]

When an issue is not at the center of an organization's agenda, it seems, its commitment to the coalition addressing the issue is often weak. Thus, coalition-based efforts can prove fragile if a major player pulls out or if the key players do not have the resources to keep the effort going or the coalition together. This is particularly troubling because issues affecting disadvantaged subgroups are least likely to be central to an organization's mission.

## MARGINALIZING OUTSIDERS

As I discussed earlier, ideological commitments often can facilitate coalition formation and longevity and can even encourage activity on disadvantaged-subgroup issues. In addition to these *benefits*, scholars also have documented many *challenges* posed by ideology, particularly by ideological differences among coalition member organizations (G. Arnold 1995; Bernstein 1997; Levi and Murphy 2006; Sawyers and Meyers 1999; Staggenborg 1986; Van Dyke 2003). Disagreements about ideological principles can lead to distrust. Distrust in turn can lead organizations to avoid collaborative efforts, viewing them as too difficult or as potentially undermining their organization's collective identity and solidarity (G. Arnold 1995; Gerhards and Rucht 1992; Levi and Murphy 2006; Zald and McCarthy 1987).

Ideological differences are the source of a more specific impediment to the use of coalitions as a vehicle for representing intersectionally disadvantaged subgroups, one that provides another illustration of the predicament faced by advocacy organizations as they try to maintain their credibility with both political elites and marginalized constituents. Concerned about the harmful effects of ideological differences on the ability of organizations to work together, coalitions often exclude organizations that are understood to be political outsiders or "radicals" in spite of the grassroots credibility that they can derive from such organizations that I have discussed previously. Both outsider status and perceived radicalism are likely to characterize many of the organizations that represent intersectionally marginalized groups. For example, the organizations that represent intersectionally disadvantaged subgroups such as low-income women are almost by definition more firmly outsiders than those women's organizations that do not focus on income inequality. These latter organizations also are likely to support extensive and fundamental changes in the policy areas in question and therefore also are more likely to be considered radical by insider groups.[38] Aversions to allying with outsiders and radicals, then, can reduce the probability that such organizations will have the opportunity to influence the agendas of the coalitions that form around the issues that affect many of their constituents. In their examination of the 1999 "Battle in Seattle," for example, Levi and Murphy found that "anarchist groups whose ideological positions made them unable to pledge to abide by the rules of the engagement were unwelcome to participate in the otherwise inclusive" coalitional efforts coordinated by the Direct Action Network (DAN; Levi and Murphy 2006, 663). When purportedly radical organizations are included in coalitions, the other members of the effort often compel the more radical groups to moderate or otherwise alter their positions in ways that forfeit issues affecting disadvantaged subgroups.

Some respondents expressed worries that allying with groups that seem too radical risked undermining their credibility with policy makers. While I have shown that many organizations are eager to enter broad coalitions with a wide array of organizations and that many see benefits associated with the expanded grassroots constituencies such eclecticism can bring, others mentioned that they were typically quite hesitant to enter coalitions with organizations that might threaten their respectability or standing with elected officials or the public. For example, the executive director of an antihunger organization explained that his organization is "very careful" about his group's choices of allies because it is worried about inadvertently associating with "extremists." These extremists, he explained, "are very dishonest. . . . They don't say that they have a [specific] agenda."[39] In other words, while this organization welcomes the support of other organizations that want to end hunger, it avoids organizations that it considers ideologically extreme, preferring to ally with organizations whose agendas and beliefs are similar to its own.[40]

When advocacy organizations do ally with groups that they consider ideologically radical, they frequently hold these other organizations to strict rules or explicitly restrict their own level of involvement as well as the extent to which they will allow the coalition to influence their actions and positions on issues (Levi and Murphy 2006). For example, the political director of a well-connected education-oriented economic justice organization told me that her organization allies quite often with teachers' unions around issues of educational policy. However, she explained, it is important that her organization maintain its image of political neutrality, and so while it is committed to its coalition with teachers' unions, her group does not allow its involvement with these organizations to influence its positions on unions more generally. Her organization is not explicitly opposed to working with unions, and "they've certainly supported us on some things and we've supported them on other things." However, she said, they will not take a position on union-related issues. Instead, she explained, the organization stays "hands off" on these questions, even when its union allies have asked it to support them on labor-related matters.[41]

Advocacy organizations rely heavily on their credibility with and access to policy makers in order to effectively press their agendas. They are therefore understandably loath to compromise this legitimacy by being publicly associated with "disreputable" or controversial organizations. Like the capture of intersectionally marginalized subgroups by the advocacy groups that claim to represent them in national politics, however, weaker organizations are similarly dependent upon the more mainstream organizations in their interest community for access and resources (Frymer 1999). As a consequence, the concerns of more mainstream organizations that their credibility and ability to attract members and resources will be tainted by association with more radical groups weighs heavily on organizations with fewer resources and on groups that are trying to represent intersectionally disadvantaged populations. Such concerns can lead captured organizations to accommodate the demands of their mainstream allies by moderating or otherwise altering their positions, usually in favor of issues and goals that appeal to more powerful coalition members (G. Arnold 1995; Bernstein 1997; Gomes and Williams 1995a).[42] For example, in response to a question I asked about whether she ever finds that she has to adjust her goals in doing coalition work, the political director of an LGBT group said, "Do you tone it down because you're jumping into a coalition fight? Have I shifted the strategies because we're playing with a broader group of people? Yes, I suppose so." Such adjustment, she argued, is part of the "very nature" of working in coalition with other organizations. "You're in it together," she said, and so "you're not necessarily going to get your way all the time. You hope that in making those compromises and in deciding to take a secondary role in this case that you're building a better product or a better strategy to get your end result."[43]

Similarly, the federal legislative counsel of a reproductive rights organization explained that coalition work sometimes forced her organization to choose between moderating its goals and rhetoric or pursuing issues on its own. Speaking about efforts to overturn the "global gag rule" (restrictions that bar foreign nongovernmental organizations from receiving any money from the American government from providing a range of abortion-related services), she said that her organization had been a member of a coalition that included groups that "do not want to even use the A-word [abortion] at all" in addressing the issue, preferring to focus on the policy's silencing effect on counseling about family planning and sexually transmitted diseases.[44] Her organization, however, insists that this policy must be addressed within the context of abortion and reproductive rights. "So," she said, "when we can't do it in coalition, we've done it on our own . . . once we'd agreed that we couldn't agree, we all moved in our own directions on it."[45] In this case, the organization did not moderate its own position but instead pulled out of the coalition.[46]

## THE LOWEST COMMON DENOMINATOR

Another way in which coalitions can reproduce impediments to advocacy on disadvantaged-subgroup issues stems from the fact that coalitions get much of their strength from their ability to settle disputes among organizations, determine their common interests, and therefore present a clear message and a united front to policy makers, the media, and the public (Levi and Murphy 2006; Tarrow 2005). As a consequence, coalitions often are organized to address the "lowest common denominator" aspects of issues—that is, to assemble "minimum winning coalitions" that address a small piece of a broader issue in which all participating organizations perceive a common interest (Levi and Murphy 2006; Riker 1962).

While it might seem neutral and perhaps even logical that coalitions will come together over issues that are of common interest and concern, statements from the face-to-face interviews illustrate the ways in which something so seemingly benign can detract from coalition work addressing disadvantaged-subgroup issues. The vice president of a feminist group explained, for example, that when her organization works in coalitions, it tries to achieve a consensus among all participating organizations and to frame the issue with a "message that works [from] all of our perspectives."[47]

While trying to achieve consensus is an understandable goal, doing so often is achieved at the expense of those aspects of issues that affect intersectionally disadvantaged subgroups since, as I showed in chapter 4, these issues are characterized by lower levels of support among members of their constituencies. In addition, as I have discussed in previous chapters, it is majority and advantaged-subgroup issues that are most often framed as being the ones in which all members of a constituency have a "common interest." Such framings regularly are applied to issues that may have little chance of affecting members of disadvantaged subgroups of the constituency in question. Nonetheless, it is assumed that feelings of linked fate will lead members of disadvantaged subgroups to identify their interests with those of more advantaged subgroups of their communities. Even in cases in which linked fate does not lead members of disadvantaged subgroups to identify with these interests, as captured constituencies, they likely will feel compelled to support them. Disadvantaged-subgroup issues, on the other hand, more often are framed by officers particularistically, as having a narrow impact, and as being outside of an organization's niche. These issues consequently are considered more expendable, and organization officers are less worried if they feel compelled to jettison them in order to maintain the coalition. As a result, focusing on lowest common denominator issues often means that coalitions exclude those aspects of an issue that affect intersectionally marginalized subgroups while at the same time relying on the support of and claiming to represent the members of these subgroups.

The comments of the executive director of a civil rights group that focuses on criminal justice issues illustrate this point. His organization frequently works in coalition with traditional civil rights organizations on criminal justice–related civil rights issues. However, these coalition efforts tend to shortchange many aspects of the criminal justice issues that his organization addresses, particularly those affecting low-income people, because other organizations within the coalition are uncomfortable with the kinds of issues that affect this intersectionally disadvantaged group. He observed, "With the civil rights groups, they're most comfortable with issues like racial profiling. That's a mainline issue. It affects fliers and drivers. Not the people you see when you come to criminal court. They take the bus to the courthouse and don't fly [in] an airplane."[48] As a consequence, the weight and resources of the coalition are brought to bear only on the aspects of criminal justice issues that these more "traditional" organizations have in common with his group. The coalition's access and resources, then, are not made available for advocacy on issues such as access to public housing and Temporary Assistance to Needy Families (or TANF, the current name for financial assistance to low-income people that previously had been called Assistance to Families with Dependent Children) for people with felony convictions—issues that have a disparate impact on low-income criminal defendants. When coalitions fail to take on such issues, they neglect the groups that are affected by them and, in this case, also pass up crucial opportunities to address the ways in which racial discrimination intersects with economic disadvantage as manifested in criminal justice–related issues.

Emphasizing the lowest common denominator among participating organizations, then, functions within coalitions in much the same way that concerns for "common interests" function within organizations. That is, emphasizing the lowest common denominator suppresses activity on disadvantaged-subgroup issues and intensifies activity on majority and advantaged-subgroup issues. Because majority and advantaged-subgroup issues are most likely to be universalized while disadvantaged-subgroup issues are likely to be particularized, a focus on lowest common denominator issues often leads coalitions to exclude those aspects of an issue that affect intersectionally marginalized groups. The negative implications of such a framing are highlighted by the following remarks by the executive director of an economic justice organization. Commenting on the strategic benefits of coalescing around a narrow, common issue, he said that doing so often comes at the expense of addressing issues in his organization's "broader context and with other areas." This is unfortunate, he argued, because "the whole movement benefits" when issues are addressed in broad contexts and in ways that illuminate the connections among them.[49]

## CONCLUSION

Coalitions allow organizations that represent small and marginalized groups to consolidate their strength and resources, increase their credibility with both political elites and grassroots constituents, and engage in prefigurative political activities that advance their ideological goals. The evidence presented in this chapter also reinforces the contention that coalition politics are, at their core, about intersectional politics. Indeed, coalitions hold a great deal of potential as a form of advocacy for intersectionally disadvantaged subgroups, and they account for a disproportionately large share of the activity devoted to disadvantaged-subgroup issues by advocacy organizations. Moreover, coalitions among organizations can encourage advocacy on behalf of disadvantaged subgroups by highlighting connections among issues and constituencies; by promoting feelings of trust, solidarity, and intersectionally linked fate; and by advancing more comprehensive solutions to the complex issues that face marginalized groups.

However, rather than simply alleviating or rectifying the biases that conspire to suppress activity on issues affecting disadvantaged subgroups, coalitions often mirror and perpetuate the very problems associated with advocacy on such issues that permeate the broader political universe. When organizations are involved in coalitions devoted to disadvantaged-subgroup issues—issues that they rarely consider central to their public policy areas—their commitments are weaker, their participation tends to be more symbolic than it is on majority issues, and they are unlikely to take the lead in advocacy activities. Organizations instead initiate coalition efforts mainly when it comes to issues that they perceive as central to their advocacy goals—issues that, as we have seen in previous chapters, are likely to be majority or advantaged-subgroup issues. Coalitions often marginalize or ignore issues that affect disadvantaged subgroups or allow efforts to address them to fall apart.

Consequently, it is frequently left to the weakest, most resource-poor organizations to lead the difficult work of building and maintaining those coalitions whose missions it is to work on disadvantaged-subgroup issues. Larger, stronger groups habitually avail themselves of what Albert Hirschman (1970) labels an "exit option," withdrawing support from causes to which they object. This option is not available to weaker organizations, which are more dependent upon, and therefore captured within, coalitions. They therefore often are compelled to temper their policy goals in order to retain the support of stronger, often more moderate organizations that have greater resources, political legitimacy, and clout. Many of these disparities originate in reasonable considerations about maintaining access to policy makers, organizational maintenance, reputation, and scarcity of resources. Nonetheless, their cumulative effect is that coalitions frequently marginalize issues affecting intersectionally disadvantaged subgroups, thereby reinforcing the mobilization of bias in representation observed in other aspects of the work of interest groups and reproducing many of the biases in politics and policy making more generally.

In spite of these challenges, the evidence shows that many organizations do exploit the opportunities presented by coalitions to more effectively advocate on behalf of intersectionally disadvantaged groups. Under some circumstances, for example, coalitions compel organizations to expand their agendas by taking part in advocacy on issues that they might otherwise ignore. In addition, the relationships that are fostered by coalitions allow organizations to act as mediators for their constituents within their interest community. These relationships help cultivate intersectional understandings of issues and constituencies, and, as a consequence, coalitions can help nurture feelings of intersectionally linked fate among the organizations that are working together. Both of these practices are manifestations of the principle of affirmative advocacy for intersectionally disadvantaged subgroups. In the next chapter, I conclude by bringing these practices together with those suggested by the findings presented in other chapters to develop the affirmative advocacy framework.

# SEVEN

# Conclusion: Affirmative Advocacy

With the mobilization of new interests and the formation of new advocacy organizations since the 1960s, much has changed in the interest group universe since E. E. Schattschneider ([1960] 1975) proffered his gloomy critique of the "pluralist heaven." As James Q. Wilson observes in the introduction to the revised version of his 1974 classic *Political Organizations*, "Since roughly 1970 we have entered a new era. Groups once excluded are now included. Pluralism that once was a distant promise is now a baffling reality." However, he continues, "we are all represented by groups, and yet we all feel unrepresented. A thousand voices are heard in Washington, but none sounds like our own" (J. Wilson [1974] 1995, xxii).

This book has sought to address some key elements of that bafflement. It is, in fact, less and less the case that once excluded groups such as women, racial minorities, and low-income people simply have no representation in national politics and policy making. Indeed, there are many organizations (and increasing numbers of elected representatives) that advocate on their behalf in the policy process. However, the nature and extent of this advocacy is extremely uneven, and its net result is to privilege advantaged subgroups of those constituencies and to marginalize the interests of disadvantaged ones. Organizations are simply far less active when it comes to issues affecting intersectionally marginalized groups. They compensate somewhat for these low levels of activity by engaging in coalitions that address disadvantaged-subgroup issues and by making relatively generous use of court tactics when it comes to such issues (at least when compared with majority issues). Nonetheless, activities in these two realms more often reinforce rather rectify the biases against intersectionally disadvantaged subgroups that are present in the broader political environment in which the relative power of organizations that speak for marginalized groups remains far less that that of the multitude of other organizations that represent advantaged constituencies.

Although these findings might seem logical from a strategic point of view, especially in light of concerns about organizational maintenance and in the context of a hostile political climate and limited resources, they are cause for concern. It may indeed be reasonable for organizations to focus their energies on the issues that they believe hold the greatest interest or have the broadest impact on their constituency or on issues that demand immediate attention, but I have shown that neither of these logics governs how organizations actually allocate their time and resources or explains their low levels of attention to disadvantaged constituents. Instead, organizations employ a double standard that determines the level of energy they devote to issues affecting subgroups of their broader constituency, a double standard based on the status of the subgroup affected rather than on the breadth or depth of the impact of the policy issue in question. As a consequence, the issues affecting advantaged subgroups receive disproportionately high levels of attention and resources, while issues affecting marginalized and disadvantaged subgroups, with some important exceptions, receive disproportionately *low* levels. This imbalance persists even in cases where the disadvantaged-subgroup issues affect a substantial portion of a constituency and when they are on the legislative, administrative, or judicial agenda.

Even if it were true that low levels of activity on disadvantaged-subgroup issues were the result of calculated decisions to focus on salient issues that have a broad impact, it would nonetheless be neither logical nor fair to sacrifice the interests of intersectionally disadvantaged groups to those of the majority. Asking weak constituencies to subsume their interests to those of privileged subgroups is even more troubling. Moreover, it is clear from the survey and interview data that the dedicated and well-intentioned officers at these organizations do not *want* to underserve intersectionally marginalized subgroups of their constituencies. In fact, the evidence shows just the opposite: The advocacy groups in this study position themselves as advocates for the weak and voiceless and lay claim to the egalitarian goals of the social movements with which they are affiliated. With the political legitimacy and power that derive from these claims comes the expectation that they will represent all members of their constituencies, using their positions to mediate among these constituencies as well as between their constituents and the constituents of other marginalized groups.

Not every organization can represent every constituent or potential constituent at all times, nor can organizations flout the exigencies of organizational maintenance or focus exclusively on disadvantaged subgroups to the exclusion of majorities and advantaged subgroups. Advocacy organizations must walk a fine line as they negotiate the task of using insider tactics to fight for outsider groups in national politics, balancing the need for legitimacy with both grassroots constituencies and affluent donors and policy-making elites. However, an intersectional approach helps us appreciate that neglecting the inequalities within marginalized groups widens the gaps among differently situated members of these groups and privileges those subgroups within their constituencies that are already the most advantaged. For organizations that charge themselves with narrowing the gaps among racial, gender, and economic groups within politics and society, the expectation that they will represent multiply marginalized constituents becomes increasingly important under conditions of advanced marginalization, as levels of political access rise and the status and living conditions of relatively privileged members of once excluded groups improve (C. Cohen 1999; see also W. Wilson 1987). Even, and perhaps especially, when these improvements are under siege, defending them ought to be accompanied by attempts to pursue changes that benefit members of marginalized groups who have benefited least from those previous victories.

In this context, many of the findings presented throughout this book raise red flags about the quality of representation afforded intersectionally disadvantaged subgroups by the organizations on which they rely to compensate for their relative lack of political power and formal representation. As such, the results reinforce the claims of scholars reaching back to Robert Michels (1911) as well as more recent work by scholars such as Frances Fox Piven and Richard Cloward (1977), Iris Young (1990, 2000), Jeffrey Berry (1999), and Theda Skocpol (2004), who have drawn our attention to a wide range of significant limitations to interest groups and other national-level staff-led organizations when it comes to improving conditions for disadvantaged populations (see also Van Til 2000; Gutmann 1998b;

Rosenblum 2000). The patterns I have described reveal that the overall level and tenor of advocacy on issues affecting intersectionally disadvantaged subgroups is lower and less rigorous than it is when it comes to other issue types. In addition, organizations pass up crucial opportunities to act as mediators for disadvantaged subgroups among the differently situated groups that make up their constituencies and between these constituencies and the larger polity. Instead, much of the mediating that they do *compounds* the problems faced by intersectionally disadvantaged groups. Rather than inspiring feelings of intersectionally linked fate by asking their *more*-advantaged constituents to help their less-advantaged ones, they are more likely to ask *less*-advantaged constituents to make do with those benefits that eventually trickle down to them. Failing to make the case for these multiply marginalized subgroups within their constituencies and within the broader community of organizations representing marginalized groups limits the possibility that they will do so effectively to the larger polity. This limitation reinforces rather than alleviates the marginalization of intersectionally disadvantaged constituents. In spite of sincere ambitions to advocate on behalf of their least advantaged constituents, then, the organizations that claim to speak for intersectionally disadvantaged subgroups are not effectively representing them in national politics. Instead, the voices and concerns of these groups are drowned out and marginalized by the majority and especially by advantaged subgroups. As a consequence, for intersectionally marginalized groups, the quality of representation is inferior to that received by advantaged subgroups.

The implications of this state of affairs are even more profound when considered in light of the modest proportion of the larger interest group universe that continues to be constituted by organizations that represent marginalized groups. Using data collected by Kay Lehman Schlozman, Sidney Verba, and Henry Brady as part of the Project on Political Equality, Scholzman and Traci Burch show that of the nearly 12,000 organizations listed in the 2001 edition of *Washington Representatives*, 35 percent represent corporations, 13 percent represent trade and other business associations, and 7 percent represent occupational groups (Schlozman and Burch forthcoming). Less than 5 percent are public interest groups, less than 4 percent are identity-based organizations representing groups such as women, racial minorities, and LGBT people, and only 1 percent are labor unions (Schlozman and Burch forthcoming). Only a fraction of 1 percent of the organizations are social welfare organizations or organizations that represent poor and low-income people (Schlozman and Burch forthcoming), a proportion that remains almost identical to the proportion that Schlozman and Tierney (1986) found almost twenty years earlier.

Considered together, the small proportion of social and economic justice organizations within the overall interest group system and the biases within these organizations themselves powerfully demonstrate the tremendous hurdles and disadvantages faced by groups such as women, racial minorities, and low-income people in their quest for representation in national politics.

## STORY OF POSSIBILITY

Despite this rather dreary picture, the data also reveal that advocacy organizations play a crucial role in combating a broader mobilization of bias in politics and public opinion. Consequently, these organizations offer an alternative conception of representation that foregrounds the importance of advocacy, redistribution, and the pursuit of social justice as some of its central goals. A wide array of evidence demonstrates that advocacy organizations *want to* represent intersectionally disadvantaged subgroups of their constituencies, and there are circumstances and conditions under which they do so. Consequently, in spite of the current shortcomings, such organizations serve as some of the best possibilities that marginal groups have for gaining an institutionalized voice in American politics (Berry and Arons 2003; Boris and Mosher-Williams 1998; Boris 1999; Mark E. Warren 2001, 2004; Weldon 2002, 2004). Conceived in this way, interest groups are an underused and undervalued democratic form of the sort that Young (1992) suggests we look to in order to improve representation for marginalized groups, building on and working within the structure and strictures of the American electoral system while simultaneously working to transform it.

Indeed, for examples of measures they can take to make the meaningful and structural changes necessary to fulfill this potential, organizations need look no further than their own advocacy communities. Organizations wishing to remedy extant disparities in representation and wanting to truly speak for all of their constituents can follow the lead of those organizations that already provide vigorous representation for intersectionally marginalized groups by making concerted efforts to amplify the voices of disadvantaged subgroups of their constituencies and to demarginalize and draw attention to the issues that affect them. In this chapter, I describe some of the remedial efforts that organizations might make in order to better represent intersectionally disadvantaged subgroups of their constituencies. Using information and examples from the survey and interviews, I describe the "best practices" of the organizations in this study, specifying conditions that increase the likelihood that an organization will be active on disadvantaged-subgroup issues.

Implicit in these practices is an underlying principle that I call *affirmative advocacy*. Applied to organizations that represent disadvantaged groups, affirmative advocacy provides a framework for proactively addressing the difficulties of achieving equitable representation for intersectionally marginalized groups. Although, as I began to articulate in chapter 1, the measures within the affirmative advocacy framework are derived inductively from the particular practices of the organizations in the study, their animating ideas echo and are inspired by calls for redistribution such as those put forth by John Rawls, who argues that distributive schemes should be designed to benefit the least well-off (Rawls 1971). The evidence from my examination suggests further that those organizations that go to the greatest lengths to represent intersectionally marginalized groups reflect the spirit of Iris Young's argument that oppressed groups should receive extra representation within policy debates and arenas of representation in order to counteract the privilege of well-represented interests (Young 1992, 530; 2000).[1] This commitment to extra representation for disadvantaged groups also reflects and draws on Lani Guinier's notion that democratic representation should provide a mechanism through which groups are able to "take turns" so that majorities do not consistently quash the abilities of marginalized groups to achieve their goals. By emphasizing the interests of disadvantaged constituents and framing disadvantaged-subgroup issues broadly and in ways that emphasize their connections to advantaged ones, organizations also reflect the expectation that they will act as mediators and nurture intersectionally linked fate on behalf of disadvantaged subgroups (Dawson 1994; M. Williams 1998; see also Mansbridge 1983; Schwartz 1988; Urbinati 2000, 2002).

Reflecting as it does the ideas of scholars such as John Rawls, Iris Young, Lani Guinier, Melissa Williams, Michael Dawson, Nancy Schwartz, and Nadia Urbinati, the framework that I describe presupposes that in order for interest groups that speak for marginalized populations to perform their compensatory role in an effective and equitable manner, it does not suffice to dedicate resources in proportion to the subgroups that are affected, nor is it effective to devote disproportionately high levels of advocacy to issues that benefit advantaged subgroups (as is currently the case). To avoid reinforcing the weak and marginalized positions of disadvantaged sub-groups, advocacy organizations (and, ideally, other political institutions as well) should instead privilege a redistributive conception of representation that treats representation itself as a way to further social justice. Conceptualizing representation in this way entails devoting *extra* resources and energies to issues affecting disadvantaged subgroups. Organizations cannot flout the dictates of organizational maintenance, nor can they ignore the preferences of their current members and supporters in favor of potential ones. However, keeping in mind the Rawlsian notion that inequalities are acceptable only if they work to the benefit of the least advantaged, these "extras" are aimed at offsetting the power of the advantaged subgroups that usually are privileged by advocacy groups or through formal representation in legislatures in order to equalize representation and policy outcomes for all groups. As Young points out, extra representation for disadvantaged subgroups also helps encourage participation by members of these groups, brings their perspectives to bear on discussions about the causes of and solutions to issues of public policy, and decenters the members of advantaged groups whose perspectives have been "taken as neutral and universal" and who traditionally have dominated the terms of debate (Young 2000, 144).

The idea of "extra" representation for disadvantaged groups, though it may seem antidemocratic at first blush, has deep roots in much democratic thought as well as in American political traditions and institutions.[2] Many American representative institutions already employ mechanisms that overrepresent select subgroups of the population. For example, the United States Senate was structured specifically to overrepresent the voices of small states, as was the electoral college that is used to aggregate votes in presidential elections. In spite of conventions such as these, neither the public nor the broader constituency of an organization will be likely to voluntarily adopt extra representation for disadvantaged subgroups. Such resistance, however, underscores one of the main points of affirmative advocacy. That is, the very fact of insufficient political support for measures designed to amplify the voices of intersectionally disadvantaged subgroups demonstrates that there remain major barriers to the representation of their interests and therefore that extra efforts must be made to rectify their marginalization.

Moreover, just as the idea of extra representation is not new, neither is resistance to suggestions such as these. Most reforms for egalitarian changes that would improve the position of marginalized groups have been regarded as unrealistic when they were initially proposed. To say that measures to improve representation for intersectionally disadvantaged groups will simply never be possible is to relegate the members of these groups to the fate of chronic underrepresentation. As many of the activists I interviewed reinforced, everything from an eight-hour workday to women's suffrage to racial equality in public accommodations had, at some point, been dismissed as radical and unattainable before it was instituted. It has only been through the tireless advocacy of interest groups and social movements like the ones in this study that such reforms have been achieved. In the words of political scientists Margaret Keck and Kathryn Sikkink, one of the main tasks of social movements and advocacy organizations "is to make possible the previously unimaginable by framing the problems in such a way that their solution comes to appear inevitable" (1998, 40; see also Guidry and Sawyer 2003).

Finally, the fact that I derive these proposals from the practices of organizations demonstrates that the value of recognizing the intersectional approach that underlies affirmative advocacy is itself gaining traction in many corners of the advocacy world—in the U.S. and internationally. In 1995, for example, the United Nations Beijing Platform for Action decried the multiple forms of discrimination that converge to disadvantage women, calling on governments to "ensure equal enjoyment of all human rights and fundamental freedoms for all women and girls who face multiple barriers to their empowerment and advancement because of such factors as their race, age, language, ethnicity, culture, religion, or disability, or because they are indigenous people" (Center for Women's Global Leadership 2001, 3). Similarly, in 2001, the United Nations Commission on the Status of Women called on governments, the United Nations, and civil society to "develop methodologies to identify the ways in which various forms of discrimination," including racism, xenophobia, and related intolerance, "converge and affect women and girls" (Center for Women's Global Leadership 2001, 5). Together with the evidence from my study, efforts such as these demonstrate that intersectional approaches to understanding inequality and marginalization resonate with organizations in very pragmatic ways and that many are making efforts to implement measures that enact the implications of such analyses.

## BEST PRACTICES

Indeed, despite overwhelming evidence of the marginalization of disadvantaged-subgroup issues by the organizations in this study, some advocacy organizations, under some circumstances, address such issues in meaningful and effective ways. In this section, I detail the practices of these organizations that lead to increased representation for disadvantaged subgroups. These "best practices" include the following: using organizational mandates to reframe and address disadvantaged-subgroup issues; using information-collection processes and decision rules to elevate such issues on organizational agendas; using internal processes and practices to improve the status of intersectionally disadvantaged groups; promoting descriptive representation and staff interest and initiative; fostering relationships with state and local organizations; being willing to evolve; making effective use of coalitions; and embracing a concern to balance self-interest with ideological and solidaristic commitments.

By adopting practices such as these, the organizations that employ them transcend traditional majoritarian and rationalist notions of representation, demonstrating that speaking for intersectionally marginalized subgroups entails conceptualizing representation as part and parcel of the pursuit of social justice. These organizations use their roles as representatives to mediate on behalf of disadvantaged subgroups and to nurture intersectionally linked fate among the subgroups that make up their constituencies by redistributing representational resources and energies to their least well-off constituents.

## ORGANIZATIONAL MANDATES

Although the results of the SNESJO demonstrate a clear pattern of greater and more vigorous activity on advantaged-subgroup issues, many officers expressed concern for disadvantaged subpopulations, and certain organizations try to pay special attention to issues that affect these groups. An explicit mandate to represent intersectionally disadvantaged subgroups of a constituency is one practice that makes it much more likely that an organization will be active on issues that affect those groups. Although self-evident to some degree, this practice bears mention because, while declarations of desires to represent disadvantaged subgroups are quite common, explicit commitments to do so are less widespread. Such mandates often can make the difference between good intentions and actual engagement, between inactivity and activity. Many of the organizations that are most active on disadvantaged-subgroup issues are also the ones that explicitly recognize that those issues are inadequately addressed. They therefore make advocacy on these issues central to their goals and organizational missions in order to offset what they perceive as a lack of energy on important issues and neglected groups (see Spalter-Roth and Schreiber 1995).

Officers at those organizations that were most active on disadvantaged-subgroup issues repeatedly emphasized their groups' particular concerns for multiply marginalized subgroups of their constituencies. The executive director of a Latino organization that, unlike many of the Latino organizations in the study, has been very involved in advocacy concerning welfare reform captured the effects of this orientation in some of his comments to me. He explained that while his organization tries to "represent all of the Hispanic community," it is "particularly concerned about poor people and moderate-income folks." In addition, in deciding whether to pursue a policy issue, the leaders in his organization do take into account "the number of people [an issue] will affect" but also place a great deal of weight on how important an issue is to the lives of the constituents that it affects. As a consequence of these considerations, his group is very involved in welfare reform because, while it "doesn't impact the majority of folks," he explained, "for those who it does, it impacts them in a very dramatic way."[3] The associate director of an economic justice organization echoed this logic, explaining that her organization focuses on issues that affect what she labeled the "most disadvantaged" groups of welfare recipients. As such, one central criterion that the organization uses "for choosing some work over other work" is an evaluation that, she said, asks, "How dire is the situation of a particular population? How poor are they, relative to other people who are also low-income or disadvantaged?" Consequently, hers has been one of the few organizations to advocate explicitly for policies addressing the needs of welfare recipients who have disabilities, which it has done because "that's a population that will tend to be most disadvantaged or tend to find it harder to get off the rolls."[4]

Similarly, the director of public policy at a women's organization that has been active on welfare reform and on HIV/AIDS—two disadvantaged-subgroup issues that have not been high on the agendas of most women's organizations—said that the focus of her organization's work "is always on low-income women and the intersection of race and class . . . and gender issues." Because of its focus on such intersectional issues, she said, her organization began to work on HIV/AIDS at a time when it "[wasn't] on a lot of women's agendas because it was an issue that affected low-income women and," she added, "sadly, often women of color."[5]

These examples emphasize that organizations that make special efforts to prioritize an explicit concern for representing the disadvantaged subgroups of their broader constituency are the ones that are most likely to be active on issues affecting intersectionally marginalized groups. What is most striking about these illustrations and the approaches to advocacy they exemplify is that each one takes into account the vulnerability of subgroups of their constituencies to changes in public policy and recognizes that because of their relative size, status, and power, the needs of disadvantaged subgroups are likely to be overlooked unless special care is taken to foreground them. As a consequence, such an orientation helps reverse the more typical tendencies to yield to the will of the majority, to listen to the most vocal constituents, and to frame issues affecting disadvantaged subgroups narrowly and particularistically. Moreover, by emphasizing the ways in which the issues that affect the most vulnerable members also affect the broader community, officers at organizations that frame disadvantaged-subgroup issues in this fashion are implicitly asking more-advantaged members of these constituencies to identify their needs with the needs of less-advantaged members rather than the reverse. By mediating among their constituencies in this way, officers nurture and validate a sense of intersectionally linked fate—a belief among constituents that their own interests are linked to the interests of disadvantaged members of the groups with which they identify (Dawson 1994, 77).

## INFORMATION COLLECTION AND DECISION RULES

The examples of these organizations also demonstrate that another important step toward increasing activity on issues affecting intersectionally marginalized groups is to prioritize them in explicit and systematic ways at the agenda-setting stage. While somewhat tautological, this is an important practice because one recurring theme throughout this book has been that there is an enormous disjuncture between the professed desires of the majority of organizations to represent disadvantaged subgroups of their constituencies and the actual low levels of advocacy on behalf of these subgroups by these same organizations. Some of this disjuncture stems from a "hollow core" in the community of organizations representing disadvantaged groups. That is, there is no single organization in the middle of the community that is in a position to coordinate activity and information sharing about the activities of its many members (Heinz et al. 1993; for an earlier version of a similar argument, see McIver 1951 and J. Wilson [1974] 1995).[6] As a consequence, two types of misinformation afflict this advocacy community.

The first type of misinformation involves a lack of knowledge about the activities and policy priorities of other organizations in the community. Organization officers often misapprehend and overestimate the levels of energy and resources that other advocacy organizations are devoting to an issue, leading them to assume that additional efforts on the issue are re- dundant, unnecessary, and possibly wasteful (Pease and Associates 2003). We saw that this was especially true in the case of Social Security, an issue that officers repeatedly referenced as being adequately covered by other groups, when in fact even labor and antipoverty organizations displayed relatively low levels of engagement with it. We saw in the discussion of niches in chapter 4 that a similar lack of information also contributed to low levels of activity on welfare reform and public funding for abortion. One key step toward prioritizing disadvantaged-subgroup issues, then, involves collecting information about the policy activities and priorities of other organizations in their interest communities and sharing these data with allies. Armed with this information, organizations can coordinate with other groups working in related and overlapping policy areas. This coordination can help ensure that every issue is being adequately dealt with while allowing organizations to carve out niches that do not replicate one another's efforts or unnecessarily concentrate resources on certain issues.

Indeed, several of the organizations in this study that take the most action on issues affecting intersectionally disadvantaged subgroups of their constituencies do so based on information that they collect about the activities and priorities of other groups in their interest communities. The director of a women's organization, for example, explained to me that her organization regularly conducts what she called "environmental scans" to assess the priorities of the organizations that her group "considers to be [its] allies." Based on these scans, the organization decides which of the efforts of other groups it should join, and it also is able to determine whether there are issues that are *not* being addressed by any of its allies that might create niches for her own group. Through this process, she said, her organization is able to exploit "opportunities that [it] would have missed otherwise," partnering with other organizations when it seems necessary and taking on issues that are being overlooked.[7]

In addition to a lack of knowledge about the activities of their allies, organizations also habitually misapprehend the proportion of their con- stituency that is affected by an issue. In particular, as illustrated by the examples about welfare reform and affirmative action in chapter 4, the scope of the impact of disadvantaged-subgroup issues tends to be drastically underestimated, whereas the effects of advantaged-subgroup issues more often are overestimated. These poor estimates contribute to the double standard that determines so much about the levels of energy that will be devoted to an issue. When organizations make themselves aware of the actual impact of policy issues, they are better able to calibrate their advocacy and resources accordingly.

With data about the priorities of their allies and about the impact of policy issues on their constituents as an informational arsenal, organizations can rationally and deliberately ensure that their own policy agendas attend to the interests of disadvantaged subgroups. One way in which organizations can formalize this process is to create a protocol for selecting issues that maps out the subgroups of their constituency along one axis and the policy issues that affect them along the other axis. Along the vertical axis, a women's organization might list subgroups including low-income women; bisexual, lesbian, and transgender women; Asian Pacific American women; African American women; women in nontraditional jobs; and so forth. They could then estimate the relative power or advantages of each of these subgroups. Along the horizontal axis, they would list policy issues that affect each subgroup, particularly those areas that fall at the intersection of two or more identities or forms of disadvantage and those that affect weak or underserved subgroups. Issues can then be coded and eventually weighted according to a variety of relevant criteria: How many other allies are working on each issue? How extensive are their efforts? Are there any immediate threats or opportunities looming in any branch of government that require an immediate or forceful response? What is the breadth of each issue's impact? Organizations also can use agenda setting as an opportunity to, in the words of legal scholar Mari Matsuda, "ask the other questions," exposing the intersectional implications of policy issues by looking for the ways in which policies that harm or benefit one subgroup might affect other groups as well so that advocacy efforts can address all of these dimensions (Matsuda 1991). For example, policies designed to address the gender-based wage disparities that I discussed in chapter 2 could be analyzed in terms of their particular benefits for intersectionally disadvantaged subgroups of women, such as women of color, gender-nonnormative men and women, and low-income women. Asking such questions provides a process through which organizations can frame intersectionally disadvantaged subgroups and the issues that affect them *into* rather than *out of* their mandates and constituencies.

As with affirmative action in admissions or employment, issues then can be ranked on a point system. Although issues certainly should receive points for strategic considerations, such as immediate threats or political opportunities and concerns about organizational maintenance, extra points also can be given to issues that affect disadvantaged subgroups. Based on this point system, organizations then can prioritize the issues on their agendas. Disadvantaged-subgroup issues will be high on the list of priorities, and organizations can accordingly designate the extra energy and resources that these issues will be afforded. This point system also can be used to more fairly allocate the use of scarce political resources such as judicial strategies to ensure that they are not deployed disproportionately on behalf of advantaged subgroups of their constituencies.

Although it may sound cumbersome, versions of this type of issue protocol and selection process frequently are employed by organizations in this study as a way to rationalize their agenda-setting procedures. For example, the executive director of a Latino organization explained to me that his group uses what he called a "decision tree" to rank issues on its agenda. The formula that his organization employs tries to balance three specific criteria: the importance of the issue; the immediacy of the issue; and whether the organization's actions on the issue are likely to make a difference.[8] The executive director of a women's health organization explained a similar process that her organization had begun to use to determine its level of advocacy on potential policy issues. While its process of issue selection had been somewhat ad hoc in the past, when I spoke to her, the organization staff members had just finished implementing a new process whereby they assess their strategic priorities on an annual basis using decision rules that balance three considerations: the extent to which a policy is in an area that exploits their organizational strengths; the extent to which other organizations are working on the issue; and the extent of the impact they are likely to have on the issue.[9]

On their own, the particular criteria used by each of the aforementioned organizations do not prioritize issues affecting intersectionally disadvantaged subgroups of their constituencies. However, there are organizations that do use these processes for precisely this purpose. For example, in its brochure, "Intersectionality: A Tool for Gender and Economic Justice," the Association for Women's Rights in Development, a Canadian women's organization, suggests that "when setting priorities for projects," organizations should allocate resources to those who are most marginalized, as revealed by analyzing intersecting discriminations" (Association for

Women's Rights in Development 2004). To do so, they suggest that organizations initiate their work by asking questions such as, "Who are the most marginalized women, girls, men, and boys in the community and why? Which groups have the lowest and the highest levels of public representation and why? What laws, policies, and organizational practices limit opportunities of different groups? What opportunities facilitate the advancement of different groups? What initiatives would address the needs of the most marginalized or discriminated groups in society?"

It is clear that many organizations already engage in forms of planning and agenda setting that are amenable to explicitly intersectional analyses and selection criteria. If such criteria are not already being deployed, they can be added to the list of decision rules that are in use in order to retrofit an organization's processes for the purpose of prioritizing issues that affect intersectionally disadvantaged groups. Not every organization can work on every issue; all groups must pick and choose among a huge array of pressing concerns. Selecting these issues in a manner that highlights and elevates disadvantaged-subgroup issues is one way to make certain that intersectionally disadvantaged groups do not bear more than their share of the practical limitations of the time, energy, and resources faced by all organizations.

## INTERNAL PROCESSES AND PRACTICES

All of the foregoing suggestions can increase the chances that organizations will represent the policy interests of intersectionally disadvantaged subgroups of their constituencies in politics and public policy processes by giving a mandate to do so to organizations that are so disposed. Sometimes, however, the political climate is so hostile to the claims of these groups that simply having such a mandate will not suffice. At these times, organizations need not discontinue their attempts to represent intersectionally disadvantaged groups. Instead, they can increase their attention to intersectional disadvantage by addressing these issues prefiguratively within their own organizations through internal processes and practices (D. Warren 2005; see also Barakso 2004; Gabin 1991; Kurtz 2002; McCann 1994; Zald, Morrill, and Rao 2005). These practices can take many forms, a few of which I will sketch out.

One illustration of such a practice is apparent in the case of labor unions. Contracts provide unions with a clear route to take on issues affecting disadvantaged members of their broader constituencies—issues that might otherwise be ignored. As the executive director of a women's labor organization told me, "You can negotiate anything. That's our position."[10] Based on this logic, her organization lobbies unions to address issues such as abortion and domestic partner benefits in their contracts, even if these same unions do not do so at the level of public policy. Many unions that had not been vocal supporters of the 1998 Violence against Women Act had been very receptive to her organization's suggestion that the labor movement address violence against women as a workplace issue by integrating into contracts provisions for addressing the effects of such violence on women's work life.

As another example of addressing issues within an organization when it is not possible to engage them politically, consider the case of one large industrial union. The president of this union explained to me that his organization officially supports reproductive rights. However, because many of this union's members oppose abortion, the organization is not involved in public policy debates about the issue. The union does, however, include abortion coverage in contracts and negotiations. He put it this way:

> The men in our union . . . don't want to see us become actively engaged pro or con. But the union has a policy . . . that the women members have the right to make that choice. . . . I don't know if we should even get [politically] involved in the issue because it's not a trade union issue. But it becomes one when we go to the bargaining table and we try to get benefits for our members . . . we have to fight to have birth control pills covered under the medical insurance, but men don't have to fight to get certain things covered for them. . . . That's where we come in on it.[11]

Contracts, in this case, provide his organization with an opportunity to represent the interests of female union members by addressing gender issues as part of "regular 'union business,'" without spending political capital or contravening members' policy preferences (Kurtz 2002, 87; see McCann 1994 for a discussion of a similar phenomenon in the case of comparable worth and pay equity).

Similarly, lesbian, gay, bisexual, and transgender (LGBT) issues often make their way onto the agendas of labor organizations initially as contract issues rather than as policy advocacy, allowing unions to support these intersectionally disadvantaged members of their larger constituency and to demonstrate this support to other union members (Sweeney 1999; D. Warren 2005). Asked about his organization's activities on the

Employment Non-Discrimination Act (which would protect LGBT people against workplace discrimination), for example, the president of a union pointed instead to a contract he had negotiated that included benefits for same-sex domestic partners. "We broke the mold for the airline industry," he boasted, by insisting that "if a heterosexual couple can have coverage, what about a homosexual couple? . . . We got it and now it's standard in our contracts."[12]

Unions are somewhat unique in their capacity to use internal practices as a prefigurative form of politics and advocacy for their constituents through the mechanism of negotiating binding contracts that affect hundreds and sometimes thousands of people. Other organizations can, however, take a page from unions' use of these contracts to incorporate activity on disadvantaged-subgroup issues and apply this model in ways that are appropriate to their own organizations. Professional organizations, for example, do not normally negotiate contracts for their members, but many do issue guidelines for professional standards or ethical conduct. Professional organizations can organize to use these guidelines as a way to press employers to, for example, provide domestic partner benefits even if there is no hope of passing legislation that would do so or if their membership does not endorse official organizational opposition to the Defense of Marriage Act. In addition, all organizations can promote these same standards within their own organizations.

There is, of course, no guarantee that labor contracts or professional guidelines will benefit disadvantaged subgroups, and inclusion in such fora will not necessarily translate into policy advocacy, even in the long term. Moreover, this and other "below the radar screen" strategies—what Sharon Kurtz characterizes as a "do it but don't talk too much about it" approach—runs the risk of perpetuating the often stigmatized positions of disadvantaged-subgroup issues if efforts are not made to supplement these stealth forms of representation with more public methods as well (Kurtz 2002, 87). Nonetheless, contracts, professional standards, and internal policies represent a few ways in which issues that might otherwise be ignored are sometimes addressed by organizations. Such an approach can be particularly useful during periods of an inhospitable political climate. During these periods, organizations can focus more of their efforts on embodying changes that they hope will eventually take root in public policy by mediating within their constituencies, fostering intersectional understandings among them about the various policy issues that affect them, and making efforts to illuminate the connections among these issues. By practicing prefigurative politics during the "doldrums," they will be in better shape to make the demands for these changes when the political winds begin to blow in their favor.

## DESCRIPTIVE REPRESENTATION

*Descriptive representation*—the idea that if representatives resemble those they represent, they will provide better "substantive" representation because a member of a given group better understands the interests and needs of that group—has been, as I discussed in chapter 2, roundly and rightly criticized as an essentialist and impractical criterion for selecting representatives and conferring legitimacy (Dovi 2002; Kenney 2005; Mansbridge 1999; Phillips 1995, 1998a; Pitkin 1967). While no panacea, an organizational commitment to descriptive representation often stimulates activity on policy issues affecting disadvantaged subgroups. Moreover, justifying descriptive representation need not rely on essentialist notions that women have different "ways of knowing" or that members of racial minorities are the only "authentic" political voices of these groups (Belenky et al. 1996; Gilligan 1993). Without accepting that there are inherent and essential differences among groups or clearly delineated boundaries dividing them, we can appreciate that marginalization and discrimination foster different life experiences—what Young refers to as different "perspectives"—for members of marginalized groups (Young 2000; see also Kenney 2005; M. Williams 1998).

As a consequence of these different perspectives and experiences, elevating women, low-income people, LGBT people, and members of racial minority groups to positions of power and authority brings different voices to conversations about public policy and fosters their participation and empowerment. These voices report different experiences, ask different questions, and present, in Young's terminology, different "starting points for discussion," while fostering the legitimacy of these representatives among the represented (Young 2000, 140; see also Kenney 2005; Mansbridge 1999; Mueller 1995; M. Williams 1998). Jane Mansbridge argues further that descriptive representation can also help crystallize interests and build trust among constituents, providing them with evidence that there is someone "fighting for them" (Mansbridge 1999). Descriptive representatives, Suzanne Dovi argues, are particularly helpful when they have strong "mutual relationships with dispossesed groups" (Dovi 2002, 730). As Young writes, one of the things that makes us "feel represented" is "when at least some of those discussing and voting on policies understand and express the kind of social experience" that we have had because of our group positions "and the history of social group relations" (Young 2000, 134).

In organizations such as the National Women's Studies Association (NWSA), for example, the oversampling of marginalized groups within representational structures has aided the building and maintenance of coalitions among women with different identities, perspectives, and interests (Sirianni 1993, 307). Carol Mueller (1995) gives a similar account of the ways in which the National Women's Political Caucus (NWPC) countered factionalism and charges of elitism by implementing formal rules and mechanisms that ensure representation along lines of race, ethnicity, sexuality, age, and partisanship among organization members, activists, and high-level officers. Maryann Barakso argues that the requirement of the National Organization for Women (NOW) that a certain minimum number of seats on their board be occupied by people of color brought similar benefits to that organization (Barakso 2004).

Although it is neither a necessary nor a sufficient condition, descriptive representation in leadership and on boards features prominently in the interviews as one way to encourage activity on disadvantaged-subgroup issues—and in ways that echo many of the foregoing arguments. For example, respondents from organizations that are especially concerned with intersectionally disadvantaged populations often assert that descriptive representation helps achieve diversity among members of their staffs and boards and that diversification and having members of these groups "in the room" changes the public policy agendas of the organizations themselves (Kenney 2005). As Jeffrey Berry (1977) has noted, staff members tend to dominate decision making about policy involvement, and so it is not surprising that many respondents reported that a diverse staff with diverse interests and experiences has a significant impact on the policy agendas of the organizations at which they work (see also J. Wilson [1974] 1995). Thus, the value of descriptive representation is enhanced when organizations have a diverse staff and board and when the interests and initiatives of these staff and board members are taken seriously.

As one director of public policy at a women's organization explained to me, when she joined the staff of this organization a few years back, she came with strong interests in LGBT rights and drug policy reform. After making her case to the other staff and officers, the organization began to focus a great deal of energy and resources on these two issues—both of which affect intersectionally disadvantaged subgroups of women (low-income women and women in prison for drug-related offenses). Because "the interests of the particular individuals who are employed" at her organization are extremely important in determining what issues the organization will pursue, these issues moved to the center of the organization's agenda.[13] Organization leaders, too, can similarly lead the organization to increase its attention to disadvantaged-subgroup issues. Several respondents credited their organization's presidents or executive directors with expanding the agendas of their organizations beyond a single-axis set of issues.[14] The previously quoted respondent explained that her organization is committed to issues affecting low-income women and women of color because, when the current president arrived, "she reinvigorated that as the niche or mission at the [organization] in a more explicit and focused way. . . . She came on board and . . . redirected the [organization toward] picking . . . issues that exemplified the intersection of race, gender, and class."[15]

Unions seem particularly amenable to this type of change in policy advocacy. Though neither descriptive representation nor changing labor force composition inevitably translate into changes in policy activity, many scholars argue that these factors, at least under some circumstances, make it more likely that unions will be attentive to the concerns of women and members of racial minorities (Kurtz 2002; D. Warren 2005; J. Wong 2006). That is, as women and members of racial minorities have come to make up increasingly large portions of the labor force, particularly in service-sector industries where unionization is more possible, some unions have begun to work more extensively on issues that affect these constituents. For example, the president of a large labor union explained that at its founding, his union had been comprised of "nineteen white men, members of a Masonic organization." While the organization's early practices and constitution focused "heavily on men," today, he explained "25 percent of the . . . union is female, about 10 percent is African American, 8 percent is Hispanic." The new diversity of the union members, he said, means that doing "a good job for all those members" and keeping "the purpose for which we were founded intact and operational, vibrant and alive," entails demonstrating "that there's room for everybody. . . . To make it work requires constant change. You have to keep molding and shaping to make it work for you."[16] Consequently, his organization has gone to great lengths to make sure that there are women, immigrants, and members of racial minority groups on its staff and board and also has become much more active on issues that affect women, immigrants, and racial minorities.

The beneficial effects of descriptive representation also can be illustrated by considering cases in which it is absent. For example, the executive director of a Latino organization explained that in his experience, many labor and Latino organizations want very much to do "good work" on behalf of migrant laborers or undocumented immigrants. However, without "diverse enough representation" in leadership positions or on boards, he said, most of the organizations become complacent because there is often nobody "in the room" pushing them to prioritize the issues that actually affect these intersectionally disadvantaged subgroups of workers and Latinos.[17]

The director of legal services and public policy at a women's organization was even more emphatic about the importance of descriptive representation. In the case of welfare reform, she argued, the policy debates and agendas have been and remain severely limited because "the people having the debate are not like the people who are experiencing the issues. It's not a diverse group of people." Echoing Young, Mansbridge, and Dovi, she noted that "it is rare that you see people who have been welfare recipients participating in the discussions ... [so] it's not as diverse as it should be, and that has an enormous impact on the type of debate" that is conducted about this issue. In particular, she argued that negative stereotypes about welfare recipients as promiscuous and lazy are easily perpetuated under such conditions, while policy initiatives do not respond to the lived experiences of people who are trying to raise children while working long hours at low-wage jobs.[18]

In a similar vein, the executive director of a women's health organization attributed "some of what was done badly or done wrong in past decades" when it came to issues such as sterilization to the fact that women's organizations did not listen to leaders among women of color who "screamed about how [sterilization] was being inappropriately marketed or pushed onto poor women." These women, she said, "were very vocal about possible coercive use" but were largely ignored by white feminists. Had they been brought "to the table very early on, [white feminists] would have known that these were potential problems, they could have dealt with them earlier on, and perhaps avoided all the problems that happened down the road." In contrast, her organization now addresses the racialized implications of sterilization head-on, a development that she attributed to the fact that her group has an advisory board that "brings to the table" groups of representatives from organizations of women of color to help set the organization's agenda. She explained, "Group after group said, 'This is really important. This is an issue that my community should know about.'"[19] Based on the recommendations of the advisory board, hers is one of the few women's health organizations that addresses issues such as sterilization as a central component of their reproductive rights agenda.

Thus, although descriptive representation may not be a cure-all, its absence can limit the policy agenda, hamper effective engagement with disadvantaged-subgroup issues, and perpetuate problematic paradigms within public policy debates.[20] To avoid the tokenism that so often accompanies descriptive representation, however, organizations also should make efforts not to take a "one of each" approach to diversity within their organizations. Instead, in keeping with the idea of affirmative advocacy, the goal should be to achieve *overrepresentation* of members of disadvantaged subgroups. To maximize the benefits of descriptive representation, organizations should make sure to promote *meaningful* descriptive representation among their staff and board members by adopting formal procedures that facilitate participation by members of underrepresented and intersectionally disadvantaged groups. For example, to compensate for the typical, if unintentional, tendency to dismiss ideas that are put forward by members of marginalized groups, a point system similar to the one described earlier for agenda setting should be employed to evaluate and implement their agenda and strategy suggestions. In addition, organizations should provide space and resources for members of these subgroups to meet and organize (by, for example, facilitating the formation of caucuses).

## RELATIONSHIPS WITH STATE AND LOCAL ORGANIZATIONS

Some observers suggest that state and local organizations such as civic organizations, service providers, and state and local chapters of national groups are more likely to address issues affecting disadvantaged groups than are national-level organizations (Brecher and Costello 1990). The members of and populations served by state and local groups are less likely to be affluent professionals than are the members of national organizations, and these organizations therefore tend to emphasize policy priorities that differ from those of national groups (Berry and Arons

2003; Skocpol 2004; Verba, Schlozman, and Brady 1995). National organizations with strong ties to state and local groups are therefore likely to respond to a wider range of constituencies and to be active on a broader range of issues than organizations without such connections (Almeida and Stearns 1998; Brecher and Costello 1990; Fung 2004; Gelb and Palley 1987; McCarthy 2005; Putnam 2001; Skocpol 2004; Mark R. Warren 2001; Young 1992; for an alternate view, see Scipes 1991; D. Warren and C. Cohen 2000). Indeed, the survey data indicate that at the bivariate level, the more that organizations are influenced by state or local organizations (including chapters of their own organization), the more active they are on disadvantaged-subgroup issues.[21] That is, the more important their relationships with state and local organizations, the more active national organizations are on behalf of intersectionally disadvantaged subgroups of their constituencies.

The interviews confirm that relationships with state and local organizations are one key route through which issues can "trickle up" to Washington-based organizations and make their way onto the national advocacy agenda.[22] Having ties to state and local groups increases organizations' activity on disadvantaged-subgroup issues in part by serving as a democratic "check" on national organizations, making them more responsive and accountable to their constituents. For example, the executive director of an economic justice group that focuses on migrant farm workers and that has close ties to migrant worker groups around the country explained that when he works with these groups, he is "very conscious that we're outsiders coming in from D.C."[23] As a consequence, he does not try to set an agenda for the local groups but instead solicits their insights on issues and incorporates them into his group's agenda. Similarly, the executive director of an economic justice organization that represents more than one thousand local organizations said that he turns quite deliberately to local groups to help him "identify needs" and "to point out shortcomings . . . in law or policies." As an example, he said, "the guys at community agencies were talking about . . . homelessness two years before I heard about it in Washington."[24] The executive director of another economic justice organization told me that his group became active on the issue of restoring public benefits such as welfare and Medicaid for immigrants—an issue that affects primarily an intersectionally disadvantaged subgroup of all immigrants—in large part because his national organization is in a "pretty deep relationship" with many state and local organizations for which this issue was important.[25]

Some organizations have formalized the kinds of mechanisms that facilitate the transmission of state and local issues to the national level. The chair of the board of a civil rights organization explained that many "cutting-edge" issues make their way onto his group's agenda at its annual conference, at which the executive directors from state and local chapters bring issues that are of concern to their communities to the floor. Recounting an example from a recent convention, he said, "While we were [at the annual convention] . . . a kid in Baltimore was discovered with lead-paint damage. . . . So [the executive director from Baltimore] announced that we were considering a lawsuit against the industry to make them do more. So an issue comes up in that direction."[26]

Not only do such relationships help put issues on the agenda, but they also help national organizations maintain a grassroots base, which can be mobilized when organizations need mass support for their policy advocacy. The political director at a large LGBT group explained, for example, that in order to maintain a "field presence," her organization partners with "state and local organizations that are out there on the front lines fighting." This grassroots base helps her organization when it needs to get "letters, calls, e-mails and faxes to members of Congress in support of a federal issue."[27]

In all of these ways, robust ties to state and local organizations provide routes through which national organizations undertake advocacy on issues affecting disadvantaged subgroups of their constituencies. Organizations wishing to enhance their representation of intersectionally marginalized groups can foster such ties, including ties to groups with mandates that are not explicitly political (Berry and Arons 2003; J. Cohen and Rogers 1992; Mansbridge 1999; Schmitter 1992; Skocpol 2004; Young 1990, 1992). By working on the issues that concern the leaders and constituents of these organizations, national groups can foster accountability to the differently situated subgroups of their broadly defined constituencies.[28]

## WILLINGNESS TO EVOLVE

Another factor that stimulates greater advocacy activity on issues affecting intersectionally disadvantaged subgroups derives from organizations' active dedication to evolving, changing, and embracing new, proactive issues on their agendas. Many respondents whose organizations are particularly active on disadvantaged-subgroup issues attributed this activity to their organizations' ability and desire to learn from and rectify past mistakes, especially with regard to issues such as immigration, criminal justice, and sterilization (Murakawa 2005).

For example, the executive director of a civil rights organization distinguished between what he labeled the first and second "generations" of civil rights issues. He argued that the United States has dealt relatively well with "the first generation of civil rights problems," such as "ending legal segregation and . . . establishing a statutory framework for the consideration of fundamental civil rights." However, he continued, while the United States has quite successfully dismantled the most egregious and obvious de jure discrimination, "we've been less successful in achieving meaningful equality in opportunity in public education . . . [or] dealing with ending and resolving the problems of housing discrimination and segregation." These issues—ones that he labeled "the second generation of civil rights issues"—are at the intersection of racial and other forms of inequality such as class, gender, or sexuality, and as such affect intersectionally disadvantaged subgroups of women, people of color, and low-income people. Issues such as these deal with what he characterized as "closing the equality gap" and determining how to "address the disparities that continue to exist in a democratic society in which race is supposed to have had a declining significance."[29]

As a particular instance of this evolution, this executive director cited his organization's work on immigration. Until 1965, American immigration policy contained many race-based and ethnicity-based restrictions, and it almost entirely prohibited immigration from Asian countries (R. M. Smith 1999). The 1965 Immigration and Nationality Act finally abolished these explicitly racist quotas and exclusions that had discriminated against people of particular nationalities. Although the immigration quotas were undeniably racist in their intent and effect and removing them represented, in the words of this executive director, "a dramatic change" in civil rights law, he explained that changing immigration policy in this way had not been "of particular concern to the civil rights community." Because, he argued, the number of Latinos and Asian Pacific Americans was "relatively small on the national scene," they were not major "factors in the policy debates [within the civil rights community] at that time." He compared the movement's lack of engagement with immigration in the 1960s with the engagement of civil rights organizations with immigration policy in the current era. These days, he argued, "immigration is now recognized as a four-square component of the national civil rights debate, and there is absolutely no debate . . . about whether we should be working on this."

This change, he argued, "reflects the evolution of thinking and not just a self-interest. Things do change, and the civil rights movement is a living entity" that changes with them.[30]

In some cases, attention to disadvantaged-subgroup issues grows directly out of an organization's recognition of past failures and a desire to ameliorate them. An instance of this process was illustrated by the earlier comments of the executive director of the women's health organization who explained that her group focuses on issues connected to the reproductive rights of women of color. The organization's interest in these issues grew out of its desire to "try to undo some of what was done . . . wrong in past decades" on issues such as forced sterilization of poor women and women of color.[31] To address these problems, her organization does not simply recognize and apologize for the mistakes of the past; it makes sure that this recognition explicitly informs and influences its current approach to contemporary issues. Consequently, this organization has proactively addressed its constituents' concerns that the long-acting and surgically implanted contraceptive Norplant is being deployed against low-income women and women of color in ways that are reminiscent of the forced sterilization of earlier eras.

Evolution, of course, does not always move in a direction that benefits disadvantaged groups. In conservative political climates, organizations might instead be driven to evolve in ways that move *away* from the issues that affect intersectionally disadvantaged groups. Rather than suggesting an inevitable progression toward more inclusiveness, however, all of the examples in this chapter clearly show the importance of a proactive and explicit commitment to engage in affirmative advocacy in all political climates, taking seriously critiques of past omissions and mistakes and making a commitment to take the necessary measures to correct them. Organizations might further these goals by engaging in regular self-studies in order to learn from the past, by remaining open to change, and by using their recognition of problematic histories to try to avoid similar mishaps and oversights in the present.

COALITIONS

Coalitions, as I discussed in chapter 6, are a double-edged sword when it comes to advocacy on disadvantaged-subgroup issues. On the one hand, coalitions often marginalize the concerns of intersectionally disadvantaged subgroups in ways that depress activity on issues affecting these groups. When organizations engage in coalition work on issues affecting intersectionally disadvantaged subgroups of their constituencies, their level of participation is usually weaker and more symbolic than it is when it comes to other issues types. As a consequence, coalitions can easily reproduce the mobilization of bias against intersectionally disadvantaged issues that we see in individual organizations.

While these limitations are persistent, coalition work is nonetheless an extremely important conduit for activity on disadvantaged-subgroup issues. By bringing together organizations in ways that transcend the usual boundaries around issues and constituencies, coalitions help advocacy groups draw connections among issues and illuminate aspects of these issues that remain in the shadows when organizations work alone. In spite of their potential pitfalls, then, coalitions provide organizations with unparalleled opportunities to improve their representation of intersectionally disadvantaged groups. Organizations should therefore give priority to coalition work, but they should do so in tandem with explicit measures to avoid using coalitions in ways that give disadvantaged-subgroup issues short shrift.

The rich potential of coalitions to represent intersectionally disadvantaged subgroups can be maximized, and many of their common pitfalls can be avoided, by incorporating into the structures and processes of coalitions many of the recommendations that I have discussed thus far regarding organizations more generally. For example, when organizations join forces with one another, they can engage in the processes of information collection and policy selection that I described earlier to ensure that they recognize and prioritize issues that affect disadvantaged subgroups of the constituencies they represent. By taking proactive measures such as these to nurture intersectional understandings of policy issues and approaches to advocacy, organizations also can make the most of the unparalleled opportunities for mediation that are offered by coalitions among many groups.

In addition to measures such as these, partners in coalitions can make explicit agreements with one another to pursue common and clearly articulated goals and to pool their relevant resources, as Ralph Gomes and Linda Williams suggest with regard to electoral coalitions (Gomes and Williams 1995a). Moreover, in the process of articulating their goals, they can make self-conscious efforts to ensure that inequities in power, resources, and social standing do not lead to taking disadvantaged-subgroup issues "off the table." Instead, coalition members can make explicit attempts to place such issues high on their agendas. In addition, when organizations pool their resources, stronger and wealthier organizations might be expected to provide extra resources to the coalitions. Those organizations that bring more resources to the table might be asked explicitly to agree that they will not wield these resources over less well-resourced organizations and that they will refrain from using the threat of pulling their resources as an exit strategy if they disapprove of decisions that are made or directions that are taken by the alliance.[32]

## IDEOLOGICAL AND SOLIDARISTIC COMMITMENTS

Another factor associated with higher levels of activity on disadvantaged-subgroup issues is an organizational commitment to an overall vision of social justice, especially one that emphasizes the interconnectedness of issues and inequalities. The way in which this approach leads to activism on intersectionally disadvantaged issues is exemplified by the following exchange that I had with an economist in the public policy department of a labor organization. I asked him why he believes that his organization should be active on a policy issue such as workfare (policies which require recipients of public assistance to fulfill a certain number of hours of labor in exchange for their benefits), even though this policy issue does not directly affect the union members who comprise his membership, since they, by definition, are employed and not receiving public assistance. Without hesitating, he responded that the organization's investment in this issue is based on a combination of what he termed "social justice and self-interest." He explained, "People who've been forced into workfare [are] being pitted against union workers, so it's natural self-interest that we shouldn't want a superexploited group of workers . . . competing with our members' jobs." Just as important, however, is what he labeled "the social justice side." He continued, "People can't survive on the wages that many of these jobs pay, creating a lot of social misery."[33] From this perspective, even though workfare does not affect union members directly, it is connected to the mission of the labor movement because it is an issue of social justice, something their overarching ideology allows them to see. Moreover, as this respondent's statements reveal so clearly, an ideological commitment to social justice need not be completely divorced from self-interest. In fact, self-interest, or at least enlightened self-interest (the idea that we can best achieve what is in our own self-interest by taking into account shared interests and the interests of others), can help reveal the interconnectedness of issues and forms of marginalization (Mansbridge 1983).

The role of an overarching ideology and set of commitments in encouraging activity on disadvantaged-subgroup issues is perhaps best articulated by the executive director of the civil rights organization that was referenced earlier as having embraced immigration as a central issue on its agenda. This respondent attributed his group's adoption of this issue to the fact that the organization is "guided a by a core set of fundamental principles that allow you to take new facts [and] situations and apply those principles and determine whether the issue that emerges should be considered as a part of the portfolio."[34] In similar fashion, the executive director of a large African American organization affirmed the centrality of ideological frameworks in prompting his group to work on issues that might not seem, at first glance, to be "black issues." He explained, for example, that even though racially motivated crimes are already covered by existing anti–hate crime legislation, African American organizations have been at the forefront of recent efforts to expand this legislation so that it would cover crime motivated by gender, sexuality, or disability. He attributed this commitment to both solidaristic and ideological sources, explaining that the organization's activity on this issue stemmed from a "desire to support and be in solidarity with other groups [in particular LGBT people] that would benefit" from it, as well as from a desire "to be included because to be [on the] left says something."[35] As this example demonstrates, ideological commitments and solidaristic impulses can lead organizations that might not seem to have a direct interest in the outcome of a campaign to contribute to the effort. Although we might not expect such efforts in the absence of these ideological commitments, self-consciously *emphasizing* these commitments and making them explicit is an important component of effective representation for intersectionally marginalized groups.

One way that organizations can emphasize ideological commitments is to maintain a utopian vision—an overarching set of ideals that encompasses both critical ideas about the problems with the world as it is and constructive ideas about what the "good life" would be. Although a pragmatic, incrementalist approach is certainly important for short-term gains and successes, a broader vision fosters motivation during difficult periods and also provides a set of long-term goals against which current actions and demands can be compared. While this might, at first glance, seem amorphous and naively utopian, it can be "operationalized" in at least two ways: by taking a long-term view and by having a proactive agenda.

*Long-Term View* | First, as I discussed in chapter 4, the interviews suggest that one way that organizations operationalize a utopian vision is by taking a long-term view of social change. Egalitarian agendas take a very long time to realize, but over these long periods of time, ideas once considered radical often become commonsensical—votes for women seemed as much of a pie-in-the-sky idea at one point in history as voting rights for felons might seem now (Baumgartner and Jones 1993; Guidry and Sawyer 2003; Keck and Sikkink 1998).[36] It is only by putting seemingly "radical" ideas out for policy makers and the public to debate over years and even decades that they will eventually be integrated into a practical political and public policy agenda.

While all such changes require long and difficult struggles before they are attained and integrated into the political landscape, policies benefiting advantaged members of formerly excluded groups have proven easier to attain than ones that might benefit multiply marginalized people (Klinkner and Smith 1999). For example, recall the executive director of the civil rights coalition who was quoted earlier, speaking about economic justice and criminal justice issues as "second-generation" civil rights issues. His statement does not mean that the economic and criminal justice issues that he referenced were absent in the 1950s and 1960s. Instead, his point is that the issues that we now think of as "basic" civil rights issues—consensus issues such as the rights to vote and to be served in public accommodations, for example (C. Cohen 1999)—were more readily (though not by any means easily) attained than these other issues that intersect race and class disadvantages or affect stigmatized subgroups. As issues affecting disadvantaged subgroups of African Americans, they are more difficult to address and have taken longer even to become agenda items, much less to solve.

Many respondents referenced the importance of taking a long-term view and working on issues that might seem to be futile at the moment. The executive director of a large civil rights organization said, for example, that while he certainly likes to work on issues that have high probability of a victory, he also argued that "on some issues of principle, it is important that the organization be counted—even though you know going in that it's going to be a tough fight and may be a fight that you can't win."[37] The executive director of an antipoverty organization made a similar point. He said that while advocacy organizations certainly have to account for immediate needs and figure out how to prioritize battles, "the opportunity for immediate success should not dictate your policy. Sometimes the same issue has to come in front of the Congress every year for a bunch of years before they get the message.... So you don't look at [the] short term."[38] It also is important not to be discouraged by short-term losses. As the president of an economic justice group said, organizations have to "deal with all the little things that pop up, obstacles and stones in the road" and "be fluid enough to dodge and step over and pick up and move so that you could move on."[39]

The political director of a LGBT organization put it this way: "The Employment Nondiscrimination Act," she began, referencing the bill that would protect LGBT people from workplace discrimination, "was just reintroduced for the fifth time in the 107th Congress.... Some people look and say, 'Seven years is an awfully long time and what are you doing?' But in the world of civil rights legislation . . . seven years really isn't that long."[40] Similarly, the executive director of a women's health organization told me that her organization worked for thirteen years to get the Federal Drug Administration to approve mifepristone (RU-486, commonly known as the "morning after pill") even though "at times it seemed like it would never happen."[41] While short-term goals must be pursued strategically, they should not preclude activity on "utopian" goals that will likely take longer to achieve. One respondent summed it up this way: the members of his organization, he said, "are interested in getting results, they're just not interested in how long it takes."[42]

*Proactive Agendas* | The second way in which organizations can "operationalize utopianism" is by maintaining a proactive agenda. Organizations must, of course, respond to assaults and opportunities, taking action on issues that are high on the legislative, administrative, or judicial agenda in order to exploit opportunities for change or block initiatives they see as detrimental (Kingdon 1995; Meyer and Minkoff 2004). Assaults on issues from reproductive rights to affirmative action certainly demand immediate reactions, high-priority positions on agendas, and the use of all of the legislative, judicial, and executive strategies in an organization's tactical arsenal. However, the need to focus on defending programs such as these often means that disadvantaged-subgroup issues are ignored. The reasonable impulse to do everything possible to protect extant rights should therefore be tempered by an awareness that doing so tends to concentrate energy and resources on protecting policies that have had disproportionate impact on relatively advantaged subgroups. In contrast to such issues, most disadvantaged-subgroup issues have yet to win a spot on the mainstream political agenda. To counteract such a lack of mainstream attention, organizations should always have several items on their agendas that are aimed at promoting public debate about and introducing legislation that would codify *new* rights or confer *new* benefits, particularly rights and benefits that help disadvantaged and multiply marginalized subgroups of their constituencies. For example, Roberta Spalter-Roth and Ronnee Schreiber examined the activities and agendas of feminist organizations during the hostile period of the Reagan and Bush administrations of the 1980s and early 1990s. They argue that those organizations that managed to survive and thrive during this period did so, in part, because they committed their organizations to expanding their agendas to include issues such as sexual orientation, abortion rights, and racism (Spalter-Roth and Schreiber 1995, 125–26).

One specific way in which organizations can be proactive is by maintaining and pursuing a research agenda that allows them to continue to collect information and develop analyses about issues during periods when there is little chance that they will succeed politically (Spalter-Roth and Schreiber 1995). The executive director of a women's health organization explained to me, for example, that in addition to its policy arm, her group has a clearinghouse for information. The staff uses the clearinghouse for public education and for working with members on issues that have not yet made it onto the national agenda. This clearinghouse allows the organization to continue to work reactively to stave off rollbacks, while guaranteeing that it will devote energy and resources to issues that are, as the director put it, political "long shots."[43]

Maintaining a proactive agenda is no small feat in political climates inhospitable to many of the goals of the groups in this study. Indeed, in addition to the usual constraints associated with organizational maintenance, organizations that represent marginalized groups face difficult decisions during times of backlash against progressive social and economic change. The following statement from the executive director of a Latino organization captured the spirit of many that I heard in my conversations with advocacy group officers in the spring of 2001. "Unfortunately," he began, reflecting on the recent election of President George W. Bush, "of late, it's playing a lot more defense than playing offense, ... trying to keep bad things from happening [rather] than making good things happen."[44]

Indeed, many observers argue that the most that can be expected of advocacy organizations in unreceptive political climates or during times of national crises is that they do their best to forestall the impact of attacks on the rights and resources of the marginalized groups they represent. But advocacy organizations can also endeavor to use the access that they have to make sure that the most vulnerable and marginalized members of their communities do not bear the lion's share of the burdens of such retrenchments. The current practices of many of these organizations unfortunately do not point in that direction. There is too much at stake, however, to normalize the fact that most organizations do not work on behalf of their disadvantaged constituents by taking it as given that they will fail to do so.

Affirmative advocacy offers a set of principles and suggestions to put advocacy organizations on a course that would help them truly realize their roles as representatives of marginalized groups by doing what they can to protect intersectionally disadvantaged members of their constituencies. By looking to the extant practices of actual organizations for models of ways that this can be done, affirmative advocacy reminds us that many organizations *already* rise to the task of working vigorously and effectively on behalf of their least advantaged constituents. Rather than exceptionalizing these practices or dismissing them as either unexplainably altruistic or cynically rational, we can take them as evidence that another way is possible and hold them up as a standard for others to emulate.

## CONCLUSION

Although they address many different aspects of organizational structures and behavior, the practices that I have highlighted in this chapter are united by a conception of redistributive representation that is itself a form of social justice. They are united as well by the premise that affirmative advocacy is necessary to rectify the inequalities in representation that, I have shown, are endemic to and deeply entrenched within contemporary politics. None of the suggestions that I have made based on these practices is the silver bullet that will allow organizations to overcome the hurdles associated with their roles as representatives for marginalized and often unpopular groups, particularly in the context of challenging political moments. However, these propositions call attention to some of the concrete ways in which many organizations can and do make concerted and institutionalized efforts to recognize intersectionally disadvantaged subgroups and to redistribute resources and energies to issues affecting them. As a consequence, these suggestions bring to light some of the many ways in which advocacy organizations might bolster the important work they do on behalf of marginalized groups by more effectively and energetically representing intersectionally disadvantaged subgroups of these constituencies.

The intersectional approach to representation promoted by affirmative advocacy asks that organizations reframe the ways in which they think about the relationships among power, interests, and representation. Affirmative advocacy departicularizes and universalizes the interests and experiences of intersectionally disadvantaged groups and asks organizations to focus on, rather than avoid, points of intersection and complexity in policy areas and constituency groups. By valuing the groups and issues at these intersections, and by evaluating their own actions in terms of their implications for multiply disadvantaged constituents, organizations can make the needs of these constituents a central part of their purpose and agenda.

To accomplish these objectives, affirmative advocacy requires that organizations invest substantially in retooling the ways in which they typically mediate among their constituencies. It entails that organizations model to their advantaged constituents how their fates are linked to, rather than isolated from, the fates of the multiply disadvantaged members of their communities and that they make clear through their actions that addressing these other forms of disadvantage is fundamental, rather than incidental, to their missions. From the vantage point of affirmative advocacy, it is in everyone's interest to address the needs of intersectionally disadvantaged groups because these groups are, in the words of Lani Guinier and Gerald Torres (2002), the "canary in a coal mine." Their distress serves as a warning about trouble ahead for all; when good things happen to these subgroups, it heralds imminent benefits for everyone else as well. In this light, organizations' efforts to give priority to issues affecting intersectionally disadvantaged subgroups are important not only for these subgroups but also because policies that benefit these subgroups provide broader social benefits by trickling *up* to all members of their constituencies and ultimately to the polity as a whole. In these ways, affirmative advocacy can help maximize the strengths of advocacy organizations and the possibilities of civil society, engaging both of them in efforts to fulfill the promises of democratic representation.

# Study Design: Methodology and Data Collection

This book uses data that I collected in two principal ways: (1) through a telephone survey conducted with officers and professional staff at 286 advocacy organizations; and (2) via face-to-face interviews with officers and professional staff at forty organizations. Many important features of the methods used to collect these data are described in chapter 2, and particular survey questions and methodological decisions are detailed as necessary in subsequent chapters. I elaborate on the data collection here for readers who desire more specific details regarding the survey design, execution, and question wordings, as well as for readers who would like more information about the face-to-face interviews (Berry 1999).

## THE 2000 SURVEY OF NATIONAL ECONOMIC AND SOCIAL JUSTICE ORGANIZATIONS

I collected the survey data in 2000 using a study I titled the Survey of National Economic and Social Justice Organizations (SNESJO), a telephone survey of officers and professional staff at 286 women's, racial minority, and economic justice organizations that are active in domestic policy issues at the national level.

SURVEY SAMPLE

The categories "women's, racial minority, and economic justice organizations" encompass a broad range of organizations and subtypes of organizations. In compiling the survey sample of organizations in each category,
I endeavored to balance several goals. First, I attempted to be as inclusive as
possible of the many types of organizations that represent women, racial
minorities, and low-income people in national politics.

To that end, I define *national organizations* to include ones outside of
Washington, D.C., because some of the populations of organizations in
which I am interested are geographically concentrated in other regions or
cities. For example, while 74 percent of African American and 70 percent of
national economic justice groups are based in the Washington, D.C. area,
only 44 percent of Asian Pacific American, 55 percent of Latino, 65 percent
of women's, and 25.5 percent of Native American organizations are based
there. While many maintain D.C. offices, a disproportionate number of
these organizations are based instead in California, the Southwest, New
York City, and the Midwest. Organizations included in the survey therefore
either maintain a Washington, D.C., office or play a leadership role in
the national policy activities of the movements of which they are a part
(Minkoff 1997; Minkoff and Agnone 2003).

In addition, as I show in chapter 2, the organizations in this study
represent marginalized and "outsider" groups and therefore have fewer resources and fewer of the organizational and political tools available to other
interests such as corporate, business, and professional organizations. As
such, many of the organizations that ideally would be surveyed are difficult
to "find." Because, for example, these organizations are less likely to be registered to lobby, to employ lobbyists, or to have political action committees
(PACs), they are also less likely to be listed in two of the main sources of
information about advocacy organizations and interest groups, *Washington Representatives* and the *Washington Information Directory*. Consequently,
meeting the goal of inclusivity also entailed consulting a broader range of
directories and lists than have been used by most surveys of organizations.
I therefore compiled the sample of organizations by assembling a database
using information from a wider-than-usual range of published directories of organizations, media sources, and movement publications. These
sources also were used to collect preliminary data about the organizations
in order to test for nonresponse and other types of bias in the survey data.

The published directories that I consulted include the *Encyclopedia of Associations* (Gale Research 2000), *Public Interest Profiles* (Foundation for Public Affairs 1999), *Washington Information Directory* (CQ Press 1998), *Washington Representatives* (Columbia Books 1999), and *Who's Who in Washington Nonprofit Groups* (Congressional Quarterly 1995). In addition, I consulted specialized directories, including the *National Directory of Asian Pacific American Organizations* (Organization of Chinese Americans 1999), the *National Directory of Hispanic Organizations* (Congressional Hispanic Caucus, Inc. 1999), and the *Women of Color Organizations and Projects National Directory* (Women of Color Resource Center 1998). I also consulted lists of organizations on approximately thirty Web sites, including those of umbrella organizations such as the Leadership Conference on Civil Rights (LCCR).[1] All of the organizations in the sample appeared in at least one source, 42 percent appeared in at least two sources, and 14 percent were found in at least three of the sources listed here.

In addition to striving for inclusivity, I also endeavored to achieve an appropriate level of specificity by refining the categories used to classify organizations so that each one was precise enough to make it possible to ask respondents questions about policies appropriate to their organizations. Doing so required disaggregating the broad categories of "women's, racial minority, and economic justice organizations" into smaller subgroupings. While the organizations in some categories are relatively straightforward, others are more complex and demand definition and clarification.

*Women's organizations* | The organizations that are classified in the tables as "women's rights/feminist" organizations include a broad array of women's, feminist, and women of color organizations. Organizations were included in this category if either their name or their description indicated that they engage in policy advocacy to advance gender equality or women's rights. Some conservative but nonetheless feminist groups were included, while explicitly antifeminist groups were not. To allow for the administration of appropriate questions, I separated reproductive rights and women's health organizations from organizations concerned with women's rights and feminism more generally. Service providers were included only if their name or description indicated that they engage in policy advocacy in addition to service provision.

*Racial minority organizations* | This category encompasses Asian Pacific American, Black/African American, Hispanic/Latino, and Native American/

American Indian organizations. Organizations were included in this category if either their name or their description specified that they engage in policy advocacy to advance equality or rights for a specific racial group or groups. In order to include organizations that represent members of racial minority groups but that do not refer to one particular racial or ethnic group, the sample also includes organizations that I have categorized as "civil rights—other." In addition to these other minority organizations, this category also includes relevant broadly based civil rights and civil liberties organizations; lesbian, gay, bisexual, and transgender (LGBT) rights organizations; criminal justice organizations; Arab/Muslim organizations; antiracist organizations; some religious minority groups; and multiculturalism organizations. I separated out immigrants' rights groups so that respondents from these groups could be asked about immigrants' rights issues. However, these groups have been folded into the "civil rights" category in most tables and analyses.

*Economic justice organizations:* | Organizations were included in this category if either their name or their description specified that they engage in policy advocacy on issues such as antipoverty policy, welfare rights, homelessness, or hunger. Some of these organizations are oriented toward children, and many are religiously affiliated. In such cases, organizations were included only if their name or their description indicated that they engage in policy advocacy related to economic justice. They have not been included if their advocacy relates only to advancing religious matters, nor if their poverty-related activities are primarily service-oriented. In order to be as inclusive as possible of the broad range of organizations that advocate in the area of economic justice, I also surveyed unions and labor organizations.

Finally, the survey also included public interest groups that indicated an interest in racial or gender equality or in economic justice. Note that I use the term *public interest* to designate a set of organizations that is more circumscribed than the organizations that are usually labeled this way. Researchers typically use the term *public interest* to distinguish those organizations that seek "a collective good" from those organizations that seek goods that benefit "selectively and materially... the membership or activists of the organization" (Berry 1977, 7). With the exception of labor unions, this more common designation encompasses *most* of the organization types that are the focus of my survey (see, however, Gerber 1999). The organizations that I have classified as "public interest" groups are primarily consumer, environmental, and "good government" organizations whose names or descriptions indicated that they advocate in the areas of racial, gender, or economic justice.

## SURVEY EXECUTION

The initial search for organizations yielded 987 organizations, and solicitation letters were sent to all of these groups. Of these, 273 were defunct, resulting in a universe of 714 organizations. Six weeks into the survey, a second solicitation letter was sent to organizations that had not yet been interviewed but had not yet refused to participate. To ensure that all of the organizations contacted are indeed advocacy groups, the survey began with the screening question, "On a scale of 1 to 5, if 1 is 'not important' and 5 is 'very important,' how important is influencing national public policy as a part of your organization's mandate and activities?" Interviews were not completed with respondents who answered "1" to this question.

The telephone interviews were conducted by Zogby International between June 26 and November 11, 2000, and took an average of thirty-three minutes to complete. Interviews were completed with 286 organizations for a 40 percent completion rate. According to Jeffrey Berry and his four coauthors (Berry et al. 2003, 12), surveys of organizations often have response rates between 17 percent and 50 percent. Respondents were promised anonymity for themselves and for their organizations.

The results of the survey compare closely to previous studies, and data on criterion variables such as location, number of employees, and year founded do not differ significantly from the data on these measures that I collected from publicly available sources for the universe of organizations as a whole in the course of compiling the master list of organizations. For example, 61.4 percent of the groups in the sample are located in or around the Washington, D.C., area, as are 61.1 percent of the groups on the master list. Similarly, the average age (in 2002) of the groups in the master list was 37.5 years old, while the average for the respondent groups is 38.4 years old. The average number of staff members among the organizations in the survey is 39, compared with an average of 37 staff members among the organizations on the master list.

## SURVEY QUESTIONS

The questions in the SNESJO (see appendix B) focus on organizations' activities on policy issues of the 1990s that have significant implications for rights and resources for marginalized groups, including women, racial minorities, LGBT people, immigrants, and low-income people. To contextualize these activities and facilitate comparisons with existing work, the survey replicates key questions from earlier surveys (Berry 1977; Heinz et al. 1993; Knoke and Adams 1984; Kollman 1998; Laumann and Knoke 1987; Schlozman and Tierney 1986; Walker 1991) such as questions about organizations' age, sources of funding, ideology, and size, as well as measures of political context factors such as partisan control of Congress.

## POLICY ISSUE SELECTION

The policy issues that were used in the survey questions are all domestic policy issues that can be pursued at the national level and through all three branches of the federal government—legislative, administrative, and judicial. Using a two-step method, I also stipulated that the policy issues must have been on the national political "agenda" during the period covered by the study (i.e., issues had to involve pending court cases being heard by the Supreme Court; pending legislation being debated in Congress; or pending policy being set in an executive branch department or agency). To select appropriate questions, I compiled a list of issues from the *Congressional Quarterly* for 1990, 1993, 1996, and 1999, and another from the "Supreme Court Roundup" (a regular feature in the *New York Times*) for the period from 1990 through 2000. After selecting all issues that were potentially relevant to the groups in the survey, I then searched the 1990–2000 volumes of the *Congressional Record* and of the *Federal Register* to confirm that the issues were on the agendas in the legislative and executive branches as well, noting how many times each issue had been mentioned in each of these sources. (The resulting "counts" also are used as measures of salience in the analyses in chapters 4 and 5.) I repeated this "reverse" search for the "Supreme Court Roundup." Although appearing in any one of these sources would constitute sufficient evidence that issues were on the "radar screen" and could reasonably be expected to be on the agenda of advocacy groups, all twenty-two issues that I selected were found in at least two of the sources, and twenty of the twenty-two issues were found in all three sources. While there are certainly biases inherent in basing the selection of policies on these sources, this method avoids asking respondents about their work on issues for which a lack of activity could be explained simply as a function of issues not being "on the agenda."

The policy issues are as follows:

> Alleviating the green card backlog for resident alien citizens
> Banning racial profiling in law enforcement
> Denial of federal safety-net benefits to immigrants
> Efforts to unionize white-collar workers
> Identifying, preventing, and rectifying gender-based wage disparities
> Preventing racial discrimination in environmental policy making and in the enforcement of environmental laws
> Protecting access to late-term abortion
> Protecting gay, lesbian, bisexual, and transgender people from workplace discrimination
> Protecting or expanding affirmative action for minority-owned businesses in government contracting
> Protecting or expanding affirmative action in higher education
> Protecting or expanding hate crime laws
> Protecting or expanding laws against violence against women
> Protecting or expanding tribal sovereignty or self-government
> Protecting or raising the minimum wage
> Protecting privacy on the Internet
> Raising the H-1B Visa ceiling for temporary high-skilled immigrant workers
> Rectifying the underrepresentation of poor people and racial minorities in the U.S. Census
> Reforming the system of campaign finance
> Regulating abortion coverage by insurance companies and HMOs
> Restrictions or cuts to public funding for abortion
> Social Security reform
> Welfare reform

In order to determine which issues should be addressed to each type of organization, I constructed a grid arraying each organization type along one axis and each issue type along the other axis. I listed the subgroups of a constituency that could be affected by each policy issue and then selected four policy issues for each organization type, the first three of which included one majority issue, one advantaged-subgroup issue, and one disadvantaged-subgroup issue (see table 2.2). The same universal issue—Social Security—was used as the fourth issue for all groups, thus also serving as a control issue.

DATABASE

Using the information collected through the telephone survey, I created two data sets following the method used by Ken Kollman (1998). In the first data set, the unit of analysis is the organization, with one record (row) for each of the 286 organizations surveyed. Arranging the data in this way allows me to analyze and compare the characteristics and activities of the organizations. In the second data set, there are four records for each organization—one row for each of the four policy issues about which they have been asked, resulting in a total of 1,144 cases. Using the data arranged in this fashion, I was able to pool all the information about the policy issues to predict a range of dependent variables, distinguishing organizations' levels of activity on each of the four policy issues.

FACE-TO-FACE INTERVIEWS

In addition to collecting survey data, I conducted semistructured, anonymous, face-to-face interviews with officials and professional staff at forty organizations between March 22 and August 3, 2001. The interview responses supplement the survey data by providing a window into the nuances of how, why, and in what context organization officers make the decisions that they do about how to allocate resources. Because of their small number, the interviews and the quotations are not intended to be generalizable as such but rather are used to illustrate, elaborate upon, and explain the quantitative findings. Nonetheless, the statements that are quoted in the book can be taken as typical of trends in the general substance, tone, and tenor of interviews as a whole.

The breakdown of interviews by organization type is presented in chapter 2 in table 2.1. Interviewees were not randomly sampled. Instead, groups were selected to vary based on criteria such as size and policy areas. Nonetheless, table 2.1 demonstrates that the resulting number of organizations in each category does not diverge drastically from their relative numbers in the broader universe. I recruited approximately half of the subjects by sending thank-you letters to the 286 survey respondents in which I requested follow-up interviews. The other half were recruited using a "snowball" sample generated through (1) recommendations from interviewees; (2) references from colleagues; (3) requests for interviews with officers and professional staff I had met at various events.

The questions on the semistructured interview protocol (see appendix C) were intended to gather more detailed information about issues that had been covered by survey questions, including questions about constituencies, coalition work, general policy activity, representation, and choices of policy issues and advocacy tactics (Collier and Brady 2004). The interviews also allowed me to ask respondents more detailed questions about the four policy issues from the survey, asking respondents, for example, to compare their involvement among different issues and about their policy goals.

One benefit of open-ended interviews, of course, is that they sometimes stray from the script. While I asked the interview questions consistently, some of the most interesting insights from respondents came in the course of digressions. In addition, although in general I replicated the policy issues that had been used in the telephone survey, I also added or substituted issues that were tailored to the mission of the organization in question. In particular, I asked about additional disadvantaged-subgroup issues to explore whether groups that might not be active on one disadvantaged-subgroup issue are active on another. For example, if an economic justice organization was not active on the designated disadvantaged-subgroup issue, public funding for abortion, then I often asked about another disadvantaged-subgroup issue, such as restoring the public benefits that had been eliminated by the 1996 Immigration Reform and Control Act.

# Survey Questionnaire

Hello, this is _____ calling from Zogby International on behalf of Dara Strolovitch of Yale University. I'm following up on a letter we sent you on May 22 about research we're conducting on national public interest groups.

1. First I'd like to make sure I have the right person. You are (name and position), is that correct?

2. On a scale of 1 to 5, if 1 is "not important" and 5 is "very important," how important is influencing national public policy as a part of your organization's mandate and activities?

3. On a scale of 1 to 10, where 1 is "very conservative" and 10 is "very liberal," how would you describe your organization?

4. How many groups are members of your organization?

5. How many individuals are members of your organization?
   (Ask 6 only if Q4 > 0 or Q5 > 0)

6. Which of the following statements best describes your organization?
   a. In general, the policy issues this organization attempts to influence affect its members directly.
   b. In general, the policy issues this organization attempts to influence mainly affect people other than its members.

    c. Neither (do not read)

    d. Both (do not read)

    e. Not sure (do not read)

7. On a scale of 1 to 5, if 1 is "not important" and 5 is "very important," how important is each of the following as a target of your organization's activity?

    a. Members of Congress

    b. The president and White House offices

    c. The executive agencies

    d. The federal courts

8. On a scale of 1 to 5, where 1 is "never" and 5 is "frequently," how often does your organization use each of the following influencing methods? (Systems: If Q8a–p = 1, there will be skips for Q15, 18, 21, 24)

    a. Directly lobbying members of Congress

    b. Directly lobbying members of executive agencies or the White House

    c. Grassroots lobbying of members of Congress, such as letter-writing or e-mail campaigns

    d. Working with federal government agencies to draft, enforce and administer regulations, rules, or guidelines

    e. Working with members of Congress to formulate legislation

    f. Pursuing issues through litigation by filing suits in court

    g. Filing *amicus curiae* (a-MEEK-us CUR-ee-eye) briefs in lawsuits brought by other groups or individuals

    h. Organizing public demonstrations, marches, protests, boycotts, strikes, or pickets

    i. Participating in public demonstrations, marches, or protests organized by others

    j. Seeking to influence public opinion by issuing press releases, talking with the media, or running advertisements about your position on issues

    k. Entering into coalitions or working with other organizations

    l. Giving testimony at congressional hearings

    m. Giving testimony at agency hearings

    n. Presenting research results or technical information to policy makers

    o. Working to appoint or elect public officials

    p. Serving on governmental advisory commissions or boards

9. On a scale of 1 to 5, where 1 is "not important" and 5 is "the most important," how important is each of the following issues to the activities and political concerns of your organization?

a. Antipoverty policy
b. Civil rights and civil liberties
c. Criminal justice
d. Health and human services
e. Immigration
f. Labor policy
g. Urban policy and development
h. Women's equality

10. Please tell me, on a scale of 1 to 5, with 1 being "not at all" and 5 being "a great deal," to what degree does your organization address the policy concerns of each of the following groups?
    a. Asian Pacific Americans
    b. Blacks or African Americans
    c. Latinos or Hispanics
    d. Native Americans
    e. Elderly people
    f. Gay, lesbian, bisexual, and transgender people
    g. Immigrants
    h. Poor or low-income people
    i. Women
    j. Workers

    (Ask Q11 only if Q4 > 0 or Q5 > 0)

11. Please tell me, on a scale of 1 to 5, with 1 being "not at all" and 5 being "a great deal," to what degree would you say that your members want your organization to address the policy concerns of each of those groups?
    a. Asian Pacific Americans
    b. Blacks or African Americans
    c. Latinos or Hispanics
    d. Native Americans
    e. Elderly people
    f. Gay, lesbian, bisexual, and transgender people
    g. Immigrants
    h. Poor or low-income people
    i. Women
    j. Workers

    (Ask Q12 only if Q4 = 0 and Q5 = 0)

12. Please tell me, on a scale of 1 to 5, with 1 being "not at all" and 5 being "a great deal," to what degree would you say that the people your

organization serves want your organization to address the policy concerns of each of these groups?

a. Asian Pacific Americans

b. Blacks or African Americans

c. Latinos or Hispanics

d. Native Americans

e. Elderly people

f. Gay, lesbian, bisexual, and transgender people

g. Immigrants

h. Poor or low-income people

i. Women

j. Workers

13. Now on a scale of 1 to 5, with 1 being "not at all" and 5 being "a great deal," to what degree would you say that the general public thinks that the policy concerns of each of these same groups deserve to be addressed?

a. Asian Pacific Americans

b. Blacks or African Americans

c. Latinos or Hispanics

d. Native Americans

e. Elderly people

f. Gay, lesbian, bisexual, and transgender people

g. Immigrants

h. Poor or low-income people

i. Women

j. Workers

(Each organization was asked the following questions about four policy issues. See appendix A for a list of policy issues and table 2.2 for the issues that were asked of each organization type.)

14. Please tell me, on a scale of 1 to 5, where 1 is "not active" and 5 is "very active," how active has your organization been on each of the following policy issues in the past ten years?

a. (Designated majority issue)

b. (Designated disadvantaged-subgroup issue)

c. (Designated advantaged-subgroup issue)

d. (Universal issue)

(Skip Q15–Q17 if Q14a = 1)

15. Which of the following political institutions is the most important target of your efforts in trying to influence policy on the issue of (Designated majority issue)?

a. Members of Congress
b. The president and White House offices
c. The executive agencies
d. The federal courts
e. Not sure (do not read)

16. Again, on a scale of 1 to 5, where 1 is "never" and 5 is "frequently," how often does your organization engage in the following activities in pursuing its goals on (Designated majority issue)?
    a. Directly lobbying members of Congress
    b. Directly lobbying members of executive agencies or the White House
    c. Grassroots lobbying of members of Congress, such as letter-writing or e-mail campaigns
    d. Working with federal government agencies to draft, enforce, and administer regulations, rules, or guidelines
    e. Working with members of Congress to formulate legislation
    f. Pursuing issues through litigation by filing suits in court
    g. Filing *amicus curiae* (a-MEEK-us CUR-ee-eye) briefs in lawsuits brought by other groups or individuals
    h. Organizing public demonstrations, marches, protests, boycotts, strikes, or pickets
    i. Participating in public demonstrations, marches, or protests organized by others
    j. Seeking to influence public opinion by issuing press releases, talking with the media, or running advertisements about your position on issues
    k. Entering into coalitions or working with other organizations
    l. Giving testimony at congressional hearings
    m. Giving testimony at agency hearings
    n. Presenting research results or technical information to policy makers
    o. Working to appoint or elect public officials
    p. Serving on governmental advisory commissions or boards

17. On a scale of 1 to 5, where 1 is "not at all" and 5 is "a great deal," how much would you say the issue of (Designated majority issue) affects each of the following groups?
    a. Asian Pacific Americans
    b. Blacks or African Americans
    c. Latinos or Hispanics
    d. Native Americans
    e. Elderly people

    f.  Gay, lesbian, bisexual, and transgender people

    g.  Immigrants

    h.  Poor or low-income people

    i.  Women

    j.  Workers

    (Skip Q18–Q20 if Q14b = 1)

18. Which of the following political institutions is the most important target of your efforts in trying to influence policy on the issue of (Designated disadvantaged-subgroup issue)?

    a.  Members of Congress

    b.  The president and White House offices

    c.  The executive agencies

    d.  The federal courts

    e.  Not sure (do not read)

19. On a scale of 1 to 5, where 1 is "never" and 5 is "frequently," how often does your organization engage in the following activities in pursuing its policy goals on the issue of (Designated disadvantaged-subgroup issue)?

    a.  Directly lobbying members of Congress

    b.  Directly lobbying members of executive agencies or the White House

    c.  Grassroots lobbying of members of Congress, such as letter-writing or e-mail campaigns

    d.  Working with federal government agencies to draft, enforce, and administer regulations, rules, or guidelines

    e.  Working with members of Congress to formulate legislation

    f.  Pursuing issues through litigation by filing suits in court

    g.  Filing *amicus curiae* (a-MEEK-us CUR-ee-eye) briefs in lawsuits brought by other groups or individuals

    h.  Organizing public demonstrations, marches, protests, boycotts, strikes, or pickets

    i.  Participating in public demonstrations, marches, or protests organized by others

    j.  Seeking to influence public opinion by issuing press releases, talking with the media, or running advertisements about your position on issues

    k.  Entering into coalitions or working with other organizations

    l.  Giving testimony at congressional hearings

    m. Giving testimony at agency hearings

    n.  Presenting research results or technical information to policy makers

    o. Working to appoint or elect public officials

    p. Serving on governmental advisory commissions or boards

20. On a scale of 1 to 5, where 1 is "not at all" and 5 is "a great deal," how much would you say the issue of (Designated disadvantaged-subgroup issue) affects the following groups?

    a. Asian Pacific Americans

    b. Blacks or African Americans

    c. Latinos or Hispanics

    d. Native Americans

    e. Elderly people

    f. Gay, lesbian, bisexual, and transgender people

    g. Immigrants

    h. Poor or low-income people

    i. Women

    j. Workers

    (Skip Q21–Q23 if Q14c = 1)

21. Which of the following political institutions is the most important target of your efforts in trying to influence policy on the issue of (Designated advantaged-subgroup issue)?

    a. Members of Congress

    b. The president and White House offices

    c. The executive agencies

    d. The federal courts

    e. Not sure (do not read)

22. On a scale of 1 to 5, where 1 is "never" and 5 is "frequently," how often does your organization engage in the following activity in pursuing its policy goals on the issue of (Designated advantaged-subgroup issue)?

    a. Directly lobbying members of Congress

    b. Directly lobbying members of executive agencies or the White House

    c. Grassroots lobbying of members of Congress, such as letter-writing or e-mail campaigns

    d. Working with federal government agencies to draft, enforce and administer regulations, rules, or guidelines

    e. Working with members of Congress to formulate legislation

    f. Pursuing issues through litigation by filing suits in court

    g. Filing *amicus curiae* (a-MEEK-us CUR-ee-eye) briefs in lawsuits brought by other groups or individuals

    h. Organizing public demonstrations, marches, protests, boycotts, strikes, or pickets

      i. Participating in public demonstrations, marches, or protests orga-
nized by others

      j. Seeking to influence public opinion by issuing press releases, talking
with the media, or running advertisements about your position on
issues

    k. Entering into coalitions or working with other organizations

    l. Giving testimony at congressional hearings

    m. Giving testimony at agency hearings

    n. Presenting research results or technical information to policy makers

    o. Working to appoint or elect public officials

    p. Serving on governmental advisory commissions or boards

23. On a scale of one to five, where 1 is "not at all" and 5 is "a great deal,"
how much would you say the issue of (Designated advantaged-subgroup
issue) affects each of the following groups?

    a. Asian Pacific Americans

    b. Blacks or African Americans

    c. Latinos or Hispanics

    d. Native Americans

    e. Elderly people

    f. Gay, lesbian, bisexual, and transgender people

    g. Immigrants

    h. Poor or low-income people

    i. Women

    j. Workers

    (Skip Q24–Q26 if Q14d = 1)

24. Which of the following political institutions is the most important target of your efforts in trying to influence policy on the issue of (Universal
issue)?

    a. Members of Congress

    b. The president and White House offices

    c. The executive agencies

    d. The federal courts

    e. Not sure (do not read)

25. On a scale of 1 to 5, where 1 is "never" and 5 is "frequently," how often
does your organization engage in the following activity in pursuing its
policy goals on the issue of (Universal issue)?

    a. Directly lobbying members of Congress

    b. Directly lobbying members of executive agencies or the White House

c. Grassroots lobbying of members of Congress, such as letter-writing or e-mail campaigns

d. Working with federal government agencies to draft, enforce and administer regulations, rules, or guidelines

e. Working with members of Congress to formulate legislation

f. Pursuing issues through litigation by filing suits in court

g. Filing *amicus curiae* (a-MEEK-us CUR-ee-eye) briefs in lawsuits brought by other groups or individuals

h. Organizing public demonstrations, marches, protests, boycotts, strikes, or pickets

i. Participating in public demonstrations, marches, or protests organized by others

j. Seeking to influence public opinion by issuing press releases, talking with the media, or running advertisements about your position on issues

k. Entering into coalitions or working with other organizations

l. Giving testimony at congressional hearings

m. Giving testimony at agency hearings

n. Presenting research results or technical information to policy makers

o. Working to appoint or elect public officials

p. Serving on governmental advisory commissions or boards

26. On a scale of 1 to 5, where 1 is "not at all" and 5 is "a great deal," how much would you say the issue of (Universal issue) affects each of the following groups?

a. Asian Pacific Americans

b. Blacks or African Americans

c. Latinos or Hispanics

d. Native Americans

e. Elderly people

f. Gay, lesbian, bisexual, and transgender people

g. Immigrants

h. Poor or low-income people

i. Women

j. Workers

27. In general, on a scale of 1 to 5, where 1 is "none" and 5 is "everyone," what proportion of the public would you say agrees with your organization's position on each issue?

a. (Designated majority issue)

b. (Designated disadvantaged-subgroup issue)

    c. (Designated advantaged-subgroup issue)

    d. (Universal issue)

    (Ask Q28 only if Q4 > 0 or Q5 > 0)

28. In general, on a scale of 1 to 5, where 1 is "none" and 5 is "everyone," what proportion of your members would you say agrees with your organization's position on each of the following issues?

    a. (Designated majority issue)

    b. (Designated disadvantaged-subgroup issue)

    c. (Designated advantaged-subgroup issue)

    d. (Universal issue)

    (Ask Q29 only if Q4 = 0 and Q5 = 0)

29. In general, on a scale of 1 to 5, where 1 is "none" and 5 is "everyone," what proportion of the people your organization serves would you say agrees with your organization's position on each of the following issues?

    a. (Designated majority issue)

    b. (Designated disadvantaged-subgroup issue)

    c. (Designated advantaged-subgroup issue)

    d. (Universal issue)

30. In general, on a scale of 1 to 5, where 1 is "not at all controversial" and 5 is "extremely controversial," how controversial is each of these issues?

    a. (Designated majority issue)

    b. (Designated disadvantaged-subgroup issue)

    c. (Designated advantaged-subgroup issue)

    d. (Universal issue)

    (Ask Q31 only if Q4 > 0 or Q5 > 0)

31. On a scale of 1 to 5, where 1 is "none" and 5 is "almost all," what proportion of your members would you say is directly affected by the following issues?

    a. (Designated majority issue)

    b. (Designated disadvantaged-subgroup issue)

    c. (Designated advantaged-subgroup issue)

    d. (Universal issue)

    (Ask Q32 only if Q4 = 0 and Q5 = 0)

32. On a scale of 1 to 5, where 1 is "none" and 5 is "almost all," what proportion of the people your organization serves would you say is directly affected by the following issues?

    a. (Designated majority issue)

    b. (Designated disadvantaged-subgroup issue)

    c. (Designated advantaged-subgroup issue)

d. (Universal issue)

(Ask Q33 only if Q4 > 0 or Q5 > 0)

33. On a scale of 1 to 5, where 1 is "none" and 5 is "almost all," what proportion of your members would you say is concerned about the following
issues?

a. (Designated majority issue)

b. (Designated disadvantaged-subgroup issue)

c. (Designated advantaged-subgroup issue)

d. (Universal issue)

(Ask Q34 only if Q4 = 0 and Q5 = 0)

34. On a scale of 1 to 5, where 1 is "none" and 5 is "almost all," what proportion
of the people you serve would you say is concerned about each of the
following issues?

a. (Designated majority issue)

b. (Designated disadvantaged-subgroup issue)

c. (Designated advantaged-subgroup issue)

d. (Universal issue)

35. Would you say that the 1992 change from Republican to Democratic
control of the presidency has made it "more likely," "less likely," or
"neither more nor less likely" that your organization will pursue your
policy objectives on the following issues in executive agencies?

  1. More likely  2. Less likely  3. No effect  4. Not sure (do not read)

a. (Designated majority issue)

b. (Designated disadvantaged-subgroup issue)

c. (Designated advantaged-subgroup issue)

d. (Universal issue)

36. Would you say that the 1994 change from Democratic to Republican
control of the House of Representatives has made it "more likely," "less
likely," or "neither more nor less likely" that your organization will
pursue your policy objectives on the following issues in Congress?

  1. More likely  2. Less likely  3. No effect  4. Not sure (do not read)

a. (Designated majority issue)

b. (Designated disadvantaged-subgroup issue)

c. (Designated advantaged-subgroup issue)

d. (Universal issue)

37. Would you say that the 1994 change from Democratic to Republican
control of the United States House of Representatives has made it "more
likely," "less likely," or "neither more nor less likely" that your organiza-

tion will pursue your policy objectives on the following issues through the courts?

      1. More likely  2. Less likely  3. No effect  4. Not sure (do not read)

a. (Designated majority issue)

b. (Designated disadvantaged-subgroup issue)

c. (Designated advantaged-subgroup issue)

d. (Universal issue)

38. Please list the three most important policy issues for your organization. These may include, but need not be limited to, the issues I have already asked you about.

    1.

    2.

    3.

39. Does this organization have tax-exempt status under the U.S. Internal Revenue Code?

    1. Yes  2. No  3. Not sure (do not read)

40. Does your organization employ a legal staff?

    1. Yes  2. No  3. Not sure (do not read)

41. Is your organization registered to lobby members of Congress?

    1. Yes  2. No  3. Not sure (do not read)

42. Does your organization regularly employ one or more registered lobbyists in Washington, D.C.?

    1. Yes  2. No  3. Not sure (do not read)

43. Does your organization have one or more political action committees?

    1. Yes  2. No  3. Not sure (do not read)

44. How many paid professional and administrative staff does your organization employ?

45. In what year was your organization founded?
(Ask Q46 only if Q4 > 0)

46. What percent of your individual members would you estimate are:

a. Asian Pacific American

b. Black or African American

c. Latino or Hispanic

d. Native American

e. White

f. Elderly

g. Gay, lesbian, bisexual, or transgender

    h. Immigrants

    i. Poor or low-income people

    j. Women

    k. Workers

47. What is the approximate budget of your organization for the current year?

48. About what percent of your organization's total budget would you say is allocated to its advocacy activities?

49. On a scale of 1 to 5, where 1 is "not a source" and 5 is "the most important," please tell me how big a source of financial support each of the following was for your organization last year. (Ask Q49a Only if Q4 > 0)

    a. Membership dues paid by organizations (Ask Q49b Only if Q5 > 0)

    b. Membership dues paid by individuals

    c. Individual contributions other than dues, including contributions from nonmembers and donations from direct mail and canvasing

    d. Foundations

    e. Government agencies

    f. Religious organizations or other nonprofit organizations

    g. Companies or corporations

50. On a scale of 1 to 5, where 1 is "no influence" and 5 is "the greatest," how much influence would you say that each of the following has in your organization's decision making about shaping public policy? (Ask Q50a only if Q5 > 0)

    a. Your individual members

    b. Contributors other than members

    c. State or local organizations, including chapters of your organization

    d. Direct service providers, such as health care providers and social workers

    e. Individual policy experts

    f. Other national organizations active in policy

    g. Foundations and nongovernmental agencies that fund your organization

    h. Political party leaders

    i. Elected and appointed public officials

    j. Organization officials and staff

51. Would you please mail or fax to Yale University. . .

    a. Surveys of your membership?

    b. Your organization's annual report?

# Interview Protocol

Reference Number _____ Date _____ Time _____ to _____
Respondent _____
Job Title _____
Organization _____
Address _____
Membership organization?  Y/N

Thank you so much for taking the time to meet with me. I know that you're very busy, and I am very grateful for your time. As I mentioned in my letter, the interview takes about sixty minutes and covers six main areas. I will start with a few general questions about the organization, followed by some questions about your constituencies, some questions about your policy activism, the targets of your activism, your coalition work, and the political climate surrounding your work.

Before I begin, I want to make sure it's all right with you if I tape this interview. Anything you say will, of course, still be kept completely anonymous, unless you explicitly specify otherwise, and the information that I am collecting will be used only for my own research. Do you have any questions before I start?

## GENERAL QUESTIONS

1. I'd like to begin with just a few background questions about your organization.
   a. Can you briefly describe the origins and general goals of this organization?

## CONSTITUENCIES

1. On whose behalf does this organization generally consider itself to be active?
2. How does the organization determine this?
3. Are there any particular subgroups of this broader constituency that you focus on?
4. How do you frame and determine this?

## GENERAL POLICY ACTIVITY

Now I'd like to talk a bit about your policy advocacy. I am most interested in your activities around national domestic policy issues, but please feel free to refer to any policy issues that you find most helpful to illustrate your points.

1. How do you decide on which specific policy issues your organization will be active, which of these issues to prioritize, and how much of the organization's energy and resources you will devote to each one?
2. In thinking about which issues to pursue, to what extent and in what ways do you consider the following factors?
   a. Which portions and the proportion of your constituency will be affected by an issue
   b. The proportion of your constituency that is interested in the issue
   c. How controversial you perceive the issue to be among members of the general public
3. How about the likelihood of success? For example, are you more likely to put in efforts when it seems that the outcome is likely to be in your favor, or doesn't this make a difference? How do you balance "pushing the envelope" with concerns about "do-ability?"
4. How do you determine which issues are important to or affect your constituents? For example, do you ever do surveys of your constituency

to find out what issues they're interested in and what issues they feel affect them?

5. How often do you get involved in issues that are already on the agenda, and how often do you try instead to get new issues on the agenda? What are some of the benefits and challenges of each approach?

6. Can you give me a few examples of policy issues your organization has been involved in over the past few years?

## STATE AND LOCAL POLICY ACTIVISM

1. Do you ever get involved in policy issues at the state and local levels, and if so, under what circumstances? Has the devolution of various policies to the state and local levels affected your decisions? How?

## SPECIFIC POLICIES

[The following battery of questions was typically asked four times regarding four separate policy issues.]

1. In the past few years, has this organization been active around [policy]?
   a. [If not at all involved] Did the organization consider getting involved in [policy]?
   b. [If yes] What made you decide not to?
   c. [If no] Why do you think this was so?
2. [If active] How active?
   a. What made you decide to get involved, and how did you decide how involved to be?
   b. What are your general policy goals when it comes to [policy]?
   c. How do you frame what is at stake when it comes to [policy]?
   d. How does this compare to the ways other organizations frame the issues associated with this policy?
   e. What specific tactics have you employed in pursuing these goals (show card)?
3. Who or what groups would you say are most affected by [policy]?

## GENERAL TARGETS OF ACTIVISM

1. In general, what factors influence which institutions your organization decides to target in pursuing its policy goals? That is, how do you

decide whether to focus on Congress, the courts, the president, or federal government agencies?

2. In general, do you find advocacy more effective in certain institutions or in certain parts of these institutions—specific agencies, offices, committees—than in others? Why?

3. Does it matter more whether it's an institution where you think in general you can get results more easily, or do you instead just target whatever institution seems to have things going on that provide opportunities—like important bills recently introduced, or lawsuits filed, or administrative rules proposed for adoption?

4. In general, do the targets of your activities change over time as you pursue your goals on an issue? Why, and in what ways?

5. In general, which political institutions, if any, do you consider more receptive to your advocacy efforts?

6. In the past ten years, for which specific issues have you focused your efforts on Congress? Federal courts (including filing amicus briefs)? President? Executive agencies?

7. How about targets other than governmental ones? For example, for what issues or under what circumstances do you try to influence public opinion?

## GENERAL TACTICS

1. In general, how do you decide what tactics to use to pursue policy goals?

2. What differences, if any, are there between the strategies you use when addressing issues that you've "initiated" versus issues that you're reacting to, such as attempts to curtail or repeal hard-won policy gains?

3. In general, what tactics, if any, do you consider most effective? Which, if any, do you consider least effective?

## COALITIONS—GENERAL

1. To what extent do you work in coalition with other organizations?

2. With what types of organizations do you enter into coalitions?

3. When does that seem to work best for you? I mean, are there particular issues or types of issues that you find more amenable to or more fruitfully pursued through coalition work?

4. Do you think that coalitions are more important for some kinds of organizations than they are for others?

5. When you work in coalitions, how do you divide up the particular tasks among the various organizations? For example, do some groups coordinate grassroots efforts while others coordinate, say, judicial strategy?

6. How about the substance of various issues? Do you try to address issues from different angles?

7. What are some of the trade-offs, if there are any, of working in coalitions?

8. In general, how do you feel about the ways in which other groups address the issues on which you're active?

9. Whether in coalitions or not, do you ever consult with other organizations in your policy area or overlapping policy areas about whether certain issues are being covered or do you engage in other types of coordination?

## POLITICAL CLIMATE

1. In general, how much conflict is there in the policy areas in which your organization is involved?

2. Thinking back a few years, did the 1992 election of Bill Clinton have an effect on your choice of strategy or have any other substantial effects on your work? In what ways?

3. Did the 1994 Republican takeover of the House of Representatives have an effect on your choice of strategy or have any other substantial effects on your work? In what ways?

4. More recently, has the [2000] election of George W. Bush affected your choice of strategy or had any other any substantial effects on your work? In what ways?

5. What issues have you been most active on this year? Has the change in administration brought about changes in your policy focus?

## ASSESSMENT AND WRAP-UP

1. How do you define "success" when it comes to policy advocacy?

2. Those are all the questions that I have for you right now, but I wonder if I could ask you two favors. First, I'm wondering if I could call you in about six months to follow up on some of the issues we've discussed. Since I

have all this interesting information, based mainly on your experiences during the Clinton presidency, I'd like to see how things progress a few months into the new administration. Second, I'm wondering if you know of anyone else at any other organizations who might be willing to speak with me about the issues we just covered.

# Notes

## CHAPTER 1

1. Commenting on Woods's statement about the right of Augusta to determine its members, Burk said, "If others had taken that view, he'd be a caddie at Augusta. He wouldn't be a player" (Ferguson 2002). In an article in *Black Issues in Higher Education*, economist Julianne Malveaux wrote that she "cringed" when she read the comment because, she explained,

> I realized that some women, right as they are on women's issues, don't get civil rights, the civil rights struggle, and the difference between bias against women and bias against African Americans. As I cringed, I also wondered how many white women, including Martha Burk, shrug off their white skin privilege around race matters. . . . Feminists have come a long way in terms of racial sensitivities, but comments like Martha Burk's suggest women still have a long way to go.
>
> It takes a history lesson to understand why Tiger may be a reluctant spokesperson for women, and why I look askance at Martha Burk's willingness to turn Tiger Woods into a pawn in her game. . . . She is acting as if Tiger is the establishment, the enemy. The real enemy is the white male patriarchy that has excluded both African Americans and women from Augusta. In the name of women's rights, should black men walk away from Augusta? When, in the name of civil rights, have white women walked away from racist institutions?
>
> African Americans and women have somewhat parallel histories in terms of having been discriminated against. But the histories are not the same.

NOTES TO PAGES 4–11 · 269

Only African Americans were enslaved. And white women, often, have enjoyed the privilege their race confers. When the many faces of bias are viewed through the lens of history, the result is a fascinating complexity absent from Martha Burk's comments about Tiger Woods. (Malveaux 2003, 34)

2. I use the terms *advocacy organization, interest group,* and *social movement organization* relatively interchangeably. For a comprehensive discussion of the many labels (and the implications of these labels) that are used to categorize organizations that are active in U.S. politics, see Frank Baumgartner and Beth Leech's book, *Basic Interests* (Baumgartner and Leech 1998). For a discussion and taxonomy of organizations that do not engage in politics, see Debra Minkoff's book *Organizing for Equality* (Minkoff 1995).

3. Political theorist Andrew Rehfeld calls the former view, associated with the tradition of social contract theorists such as Hobbes, Locke, and Rousseau, the "sociological view of legitimacy" (Rehfeld 2005, 16).

4. The notion that distributive schemes should be designed to benefit the least well-off members of society is not, of course, John Rawls's invention. Rather, it is a cornerstone of many calls for redistribution, such as Karl Marx's call for resources to be distributed "from each according to his ability, to each according to his needs" (Marx [1875] 1978). I invoke Rawls's difference principle mainly as a point of relatively common reference that provides a useful shorthand for engaging with and understanding the redistributive spirit of affirmative advocacy. I am not claiming that the organizations in the study endorse Rawls's particular brand of liberalism, nor that Rawls would necessarily endorse the precise kinds of redistributive representation implied by the framework that I sketch out in the book.

This caveat is important because Rawls's difference principle (and, in fact, his entire *Theory of Justice*) has been subjected to a wide range of powerful and important critiques. Some critics argue that its redistributive goals are overly radical and that they entail unacceptable infringements on individual liberty (Nozick 1974). Others take the opposite view, contending that the difference principle does little more than justify a minimal neoliberal welfare state. Sill others argue that it is "a disingenuous defense of capitalism and huge inequalities" (Chambers 2006, 83). Simone Chambers reminds us, however, that Rawls made it clear that his intentions in *A Theory of Justice* are far more egalitarian than anything that could be accomplished by welfare-state capitalism (Chambers 2006, 83). In that light, while I am not advocating the difference principle as a guide for individual behavior, nor as a principle for economic policy, I invoke the difference principle because it captures something important about the motivations and spirit of many of the organizations in this study. As I will demonstrate in subsequent chapters, these organizations explicitly charge themselves with fighting for justice and equality for disadvantaged groups. Officers at such organizations are therefore far more likely than most individuals or political institutions to embrace the egalitarian goals embodied in Rawls's theory. These officers also are consequently likely to interpret a concept like the difference principle in its most redistributive light and are unlikely to reject it based on its redistributive implications. In their hands, then, we might be more confident that a principle that dictates that inequalities should benefit the least well-off members will be applied in noncynical ways that are actually intended to help the "truly disadvantaged" (W. Wilson 1987).

5. Nancy Schwartz (1988) argues that representatives should engage in what she calls "constitutive representation," a process of citizen empowerment and community formation among constituents. In contrast to my invocation of this idea, Schwartz focuses on territorially based elected representation, arguing that constitutive representation works best when it is rooted in local constituencies, in particular in single-member electoral districts.

6. While I borrow Urbinati's terminology of "representation as advocacy," her conceptualization is distinct from the one that I advance here in some important ways. As I elaborate in the rest of the book, I use the term *advocacy* primarily to highlight the idea of representation as a form of and a means to social justice. Urbinati, too, emphasizes the relationship between advocacy and justice, but she also is concerned with the benefits that conceptualizing representation as a form of advocacy has for deliberation and for the expressive aspects of representation. As such, my use of the term *advocacy* shares with Urbinati's its evocation of engagement, sympathy, and partiality on the part of representatives, its "notion of citizenship that is egalitarian in principle" but that "still takes power relations into account" (Urbinati 2000, 778), as well as the alternative that it presents to "the dichotomy of representative as delegate or representative as trustee" (777). I am less concerned, however, with exploring the deliberative and expressive values of advocacy.

CHAPTER 2

1. In addition to Schattschneider's critiques of pluralist assumptions, such ideas have also been also roundly critiqued by rational choice theorists, most notably Mancur Olson (1965), who argues that the goals pursued by interest groups were almost always "public goods," equally available to everyone regardless of whether they participate in the efforts to obtain them. A "rational actor," therefore, will decline the costs of participation unless selective incentives are made available only to participants. Olson argues that these problems are particularly egregious when it comes to large groups—small groups are much more likely to organize than large ones. Subsequent research has found many conditions under which such "collective action problems" can be overcome. John Mark Hansen (1985), for example, finds that many people join organizations because they see them as having been instrumental in previously helping to win some collective benefits. Other research has identified benefits other than "selective incentives" (such as purposive and solidary incentives) and narrow economic self-interest that participants derive from group politics (Barakso 2004; Berry 1977; Cigler and Hansen 1983; Gamson 1975; McFarland 1984; Moe 1981; Rothenberg 1992; Wilson [1974] 1995). Nonetheless, the inevitability of organization and mobilization is no longer taken for granted.

2. In their recent work on the political development of interest groups in the United States, Daniel Tichenor and Richard Harris (2002–3, 2005) challenge the dominant characterization of a late-twentieth-century explosion in the

number of interest groups in the United States brought on by two world wars, New Deal–era government programs, and the movements of the 1960s. They note that the sources from which data about political organizations are typically collected—surveys, interviews, and directories of organizations—can tell us little about organizations that ceased operation before the 1950s, when directories such as the *Encyclopedia of Associations*, *Washington Information Directory*, and *Washington Representatives* began publication. They argue that most political science work has therefore ignored the "robust set of organized interests engaged in Progressive Era political life" (Tichenor and Harris 2002–3, 593).

3. There are vast and important literatures that address each of the concerns that I take up in this chapter. I limit my discussion to the ways in which each one relates to the prospects for advocacy on behalf of intersectionally disadvantaged groups.

4. While most of these critiques originate on the left, critics on the right often make similar points as a way to undermine the moral claims of progressive organizations, casting them as self-interested elitists (Rauch 1994).

5. Michels's concerns focused on Socialist parties, arguing that they would be undermined by the self-interested actions of their elite leaders (Michels 1911). For an alternative view about the potential pitfalls of working-class organizations, see Lipset 1963.

6. Note that a number of studies have found that formal organizations are more institutionalized and therefore do indeed use more moderate and less disruptive tactics than more diffuse social movements. However, a great deal of research also has found that formal organizations do not diffuse protest (Staggenborg 1988; Taylor 1989) and that they also have benefits, playing a crucial role in maintaining movements during periods of low mobilization and in following up on movements' victories through lobbying, litigation, and monitoring government agencies (Jenkins and Eckert 1986; Staggenborg 1986; Tarrow 1994). William Gamson actually finds that more bureaucratic movements were more successful than less bureaucratic ones (1975).

7. Along similar lines, Mark Smith (2000) distinguishes between particularistic, conflictual, and unifying issues and finds that, paradoxically, businesses have the least influence when it comes to unifying issues because these are the ones that tend to be salient to voters, so legislators pay more attention to their constituents. Ken Kollman (1998) also finds that organizations are attentive to the salience of an issue.

8. Young is referring here most specifically to the category of "women." Applying Jean-Paul Sartre's (1976) concept of "seriality" to theorize women's structural position, she argues that the gender position of being a woman

> does not itself imply sharing social attributes and identity with all those others called women. Instead, "women" is the name of a series in which some individuals find themselves positioned by virtue of norms of enforced heterosexuality and the sexual division of labor. Both the norms and expectations of heterosexual interaction and the habits developed in certain social activities such as caring for children will condition the dispositions and affinities of people, without constituting their identities. (Young 2000, 100)

9. For extremely helpful and detailed genealogies and overviews of the origins and core ideas of intersectionality, see Hancock 2007 and Kurtz 2002, particularly chap. 2.

10. Of course, other national organizations committed to addressing other axes of marginalization may possibly address issues that affect intersectionally disadvantaged subgroups. However, intersectionally disadvantaged subgroups are at the margins of *most* broader groups. Members of these subgroups need to look to many national organizations in order to have their interests voiced, yet they are often the very people with the fewest resources to do so (Scully and Creed 2005). Lack of resources also makes it unlikely that these subgroups will be able to form organizations themselves. Thus, it is particularly important that extant organizations advocate for intersectionally disadvantaged subgroups because ignoring them perpetuates marginalization and stigmatization and contributes to conditions of cumulative inequality (C. Cohen 1999; Parenti 1978).

11. Some of these organizations have adopted specific programs designed to address other axes of discrimination. Roberta Spalter-Roth and Ronnee Schreiber document, for example, the attempts of women's organizations such as the Women's Legal Defense Fund, the Women's International League for Peace and Freedom, and the National Committee on Pay Equity to address racism and issues of interest to women of color (Spalter-Roth and Schreiber 1995, 122). However, they note that these programs often were criticized as being "too little, too late." Moreover, these same organizations seemed far less enthusiastic about promoting working-class women's issues, about offering a class-based analysis, about promoting efforts to address lesbian issues, or about educating "their constituencies, policymakers, and the public about homophobia, despite the leadership roles lesbians often played in their organizations" (Spalter-Roth and Schreiber 1995, 123).

12. I am concerned with the constructedness of interests and identities mainly as they apply to intersectionally marginalized groups. However, many similar issues arise vis-à-vis the interests of conservative members of groups such as women, racial minorities, and low-income people, who may not accept the agendas advanced in their names by the organizations that claim to speak for them and represent their interests. For example, pro-life women reject the claim of most feminist organizations that is in women's interests to maintain access to safe and legal abortions (Schreiber 1998).

13. Other related paradigms, such as Jeffrey Berry's (1999), which distinguishes between *material* issues that appeal to low-income people and *postmaterial* issues that appeal to middle-class people, are similarly limited to two categories.

14. Mancur Olson's work suggests almost the opposite relationship between the size of the group affected by a policy issue and the level of advocacy on this issue. In his view, smaller groups will be easier to mobilize and, by extension, will therefore be more likely than large groups to have their interests represented by advocacy groups (Olson 1965). Because his focus is on the material incentives driving mobilization rather than on the social, economic, and political disadvantages faced by racial, ethnic, sexual, and other minorities, Olson does not distinguish between small advantaged groups and small disadvantaged

groups. As such, his analysis misses a key aspect of the relationship between the size of a group and its ability to mobilize and demand public goods.

15. Note that the term *majority issue* describes issues that are equally likely to affect any of an advocacy group's constituents. However, it is not necessarily the case that issues so labeled actually affect a numerical majority. I use the term *majority*, however, because other, potentially more accurate terms such as *plurality* or *predominant* are more awkward.

16. In theory, cross-tabulating size with power gives us two types of *majority* issues as well: advantaged majority and disadvantaged majority. I do not use these categories in the analysis, however, because by definition, majority issues affect both advantaged and disadvantaged subgroups of the broader identity or issue that unites a group into a constituency for a given organization.

17. Because interest group officers are strategic actors, there is reason to be concerned about the validity of the survey responses. Large-scale surveys of advocacy organizations have been used to collect data in many of the most important studies of interest groups (Berry 1977; Heinz et al. 1993; Kollman 1998; Laumann and Knoke 1987; Schlozman and Tierney 1986; Walker 1991) and are credited with having contributed to "some of the greatest advances in the past decades of research on groups" (Baumgartner and Leech 1998, 12). Most centrally, the survey results show that officers' responses are not biased in "desirable" directions. Instead, the data show a great deal of variation in levels of activity by policy issue (as well as for the other variables), suggesting that officers were quite forthcoming.

18. Though a response rate of 40 percent might be considered low if this were a survey of public opinion, it is about average for a survey of organizations (Berry et al. 2003, 12).

19. This latter category also includes organizations that Salisbury calls "associations," that is, organizations that are comprised of other organizations as members. Chapter 3 includes a discussion of the terminology that I apply to describe the different members and constituents of each type of organization.

20. Note that organizations that I have classified as "public interest" groups are primarily consumer, environmental, and "good government" organizations. Researchers usually use the designation *public interest group* to distinguish organizations that seek "a collective good" from business and professional organizations seeking goods that benefit "selectively and materially . . . the membership or activists of the organization" (Berry 1977, 7). With the exception of labor unions, this more common and much broader designation encompasses most of the organization types that are the focus of my survey.

21. Although clearly related in important ways, the "collective action" problems and other barriers associated with obtaining and maintaining public goods are beyond the scope of this discussion.

22. Even in cases when it is arguably true that "everyone" has an interest in a public good, such as a secure retirement or clean air, scholars such as Andrew McFarland (1976) and Kay Lehman Schlozman and John Tierney (1986) have pointed out that there are almost inevitably equally weighty interests in *other* public goods with which these former goods might be at odds, such as economic development.

23. To address this fear, the Immigration Act of 1990 contained a provision that amended the marriage fraud rules of the 1986 Immigration Act and allowed for waivers for hardship caused by domestic violence. However, this has been an incomplete solution because many women are unable to meet the conditions established for a waiver, which include providing reports and affadavits from officials such as medical personnel, police, and school administrators (Crenshaw 1994).

24. Some argue that the Title IX prohibition against sex discrimination in education has done much more than affirmative action to increase higher education opportunities for women. I refer mainly to affirmative action programs, however, because of their political salience during the period covered by this study.

25. The means for these measures (on the 1-to-5 scale) are 3.55 for the majority issue, 3.49 for the advantaged-subgroup issue, 2.89 for the disadvantaged-subgroup issue, and 3.75 for the universal issue. All differences are statistically significant at $p < .05$.

## CHAPTER 3

1. Other terms that have been used to describe the underlying idea of intersectional marginalization include *compound discrimination, interlinking forms of discrimination, multiple burdens,* or *double* or *triple discrimination* (Crenshaw 2000, 8).

2. Schlozman and Tierney's question was slightly broader, asking whether the group has "lawyers on staff." In addition, their study encompassed a sampling of all organized interests, including corporations, trade associations, unions, professional associations, civil rights groups, and citizens' groups. Political Action Committees (PACs) collect contributions from individuals and distribute them to political candidates (Mervin 2003).

3. That 11.4 percent of respondents place their organization at under 5, and therefore on the conservative side of the scale, indicates that there is a fair bit of variation in the responses to this question, even among groups commonly associated with "liberal" causes, such as feminism, civil rights, and the labor movement.

4. See www.cawp.rutgers.edu/Facts/Officeholders/elective.pdf.

5. Andrew Rehfeld (2005) analyzes other shortcomings associated with territory-based systems of defining constituencies. He concludes that territory is not a compelling way to define interests and that the founders did not intend territorially defined constituencies to represent communities of interest (Rehfeld 2005, 140, 159). In this work, Rehfeld explicitly limits his discussion of constituency to *electoral* constituencies because of what he characterizes as their "formal institutional role to structure political representation" (2005, 36). However, many of his arguments about the limitations of territorially defined electoral constituencies offer reasons to take seriously the value of examining the representational roles of advocacy organizations, particularly given the improbability that the random assignment to constituencies that he advocates will be implemented. In more recent work, Rehfeld himself argues that we should take seriously informal political representation that is not achieved through elections (Rehfeld 2006).

6. Note again that Berry's use of the term *public interest groups* differs from the way in which I use it. In my classification scheme, "public interest" groups are primarily consumer, environmental, and "good government" organizations.

7. According to the 1999 World Values Survey, 25.9 percent of American women belonged to women's organizations in that year. Many more women—61.7 percent—said that they had either "a great deal" or "quite a lot" of confidence in the women's movement. Similarly, while only 16.4 percent of respondents employed as manual workers (skilled, semiskilled, and unskilled) belonged to labor unions in 1999, 47 percent of these workers said that they had either "a great deal" or "quite a lot" of confidence in labor unions. Although these responses are not perfect measures of the extent to which members of a given population identify as constituents of organizations and movements, they do suggest that they rely on these organizations and see them as expressing their interests to some degree (World Values Study Group 1999).

8. As I will discuss at greater length in chapters 4 and 5, it is not necessarily the case that elected representatives actually *do* represent all constituents. Nonetheless, the normative and legal standards that dictate that they *should* represent all constituents are still more rigorous than any that exist when it comes to holding interest groups accountable.

9. See the AFL–CIO Web site, www.afl-cio.org/aboutaflcio/about/mission/index.cfm.

10. In a somewhat different context, Sharon Kurtz writes about the ways in which collective identity is constituted by movements through what she calls "identity practices," which include a movement's "demands, framing and ideology, culture, leadership, organizational structure, and support resources" (2002, xxi).

11. For an overview of the vibrant and growing literature about the role of emotions in politics, see Goodwin, Jasper, and Polletta 2001a; Hochschild 1975. See also A. Miller et al. 1981; Rhea 1997; and Sears et al. 2003 regarding the ways in which politicizing ethnic identity leads to group consciousness and collective action.

12. Social scientists have posited a wide range of ways in which frames are created and deployed by individuals, the media, and political actors in order to understand and make sense of the "complexities of the world" (Goffman 1974; Goodwin and Jasper 2003, 52). I limit my discussion here to the ways in which organizations use frames to define their constituencies and to construct the issues that are in the interests of these constituents.

13. Organization leaders typically cannot construct frames and set the terms of debate about an issue by themselves and instead must compete with the media and political elites to influence social understandings of policy issues (Tarrow 2005). In addition, they generally do not construct frames from scratch but instead try to frame issues such that their grievances have legitimacy within "existing cultural understandings" of these issues and so that these framings resonate with the "'common sense' of their target publics" (Tarrow 2005, 61). Because, as Sidney Tarrow points out, "common sense" usually "buttresses the position of elites and defends inherited inequalities," trying to frame issues in these ways can further disadvantage marginalized groups (Tarrow 1992).

14. An examination and discussion of the extent to which attitudes among marginalized groups actually feel linked fate is beyond the scope of this book. There is much evidence that supports the validity of this concept but also a great deal of evidence that linked fate is mediated by other identities and affiliations (Dawson 1994; Harris-Lacewell 2004; Simien 2005). My concern here, however, is less with whether or not groups such as women, African Americans, or low-income people actually think and behave as groups in the ways that linked fate theory would predict. Rather, I am concerned with the ways in which organizations representing these populations implicitly define and deploy that "groupness" as they define some issues as being *within* their policy purviews while they define other issues as being outside of, or tangential to, their core concerns.

15. Note that I am not saying that lesbians never require birth control or abortions. There are a variety of circumstances under which they might need access to either or both of them. Clearly, however, access to reproductive rights and controls is far less of a day-to-day concern for lesbians than it is for heterosexual women.

16. Roberta Spalter-Roth and Ronnee Schreiber (1995) found that some women's organizations had added lesbian issues and efforts to address homophobia to their organizations' agendas by the end of the 1980s but that these issues were addressed less enthusiastically and in a markedly less-integrated fashion than other issues.

17. Regarding this, some differences exist between economic justice and feminist and racial or ethnic minority organizations. Leaders of the latter organizations would typically claim membership in the group for which the organization advocates. In contrast, national-level advocates for the poor, almost by virtue of their positions, tend not to be poor themselves, even if they once were. The point remains, however, that the average constituent of all these organizations is marginalized and has little political power, while their advocates are accorded more political legitimacy by elected officials.

18. Some of the variation among organizations on this issue is probably structural in origin. For example, some groups have members who are direct beneficiaries of their policy advocacy (for example, labor unions), whereas in other cases their work generally benefits people who are not actually members of the organization (for example, antipoverty organizations that focus on children).

19. Interview with organization officer, July 2001. As I indicate in chapter 2 and in appendix A, all survey and face-to-face interviews were conducted confidentially and anonymously. Names of interviewees and their organizations therefore are withheld by mutual agreement.

20. Interview with organization officer, May 2001.

21. Interview with organization officer, April 2001.

22. Interview with organization officer, April 2001.

23. Interview with organization officer, April 2001.

24. Interview with organization officer, April 2001.

25. Interview with organization officer, April 2001.

26. Interview with organization officer, July 2001.

27. Note, however, that in the case of some other groups, organizations seem more likely to mirror and reinforce the marginalization of groups the public disfavors. In particular, LGBT people were ranked last on each question.
28. Interview with organization officer, August 2001.
29. Interview with organization officer, April 2001.
30. Interview with organization officer, May 2001.

CHAPTER 4

1. Interview with organization officer, August 2001.
2. Ibid.
3. Ibid.
4. Quoted from the NAACP Web site, www.naacp.org/about/ (accessed October 19, 2000).
5. Quoted from the NOW Web site, www.now.org/organiza/nutsbolts.html (accessed November 9, 2001).
6. Notably, although some differences exist between member and nonmember organizations, the percentage of each type of organization that is involved with each activity type follows the same pattern, as do their mean levels of involvement.
7. Transforming the dependent variable in this way (by differencing out each organization's average level of activity) is intended to control for each organization's overall level of activity. Including a measure of each organization's average level of activity as an *independent* variable would introduce posttreatment bias into the equation, as this variable measures some part of the same syndrome as the dependent variable. Incorporating it into the dependent variable, however, minimizes both the bias that would be introduced by including it as an independent variable and the "noise" that would result from failing to take account of the general "activeness" of each organization.
8. Running the analysis alternating the dummy categories that are excluded does not affect the substantive results, so I present the results of the analysis that excludes the universal category because the mean level of activity for this issue is the lowest. As such, comparing the values of the other categories to this one is the most straightforward.
9. Although the model includes variables that control for factors suggested by several theories, I am interested mainly in testing the relative value of intersectional and Downsian strategic explanations. I therefore focus my discussion on the variables that are intended to operationalize, or that have implications for, understanding the relative explanatory power of each of these concepts.
10. There are many other facets of political opportunity that might be important, and David Meyer and Debra Minkoff have demonstrated persuasively that each factor has its own nuances and that it is important to consider the ways in which political opportunities "operate through different causal mechanisms that depend on the political process" (Meyer and Minkoff 2004, 1483). The measure that I use here is intended to tap the political opportunities associated with government attention to an issue, a factor that is likely to be important to the organizations in this study.

11. Once again, this measure is estimated by respondents.

12. I elected to use the percentage of the budget that is devoted to advocacy instead of a measure of the size of the budget itself. Preliminary analyses showed that budget size is not correlated with activity at the bivariate level, nor did it have a significant effect in a multivariate model. I do not include a control for ideology. Adding such a control makes no difference to the substantive results. However, to ensure that the results are not being driven by the 10 percent of organizations that placed themselves on the conservative side of the 1-to-10 scale of ideology, I also ran the model including only organizations that placed themselves above 6 (i.e., on the liberal side) on the 1-to-10 scale of ideology. Excluding more conservative organizations did not change the results of the model. In addition, although funding is clearly a crucial aspect of organizational maintenance, none of the measures of funding sources were significantly correlated with the dependent variable at the bivariate level, nor was an index of all funding sources. These measures were not significant in the multivariate model, nor did including them (either individually or in various combinations) have any effect on the other variables in the model.

13. Because there are four observations for each organization, I used robust standard errors to correct for clustering of the standard errors. Because the dependent variable is bounded between 1 and 5, I used ordered logit regression to conduct the analysis.

14. The pseudo $R^2$ is 0.12 for membership organizations and 0.15 for nonmembership organizations.

15. I do not include a table of bivariate correlations or colinearity diagnostics. However, there is no indication that multicolinearity is a problem. Other than for the interaction terms, the strongest correlation between the independent variables is between the proportions of constituents affected by an issue and the proportion that is concerned about an issue (0.50, sig. $p < .01$). Colinearity diagnostics are within acceptable limits, with tolerance levels between 0.56 and 0.9, and VIFs between 1.06 and 1.76 (other than for the interaction terms and their component variables). For further details, please see the appendix to Strolovitch 2006.

16. Probabilities were generated using the Stata add-on program Clarify created by Micheal Tomz, Jason Wittenberg, and Gary King. Clarify "uses Monte Carlo simulation to convert the raw output of statistical procedures into results that are of direct interest to researchers, without changing statistical assumptions or requiring new statistical models" (as described on Tomz's Web site, www.stanford.edu/~tomz/software/software.shtml). Probabilities of activity were predicted while holding the values of all variables at their means.

17. 2002 Current Population Survey, as posted on the U.S. Census Bureau Web site, www.census.gov, esp. http://www.census.gov/population/www/socdemo/education/ppl-169.html and http://pubdb3.census.gov/macro/032005/pov/toc.htm (both accessed July 16, 2004).

18. Interview with organization officer, April 2001.

19. Interview with organization officer, April 2001.

20. Ibid.

21. In fact, other research has found that most national women's organizations were largely inactive around the 1996 Personal Responsibility and Work Reconciliation Act (PRWORA, i.e., welfare reform). Kent Weaver (2000) found, for example, that the key liberal organizations involved in this issue were children's rights groups, the Center on Budget and Policy Priorities, and the Center on Law and Social Policy. While these organizations worked closely with the NOW Legal Defense and Education Fund (NOW LDEF, which in 2006 changed its name to Legal Momentum and is an organization separate from but related to NOW) to keep out illegitimacy reduction measures such as "family caps," they framed the issue in a way that de-emphasized the gender-related concerns and emphasized the potential harm to "innocent children." This framing allowed them to include pro-life groups in their coalition (Weaver 2000). Linda Williams makes a similar point about African American organizations. She claims that African American groups also failed to adequately respond to "the Republicans' extreme [welfare reform] bill in the 104th Congress" and that "African American interest groups concentrated most on its failure to seriously address job creation for those whose time limits on welfare receipt had expired, as well as for poor fathers who were expected to meet child support requirements. . . . In a very real sense," she concludes, "black, Latino, and women leaders never prioritized welfare reform . . . [because] welfare reform did not inspire the kind of high-visibility mobilization that occurred over affirmative action, an issue that has a disproportionately middle-class clientele" (L. Williams 1998, 432).

   Some feminist organizations, however, were very involved in the debates leading up to the 1996 welfare reforms. The executive director of a large civil rights coalition told me, for example, that those women's organizations that recognized the importance of this issue "from the outset" spent "a considerable effort opposing the welfare reform bill." In his opinion, their activity was an example of organizations "helping on issues that are only secondary to them." In this case, it meant that "organizations representing more middle-class constituencies did not turn their back on poorer women." NOW in particular actively and vociferously opposed the Clinton plan, calling it "welfare repeal" and characterizing it as "punitive." As Maryann Barakso explains, the organization staged a twenty-one-day vigil outside the White House. NOW/PAC refused to support President Clinton's 1996 reelection, in large part because he signed the bill into law (Barakso 2004, 123). In addition, NOW LDEF was very involved in trying to influence the reauthorization of the 1996 PRWORA. However, Ange-Marie Hancock's examination of the 1996 welfare reform debate found that many white female members of Congress who had previously stated their commitment to supporting "all women" voted in favor of the PRWORA despite the lobbying efforts of women of color in Congress as well as of some women's organizations to highlight the gendered aspects of the issue (Hancock 2004; see also Dodson et al. 1995; Mink 1998; Weaver 1998, 2000).

22. Interview with organization officer, July 2001.
23. Interview with organization officer, April 2001. H-1B visas benefit relatively privileged immigrants to the United States because they are used to employ aliens who, as the Web site for U.S. Citizenship and Immigration Services

explains, "will be employed temporarily in a specialty occupation or as a fashion model of distinguished merit and ability." To qualify as a specialty occupation, a job must require "theoretical and practical application of a body of specialized knowledge along with at least a bachelor's degree or its equivalent. For example, architecture, engineering, mathematics, physical sciences, social sciences, medicine and health, education, business specialties, accounting, law, theology, and the arts are specialty occupations" (http://uscis.gov/graphics/howdoi/h1b.htm; accessed August 11, 2005).

24. Interview with organization officer, May 2001.
25. Interview with organization officer, July 2001.
26. Interview with organization officer, April 2001.
27. Interview with organization officer, April 2001.
28. Interview with organization officer, May 2001.
29. Interview with organization officer, April 2001.
30. Interview with organization officer, April 2001.
31. Interview with organization officer, April 2001.
32. Interview with organization officer, April 2001.
33. Interview with organization officer, April 2001.
34. Interview with organization officer, April 2001.
35. Interview with organization officer, July 2001.
36. Interview with organization officer, April 2001.
37. Interview with organization officer, April 2001.
38. Interview with organization officer, April 2001.
39. Interview with organization officer, April 2001.
40. Interview with organization officer, March 2001.
41. Interview with organization officer, May 2001.
42. The positive effect of the number of other organizations potentially active on an issue suggests that coalitional alliances influence decisions about activity. I will explore this idea in greater depth in chapter 6.
43. Interview with organization officer, August 2001.
44. Interview with organization officer, March 2001.
45. Interview with organization officer, August 2001.
46. Interview with organization officer, April 2001.
47. The Alan Guttmacher Institute estimates that 49 out of every 1,000 black women, 33 out of every 1,000 Latinas, and 13 out of every 1,000 non-Hispanic white women have had an abortion. They also find that women who have abortions are more likely to be poor (www.guttmacher.org/in-the-know/characteristics.html; accessed June 4, 2006).
48. Interview with organization officer, April 2001.
49. None of the institutional control variables is a significant predictor of activity. While the percentage of the budget devoted to advocacy has no effect for either membership or nonmembership organizations, funding might matter in other ways. For example, several officers I spoke with mentioned that they had become involved in some policy issues because designated grant money was available to support work in those areas. Many also spoke about a more general trend in this area, with less general-program support available from grant makers and foundations. Because fewer and fewer foundations are

giving general operating support, shifting more and more of their grants to more-restrictive program-specific support (Shuman 1998), the advocacy agendas of many organizations are likely to become increasingly tied to the priorities of their funders.

50. See Business and Professional Women/USA (BPW/USA) Web site, www.network-democracy.org/social-security/bb/whc/bpwusa.html; and Congressional Black Caucus Foundation Web site, http://cbcfinc.org/pdf/waysandmeans2.pdf (both accessed August 29, 2005).

51. Interview with organization officer, April 2001.

52. Interview with organization officer, April 2001.

53. Interview with organization officer, May 2001.

54. Interview with organization officer, May 2001.

55. Because the data were not collected with this analysis in mind, many of the issues in the SNESJO are neither purely economic nor purely social. I categorized as many as I could and omitted ones that were too ambiguous. The issues that did not fall clearly into one of the categories and which I therefore omitted from this analysis are campaign finance reform, denying safety net benefits to immigrants, green card backlog, and H1-B visas. The issues I coded as *Economic issue* are the minimum wage, Social Security, the unionization of white-collar workers, and welfare reform. The issues that I coded as *Social issue* are abortion coverage by insurance companies and HMOs; affirmative action in contracting; affirmative action in higher education; census undercount; employment discrimination against LGBT people; environmental justice; gender- and race-based wage disparities; hate crime; Internet privacy; late-term abortion; public funding for abortion; racial profiling; tribal sovereignty; and violence against women.

56. Interview with organization officer, April 2001.

57. Interview with organization officer, May 2001.

58. Respondents from organizations representing women of color were asked questions about the same policy issues as the other women's organizations in the survey: violence against women (majority issue), affirmative action in higher education (advantaged-subgroup issue), and welfare reform (disadvantaged-subgroup issue). Among organizations representing women of color, equal proportions are active on the majority and disadvantaged-subgroup issues (62.5 percent), while three quarters (75 percent) are active on the advantaged-subgroup issue. Mean scores of activity show that these organizations devote their lowest *levels* of attention to the disadvantaged-subgroup issue of welfare reform as well. Specifically, on the 1-to-5 scale of activity, the advantaged-subgroup issue is at 3.13, the majority issue is at 2.63, and the disadvantaged-subgroup issue is at 2.38.

59. As a further test of robustness of the results and to ensure that no single issue is driving them, I ran the ordered logit analysis excluding welfare reform. The results remain largely unchanged in terms of the direction, significance, and magnitude of the coefficients.

60. Note that this civil rights organization addresses civil rights broadly speaking rather than focusing specifically on civil rights for racial minority groups.

61. Interview with organization officer, May 2001.

CHAPTER 5

1. Quoted from transcript of May 17, 2004, speech released by the White House, www.whitehouse.gov/news/releases/2004/05/20040517-4.html (accessed December 25, 2004).

2. Quoted from transcript of May 17, 2004, speech released by the White House, www.whitehouse.gov/news/releases/2004/05/20040517-2.html (accessed December 25, 2004).

3. The *Goodridge* case was not a federal one but rather was pursued through the Massachusetts state court system.

4. Lisa Hilbink (2006) argues that debates about rising constitutionalism and judicial empowerment in Europe have followed these same lines of debate between what she characterizes as "sunny liberal enthusiasm" and "skeptical democratic dismay."

5. While there are important questions about the impact of the court (see, for example, Hakman 1966; Caldeira and Wright 1988; Kearney and Merrill 2000), and while these questions inform the concerns addressed here, my intention in this chapter is not to debate the impact of judicial decisions versus the impact of legislation, nor is it to argue about the correct role of the court within a majoritarian democracy. Instead, I want to take a step back to think about the use of the courts as a form of representation that is a political good and goal of its own, related to issues of efficacy and impact but independently important. I also am not attempting here to provide a complete or general explanation for organizations' decisions about which branch they target. Rather, my intention is to examine whether the choice of institutional target varies by policy type and to explore the implications of this variation if it exists.

6. Note, however, that recent research suggests that it is currently so easy for organizations to get permission to file amicus curiae briefs that the process of obtaining permission is viewed by many as pro forma (see, for example, Epstein and Knight 1999).

7. See Baumgartner and Leech 1998 for more comparisons among previous surveys of organizations.

8. When organizations representing marginalized groups do lobby the executive branch, they tend to favor agencies such as Housing and Urban Development (HUD) that are not dominated by the influence of corporations, public utilities, or trade associations (Golden 1998).

9. The survey question asked respondents, "On a scale of 1 to 5, if 1 is 'not important' and 5 is 'very important,' how important is each of the following as a target of your organization's activity? (1) Members of Congress; (2) The President and White House offices; (3) The Executive agencies; or (4) The Federal courts." Answers for choices 2 and 3 were combined into a single "Executive Branch" category.

10. Interview with organization officer, April 2001.

11. Interview with organization officer, May 2001.

12. Interview with organization officer, July 2001.

13. Interview with organization officer, May, 2001.

14. Interview with organization officer, April, 2001.

15. Although the survey asks respondents about their activities over a ten-year period, the resulting data are essentially cross-sectional, not longitudinal. It is consequently difficult to address the ways in which over-time changes in receptivity might affect venue selection. Such an examination likely would yield interesting and important findings about changes in organizations' decisions about targeting each branch. However, fluctuations in the courts' ideology and in resulting levels of receptivity are likely to affect organizations' decisions across the board rather than having a specific impact on their decisions about which venue to target for which issue type. I attempt to take into account changing ideology and levels of receptivity in the multivariate analysis that follows by controlling for levels of partisan sensitivity and for the salience of each issue within each institution.

16. Several respondents commented on the palpable decreases in their levels of access under the Bush administration when compared with the Clinton administration. One respondent commented, "From [1992] until now, we had access to administrators in the White House that we don't have now. We had people's ears, [the president of our organization] had the fax number to the kitchen in the White House . . . and Hillary and Bill knew her by name."

17. Interview with organization officer, August 2001.

18. Interview with organization officer, April 2001.

19. Interview with organization officer, April 2001.

20. This concern about maintaining good relations with government officials echoes James Q. Wilson's arguments about the tensions within the contrasting roles of organizations that must serve the needs of both government officials and their own constituents (J. Wilson [1974] 1995, 319).

21. Interview with organization officer, April 2001.

22. Intended to develop the Bush administration's energy policy, the NEPDG was chaired by Vice President Dick Cheney, himself a former energy industry executive.

23. Phillip Cooper explains that presidential signing statements are "pronouncements issued by the president at the time a congressional enactment is signed" (Cooper 2005, 516–17). These statements often provide "general commentary on the bills, identify provisions of the legislation with which the president has concerns and (1) provide the president's interpretation of the language of the law, (2) announce constitutional limits on the implementation of some of its provisions, or (3) indicate directions to executive branch officials as to how to administer the new law in an acceptable manner" (Cooper 2005, 517).

24. Twenty-one percent of respondents said they had a "great deal of trust and confidence" in "The Executive branch headed by the President." The survey interviews were conducted by Gallup, May 23–25, 2005. Complete survey results are available at http://brain.gallup.com/documents/questionnaire.aspx?STUDY=P0505024 (accessed May 28, 2006).

25. The question that they were asked was, "Which of the following political institutions is the most important target of your efforts in trying to influence policy on [the issue in question]?" Answers for "The President and White House

offices" and "The Executive agencies" were combined into a single "Executive Branch" category. Answers were then coded "1" for the least majoritarian judicial branch, "2" for the executive branch, and "3" for the most majoritarian legislative branch. Note that the question was posed so that respondents had to select only one of the institutions rather than rank them.

26. The differences between these scores are all significant ($p < .05$).

27. As with the analysis in chapter 4, because there are four observations for each organization, I used robust standard errors (RSE) to correct for clustering of the standard errors. Because the dependent variable is categorical and bounded between 1 and 3, I used ordered logit regression to conduct the analysis. I also ran the analysis using unordered logit (multinomial regression), but I use the ordered method of analysis because, while the results are quite similar, the ordered model is more appropriate theoretically given my argument about the ordered scale of majoritarianism represented by the three branches. I also ran separate analyses for membership and nonmembership organizations. Unlike the results for the level of advocacy, there were no major differences between the two except that the effect for disadvantaged-subgroup issues is somewhat smaller for nonmember organizations. However, this coefficient remains significant and in the same direction. The model reported here therefore includes all organizations. I also ran this model with an additional dummy measure to control for whether or not an organization is a membership organization, but the effect was not significant, and including this variable had no perceptible effect on the direction, magnitude, or significance of the other variables in the model. A measure of the number of members (in thousands) had a small but significantly positive effect in the model for membership organizations, suggesting that the more members such organizations have, the more likely they are to target majoritarian institutions. Once again, omitting this variable has no effect on the other variables, so I report one model for all organizations. Note that Hansford (2004) found that membership organizations were more likely than the organizations that he classifies as "institutions" (following Salisbury's [1984] categorization) to take into account media attention to an issue when deciding whether to file amicus curiae briefs (see also Solberg and Waltenberg [2006], however, who find that membership organizations were less likely than institutions to engage the courts).

28. Because universal issues show the strongest positive correlation with the dependent variable at the bivariate level, I designated those issues as the excluded category, with the expectation that the slopes for the three other categories will be negative, indicating less-majoritarian targeting.

29. The model includes measures of several factors that are likely to affect the choice of institution targeted. Recall, however, that the intention is not an exhaustive examination of all factors that might affect this targeting, nor is it to predict choice of target generally. Rather, my intention is to examine whether policy type remains a significant predictor of target once we control for other factors.

30. These measures are the three (disaggregated) components of the variable *Agenda salience* that was used in the analyses in chapter 4.

31. The Alpha for this scale is 0.54.

32. This measure is similar to the one used by Hansford (2004) to measure previous court involvement (he does not include analogous measures of legislative and executive involvement).

33. Note that the two prominent University of Michigan cases, *Grutter v. Bollinger* and *Gratz v. Bollinger*, both were decided by the Supreme Court in 2003, after the period covered by this study.

34. The dependent variable uses answers to the SNESJO question, "Which of the following political institutions is the most important target of your efforts in trying to influence policy on [the issue in question]?" As I described previously in note 25, answers for the two categories of the executive branch—"The President and White House offices" and "The Executive agencies"—were combined into an "Executive Branch" category, and responses were coded "1" for the courts, "2" for the executive branch, and "3" for the legislative branch. I also ran the analysis without aggregating the two executive branch categories. In this case, the dependent variable had four categories, and the legislative branch was coded "4" at the most majoritarian end of the scale. The judicial branch remained coded "1" at the least majoritarian end. "The President and White House offices" was coded "3" as slightly more majoritarian than "The Executive agencies," which was placed at "2" on the scale. The alternative scale produces substantively the same results regarding the relationship between issue type and advocacy target, and conducting the analysis in this way did not change any of the other results in substantively important ways. The only substantial difference is that the effect of the measure of the importance of the courts to organizations' overall advocacy activities no longer reaches statistical significance in the disaggregated model. I have reported only the results for the model that uses the aggregated executive category in the dependent variable. The aggregated categories are more streamlined and more aptly convey the theoretical points about majoritarianism and the advocacy activities of interest groups.

35. The pseudo $R^2$ for the model is 0.15. Recall that the intention of the model is not to explain the determinants of targeting in toto but rather to test whether specific independent variables help us predict and understand the relationships among policy type, advocacy activity, and representation. As such, the magnitude, direction, and significance of the slope coefficients for the variables of interest are the important factors.

36. Because ordered logit results indicate only that dummy categories are different from the excluded category, relative levels of judicial targeting are in comparison with the levels for universal issues. I also used the Clarify statistical software program to test for differences between the categories. Created by Michael Tomz, Jason Wittenberg, and Gary King, Clarify "uses Monte Carlo simulation to convert the raw output of statistical procedures into results that are of direct interest to researchers, without changing statistical assumptions or requiring new statistical models" (as described on Tomz's Web site, www.stanford.edu/~tomz/software/software.shtml). The Clarify analysis tests and confirms the differences between the categories of the dummy variables in the aforementioned findings—organizations are indeed more likely to pursue majority issues through Congress and more likely to pursue them administratively as well. However, they are less likely to employ court strategies

for this issue type. In the case of disadvantaged-subgroup and advantaged-subgroup issues, groups are more likely to use court tactics and to target the administration and less likely to target Congress.

37. Probabilities also were generated using the Stata add-on program Clarify. See note 36 for details about this program.

38. These probabilities were predicted while holding the values of all variables at their means, except the controls for the salience of the issues in each branch, which were set at zero.

39. Because these variables are included mainly as controls, I also ran the model without these measures. Omitting them does not change significantly the magnitude or direction of any of the other variables.

40. The measure of partisan sensitivity is quite a blunt instrument, which may explain its lack of significance.

41. Note that Hansford (2004) also finds uneven but somewhat different results regarding the relationship between political opportunity and institutional targets. In particular, he finds that interest groups are more likely to submit amicus curiae briefs when the court is more receptive to their arguments. However, he finds that measures of receptivity are not useful in predicting lobbying activity directed at the president or Congress.

42. Interview with organization officer, April 2001.

43. Interview with organization officer, April 2001.

44. Interview with organization officer, August 2001.

## CHAPTER 6

1. The LCCR had 192 member organizations as of June 2006. The A. Philip Randolph Institute is a black labor organization that fights "for racial equality and economic justice," working with black trade unionists and heading the "'Black-Labor Alliance' an initiative to build black community support for the trade union movement, and to convey to labor the needs and concerns of black Americans" (according to the organization's Web site, www.apri.org, accessed June 11, 2006). The American Association of Retired People is "a nonprofit membership organization of persons 50 and older dedicated to addressing their needs and interests" (AARP Web site, www.aarp.org/about_aarp/aarp_overview, accessed June 11, 2006). The Women's International League for Peace and Freedom "works to achieve through peaceful means world disarmament, full rights for women, racial and economic justice, an end to all forms of violence, and to establish those political, social, and psychological conditions which can assure peace, freedom, and justice for all" (Web site http://wilpf.org/us-wilpf/default.htm, accessed June 11, 2006). The Zeta Phi Beta Sorority is a predominantly African American service and social sorority "founded on the simple belief that sorority elitism and socializing should not overshadow the real mission for progressive organizations—to address societal mores, ills, prejudices, poverty, and health concerns of the day" (Web site www.zphib1920.org/heritage, accessed June 11, 2006).

2. See http://www.civilrights.org/issues/immigration/details.cfm?id=41532 (accessed June 11, 2006).

3. Sidney Tarrow (2005) describes four types of coalitions which are differentiated by their duration and the level of involvement required by participants. *Instrumental coalitions* are short-term cooperative efforts that entail low levels of involvement and are unlikely to produce the bases for continued collaboration or issue broadening. *Event coalitions* are also short-term but entail higher levels of involvement and harbor more potential for future collaboration if they "solder alliances among people who recognize their shared identities in the process of collective action." Such coalitions are nonetheless difficult to transform into enduring cooperation against more concrete targets. *Federated coalitions* are long-term collaborations that nonetheless demand a low level of involvement for member organizations. *Campaign coalitions* are also long-term collaborations that demand high-intensity involvement from member organizations (Tarrow 2005, 166–67). For other discussions of the various forms that coalitions can take see, for example, Berry 1977; Evans 1991; Loomis 1986; Meyer and Corrigall-Brown 2005; Salisbury 1983; Staggenborg 1986; Wilson [1974] 1995.

4. Previous research has taught us a great deal about issues such as the origins, benefits, and stability of coalitions (see, for example, G. Arnold 1995; Diaz-Veizades and Chang 1996; Gamson 1975; Hathaway and Meyer 1997; McCammon and Campbell 2002; Rochon and Meyer 1997; Staggenborg 1986; Zald and McCarthy 1987). This chapter draws on the many findings in this literature but focuses on coalitions primarily as they relate to advocacy for intersectionally disadvantaged groups.

5. Interview with organization officer, May 2001.

6. In this usage of the term *public interest group*, I mean organizations whose primary goal is not to "selectively and materially benefit the membership and activists of the organization" (Berry 1977, 7).

7. Interview with organization officer, August 2001.

8. Interview with organization officer, August 2001.

9. Interview with organization officer, April 2001.

10. Interview with organization officer, March 2001.

11. Interview with organization officer, April 2001.

12. Interview with organization officer, April 2001.

13. Interview with organization officer, April 2001.

14. Organizational forms other than coalitions—such as collectives or nonhierarchical associations—also often are seen as such prefigurative opportunities by movements that try to use them to embody normative ideals such as egalitarianism and participatory democracy (G. Arnold 1995; Breines 1989).

15. Surveys of interest groups have consistently reported that over 90 percent of organizations make at least occasional use of coalitions (Berry 1977, 1989; Heinz et al. 1993; Kollman 1998; Nownes and Freeman 1998; Schlozman and Tierney 1986; see also C. Tilly 1978, 1984). Knoke (1990), however, found that only 58 percent of the groups he surveyed had entered coalitions with other organizations. His survey included many nonpolitical associations, which likely accounts for this low incidence.

16. Interview with organization officer, April 2001.

17. Interview with organization officer, March 2001.

18. Interview with organization officer, April 2001.

19. Interview with organization officer, April 2001.

20. The important role of relationships corroborates the finding in chapter 4 regarding niches, that organizations often become involved in issues because they follow the lead of their allies.

21. Interview with organization officer, April 2001.

22. Interview with organization officer, April 2001.

23. Ibid.

24. Interview with organization officer, April 2001.

25. Interview with organization officer, April 2001.

26. Interview with organization officer, May 2001.

27. Interview with organization officer, May 2001.

28. Interview with organization officer, April 2001.

29. Interview with organization officer, May 2001.

30. Ibid.

31. Interview with organization officer, May 2001.

32. Scholars have documented a wide variety of additional difficulties associated with maintaining coalitions, such as the need to expend resources to maintain them; the effects of competition on the ability and will of coalition members to cooperate with one another; the threats to their survival posed by changing circumstances; and tensions resulting from differences in goals, strategies, ideology as well as from perceptions that some coalition members are contributing or benefiting more than others (Levi and Murphy 2006; Meyer and Corrigall-Brown 2005; Tarrow 2005).

33. Interview with organization officer, May 2001.

34. Interview with organization officer, May 2001.

35. Interview with organization officer, April, 2001.

36. Interview with organization officer, May 2001.

37. Interview with organization officer, April 2001.

38. Note, however, that Berry (1977) found that none of the groups in his study mentioned this fear.

39. Interview with organization officer, April 2001.

40. Some organizations also are wary about entering into coalitions that include groups associated with negative stereotypes and images such as deviance, criminality, or laziness, from a concern that such images might rub off on them and bring negative press, threatening their already precarious access and respectability (C. Cohen 1999; Hall 1969). For example, women's organizations were long reluctant to support lesbian and gay rights organizations, not wanting to be tainted by association with the deviant image that the public held of these groups. For their part, many LGBT organizations continue to deny their support to organizations that work on controversial issues, such as transgender rights. As shown in chapter 4, some women's organizations and civil rights organizations also avoid association with issues associated with the poor, such as welfare reform. Because the effects of welfare policy are intensely gendered and racialized, this issue invites associations with populations popularly labeled undeserving, and therefore some organizations feel compelled to make clear that it is not their "cup of tea," as the respondent quoted in chapter 4 made clear.

41. Interview with organization officer, April 2001.

42. Although the observational data from interviews make it difficult to determine the causal direction of this relationship—Do coalitions lead to moderation, or do moderate organizations join coalitions?—the interviews on which I base this analysis represent an implicit time series design that helps deal with this methodological issue. That is, the recollections of the respondents give us a sense of the changes that their organizations and advocacy have experienced over time. In addition, while it is possible that more moderate organizations are more likely to enter coalitions, note that the organizations in this study represent a range of ideological positions but that almost all of them participate in coalitions at least occasionally. It seems more likely, then, that it is participation in these alliances that leads to moderation of goals and not the reverse.

43. Interview with organization officer, August 2001.

44. The "global gag rule," officially termed the Mexico City Policy, mandates "that no U.S. family planning assistance can be provided to foreign NGOs that use funding from any other source to: perform abortions in cases other than a threat to the woman's life, rape or incest; provide counseling and referral for abortion; or lobby to make abortion legal or more available in their country" (quoted from the Web site of the coalition-sponsored Global Gag Rule Impact Project, www.globalgagrule.org, accessed July 6, 2005).

45. Interview with organization officer, April 2001.

46. In her examination of a battered-women's coalition, Gretchen Arnold (1995) finds that coalitions among ideologically disparate groups can lead to conflicts over structure that can result in moderation of goals or dissolution of the coalition. Anya Bernstein (1997) also finds that coalitions lead to moderation in policy goals, but she argues that this may be a positive phenomenon. That is, she finds that coalitions of moderate insiders are more likely to get policies enacted, both because they have more clout and because they are likely to propose moderate bills and be willing to compromise. On the other hand, Bernstein writes, outsiders help the cause by expanding the scope of the debate and by making insiders' demands look moderate by comparison. In the case that she examines, the Family and Medical Leave Act, moderation came at a cost—that is, the policies that were adopted at the state and national levels generally cover less than half the population and offer only unpaid leave.

47. Interview with organization officer, April 2001.

48. Interview with organization officer, April 2001.

49. Interview with organization officer, April 2001.

CHAPTER 7

1. Chapter 2 includes an extended discussion of how to determine which groups might be considered oppressed, and further elaboration of this discussion is beyond the scope of this chapter. For in-depth treatment of this issue, see, for example, the work of Laurel Weldon (2002), Melissa Williams (1998), and Iris Young (1990). Similarly, chapters 2 and 3 include extended discussions

validating the idea of "group politics" within the American political system, so I do not revisit this issue in depth here. See, however, Lani Guinier (1994), for an argument that all politics is essentially "group politics," and Nancy Schwartz (1988, 46–47), for a discussion of the U.S. Supreme Court's "experimentation" with the idea of group representation.

2. Extra representation may also seem excessive, since proportional representation would be an improvement.

3. Interview with organization officer, April 2001.

4. Interview with organization officer, March 2001.

5. Interview with organization officer, March 2001.

6. A few prominent coalitions of organizations, such as the Leadership Conference on Civil Rights (LCCR), the National Council of Women's Organizations (NCWO), and the American Federation of Labor–Congress of Industrial Organizations (AFL-CIO) do play such a "broker" role to some degree.

7. Interview with organization officer, April 2001.

8. Interview with organization officer, April 2001.

9. Interview with organization officer, April 2001.

10. Interview with organization officer, April 2001.

11. Interview with organization officer, May 2001.

12. Interview with organization officer, May 2001.

13. Interview with organization officer, March 2001.

14. It should be noted, however, that having a liberal executive director does not inevitably mean that she or he will push the organization to be similarly liberal. Some respondents expressed frustration about having joined organizations out of specific commitments that they were then not able to pursue. For example, the executive director of an economic justice organization said,

> My commitment to the antihunger effort and things that I've done . . . I get involved in doing these things, but the association's position is frequently more conservative than my position or my boss's position for that matter, who I know is also very committed to these issues. . . . My employers are sixty thousand members of this association. What I believe is not necessarily what they believe and . . . our public positions reflect our members' interests. There have been times when I have lobbied on behalf of issues because that's what our members decided that I didn't necessarily agree with. . . . I would do it differently or go after something else, but once through the representative process, the association makes a decision . . . that's what we do (interview with organization officer, April 2001).

15. Interview with organization officer, March 2001.

16. Interview with organization officer, May 2001.

17. Interview with organization officer, April 2001.

18. Interview with organization officer, July 2001.

19. Interview with organization officer, April 2001.

20. For a contrary view, see D. Warren 2005.

21. Although the bivariate correlation is significant (0.2, $p < .001$), it was not significant in the multivariate analysis and was not included in the model presented in chapter 4.

22. A related phenomenon is evident in organizations that have relationships with international groups. For example, an economist in the public policy department at a labor organization with a federated structure explained that in addition to consulting with state and local organizations about state, local, and national issues, "Through our relationships with other countries, there's a lot of interest in global, multilateral, multilevel policy issues" (interview with organization officer, July 2001).

23. Interview with organization officer, April 2001.

24. Interview with organization officer, May 2001.

25. Interview with organization officer, April 2001.

26. Interview with organization officer, August 2001.

27. Interview with organization officer, August 2001.

28. This is not necessarily a call for increased internal democracy or for any specific state mandate about accountability or democracy within advocacy groups. If organizations do employ democratic means to enhance their accountability to their constituents, however, they should do so with the point-system guidelines suggested here to avoid a "tyranny of the majority" that would further marginalize disadvantaged subgroups.

29. Interview with organization officer, May 2001.

30. Interview with organization officer, May 2001.

31. Interview with organization officer, April 2001.

32. There may, however, be circumstances under which the threat of withholding resources could lead to the *inclusion* rather than the exclusion of disadvantaged-subgroup issues.

33. Interview with organization officer, July 2001.

34. Interview with organization officer, May 2001.

35. Interview with organization officer, August 2001.

36. It is not inevitable, of course, that the trajectory will be from radical to accepted. Many ideas that once seemed commonsensical, such as Social Security, now are considered by many people to be less so. On the other hand, ideas that had seemed outdated, such as biological explanations for racial or gender differences in intellectual capacities, have seen a resurgence.

37. Interview with organization officer, May 2001.

38. Interview with organization officer, April 2001.

39. Interview with organization officer, May 2001.

40. Interview with organization officer, August 2001. Note that at the time of publication (2007), ENDA has still not become law and organizations are lobbying to have the bill reintroduced in the 110th congress.

41. Interview with organization officer, April 2001.

42. Interview with organization officer, April 2001.

43. Interview with organization officer, April 2001.

44. Interview with organization officer, April 2001.

APPENDIX A

1. Unlike most of the other large directories that I consulted, the *Encyclopedia of Associations* lists local and international groups as well as many nonpolitical

groups such as cultural organizations, self-help groups, and educational organizations. I confined my search to organizations classified as "National Associations," and such organizations were included in the sample only if the entries about them made direct references to their engagement in national policy. Similarly, organizations such as women's and minority professional organizations, no matter where they were listed, were included in the sample only if information about them indicated that they are involved in policy advocacy. Professional associations that are involved only in advancing the interests of women or minorities within their particular professions have not been included.

# Bibliography

Abel, Richard. 1985. "Lawyers and the Power to Change." *Law and Policy* 7:1–18.

Abzug, Rikki, and Joseph Galaskiewicz. 2001. "Nonprofit Boards: Crucibles of Expertise or Symbols of Local Identities?" *Nonprofit and Voluntary Sector Quarterly* 30 (1): 51–73.

Achen, Christopher. 1978. "Measuring Representation." *American Journal of Political Science* 22:475–510.

Ainsworth, Scott. 2002. *Analyzing Interest Groups: Group Influence on People and Policies*. New York: Norton.

Alcoff, Linda Martìn. 1996. "The Problem of Speaking for Others." In *Who Can Speak? Authority and Critical Identity*, edited by Judith Roof and Robyn Wiegman, 97–119. Chicago: University of Illinois Press.

Almeida, Paul, and Linda Brewster Stearns. 1998. "Political Opportunities and Local Grassroots Environmental Movements: The Case of Minamata." *Social Problems* 45:37–60.

Aminzade, Ronald, Jack A. Goldstone, Doug McAdam, Elizabeth J. Perry, William H. Sewell Jr., Sidney Tarrow, and Charles Tilly, eds. 2001. *Silence and Voice in Contentious Politics*. Cambridge: Cambridge University Press.

Anderson, Benedict. 1991. *Imagined Communities: Reflections on the Origin and Spread of Nationalism*. Rev. ed. London: Verso.

Anderson, Ellen Ann. 2004. *Out of the Closets and into the Courts*. Ann Arbor: University of Michigan Press.

Ansolabehere, Stephen, James M. Snyder, and Charles Stewart III. 2001. "Candidate Positioning in US House Elections." *American Journal of Political Science* 45 (1):136–59.

Appiah, K. Anthony, and Amy Gutman. 1996. *Color Conscious: The Political Morality of Race*. Princeton, NJ: Princeton University Press.

Arnold, Douglas. 1993. "Can Inattentive Citizens Control Their Elected Representatives?" In *Congress Reconsidered*, 5th ed., edited by Lawrence Dodd and Bruce
Oppenheimer, 401–16. Washington, DC: CQ Press.

Arnold, Gretchen. 1995. "Dilemmas of Feminist Coalitions: Collective Identity and
Strategic Effectiveness in the Battered Women's Movement." In *Feminist Organi-
zations: Harvest of the New Women's Movement*, edited by Myra Marx Ferree and
Patricia Yancey Martin, 276–90. Philadelphia: Temple University Press.

Aronowitz, Stanley. 1992. *The Politics of Identity: Class, Culture, and Social Movements.*
New York: Routledge.

Association for Women's Rights in Development. 2004. "Intersectionality: A Tool for
Gender and Economic Justice." *Women's Rights and Economic Change* 9 (August):
1–8.

Austen-Smith, David, and John R. Wright. 1994. "Counteractive Lobbying." *American
Journal of Political Science* 38:25–44.

———. 1996. "Theory and Evidence for Counteractive Lobbying." *American Journal of
Political Science:* 40:543–64.

Baca Zinn, Maxine, and Bonnie Thornton Dill. 1996. "Theorizing Difference from
Multiracial Feminism." *Feminist Studies* 22 (2): 321–31.

Bachrach, Peter, and Morton S. Baratz. 1962. "The Two Faces of Power." *American
Political Science Review* 56:947–62.

Baker, Lee D. 1998. *From Savage to Negro: Anthropology and the Construction of Race,
1896–1954.* Berkeley and Los Angeles: University of California Press.

Banaszak, Lee Ann. 1996. *Why Movements Succeed or Fail.* Princeton, NJ: Princeton
University Press.

Barakso, Maryann. 2004. *Governing NOW: Grassroots Activism in the National Organization for Women.* Ithaca, NY: Cornell University Press.

Barker, Lucius. 1967. "Third Parties in Litigation: A Systematic View of Judicial Education." *Journal of Politics* 29:49–69.

Bartels, Larry M. 1991. "Constituency Opinion and Congressional Policy Making: The
Reagan Defense Buildup." *American Political Science Review* 85:457–74.

———. 2005. "Economic Inequality and Political Representation." Revised paper
presented at the annual meeting of the American Political Science Association,
Boston.

Bartley, Numan V. 1969. *The Rise of Massive Resistance.* Baton Rouge: Louisiana State
University Press.

Bass, Marie. 1998. "Toward Coalition: The Reproductive Health Technologies Project."
In *Abortion Wars: A Half Century of Struggle*, edited by Rickie Solinger, 251–68.
Berkeley and Los Angeles: University of California Press.

Bauer, Raymond, Ithiel de Sola Pool, and Lewis A. Dexter. 1963. *American Business and
Public Policy: The Politics of Foreign Trade.* New York: Prentice-Hall, Atherton Press.

Baum, Lawrence. 2001. *The Supreme Court.* 7th ed. Washington, DC: CQ Press.

Baumgartner, Frank R., and Bryan D. Jones. 1993. *Agendas and Instability in American
Politics.* Chicago: University of Chicago Press.

Baumgartner, Frank R., and Beth L. Leech. 1998. *Basic Interests: The Importance of Groups
in Politics and Political Science.* Princeton, NJ: Princeton University Press.

Bawn, Kathleen. 1999. "Constructing 'Us': Ideology, Coalition Politics, and False Consciousness." *American Journal of Political Science* 43 (2): 303–34.

Beard, Charles. 1913. *An Economic Interpretation of the Constitution of the United States.* New York: Macmillan.

Belenky, Mary, Blythe Clinchy, Nancy Goldberger, and Jill Tarule. 1996. *Women's Ways of Knowing.* New York: HarperCollins.

Bell, Derrick A. Jr. 1976. "Serving Two Masters: Integration Ideals and Client Interests in School Desegregation Litigation." *Yale Law Journal* 85:470–516.

Bell, Ella Louise. 1990. "The Bicultural Life Experience of Career-Oriented Black Women." Journal of Organizational Behavior 11 (6): 469–77.

Bentley, Arthur F. 1908. *The Process of Government.* Chicago: University of Chicago Press.

Bernstein, Anya. 1997. "Inside or Outside? The Politics of Family and Medical Leave." *Policy Studies Journal* 25 (1): 87–99.

Berry, Jeffrey M. 1977. *Lobbying for the People.* Princeton, NJ: Princeton University Press.

———. 1989. *The Interest Group Society.* 2nd ed. New York: HarperCollins.

———. 1999. *The New Liberalism: The Rising Power of Citizen Groups.* Washington, DC: Brookings Institution Press.

Berry, Jeffrey M., and David F. Arons. 2003. *A Voice for Nonprofits.* Washington, DC: Brookings Institution Press.

Berry, Jeffrey M., David F. Arons, Gary D. Bass, Matthew F. Carter, and Kent E. Portney. 2003. *Surveying Nonprofits: A Methods Handbook.* Washington, DC: Nonprofit Sector Research Fund, Aspen Institute.

Bickel, Alexander M. 1986. *The Least Dangerous Branch: The Supreme Court at the Bar of Politics.* 2nd ed. New Haven, CT: Yale University Press.

Black, Duncan. 1948. "On the Rationale of Group Decision-making". *Journal of Political Economy* 56:23–34.

Boles, Janet K. 1991. "Form Follows Function: The Evolution of Feminist Strategies." *Annals of the American Academy of Political Science and Sociology* 51:38–49.

Boris, Elizabeth T. 1999. "Nonprofit Organizations in a Democracy: Varied Roles and Responsibilities." In *Nonprofits and Government: Collaboration and Conflict*, edited by Elizabeth T. Boris and C. Eugene Steuerle. Washington, DC: Urban Institute Press.

Boris, Elizabeth T., and Rachel Mosher-Williams. 1998. "Nonprofit Advocacy Organizations: Assessing the Definitions, Classifications, and Data." *Nonprofit and Voluntary Sector Quarterly* 27 (4): 488–506.

Bork, Robert. 2003. *Slouching towards Gomorrah: Modern Liberalism and American Decline.* New York: Regan Books.

Boswell, Holly. 1997. "The Transgender Paradigm Shift toward Free Expression." In *Current Concepts in Transgender Identity*, edited by Dallas Denny, 55–61. New York: Garland.

Bradburn, Norman M., and Seymour Sudman. 1979. *Improving Interview Method and Questionnaire Design.* Washington, DC: Jossey-Bass.

Brecher, Jeremy, and Tim Costello, eds. 1990. *Building Bridges: The Emerging Grassroots Coalition of Labor and Community.* New York: Monthly Review Press.

Breines, Wini. 1989. *Community and Organization in the New Left: The Great Refusal.* New Brunswick, NJ: Rutgers University Press.

Bright, Charles, and Susan Harding, eds. 1984. *Statemaking and Social Movements: Essays in History and Theory.* Ann Arbor: University of Michigan Press.

Brod, Harry, and Michael Kaufman, eds. 1994. *Theorizing Masculinities.* Newbury Park, CA: Sage.

Browne, William. 1990. "Organized Interests and Their Issue Niches." *Journal of Politics* 52:477–509.

———. 1998. *Groups, Interests, and U.S. Public Policy.* Washington, DC: Georgetown University Press.

Bull, Chris. 1998. "The Power Brokers." *Advocate,* June 23.

Bunch, Charlotte. 1987. *Passionate Politics: Feminist Theory in Action.* New York: St. Martin's Press.

Burke, Edmund. [1792] 1889. "Letter to Sir Hercules Langriche." In *The Works of the Right Honorable Edmund Burke.* Vol. 3. Boston: Little, Brown.

———. [1774] 1889. "Speech to the Electors of Bristol." In *The Works of the Right Honorable Edmund Burke.* Vol. 2. Boston: Little, Brown.

Burstein, Paul. 1991. "Legal Mobilization as a Social Movement Tactic: The Struggle for Equal Employment Opportunity." *American Journal of Sociology* 96:1201–25.

Bussiere, Elizabeth. 1997. *(Dis)Entitling the Poor: The Warren Court, Welfare Rights, and the American Political Tradition.* University Park: Pennsylvania State University.

Bykerk, Loree, and Ardith Maney. 1995. "Consumer Groups and Coalition Politics on Capitol Hill." In *Interest Group Politics,* 4th edition, edited by Alan Cigler and Burdett Loomis, 259–80. Washington, DC: CQ Press.

Caldeira, Gregory A., and John R. Wright. 1988. "Organized Interests and Agenda Setting in the U.S. Supreme Court." *American Political Science Review* 82:1109–27.

———. 1989. "Why Organized Interests Participate as Amicus Curiae in the U.S. Supreme Court." Paper presented at the annual meeting of the Law and Society Association, Madison, WI.

———. 1990. "Amici curiae before the Supreme Court: Who Participates, When, and How Much?" *Journal of Politics* 52:782–806.

Calhoun, Craig, ed. 2002. *Dictionary of the Social Sciences.* New York: Oxford University Press.

Campbell, Andrea Louise. 2003. *How Policies Make Citizens: Senior Political Activism and the American Welfare State.* Princeton, NJ: Princeton University Press.

Canon, David. 1999. *Race, Redistricting, and Representation: The Unintended Consequences of Black-Majority Districts.* Chicago: University of Chicago Press.

Carroll, Susan J., ed. 1991. *Women, Black, and Hispanic Elected Leaders.* New Brunswick, NJ: Rutgers University, Eagleton Institute of Politics.

———. 2002. "Representing Women: Congresswomen's Perceptions of Their Representational Roles." In *Women Transforming Congress,* edited by Cindy Simon Rosenthal, 51–74. Oklahoma City: Oklahoma University Press.

Carter, Prudence, Sherrill Sellers, and Catherine Squires. 2002. "Reflections on Race/ Ethnicity, Class and Gender Inclusive Research." *African American Research Perspectives* 8 (1): 111–24.

Casper, Jonathon D. 1976. "The Supreme Court and National Policy Making." *American Political Science Review* 70:50–63.

Center for American Women and Politics. 2006. "Women in Elective Office 2006," Center for American Women and Politics, Eagleton Institute of Politics, Rutgers the State University of New Jersey, New Brunswick, NJ, http://www.cawp.rutgers.edu/ Facts/Officeholders/elective.pdf.

Center for Women's Global Leadership. 2001. "A Women's Human Rights Approach to the World Conference against Racism." http://www.cwgl.rutgers.edu/globalcenter/policy/gcpospaper.html.

Chambers, Simone. 2006. "The Politics of Equality: Rawls on the Barricades." *Perspectives on Politics* 4 (1): 81–89.

Chesler, Mark. 1996. "White Men's Roles in Multicultural Coalitions." In *Impacts of Racism on White Americans*, 2nd ed., edited by Raymond Hunt and Benjamin Bowser, 202–29. Thousand Oaks, CA: Sage.

Chong, Dennis. 1991. *Collective Action and the Civil Rights Movement*. Chicago: University of Chicago Press.

Cigler, Allan. 1986. "From Protest Group to Interest Group: The Making of the American Agriculture Movement, Inc." In *Interest Group Politics*, 2nd ed., edited by Alan Cigler and Burdett Loomis, 46–69. Washington, DC: CQ Press.

Cigler, Allan J., and John Mark Hansen. 1983. "Group Formation through Protest: The American Agriculture Movement." In *Interest Group Politics*, edited by Alan Cigler and Burdett Loomis, 84–109. Washington, DC: CQ Press.

Cigler, Allan, and Burdett Loomis, eds. 1983. *Interest Group Politics*. Washington, DC: CQ Press.

———. 1986. *Interest Group Politics*. 2nd edition. Washington, DC: CQ Press.

———. 1998. *Interest Group Politics*. 5th edition. Washington, DC: CQ Press.

Clemens, Elizabeth S. 1997. *The People's Lobby: Organizational Innovation and the Rise of Interest Group Politics in the United States, 1890–1925*. Chicago: University of Chicago Press.

———. 2005. "Two Kinds of Stuff: The Current Encounter of Social Movement Organizations." In *Social Movements and Organization Theory*, edited by Gerald Davis, Doug McAdam, W. Richard Scott, and Mayer N. Zald, 351–66. New York: Cambridge University Press.

Cohen, Cathy J. 1997: "Straight Gay Politics: The Limits of an Ethnic Model of Inclusion." In *Ethnicity and Group Rights*, edited by Ian Shapiro and Will Kymlicka. New York: New York University Press.

———. 1999. *The Boundaries of Blackness: AIDS and the Breakdown of Black Politics*. Chicago: University of Chicago Press.

———. 2001. "Punks, Bulldaggers, and Welfare Queens: The Radical Potential of Queer Politics?" In *Sexual Identities, Queer Politics*, edited by Mark Blasius, 200–208. Princeton, NJ: Princeton University Press.

Cohen, Joshua, and Joel Rogers. 1992. "Secondary Associations and Democratic Governance." *Politics and Society* 20 (4): 393–472.

Coles, Romand. 1996. "Liberty, Equality, Receptive Generosity: Neo-Nietzschean Reflections and the Ethics and Politics of Coalition." *American Political Science Review* 90 (2): 375–88.

Collier, David, and Henry Brady, eds. 2004. *Rethinking Social Inquiry: Diverse Tools, Shared Standards*. Lanham, MD: Rowman and Littlefield.

Collins, Patricia Hill. 1990. *Black Feminist Thought*. Boston: Unwin Hyman.

Columbia Books. 1999. *Washington Representatives*. Washington, DC: Columbia Books.

Combahee River Collective. [1977] 1981. "A Black Feminist Statement." In *This Bridge Called My Back: Writings by Radical Women of Color*, edited by Cherrie Moraga and Gloria Anzaldua, 210–18. New York: Kitchen Table.

Congressional Hispanic Caucus. 1999. *National Directory of Hispanic Organizations.* Washington, DC: Congressional Hispanic Caucus.

Congressional Quarterly. 1995. *Who's Who in Washington Nonprofit Groups.* Washington, DC: Congressional Quarterly.

Connolly, William A. 1972. "On 'Interests' in Politics." *Politics and Society* 2:459–77.

Cook, Constance. 1998. "The Washington Higher Education Community: Moving Beyond Lobbying 101." In *Interest Group Politics*, 5th ed., edited by Alan Cigler and Burdett Loomis, 97–117. Washington, DC: CQ Press.

Cook, Karen. S., Russel Hardin, and Margaret Levi. 2005. *Cooperation without Trust?* New York: Russell Sage Foundation.

Cooper, Phillip J. 2005. "George W. Bush, Edgar Allan Poe, and the Use and Abuse of Presidential Signing Statements." *Presidential Studies Quarterly* 35: 515–32.

Cortner, Richard C. 1968. "Strategies and Tactics of Litigants in Constitutional Cases." *Journal of Public Law* 17:287–307.

Costain, Anne. 1981. "Representing Women: The Transition from Social Movement to Interest Group." In *Women, Power, and Policy*, edited by E. Bonaparth, 26–47. New York: Pergamon Press.

———. 1992. *Inviting Women's Rebellion: A Political Process Interpretation of the Women's Movement.* Baltimore: Johns Hopkins University Press.

Costain, Anne, and Andrew McFarland, eds. 1998. *Social Movements and American Political Institutions.* New York: Rowman and Littlefield.

CQ Press. 1998. *Washington Information Directory.* Washington, DC: CQ Press.

Crenshaw, Kimberlé. 1989. "Demarginalizing the Intersection of Race and Sex." *University of Chicago Legal Forum* 39:139–67.

———. 1994. "Mapping the Margins: Intersectionality, Identity Politics, and Violence against Women of Color." In *The Public Nature of Private Violence*, edited by Martha Albertson Fineman and Rixanne Mykitiuk, 93–118. New York: Routledge.

———. 2000. "The Intersectionality of Race and Gender Discrimination." Background paper presented at Expert Group Meeting on Gender and Race Discrimination, Zagreb, Croatia, November 21–24.

Cummings, Scott L., and Ingrid V. Eagly. 2001. "A Critical Reflection on Law and Organizing." *UCLA Law Review* 48:443.

Dahl, Robert A. 1957. "Decision-Making in a Democracy: The Supreme Court as a National Policy-Maker." *Journal of Public Law* 6:279–95.

———. 1967. *Pluralist Democracy in the United States.* Chicago: Rand McNally.

Danielian, Lucig H., and Benjamin I. Page. 1994. "The Heavenly Chorus: Interest Group Voices on TV News." *American Journal of Political Science* 38 (4): 1056–78.

Dao, James. 2005. "At N.A.A.C.P. Helm, an Economic Approach to Rights." *New York Times*, July 5.

Davis, Angela Y. 1981. *Women, Race, and Class.* New York: Random House.

———. 2000. "The Color of Violence against Women." *Colorlines* 3:3.

Davis, Gerald, Doug McAdam, W. Richard Scott, and Mayer N. Zald, eds. 2005. *Social Movements and Organization Theory.* New York: Cambridge University Press.

Davis, Martha S. 1993. *Brutal Need: Lawyers and the Welfare Rights Movement, 1960–1973.* New Haven, CT: Yale University Press.

Dawson, Michael C. 1994. *Behind the Mule.* Princeton, NJ: Princeton University Press.

Delgado, Gary. 1986. *Organizing the Movement: The Roots and Growth of ACORN*. Philadelphia: Temple University Press.

Denny, Dallas, ed. 1997. *Current Concepts in Transgender Identity*. New York: Garland.

Diamond, Irene. 1977. *Sex Roles in the State House*. New Haven, CT: Yale University Press.

Diaz-Veizades, Jeannette, and Edward T. Chang. 1996. "Building Cross-Cultural Coalitions: A Case-Study of the Black-Korean Alliance and the Latino-Black Roundtable." *Ethnic and Racial Studies* 19:680–700.

Dietz, Mary G. 2003. "Current Controversies in Feminist Theory." *Annual Review of Political Science* 6:399–431.

Dillman, Don A. 1978. *Mail and Telephone Surveys: The Total Design Method*. New York: John Wiley and Sons.

DiMaggio, Paul J., and Helmut K. Anheier. 1990. "The Sociology of Nonprofit Organizations and Sectors." *Annual Review of Sociology* 16:137–59.

Dionne, E. J., ed. 1998. *Community Works: The Revival of Civil Society in America*. Washington, DC: Brookings Institution Press.

Disch, Lisa. 2006. "Rethinking 'Re'-presentation." Paper presented at the annual meeting of the Midwest Political Science Association, Chicago, April.

Dodd, Lawrence, and Bruce Oppenheimer, eds. 1993. *Congress Reconsidered*. 5th ed. Washington, DC: CQ Press.

Dodson, Debra L., Susan J. Carroll, Ruth B. Mandel, Katherine E. Kleeman, Ronnie Schreiber, and Debra Liebowitz. 1995. *Voices, Views, Votes: The Impact of Women in the 103rd Congress*. New Brunswick, NJ: Center for the American Woman and Politics, Rutgers University.

Dovi, Suzanne. 2002. "Preferable Descriptive Representatives." *American Political Science Review* 96:729–43.

Downs, Anthony. 1957. *An Economic Theory of Democracy*. New York: Harper and Row.

Druckman, James N., and Lawrence R. Jacobs. 2006. "Lumpers and Splitters: The Public Opinion Information That Politicians Collect and Use." *Public Opinion Quarterly*.

Duberman, Martin. 2002. *Left Out: The Politics of Exclusion*. Boston: South End Press.

DuBois, W. E. B. 1903. *The Souls of Black Folk*. Chicago: A. C. McClurg.

———. 1935. *Black Reconstruction*. New York: Harcourt, Brace.

Duggan, Lisa. 2005. *The Twilight of Equality? Neoliberalism, Cultural Politics, and the Attack on Democracy*. Boston: Beacon Press.

Dworkin, Ronald. 1977. *Taking Rights Seriously*. Cambridge, MA: Harvard University Press.

———. 1986. *Freedom's Law: The Moral Reading of the American Constitution*. Cambridge, MA: Harvard University Press.

Edsall, Thomas B. 1991. *Chain Reaction: The Impact of Race, Rights, and Taxes on American Politics*. New York: Basic Books.

Ely, John Hart. 1980. *Democracy and Distrust: A Theory of Judicial Review*. Cambridge, MA: Harvard University Press.

Epp, Charles R. 1998. *The Rights Revolution: Lawyers, Activists, and Supreme Courts in Comparative Perspective*. Chicago: University of Chicago Press.

Epstein, Lee. 1985. *Conservatives in Court*. Knoxville: University of Tennessee Press.

———. 1993. "Interest Group Litigation During the Rehnquist Court Era." *Journal of Law and Politics* 9:639–717.

Epstein, Lee, and Jack Knight. 1999. "Mapping out the Strategic Terrain: The Informational Role of Amici Curiae." In *Supreme Court Decision-Making: New Institutional Approaches*, edited by C. W. Clayton and H. Gillman. Chicago: University of Chicago Press.

Erikson, Robert S., Gerald C. Wright, and John P. McIver. 1993. *Statehouse Democracy: Public Opinion and Policy in the American States*. New York: Cambridge University Press.

Esterling, Kevin M. 1999. "Coalitions of Coalitions: Interest Group Internal Deliberation and Policy Alliances." Paper presented at the annual meeting of the Midwest Political Science Association, Chicago, April.

———. 2004. *The Political Economy of Expertise: Information and Efficiency in American National Politics*. Ann Arbor: University of Michigan Press.

Evans, Diana M. 1991. "Lobbying the Committee: Interest Groups and the House Public Works Transportation Committee." In *Interest Group Politics*, 3rd edition, edited by Alan Cigler and Burdett Loomis, 257–76. Washington, DC: CQ Press.

Fausto-Sterling, Anne. 1993. "The Five Sexes: Why Male and Female Are Not Enough." *Sciences* 33:20–25.

Fenno, Richard F. 1978. *Home Style: House Members in Their Districts*. Boston: Little, Brown.

———. 2003. *Going Home: Black Representatives and Their Constituents*. Chicago: University of Chicago Press.

Ferejohn, John. 1986. "Incumbent Performance and Electoral Control." *Public Choice* 50:5–25.

Ferguson, Doug. 2002. "Woods: Augusta flap 'not players' fault.'" *USA Today*, November 1.

Ferree, Myra Marx, and Patricia Yancey Martin, eds. 1995. *Feminist Organizations: Harvest of the New Women's Movement*. Philadelphia: Temple University Press.

Fineman, Martha Albertson, and Roxanne Mykitiuk, eds. 1994. *The Public Nature of Private Violence*. New York: Routledge.

Fiorina, Morris P. 1981. *Retrospective Voting in American National Elections*. New Haven, CT: Yale University Press.

Fishkin, James. 1991. *Democracy and Deliberation*. New Haven, CT: Yale University Press.

Flammang, Janet A. 1997. *Women's Political Voice: How Women Are Transforming the Practice and Study of Politics*. Philadelphia: Temple University Press.

Foundation for Public Affairs. 1999. *Public Interest Profiles*. Washington, DC: Foundation for Public Affairs.

Fowler, Floyd J. Jr. 1993. *Survey Research Methods*. 2nd ed. Newbury Park, CA: Sage.

Fraga, Luis, Valerie Martinez-Ebers, Linda Lopez, and Ricardo Ramirez. 2005. "Strategic Intersectionality: Gender, Ethnicity, and Political Incorporation." Paper presented at the annual meeting of the American Political Science Association, Washington, DC.

Frank, Thomas. 2004. *What's the Matter with Kansas? How Conservatives Won the Heart of America*. New York: Metropolitan Books.

Fraser, N. 1997. *Justice Interruptus: Critical Reflections on the "Postsocialist" Condition*. New York: Routledge.

Freeman, Alan David. 1978. "Legitimating Racial Discrimination through Antidiscrimination Law: A Critical Review of Supreme Court Doctrine." *Minnesota Law Review* 62:1049–1119.

———. 1998. "Antidiscrimination Law from 1954 to 1989: Uncertainty, Contradiction, Rationalization, Denial." In *The Politics Of Law: A Progressive Critique*, edited by David Kairys, 285–311. New York: Basic Books.

Freeman, Jo. 1972–73. "The Tyranny of Structurelessness." *Berkeley Journal of Sociology* 17:151–165.

———. 1975. *The Politics of Women's Liberation*. New York: David McKay.

Freeman, Jo, and Victoria Johnson, eds. 1999. *Waves of Protest: Social Movements since the Sixties*. New York: Rowman and Littlefield.

Frymer, Paul. 1999. *Uneasy Alliances: Race and Party Competition in America*. Princeton, NJ: Princeton University Press.

———. 2005. "Opportunities for Court Activism in a Conservative Era." Paper presented at Inequality and Representation in American Politics meeting, Minneapolis.

———. 2006. "Distinguishing Formal from Institutional Democracy." *Maryland Law Review* 65 (1): 125–38.

Frymer, Paul, Dara Z. Strolovitch, and Dorian T. Warren. 2006. "Race, Class, and the Federalism of American Disasters." *DuBois Review* 3 (1): 37–57.

Fung, Archon. 2004. *Empowered Participation: Reinventing Urban Democracy*. Princeton, NJ: Princeton University Press.

Furlong, Scott R. 1997. "Interest Group Lobbying: Differences between the Legislative and Executive Branches." Paper presented at the annual meeting of the American Political Science Association, Washington, DC.

Gabin, Nancy. 1991. "Time Out of Mind: The UAW's Response to Female Labor Laws and Mandatory Overtime in the 1960s." In *Work Engendered: Toward a New History of American Labor*, edited by Ava Baron, 351–74. Ithaca, NY: Cornell University Press.

Galanter, Marc. 1974. "Why the 'Haves' Come Out Ahead: Speculations on the Limits of Legal Change." *Law and Society Review* 95:149–50.

Gale Research. 2000. *Encyclopedia of Associations/Associations Unlimited*. Detroit: Gale Research.

Gamson, William A. 1961. "A Theory of Coalition Formation." *American Sociological Review* 26 (3): 373–82.

———. 1975. *The Strategy of Social Protest*. Homewood, IL: Dorsey.

Gamson, William A., and Emilie Schmeidler. 1984. "Organizing the Poor." *Theory and Society* 13:567–85.

Gaventa, John. 1982. *Power and Powerlessness: Quiescence and Rebellion in an Appalachian Valley*. Chicago: University of Illinois Press.

Gay, Claudine. 2001. "The Effect of Black Congressional Representation on Political Participation." *American Political Science Review* 95:589–602.

———. 2002. "Spirals of Trust: The Effect of Descriptive Representation on the Relationship between Citizens and their Government." *American Journal of Political Science* 46:717–32.

Gelb, Joyce, and Marion Lief Palley. 1987. *Women and Public Policies*. Princeton, NJ: Princeton University Press.

Gerber, Elisabeth R. 1999. *The Populist Paradox*. Princeton, NJ: Princeton University Press.

Gerhards, Jurgen, and Dieter Rucht. 1992. "Mesomobilization: Organizing and Framing in Two Protest Campaigns in West Germany." *American Journal of Sociology* 98:555–95.

Geron, Kim, Enrique DeLa Cnrz, and Jaideep Singh. 2001. "Asian Pacific American Social Movements and Interest Groups." *PS: Political Science and Politics* 34:619–24.

Gibson, James L., and Richard D. Bingham. 1985. *Civil Liberties and Nazis: The Skokie Free Speech Controversy.* New York: Praeger.

Giddings, Paula. 1984. *When and Where I Enter: The Impact of Black Women on Race and Sex in America.* New York: Bantam.

Gilens, Martin. 2005. "Inequality and Democratic Responsiveness." *Public Opinion Quarterly* 69 (5): 778–96.

Gilliam, Frank D. Jr. 1996. "Exploring Minority Empowerment." *American Journal of Political Science* 40 (1): 56–81.

Gilligan, Carol. 1993. *In a Different Voice: Psychological Theory and Women's Development.* Cambridge, MA: Harvard University Press.

Gitlin, Todd. 1995. *The Twilight of Common Dreams: Why America is Wracked by Culture Wars.* New York: Henry Holt.

Goffman, Erving. 1974. *Frame Analysis: An Essay on the Organization of Experience.* New York: Harper and Row.

Golden, Marissa Martino. 1998. "Interest groups in the rule-making process: Who Participates? Whose Voices Get Heard?" *Journal of Public Administration Research and Theory* 8:245–70.

Goldstone, Jack A., and Charles Tilly. 2001. "Threat (and Opportunity): Popular Action and State Response in the Dynamics of Contentious Action." In *Silence and Voice in Contentious Politics*, edited by R. Aminzade, Jack A. Goldstone, Doug McAdam, Elizabeth J. Perry, William H. Sewell, Sidney Tarrow, and Charles Tilley, 179–94. Cambridge: Cambridge University Press.

Gomes, Ralph C., and Linda Faye Williams. 1995a. "Coalition Politics: Past, Present, and Future." In *From Exclusion to Inclusion: The Long Struggle for African American Political Power*, edited by Ralph C. Gomes and Linda Faye Williams, 129–60. Westport, CT: Praeger.

———, eds. 1995b. *From Exclusion to Inclusion: The Long Struggle for African American Political Power.* Westport, CT: Praeger.

Gonen, Julianna S. 2003. *Litigation as Lobbying: Reproductive Hazards and Interest Aggregation.* Columbus: Ohio State University Press.

Goodwin, Jeff, and James M. Jasper. 2003. *The Social Movements Reader: Cases and Concepts.* Malden, MA: Blackwell Publishing.

———, eds. 2004. *Rethinking Social Movements: Structure, Meaning and Emotion.* New York: Rowman and Littlefield.

Goodwin, Jeff, James M. Jasper, and Francesca Polletta. 2001a. "Introduction: Why Emotions Matter." In *Passionate Politics: Emotions and Social Movements*, edited by Jeff Goodwin, James M. Jasper, and Francesca Polletta, 1–24. Chicago: University of Chicago Press.

———, eds. 2001b. *Passionate Politics: Emotions and Social Movements.* Chicago: University of Chicago Press.

Gould, Deborah B. 2004. "Passionate Political Processes: Bringing Emotions Back into the Study of Social Movements." In *Rethinking Social Movements: Structure, Meaning and Emotion*, edited by Jeff Goodwin and James M. Jasper, 155–75. New York: Rowman and Littlefield.

Gray, Virginia, and David Lowery. 1996. *The Population Ecology of Interest Representation*. Ann Arbor: University of Michigan Press.

Groves, Robert M., and Robert L. Kahn. 1979. *Surveys by Telephone: A National Comparison with Personal Interviews*. New York: Academic Press.

Guidry, John A., and Mark Q. Sawyer. 2003. "Contentious Pluralism: The Public Sphere and Democracy." *Perspectives on Politics* 1 (2): 273–89.

Guinier, Lani. 1994. *The Tyranny of the Majority*. New York: Free Press.

Guinier, Lani, and Gerald Torres. 2002. *The Miner's Canary*. Cambridge, MA: Harvard University Press.

Gutmann, Amy, ed. 1998a. *Freedom of Association*. Princeton, NJ: Princeton University Press.

———. 1998b. "Freedom of Association: An Introductory Essay." In *Freedom of Association*, edited by Amy Gutmann, 3–32. Princeton: Princeton University Press.

Gutmann, Amy, and Dennis Thompson. 1996. *Democracy and Disagreement*. Cambridge, MA: Harvard University Press.

Habermas, Jurgen. 1987. *The Theory of Communicative Action*. Boston: Beacon Press.

Hakman, Nathan. 1966. "Lobbying the Supreme Court—An Appraisal of Political Science Folklore." *Fordham Law Review* 35:50–75.

Hall, Donald. 1969. *Cooperative Lobbying—The Power of Pressure*. Tucson: University of Arizona Press.

Haltom, William, and Michael McCann. 2004. *Distorting the Law: Politics, Media, and the Litigation Crisis*. Chicago: University of Chicago Press.

Hamilton, Donna Cooper, and Charles V. Hamilton. 1992. "The Dual Agenda of African American Organizations since the New Deal: Social Welfare Policies and Civil Rights." *Political Science Quarterly* 107 (3): 435–53.

Hancock, Ange-Marie. 2004. *The Politics of Disgust: The Public Identity of The Welfare Queen*. New York: New York University Press.

———. 2007. "When Multiplication Doesn't Equal Quick Addition: Examining Intersectionality as a Research Paradigm" *Perspectives on Politics* 5 (1): 63–79.

Handler, Joel F. 1978. *Social Movements and the Legal System: A Theory of Law, Reform and Social Change*. New York: Academic Press.

Hansen, John Mark. 1985. "The Political Economy of Group Membership." *American Political Science Review* 79:79–96.

Hansford, Thomas G. 2004. "Lobbying Strategies, Venue Selection, and Organized Interest Involvement at the U.S. Supreme Court." *American Politics Research* 32 (2): 170–97.

Harris-Lacewell, Melissa V. 2004. *Barbershops, Bibles, and BET: Everyday Talk and Black Political Thought*. Princeton, NJ: Princeton University Press.

Hathaway, Will, and David S. Meyer. 1997. "Competition and Cooperation in Movements Coalitions: Lobbying for Peace in the 1980s." In *Coalitions and Political Movements: Lessons of the Nuclear Freeze*, edited by Thomas R. Rochon and David S. Meyer, 61–79. Boulder, CO: Lynne Rienner.

Hawkesworth, Mary. 2003. "Congressional Enactments of Race-Gender: Towards a Theory of Race-Gendered Institutions." *American Political Science Review* 97 (4): 529–50.

Hayward, Clarissa Rile. 2000. *Defacing Power*. New York: Cambridge University Press.

Heaney, Michael. 2004. "Outside the Issue Niche: The Multidimensionality of Interest Group Identity." *American Politics Research* 32 (6): 611–51.

Heclo, Hugh. 1978. "Issue Networks and the Executive Establishment." In *The New American Political System*, edited by Anthony King, 87–124. Washington, DC: American Enterprise Institute.

Heinz, John P., Edward O. Lauman, Robert L. Nelson, and Robert H. Salisbury. 1993. *The Hollow Core: Private Interests in National Policy Making.* Cambridge, MA: Harvard University Press.

Henry, Gary T. 1990. *Practical Sampling.* Newbury Park, CA: Sage.

Hero, Rodney E. 1992. *Latinos and the U.S. Political System: Two-Tiered Pluralism.* Philadelphia: Temple University Press.

Herring, E. Pendleton. 1929. *Group Representation before Congress.* Baltimore: Johns Hopkins University Press.

Hilbink, Lisa. 2006. "Beyond Manicheanism: Assessing the New Constitutionalism." *Maryland Law Review* 65 (1): 15–31.

Hirschl, Ran. 2004. *Towards Juristocracy: The Origins and Consequences of the New Constitutionalism.* Cambridge, MA: Harvard University Press.

Hirschman, Albert O. 1970. *Exit Voice and Loyalty: Responses to Decline in Firms, Organizations, and States.* Cambridge, MA: Harvard University Press.

Hochschild, Arlie Russell. 1975. "The Sociology of Feeling and Emotion: Selected Possibilities." *Sociological Inquiry* 45:2–3.

Hojnacki, Marie. 1997. "Interest Groups' Decisions to Join Alliances or Work Alone." *American Journal of Political Science* 41:61–87.

———. 1998. "Organized Interests' Advocacy Behavior in Alliances." *Political Research Quarterly* 51:437–59.

Hojnacki, Marie, and David C. Kimball. 1998. "Organized Interests and the Decision of Whom to Lobby in Congress." *American Political Science Review* 92:775–90.

———. 1999. "The Who and How of Organizations' Lobbying Strategies in Committee." *Journal of Politics* 61:999–1024.

hooks, bell. 1981. *Ain't I a Woman?* Boston: South End Press.

Horowitz, Donald L. 1977. *The Courts and Social Policy.* Washington, DC: Brookings Institution Press.

Huber, Gregory, and Sanford C. Gordon. 2004. "Accountability and Coercion: Is Justice Blind When It Runs for Office?" *American Journal of Political Science* 48:247–63.

Hula, Kevin. 1995. "Rounding Up the Usual Suspects: Forging Interest Group Coalitions in Washington." In *Interest Group Politics*, 5th ed., edited by Alan Cigler and Burdett Loomis, 239–58. Washington, DC: CQ Press.

———. 1999. *Lobbying Together: Interest Group Coalitions in Legislative Politics.* Washington, DC: Georgetown University Press.

Hull, Gloria T., Patricia Bell Scott, and Barbara Smith. 1982. *All the Women Are White, All the Blacks Are Men, but Some of Us Are Brave.* Old Westbury, NY: Feminist Press.

Hunt, Raymont, and Benjamin Bowser, eds. 1996. *Impacts of Racism on White Americans.* Thousand Oaks, CA: Sage.

Iglesias, Elizabeth. 1996. "Structures of Subordination." In *Critical Race Feminism*, edited by Adrien Wing, 317–32. New York: New York University Press.

Imig, Douglas R. 1996. *Poverty and Power: The Political Representation of Poor Americans.* Lincoln: University of Nebraska Press.

Inglehart, Ronald F. 1977. *The Silent Revolution.* Princeton, N.J.: Princeton University Press.

Jackson, John E., and David C. King. 1989. "Public Goods, Private Interests, and Representation." *American Political Science Review* 83:1143–64.

Jacobs, Lawrence R., and Benjamin I. Page. 2005. "Who Influences U.S. Foreign Policy?" *American Political Science Review* 99 (February): 107–24.

Jacobs, Lawrence R., and Robert Y. Shapiro. 2000. *Politicians Don't Pander: Political Manipulation and the Loss of Democratic Responsiveness.* Chicago: University of Chicago Press.

Jacobson, Matthew Frye. 1998. *Whiteness of a Different Color: European Immigrants and the Alchemy of Race.* Cambridge, MA: Harvard University Press.

Jenkins, J. Craig. 1987. "Nonprofit Organizations and Policy Advocacy." In *The Nonprofit Sector: A Research Handbook*, edited by W. W. Powell., 296–318. New Haven, CT: Yale University Press.

———. 1999. "The Transformation of a Constituency into a Social Movement Revisited: Farmworker Organizing in California." In *Waves of Protest: Social Movements since the Sixties*, edited by Jo Freeman and Victoria Johnson, 277–99. New York: Rowman and Littlefield.

Jenkins, J. Craig, and Craig M. Eckert. 1986. "Channeling Black Insurgency: Elite Patronage and Professional Social Movement Organizations in the Development of the Black Movement." *American Sociological Review* 51 (6): 812–29.

Jenkins, J. Craig, and Charles Perrow. 1977. "Insurgency of the Powerless: Farm Worker Movements (1946–1972)." *American Sociological Review* 42:249–68.

Johnson, Timothy R. 2003. "The Supreme Court, the Solicitor General, and the Separation of Powers." *American Politics Research* 31 (4): 426–51.

———. 2004. *Oral Arguments and Decision Making on the United States Supreme Court.* Albany: State University of New York Press.

Josephy, Alvin M. Jr., Joane Nagel, and Troy Johnson. 1999. *Red Power: The American Indian's Fight for Freedom.* Lincoln: University of Nebraska Press.

Kairys, David, ed. 1998. *The Politics Of Law: A Progressive Critique.* New York: Basic Books.

Kathlene, Lyn. 1994. "Power and Influence in State Legislative Policymaking: The Interaction of Gender and Position in Committee Hearing Debates." *American Political Science Review* 88 (3): 560–76.

Katz, Jonathan Ned. 1995. *The Invention of Heterosexuality.* New York: Dutton.

Katz, Michael B. 1989. *The Undeserving Poor: From the War on Poverty to the War on Welfare.* New York: Pantheon Books.

Kearney, Joseph D., and Thomas W. Merrill. 2000. "The Influence of Amicus Curiae Briefs on the Supreme Court." *University of Pennsylvania Law Review* 148:743–855.

Keck, Margaret, and Kathryn Sikkink. 1998. *Activists Beyond Borders.* Ithaca, NY: Cornell University Press.

Kenney, Sally J. 1996. "New Research on Gendered Political Institutions." *Political Research Quarterly* 49 (2): 445–66.

———. 2005. "Making the Case for Women on the Bench: Comparative Perspectives." Paper presented at Inequality and Representation in American Politics meeting, Minneapolis.

Kersh, Rogan. 2001. "State Autonomy and Civil Society: The Lobbyist Connection." *Critical Review* 14:237–58.

Kimmel, Michael S. 1994. "Masculinity as Homophobia: Fear, Shame and Silence in the Construction of Gender Identity." In *Theorizing Masculinities*, edited by H. Brod and M. Kaufman, 119–41. Newbury Park, CA: Sage.

Kingdon, John W. 1995. *Agendas, Alternatives, and Public Policies.* New York: HarperCollins.

Klinkner, Philip A., and Rogers M. Smith. 1999. *The Unsteady March: The Rise and Decline of Racial Equality in America.* Chicago: University of Chicago.

Knoke, David. 1990. *Organizing for Collective Action.* Hawthorne, NY: Aldine de Gruyter.

Knoke, David, and Richard Adams. 1984. *National Association Study.* n.p.

Kollman, Ken. 1998. *Outside Lobbying: Public Opinion and Interest Group Strategies.* Princeton, NJ: Princeton University Press.

Krislov, Samuel. 1963. "The Amicus Curiae Brief: From Friendship to Advocacy." *Yale Law Journal* 72:694–721.

Kuersten, Ashlyn K., and Jason Jagemann. 2000. "Does the Interest Group Choir Really 'Sing with an Upper Class Accent'? Coalitions of Race and Gender Groups before the Supreme Court." *Women and Politics* 21 (3): 53–73.

Kurtz, Sharon. 2002. *Workplace Justice: Organizing Multi-Identity Movements.* Minneapolis: University of Minnesota Press.

Latham, Earl. 1952. *The Group Basis of Politics.* Ithaca, NY: Cornell University Press.

Laumann, Edward O., and David Knoke. 1987. *The Organizational State: Social Choice in National Policy Domains.* Madison: University of Wisconsin Press.

Lawrence, Susan E. 1990. *The Poor in Court: The Legal Services Program and Supreme Court Decision Making.* Princeton, NJ: Princeton University Press.

Leech, Beth, and Frank Baumgartner. 1998. "Lobbying Friends and Foes in Washington." In *Interest Group Politics*, 5th ed., edited by Alan Cigler and Burdett Loomis, 217–33. Washington, DC: CQ Press.

Levi, Margaret, and Gillian Murphy. 2006. "Coalitions of Contention: The Case of the WTO Protests in Seattle." *Political Studies.* 54: 651–670.

Lewis, Andrea. 2003. "Martha Burk Takes a Swing—Protests Men-Only Policy at Augusta National Home of the Masters Golf Tournament." *Progressive*, June.

Lindblom, Charles E. 1963. *The Intelligence of Democracy.* New York: Free Press.

Lipset, Seymour Martin. 1963. *Political Man: The Social Bases of Politics.* Garden City, NY: Doubleday.

Lipsky, Michael. 1970. *Protest in City Politics: Rent Strikes, Housing and the Power of the Poor.* Chicago: Rand McNally.

Loomis, Burdett. 1986. "Coalitions of Interests: Building Bridges in the Balkanized State." In *Interest Group Politics*, 2nd ed., edited by Alan Cigler and Burdett Loomis, 258–74. Washington, DC: CQ Press.

Lorber, Judith. 1995. *Paradoxes of Gender.* New Haven, CT: Yale University Press.

Lovell, George. 2003. *Legislative Deferrals: Statutory Ambiguity, Judicial Power, and American Democracy.* New York: Cambridge University Press.

Lowi, Theodore. 1969. *The End of Liberalism.* 2nd ed. New York: Norton.

Lublin, David. 1997. *The Paradox of Representation.* Princeton, NJ: Princeton University Press.

Lugones, María C. 1992. "On Borderlands/La Frontera: An Interpretive Essay." *Hypatia* 7:31–37.

———. 1994. "Purity, Impurity, and Separation." *Signs: Journal of Women in Culture and Society* 19:458–79.

Lukcs, Georg. [1923] 1971. *History and Class Consciousness*. Cambridge, MA: MIT Press.

Luker, Kristin. 1984. *Abortion and Politics of Motherhood*. Berkeley and Los Angeles: University of California Press.

Lukes, Steven. 1974. *Power: A Radical View*. London: Macmillan.

Malveaux, Julianne. 2003. "The Many Faces of Bias." *Black Issues in Higher Education* 19, no. 24 (January 15): 34.

Manin, Bernard. 1997. *The Principles of Representative Government*. New York: Cambridge University Press.

Mansbridge, Jane J. 1983. *Beyond Adversary Democracy*. Chicago: University of Chicago Press.

———. 1986. *Why We Lost the ERA*. Chicago: University of Chicago Press.

———. 1999. "Should Blacks Represent Blacks and Women Represent Women? A Contingent 'Yes.'" *Journal of Politics* 61 (3): 628–57.

———. 2003. "Rethinking Representation." *American Political Science Review* 97 (4): 515–28.

Manwaring, David. 1962. *Render Unto Caesar: The Flag Salute Controversy*. Chicago: University of Chicago Press.

Marquez, Benjamin, and James Jennings. 2000. "Representation by Other Means: Mexican American and Puerto Rican Social Movement Organizations." *PS: Political Science and Politics* 33:541–46.

Marx, Karl. [1875] 1978. "Critique of the Gotha Program." In *The Marx-Engels Reader*, edited by Robert Tucker, 525–541. New York: Norton.

Matsuda, Mari. 1991. "'Beside My Sister, Facing the Enemy: Legal Theory out of Coalition." *Stanford Law Review* 43 (July): 1189.

Mayhew, David R. 1974. *Congress: The Electoral Connection*. New Haven, CT: Yale University Press.

McAdam, Doug. 1982. *Political Process and the Development of Black Insurgency, 1930–1970*. Chicago: University of Chicago Press.

McAdam, Doug, John D. McCarthy, and Mayer M. Zald, eds. 1996. *Comparative Perspectives on Social Movements*. Cambridge: Cambridge University Press.

McCall, Leslie. 2005. "The Complexity of Intersectionality." *Signs: Journal of Women in Culture and Society* 30 (3): 1771–1800.

McCammon, Holly J., and Karen E. Campbell. 2002. "Allies on the Road to Victory: Coalition Formation between the Suffragists and the Woman's Christian Temperance Union." *Mobilization* 7:231–51.

McCann, Michael W. 1986. *Taking Reform Seriously: Perspectives on Public Interest Liberalism*. Ithaca, NY: Cornell University Press.

———. 1994. *Rights at Work: Pay Equity Reform and the Politics of Legal Mobilization*. Chicago: University of Chicago Press.

———. 1998. "Social Movements and the Mobilization of Law." In *Social Movements and American Political Institutions*, edited by Anne N. Costain and Ander McFarland, 201–15. New York: Rowman and Littlefield.

McCarthy, John D., and Mayer N. Zald. 1973. *The Trend in Social Movements in America: Professionalization and Resource Mobilization*. Morristown, NJ: Chatham House.

McCarthy, John D. 2005. "Persistence and Change among Nationally Federated So-
cial Movements." In *Social Movements and Organization Theory*, edited by Gerald
Davis, Doug McAdam, W. Richard Scott, and Mayer N. Zald, 193–225. New York:
Cambridge University Press.

McFarland, Andrew. 1976. *Public Interest Lobbies: Decision Making on Energy*. Washington, DC: American Enterprise Institute.

———. 1984. *Common Cause*. Chatham, NJ: Chatham House.

McGrath, Charles. 2002. "Augusta's Battle of The Sexes: Will the Home of the Masters
Lay Up Short of the Gender Gap, or Will It Get in Touch With its Feminine Side—
Again?" *Golf Digest*, September. http://www.golfdigest.com/search/index.ssf?/
features/gd200209augusta.html.

McIver, Robert M. 1951. *Report on the Jewish Community Relations Agencies*. New York:
National Community Relations Advisory Council.

McLean, Iain, and Alistair McMillan, eds. 2003. *The Concise Oxford Dictionary of Politics*.
New York: Oxford University Press.

Melnick, R. Shep. 1994. *Between the Lines: Interpreting Welfare Rights*. Washington, DC:
Brookings Institution Press.

Melucci, Alberto. 1989. *Nomads of the Present*. Philadelphia: Temple University Press.

Mervin, David. 2003. "PAC." In *The Concise Oxford Dictionary of Politics*, edited by Iain
McLean and Alistair McMillan. New York: Oxford University Press.

Messere, Fritz J. n.d. "U.S. Policy: Telecommunications Act of 1996." http://www
.museum.tv/archives/etv/U/htmlU/uspolicyt/uspolicyt.htm.

Meyer, David S. 1990. *A Winter of Discontent: The Nuclear Freeze and American Politics*.
New York: Praeger.

———. 1993. "Institutionalizing Dissent: The United States Structure of Political
Opportunity and the End of the Nuclear Freeze Movement." *Sociological Forum*
8:157–79.

Meyer, David S., and Catherine Corrigall-Brown. 2005. "Coalitions and Political Context: U.S. Movements against Wars in Iraq." *Mobilization* 10 (3): 327–44.

Meyer, David S., and Debra Minkoff. 2004. "Conceptualizing Political Opportunity."
*Social Forces* 82 (4): 1457–92.

Meyer, David S., and Suzanne Staggenborg. 1996. "Movements, Countermovements,
and the Structure of Political Opportunity." *American Journal of Sociology* 101 (6):
1628–60.

Michels, Robert. 1911. *Political Parties*. New York: Free Press.

Miller, Arthur H., Patricia Gurin, Gerald Gurin, and Oksana Malanchuk. 1981. "Group
Consciousness and Political Participation." *American Journal of Political Science*
25:494–511.

Miller, Warren E., and Donald E. Stokes. 1963. "Constituency Influence in Congress."
*American Political Science Review* 57:45–56.

Mills, C. Wright. 1956. *The Power Elite*. New York: Oxford University Press.

Mink, Gwendolyn. 1990. "The Lady and the Tramp." In *Women, the State, and Welfare*,
edited by Linda Gordon, 92–122. Madison: University of Wisconsin.

———. 1998. *Welfare's End*. Ithaca, NY: Cornell University Press.

Minkoff, Debra. 1995. *Organizing for Equality: The Evolution of Women's and Racial-
Ethnic Organizations in America, 1955–1985*. New Brunswick, NJ: Rutgers University
Press.

————. 1997. "Producing Social Capital: National Social Movements and Civil Society." *American Behavioral Scientist* 40 (5): 606–19.

Minkoff, Debra, and Jon Agnone. 2003. "Protest Potential in the U.S. Social Movement Sector." Paper presented at the annual meeting of the American Sociological Association, Atlanta, GA.

Mishel, Lawrence, and Matthew Walters. 2003. "How Unions Help All Workers." Washington, DC: EPI. http://www.epinet.org/content.cfm/briefingpapers_bp143.

Mishler, William, and Reginald S. Sheehan. 1993. "The Supreme Court as a Countermajoritarian Institution? The Impact of Public Opinion on Supreme Court Decisions." *American Political Science Review* 87 (1): 87–101.

Moe, Terry M. 1981. "Toward a Broader View of Interest Groups." *Journal of Politics* 43: 531–43.

Mohanty, Chandra Talpade. 1988. "Under Western Eyes: Feminist Scholarship and Colonial Discourses." *Feminist Review* 30:61–88.

Moraga, Cherrie, and Gloria Anzaldua, eds. 1981. *This Bridge Called My Back: Writings by Radical Women of Color.* Watertown, MA: Persephone Press.

Morris, Aldon. 1984. *The Origins of the Civil Rights Movement: Black Communities Organizing for Change.* New York: Free Press.

Morris, Aldon D., and Carol McClurg Mueller. 1992. *Frontiers in Social Movement Theory.* New Haven, CT: Yale University Press.

Mueller, Carol. 1995. "The Organizational Basis of Conflict in Contemporary Feminism." In *Feminist Organizations: Harvest of the New Women's Movement*, edited by Myra Marx Ferree and Patricia Yancey Martin, 263–75. Philadelphia: Temple University Press.

Murakawa, Naomi. 2005. "Electing to Punish: Congress, Race, and the American Criminal Justice State." PhD diss., Yale University.

Nelson, Jennifer. 2003. *Women of Color and the Reproductive Rights Movement.* New York: New York University Press.

Nelson, Mariah Burton. 2003. "Women of the Year 2003: Martha Burk." *Ms. Magazine* 13:4.

Neuborne, Burt. 2005. "Addicted to the Courts." *Nation*, April 25, 23–34.

Novkov, Julie. 2001. *Constituting Workers, Protecting Women: Gender, Law and Labor in the Progressive Era and New Deal Years.* Ann Arbor: University of Michigan Press.

Nownes, Anthony J., and Patricia Freeman. 1998. "Interest Group Activity in the States." *Journal of Politics* 60 (1): 86–112.

Nowrojee, Sia, and Jael Silliman. 1997. "Asian Women's Health: Organizing a Movement." In *Dragon Ladies: Asian American Feminists Breathe Fire*, edited by S. Shah., 73–89. Boston: South End Press.

Nozick, Robert. 1974. *Anarchy, State, and Utopia.* New York: Basic Books.

O'Connor, Karen. 1980. *Women's Organizations' Use of the Courts.* Lexington, MA: Lexington Books.

O'Connor, Karen, and Lee Epstein. 1981–82. "Amicus Curiae Participation in U.S. Supreme Court Participation: An Appraisal of Hakman's 'Folklore.'" *Law and Society Review* 16:311–20.

————. 1983a. "The Rise of Conservative Interest Group Litigation." *Journal of Politics* 45:479–89.

————. 1983b. "Sex and the Supreme Court: An Analysis of Support for Gender-Based Claims." *Social Science Quarterly* 64:327–31.

Olson, Mancur. 1965. *The Logic of Collective Action: Public Goods and the Theory of Groups.* Cambridge, MA: Harvard University Press.

Omi, Michael, and Howard Winant. 1994. *Racial Formation in the United States: From the 1960s to the 1990s.* New York: Routledge.

O'Regan, Katherine, and Sharon M. Oster. 2005. "Does the Structure and Composition of the Board Matter? The Case of Nonprofit Organizations." *Journal of Law, Economics, and Organization* 21 (1): 205–27.

Organization of Chinese Americans. 1999. *Asian Pacific American Organizations.* Washington, DC: Organization of Chinese Americans.

Page, Benjamin I., and Robert Y. Shapiro. 1983. "Effects of Public Opinion on Policy." *American Political Science Review* 77:175–90.

———. 1992. *The Rational Public: Fifty Years of Trends in Americans' Policy Preferences.* Chicago: University of Chicago Press.

Parenti, Michael. 1978. *Power and the Powerless.* New York: St. Martin's Press.

Pease, Katherine, and Associates. 2003. *Inside Inclusiveness: Race, Ethnicity and Nonprofit Organizations.* Denver: Denver Foundation.

Peltason, Jack W. 1971. *Fifty-Eight Lonely Men: Southern Federal Judges and School Desegregation.* Urbana: University of Illinois Press.

Perry, Huey L., ed. 1995. *Blacks and the American Political System.* Gainesville: University of Florida Press.

Peterson, Paul. 1981. *City Limits.* Chicago: University of Chicago Press.

Phillips, Anne. 1995. *The Politics of Presence.* New York: Oxford University Press.

———. 1998a. "Democracy and Representation; Or, Why Should it Matter Who Our Representatives Are?" In *Feminism and Politics,* edited by Anne Phillips, 224–40. New York: Oxford University Press.

———, ed. 1998b. *Feminism and Politics.* New York: Oxford University Press.

Pinderhughes, Dianne M. 1995. "Black Interest Groups and the 1982 Extension of the Voting Rights Act." In *Blacks and the American Political System,* edited by H. L. Perry., 203–24. Gainesville: University of Florida Press.

Pitkin, Hanna Fenichel. 1967. *The Concept of Representation.* Berkeley and Los Angeles: University of California Press.

Piven, Frances Fox, and Richard A. Cloward. 1977. *Poor People's Movements: Why They Succeed, How They Fail.* New York: Vintage Books.

Polletta, Francesca. 2002. *Freedom in an Endless Meeting.* Chicago: University of Chicago Press.

Polletta, Francesca, and James M. Jasper. 2001. "Collective Identity and Social Movements." *Annual Review of Sociology* 27;283–305.

Prestage, Jewel L. 1977. "Black Women State Legislators: A Profile." In *A Portrait of Marginality: The Political Behavior of the American Woman,* edited by Marianne Githens and Jewel L. Prestage, 401–18. New York: Longman.

Putnam, Robert. 2001. *Bowling Alone: The Collapse and Revival of American Community.* New York: Simon and Schuster.

Quiroz-Martínez, Julie. 2001. "Missing Link." *ColorLines* 4:2. http://www.arc.org/C_Lines/CLArchive/story4_2_01.html.

Rauch, Jonathan. 1994. "The Hyperpluralism Trap." *New Republic,* June 6.

Rawls, John. 1971. *A Theory of Justice.* Cambridge, MA: Belknap Press.

Reagon, Bernice Johnson. 1983. "Coalition Politics: Turning the Century." In *Homegirls: A Black Feminist Anthology*, edited by B. Smith., 356–68. New York: Kitchen Table— Women of Color Press.

Reed, Adolph L. Jr. 2000. *Class Notes: Posing as Politics and Other Thoughts on the American Scene*. New York: New Press.

Reeve, Andrew. 2003. "Interests, individual." In *The Concise Oxford Dictionary of Politics*, edited by Iain McLean and Alistair McMillan. New York: Oxford University Press. Also in *Oxford Reference Online*. http://www.oxfordreference.com/views/ENTRY .html?subview=Main&entry=t86.e65. (accessed June 12, 2006).

Rehfeld, Andrew. 2005. *The Concept of Constituency: Political Representation, Democratic Legitimacy, and Institutional Design*. New York: Cambridge University Press.

———. 2006. "Towards a General Theory of Political Representation." *Journal of Politics* 68 (1): 1–21.

Reingold, Beth. 1992. "Concepts of Representation among Female and Male State Legislators." *Legislative Studies Quarterly* 27 (4): 509–37.

Rhea, Joseph T. 1997. *Race Pride and the American Identity*. Cambridge, MA: Harvard University Press.

Rich, Andrew. 2005. *Think Tanks, Public Policy, and the Politics of Expertise*. New York: Cambridge University Press.

Riker, William. 1962. *The Theory of Political Coalitions*. New Haven, CT: Yale University Press.

Rocco, Raymond. 2000. "Associational Rights, Civil Society, and Place." In *Democracy, Citizenship, and the Global City*, edited by Engin F. Isin, 218–40. New York: Routledge.

Rochon, Thomas R., and David S. Meyer, eds. 1997. *Coalitions and Political Movements*. Boulder, CO: Lynne Reiner.

Roediger, David. 1991. *The Wages of Whiteness: Race and the Making of the American Working Class*. New York: Verso Books.

Rose, Fred. 2000. *Coalitions across the Class Divide: Lessons from the Labor, Peace and Environmental Movements*. Ithaca, NY: Cornell University Press.

Rosen, Jeffrey. 2004. "Courting Disaster." *New York Times Magazine*, December 5.

Rosenberg, Gerald N. 1991. *The Hollow Hope: Can Courts Bring About Social Change?* Chicago: University of Chicago Press.

Rosenblum, Nancy L. 2000. *Membership and Morals: The Personal Uses of Pluralism in America*. Princeton, NJ: Princeton University Press.

Rosenthal, Cindy Simon, ed. 2002. *Women Transforming Congress*. Oklahoma City: Oklahoma University Press.

Rothenberg, Lawrence S. 1992. *Linking Citizens to Government: Interest Group Politics at Common Cause*. New York: Cambridge University Press.

Rothenberg, Sandra, and Maureen Scully. 2002. "Identity Formation in the Mobilization of the Wealthy in the Fight for Income Equity." *Proceedings of the 12th Annual Conference of the International Association for Business and Society*, 57–61.

Rutledge, J. M. 1994. *Building Board Diversity*. Washington, DC: National Center for Nonprofit Boards.

Salisbury, Robert H. 1969. "An Exchange Theory of Interest Groups." *Midwest Journal of Political Science* 13:1–13.

———. 1983. "Interest Groups: Toward a New Understanding." In *Interest Group Politics*, edited by Alan Cigler and Burdett Loomis, 354–69. Washington, DC: CQ Press.

———. 1984. "Interest Representation: The Dominance of Institutions." *American Political Science Review* 78:64–76.

Salisbury, Robert H., John P. Heinz, Edward O. Laumann, and Robert L. Nelson. 1987. "Who Works with Whom? Interest Group Alliances and Opposition." *American Political Science Review* 81:1217–34.

Sanbonmatsu, Kira. 2002. *Democrats, Republicans, and the Politics of Women's Place*. Ann Arbor: University of Michigan Press.

Sapiro, Virginia. 1981. "When Are Interests Interesting? The Problem of Political Representation of Women." *American Political Science Review* 75:701–16.

Sartre, Jean-Paul. 1976. *Critique of Dialectical Reason*. Translated by Alan Sheridan-Smith. London: New Left Books.

Sawyers, Traci M., and David S. Meyer. 1999. "Missed Opportunities: Social Movement Abeyance and Public Policy." *Social Problems* 46 (2): 187–206.

Scalia, Antonin. 1998. *A Matter of Interpretation*. Princeton, NJ: Princeton University Press.

Schattschneider, E. E. [1960] 1975. *The Semisovereign People*. New York: Harcourt Brace Jovanovich.

Scheingold, Stuart A. 1974. *The Politics of Rights: Lawyers, Public Policy, and Political Change*. Ann Arbor: University of Michigan Press.

Scheppele, Kim Lane, and Jack L. Walker Jr. 1991. "The Litigation Strategies of Interest Groups." In *Mobilizing Interest Groups in America*, edited by Jack L. Walker Jr., 157–83. Ann Arbor: University of Michigan Press.

Schlozman, Kay Lehman. 1984. "What Accent the Heavenly Chorus? Political Equality and the American Pressure System." *Journal of Politics* 46:1006–32.

———. 1990. "Representing Women in Washington: Sisterhood and Pressure Politics." In *Woman, Politics, and Change*, edited by Louise A. Tilly and Patricia Gurin, 339–82. New York: Russell Sage Foundation.

Schlozman, Kay Lehman, and Traci Burch. Forthcoming. "Political Voice in an Age of Inequality." In *America at Risk: The Great Dangers*, edited by Robert F. Faulkner and Susan Shell.

Schlozman, Kay Lehman, and John T. Tierney. 1986. *Organized Interests and American Democracy*. New York: Harper and Row.

Schmitter, Phillipe C. 1992. "The Irony of Modern Democracy and Efforts to Improve its Practice." *Politics and Society* 20:507–12.

Schneider, Anne Larason, and Helen Ingram. 1997. *Policy Design for Democracy*. Lawrence: University Press of Kansas.

Schreiber, Ronnee. 1998. "Projecting the 'Voices of Reasonable Women': The Construction of Political Legitimacy among Antifeminist Women." Paper presented at the annual meeting of the Midwest Political Science Association, Chicago, April.

Schultz, David A., ed. 1998. *Leveraging the Law: Using the Courts to Achieve Social Change*. New York: Peter Lang.

Schwartz, Nancy L. 1988. *The Blue Guitar: Political Representation and Community*. Chicago: University of Chicago Press.

Scipes, Kim. 1991. "Labor-Community Coalitions: Not All They're Cracked Up to Be." *Monthly Review*, December.

Scott, John, and Gordon Marshall. 2005. *A Dictionary of Sociology*. New York: Oxford University Press.

Scully, Maureen A., and W. E. Douglas Creed. 2005. "Subverting Our Stories of Subversion." In *Social Movements and Organization Theory*, edited by Gerald Davis, Doug McAdam, W. Richard Scott, and Mayer N. Zald, 310–32. New York: Cambridge University Press.

Sears, David, Mingyong Fu, P. J. Henry, and Kerra Bui. 2003. "The Origins and Persistence of Ethnic Identity among the 'New Immigrant' Groups." *Social Psychology Quarterly* 66 (4): 419–37.

Sears, David, and Leonie Huddy. 1990. "On the Origins of Political Disunity Among Women." In *Women, Politics, and Change*, edited by Louise A. Tilly and Patricia Gurin, 249–77. New York: Russell Sage Foundation.

Shapiro, Ian. 1999. *Democratic Justice*. New Haven, CT: Yale University Press.

Shilts, Randy. 1987. *And the Band Played On: Politics, People, and the AIDS Epidemic*. New York: St. Martin's Press.

Shipan, Charles R. 1997. "Interest Groups, Judicial Review, and the Origins of Broadcast Regulation." *Administrative Law Review* 49:549–84.

Shuman, Michael H. 1998. "Why Do Progressive Foundations Give Too Little to Too Many?" *Nation*, December 28.

Sierra, Christine Marie, and Adaljiza Sosa-Riddell. 1994. "Chicanas as Political Actors: Rare Literature, Complex Practice." *National Political Science Review* 4:297–317.

Silliman, Jael, Marlene Gerber Freid, Loretta Ross, and Elena R. Gutiérrez. 2004. *Undivided Rights: Women of Color Organize for Reproductive Justice*. Cambridge, MA: South End Press.

Simien, Evevlyn M. 2005. "Race, Gender, and Linked Fate." *Journal of Black Studies* 35 (5): 529–50.

Sinclair, Barbara. 2000. *Unorthodox Lawmaking: New Legislative Processes in the U.S. Congress*. 2nd ed. Washington, DC: CQ Press.

Sirianni, Carmen. 1993. "Learning Pluralism: Democracy and Diversity in Feminist Organizations." *Nomos* 34:283–312.

Skocpol, Theda. 1997. *Boomerang: Health Care Reform and the Turn Against Government*. New York: Norton.

———. 2003. *Diminished Democracy: From Membership to Management in American Civic Life*. Norman: University of Oklahoma Press.

Skrentny, John David. 1996. *The Ironies of Affirmative Action: Politics, Culture, and Justice in America*. Chicago: University of Chicago Press.

———. 2004. *The Minority Rights Revolution*. Cambridge, MA: Belknap Press.

Smith, Jackie. 1997. "Nonresponse Bias in Organizational Surveys: Evidence from a Survey of Groups and Organizations Working for Peace." *Nonprofit and Voluntary Sector Quarterly* 26 (3): 359–68.

Smith, Mark. 2000. *American Business and Political Power: Public Opinion, Elections, and Democracy*. Chicago: University of Chicago Press.

Smith, Robert C. 1996. *We Have No Leaders: African Americans in the Post–Civil Rights Era*. Albany: State University of New York Press.

Smith, Rogers M. 1999. *Civic Ideals: Conflicting Visions of Citizenship in U.S. History*. New Haven, CT: Yale University Press.

———. 2004. "Identities, Interests, and the Future of Political Science." *Perspectives on Politics* 2:301–12.

Smooth, Wendy G. 2001. "African American Women State Legislators: The Impact of Gender and Race on Legislative Influence." PhD diss., University of Maryland.

Snow, David A., and Robert D. Benford. 1988. "Ideology, Frame Resonance, and Participant Mobilization." *International Social Movement Research* 1:197–218.

———. 1992. "Master Frames and Cycles of Protest." In *Frontiers of Social Movement Theory*, edited by Aldon Morris and Carol M. Mueller, 133–55. New Haven, CT: Yale University Press.

Solberg, Rorie Spill, and Eric N. Waltenburg. 2006. "Why Do Interest Groups Engage the Judiciary? Policy Wishes and Structural Needs." *Social Science Quarterly* 87 (3): 558–72.

Songer, Donald R., and Reginald S. Sheehan. 1993. "Interest Group Success in the Courts: Amicus Participation in the Supreme Court." *Political Research Quarterly* 46:339–54.

Sorauf, Frank J. 1976. *The Wall of Separation: The Constitutional Politics of Church and State*. Princeton, NJ: Princeton University Press.

Spade, Dean. 2004. "Transecting the Academy." *Gay and Lesbian Quarterly* 10 (2): 240–53.

Spalter-Roth, Roberta, and Ronnee Schreiber. 1995. "Outside Issues and Insider Tactics: Strategic Tensions in the Women's Policy Network during the 1980s." In *Feminist Organizations: Harvest of the New Women's Movement*, edited by Myra Marx Ferree and Patricia Yancey Martin, 105–27. Philadelphia: Temple University Press.

Spelman, Elizabeth V. 1988. *Inessential Woman: Problems of Exclusion in Feminist Thought*. Boston: Beacon Press.

Spill, Rorie L. 1999. "The Use of Courts by Interest Groups." Paper presented at the annual meeting of the Midwest Political Science Association, Chicago, April.

Spriggs, James F. Jr., and Paul Wahlbeck. 1997. "Amicus Curiae and the Role of Information at the Supreme Court." *Political Research Quarterly* 50:365–86.

Staggenborg, Suzanne. 1986. "Coalition Work in the Pro-Choice Movement: Organizational and Environmental Opportunities and Obstacles." *Social Problems* 33 (5): 374–90.

———. 1988. "The Consequences of Professionalization and Formalization in the Pro-Choice Movement." *American Sociological Review* 53:585–605.

Starr, Paul. 2005. "Winning Cases, Losing Voters." Editorial Desk, *New York Times*, January 26, sec. A, col. 1, p. 17.

Stimson, James A., Michael B. MacKuen, and Robert S. Erikson. 1995. "Dynamic Representation." *American Political Science Review* 89 (3):543–65.

Stone, Deborah. 1989. "Causal Stories and the Formation of Policy Agendas." *Political Science Quarterly* 104:281–300.

Stone, Katherine VanWezel. 1992. "The Legacy of Industrial Pluralism: The Tension between Individual Employment Rights and the New Deal Collective Bargaining System." *University of Chicago Law Review* 59:575.

Strolovitch, Dara Z. 1998. "Playing Favorites: Public Attitudes toward Race- and Gender-Targeted Anti-discrimination Policy." *National Women's Studies Association Journal* 10:27–53.

———. 2006. "Do Interest Groups Represent the Disadvantaged? Advocacy at the Intersections of Race, Class, and Gender." *Journal of Politics* 68 (4): 893–908.

Swain, Carol. 1993. *Black Faces, Black Interests*. Cambridge, MA: Harvard University Press.

Sweeney, John J. 1999. "The Growing Alliance between Gay and Union Activists." *Social Text* 61:31–38.

Swers, Michele. 2002. *The Difference Women Make: The Policy Impact of Women in Congress*. Chicago: University of Chicago Press.

Tarrow, Sidney. 1992. "Mentalities, Political Cultures, and Collective Action Frames: Constructing Meanings through Action." In *Frontiers in Social Movement Theory*, edited by Aldon D. Morris and Carol McClurg Mueller. New Haven, CT: Yale University Press.

———. 1994. *Power in Movement: Social Movements, Collective Action, and Mass Politics in the Modern State*. Cambridge: Cambridge University Press.

———. 1996. "States and Opportunities: The Political Structuring of Social Movements." In *Comparative Perspectives on Social Movements*, edited by D. McAdam, J. McCarthy, and M. Zald, 41–61. Cambridge: Cambridge University Press.

———. 2005. *The New Transnational Activism*. New York: Cambridge University Press.

Taylor, Verta. 1989. "Social Movement Continuity: The Women's Movement in Abeyance." *American Sociological Review* 54:761–75.

———. 1995. "Watching for Vibes: Bringing Emotions into the Study of Feminist Organizations." In *Feminist Organizations: Harvest of the New Women's Movement*, edited by Myra Marx Ferree and Patricia Yancey Martin, 223–33. Philadelphia: Temple University Press.

Taylor, Verta, and Mancy Whittier. 1999. "Collective Identity in Social Movement Communities: Lesbian Feminist Mobilization." In *Waves of Protest: Social Movements since the Sixties*, edited by Jo Freeman and Victoria Johnson, 169–94. New York: Rowman and Littlefield.

Terrell, Mary Church. [1898] 2003. "The Progress of Colored Women." In Ripples of Hope: Great American Civil Rights Speeches, edited by Josh Gottheimer, 142–45. New York: Basic Civitas Books.

Thomas, Sue. 1994. *How Women Legislate*. New York: Oxford University Press.

Thompson, Becky W. 2001. *A Promise and Way of Life: White Anti-Racist Activism*. Minneapolis: University of Minnesota Press.

Tichenor, Daniel, and Richard Harris. 2002–3. "Organized Interests and American Political Development." *Political Science Quarterly* 117:587–612.

———. 2005. "The Development of Interest Group Politics in America: Beyond the Conceits of Modern Times." *Annual Review of Political Science* 8:251–70.

Tilly, Charles. 1978. *From Mobilization to Revolution*. Reading, MA: Addison Wesley.

———. 1984. "Social Movements and National Politics." In *Statemaking and Social Movements: Essays in History and Theory*, edited by Charles Bright and Susan Harding, 297–317. Ann Arbor: University of Michigan Press.

Tilly, Louise A., and Patricia Gurin, eds. 1990. *Woman, Politics, and Change*. New York: Russell Sage Foundation.

Tocqueville, Alexis de. [1835] 1965. *Democracy in America*. New York: Harper and Row.

Tom, Allison. 1995. "Children of Our Culture? Class, Power, and Learning in a Feminist Bank." In *Feminist Organizations: Harvest of the New Women's Movement*, edited by Myra Marx Ferree and Patricia Yancey Martin, 165–79. Philadelphia: Temple University Press.

Torres, Rodolpho D., and George Katsiaficas, eds. 1999. *Latino Social Movements: Historical and Theoretical Perspectives*. New York: Routledge.

Truman, David B. 1951. *The Governmental Process*. New York: Knopf.

Truth, Sojourner. 1976. "Address by Sojourner Truth." In *Black Women in Nineteenth Century American Life: Their Words, Their Thoughts, Their Feelings*, edited by Bert James Loewenberg and Ruth Bogin, 234–42. University Park: Pennsylvania State University Press.

Tushnet, Mark V. 1987. *The NAACP's Legal Strategy Against Segregated Education, 1925–1950*. Chapel Hill: University of North Carolina Press.

———. 1991. "Critical Legal Studies: A Political History." *Yale Law Journal* 100:1515–44.

Urbinati, Nadia. 2000. "Representation as Advocacy: A Study of Democratic Deliberation." *Political Theory* 28:258–786.

———. 2002. *Mill on Democracy: From the Athenian Government to Representative Government*. Chicago: University of Chicago Press.

U.S. Census Bureau. 2004. "Race and Hispanic Origin in 2004." http://www.census.gov/population/pop-profile/dynamic/RACEHO.pdf#search=%22%22race%20and%20hispanic%20origin%20in%202004%22%22.

Valocchi, Steve. 1990. "The Unemployed Workers Movement of the 1930s: A Reexamination of the Piven and Cloward Thesis." *Social Problems* 37:191–205.

———. 1993. "External Resources and the Unemployed Councils of the 1930s: Evaluating Six Propositions from Social Movement Theory." *Sociological Forum* 8:451–70.

Van Dyke, Nella. 2003. "Crossing Movement Boundaries: Factors That Facilitate Coalition Protest by American College Students." *Social Problems* 50:226–50.

Van Dyke, Nella, and Sarah A. Soule. 2002. "Structural Social Change and the Mobilizing Effect of Threat: Explaining Levels of Patriot and Militia Mobilizing in the United States." *Social Problems* 49:497–520.

Van Til, Jon. 2000. *Growing Civil Society: From Nonprofit Sector to Third Space*. Bloomington: Indiana University Press.

Verba, Sidney, Kay Lehman Schlozman, and Henry Brady. 1995. *Voice and Equality: Civic Voluntarism in American Politics*. Cambridge, MA: Harvard University Press.

Vose, Clement E. 1958. "Litigation as a Form of Pressure Group Activity." *Annals of the American Academy of Political and Social Science* 319:20–31.

———. 1959. *Caucasians Only*. Berkeley and Los Angeles: University of California Press.

Waldron, Jeremy. 2001. *Law and Disagreement*. New York: Oxford University Press.

Walker, Jack L. Jr. 1983. "The Origins and Maintenance of Interest Groups." *American Political Science Review* 77:390–406.

———. 1991. *Mobilizing Interest Groups in America: Patrons, Professions, and Social Movements*. Ann Arbor: University of Michigan Press.

Wallis, Jim. 2005. *God's Politics: Why the Right Gets It Wrong and the Left Doesn't Get It*. San Francisco: Harper San Francisco.

Walsh, Katherine Cramer. 2002. "Enlarging Representation: Women Bringing Marginalized Perspectives to Floor Debate in the House of Representatives." In *Women Transforming Congress*, edited by Cindy Simon Rosenthal, 370–96. Norman: University of Oklahoma Press.

Warren, Dorian T. 2005. "The Labor Movement's Identity Politics: Organizing around Race, Gender and Sexuality." PhD diss., Yale University.

Warren, Dorian T., and Cathy J. Cohen. 2000. "Organizing at the Intersection of Labor and Civil Rights: A Case Study of New Haven." *University of Pennsylvania Journal of Labor and Employment Law* 2 (4): 629–55.

Warren, Mark E. 2001. *Democracy and Association*. Princeton, NJ: Princeton University Press.

———. 2004. "Informal Representation: Who Speaks for Whom?" *Democracy and Society* 1:8–15.

Warren, Mark R. 2001. *Dry Bones Rattling: Community Building to Revitalize American Democracy*. Princeton, NJ: Princeton University Press.

Wasby, Steven L. 1984. "How Planned Is 'Planned' Litigation?" *American Bar Foundation Research Journal* (Winter): 83–138.

Weaver, R. Kent. 1998. "Ending Welfare as We Know It." In *The Social Divide: Political Parties and the Future of Activist Government*, edited by M. Wier., 361–416. Washington, DC: Brookings Institution Press.

———. 2000. *Ending Welfare as We Know It*. Washington, DC: Brookings Institution Press.

Weldon, S. Laurel. 2002. "Beyond Bodies: Institutional Sources of Representation for Women in Democratic Policymaking." *Journal of Politics* 64 (4): 1153–74.

———. 2004. "The Dimensions and Policy Impact of Feminist Civil Society." *International Feminist Journal of Politics* 6 (1): 1–28.

Whitby, Kenny J. 1997. *The Color of Representation: Congressional Behavior and Black Interests*. Ann Arbor: University of Michigan Press.

White, Lucie. 1987–88. "Mobilization on the Margins of the Lawsuit: Making Space for Clients to Speak." *New York University Review of Law and Social Change* 16: 535.

———. 1988. "To Learn and Teach: Lessons from Direction on Lawyering and Power." *Wisconsin Law Review* 5:699–769.

Williams, Kimberly. 2006. *Mark One or More: Civil Rights in Multiracial America*. Ann Arbor: University of Michigan Press.

Williams, Linda Faye. 1998. "Race and the Politics of Social Policy." In *The Social Divide: Political Parties and the Future of Activist Government*, edited by Margaret Weir, 417–63. Washington, DC: Brookings Institution Press.

Williams, Melissa S. 1998. *Voice, Trust, and Memory: Marginalized Groups and the Failings of Liberal Representation*. Princeton, NJ: Princeton University Press.

Willis, Ellen. 1998. "We Need a Radical Left." *Nation*, June 29, 18–21.

Wilson, James Q. [1974] 1995. *Political Organizations*. Princeton, NJ: Princeton University Press.

Wilson, William Julius. 1987. *The Truly Disadvantaged: The Inner City, the Underclass, and Public Policy*. Chicago: University of Chicago Press.

Wing, Adrien, ed. 1997. *Critical Race Feminism: A Reader*. New York: New York University Press.

Woliver, Laura R. 1998. "Abortion Interests: From the Usual Suspects to Expanded Coalitions." In *Interest Group Politics* 5th ed., edited by Alan Cigler and Burdett Loomis, 327–42. Washington, DC: CQ Press.

Women of Color Resource Center. 1998. *Women of Color Organizations and Projects*. Berkeley, CA: Women of Color Resource Center.

Wong, Carolyn. 2006. *Lobbying for Inclusion: Rights Politics and the Making of Immigration Policy.* Palo Alto, CA: Stanford University Press.

Wong, Janelle. 2006. *Democracy's Promise: Immigrants and American Civic Institutions.* Ann Arbor: University of Michigan Press.

World Values Study Group. 1999. *World Values Survey 1999.* ICPSR Study No. 6160. Ann Arbor, MI: Inter-University Consortium for Political and Social Research. 2000-03-28.

Wright, John R. 2003. *Interest Groups and Congress: Lobbying, Contributions, and Influence.* Boston: Allyn and Bacon.

Young, Iris M. 1990. *Justice and the Politics of Difference.* Princeton, NJ: Princeton University.

———. 1992. "Social Groups in Associative Democracy." *Politics and Society* 20:529–34.

———. 1997. *Intersecting Voices: Dilemmas of Gender, Political Philosophy, and Policy.* Princeton, NJ: Princeton University Press.

———. 2000. *Inclusion and Democracy.* New York: Oxford University Press.

Zald, Mayer, and John D. McCarthy. 1987. *Social Movements in an Organizational Society.* New Brunswick, NJ: Transaction Books.

Zald, Mayer, Calvin Morrill, and Hayagreeva Rao. 2005. "The Impact of Social Movements on Organizations." In *Social Movements and Organization Theory*, edited by Gerald Davis, Doug McAdam, W. Richard Scott, and Mayer N. Zald, 253–79. New York: Cambridge University Press.

# Index

Page numbers in *italic* type refer to tables.